BARRON'S
THE TRUSTED NAME IN TEST PREP

2025

T0272471

AP®
Psychology
PREMIUM

Allyson J. Weseley, Ed.D.,
and Robert McEntarffer, Ph.D.

Dedication

To Kristin, Esme, and Guy.—R.M.

To Sara, Kate, and EIi.—A.W.

AP® is a registered trademark of the College Board, which is not affiliated with Barron's and was not involved in the production of, and does not endorse, this product.

© Copyright 2024, 2023, 2022, 2020, 2018, 2016, 2014, 2012, 2010, 2007, 2004, 2000 by Kaplan North America, LLC, d/b/a Barron's Educational Series

Published by Kaplan North America, LLC, d/b/a Barron's Educational Series
1515 West Cypress Creek Road
Fort Lauderdale, Florida 33309
www.barronseduc.com

ISBN: 978-1-5062-9191-8

10 9 8 7 6 5 4 3

Kaplan North America, LLC, d/b/a Barron's Educational Series print books are available at special quantity discounts to use for sales promotions, employee premiums, or educational purposes. For more information or to purchase books, please call the Simon & Schuster special sales department at 866-506-1949.

About the Authors

Rob McEntarffer taught AP Psychology at Lincoln Southeast High School in Lincoln, NE, for 13 years and Psychology at Nebraska Wesleyan University for 7 years. He earned his teaching certificate in psychology from the University of Nebraska, a master's degree in educational psychology, and a Ph.D. in education. He has extensive experience in scoring the Advanced Placement Psychology free-response questions, having served as a Reader and Table Leader, and as the high school Question Leader. He is past chair of the national organization Teachers of Psychology in Secondary Schools, worked with the committee on the National Standards for the Teaching of High School Psychology, and is involved in writing assessment materials for high school- and college-level introductory psychology textbooks. He works as an assessment specialist for his school district.

Allyson Weseley has taught AP Psychology and run a Behavioral Science Research Program at Roslyn High School in Roslyn Heights, NY, for over 25 years. Her students have enjoyed great success on the AP exam, with a 100 percent passing rate and well over 80 percent earning 5's. She earned an undergraduate degree in psychology from Princeton University, a master's degree from the Harvard Graduate School of Education, and a doctorate from Columbia University's Teachers College. Dr. Weseley has served as a Reader and Table Leader for the AP Psychology exam, published a number of psychology-related activities, led several psychology teacher workshops, and served on the board of Teachers of Psychology in Secondary Schools.

Table of Contents

UNIT 0: SCIENCE PRACTICES

UNIT 1: BIOLOGICAL BASES OF BEHAVIOR

UNIT 2: COGNITION

UNIT 3: DEVELOPMENT AND LEARNING

UNIT 4: SOCIAL PSYCHOLOGY, PERSONALITY, MOTIVATION, AND EMOTION

UNIT 5: MENTAL AND PHYSICAL HEALTH

PRACTICE TESTS

How to Use This Book

This edition of Barron's *AP Psychology* has been completely overhauled to align with the 2024 changes to the AP Psychology curriculum and test.

Course Content

Revisions have been made to the review content, and the overall structure of the book has been altered to match the *new* 5-unit structure. The updated edition of the book includes:

- Revised "AP Psychology Course and Exam Description" and "Overview of the AP Psychology Exam"
- A Unit 0 addressing the Science Practices essential to the exam's new and greater focus on understanding research
- Vocabulary terms in **bold** aligned with terms in the College Board's Course CED items
- Science Practice Skill 2 (Research Methods) and Science Practice Skill 3 (Data Analysis) multiple-choice items included with each chapter

Multiple-Choice Questions

The new test will include 75 multiple-choice items, each with 4 answer choices. These items do not ask for definitional knowledge; they require a greater depth of understanding and ability to apply concepts. As a result, in this edition:

- All multiple-choice items at the end of each unit and in the practice test will align with the new format and reflect the emphasis on the ability to apply knowledge and analyze and interpret data
- The chapter on "Multiple-Choice Test-Taking Tips" has been revised to reflect these changes

Free-Response Questions (FRQs)

The revised exam will still include two FRQs, but their format has been entirely revised. We have included a chapter explaining the new FRQs and provide an example and how it would be scored.

Practice Exam

This edition contains a complete practice test that represents our best approximation of the exams we will see in the coming years.

BARRON'S ESSENTIAL 5

As you review the content in this book to work toward earning that **5** on your AP PSYCHOLOGY exam, here are five things that you **MUST** know above everything else:

Psychology is a science. Psychological researchers use the scientific method to gather data and test hypotheses about the mind and behavior instead of relying on intuition, what the majority of people believe, or "common sense." Often what people refer to as "common sense" offers contradictory ideas. Regarding attraction, common sense tells us both that "opposites attract" and that "birds of a feather flock together." Psychological researchers carefully gather data about topics like attraction to reach conclusions rather than rely on intuition or belief. Unit 0 describes in detail how psychologists gather data and test hypotheses. Understanding research methodology is vital to your performance on the exam and your understanding of the science of psychology.

Know the psychological perspectives. Psychological researchers study the mind and behavior from different "perspectives." Each perspective uses some unique research methods, concepts, and vocabulary to describe and explain thinking and behavior. Knowing the vocabulary and concepts associated with each perspective can help you better understand psychological theories and quickly narrow down possible answers to exam questions. For instance, if a question uses the term *classical conditioning*, you should be able to immediately identify the question as belonging in the "behavioral" area of psychology and look for answers that include other behavioral terms. The psychological perspectives are introduced in Unit 0 and form the basis for the discussion of personality, psychological disorders, and treatment of psychological disorders found in later units.

Know your terms. Psychological terms refer to specific concepts, and it is important that you don't confuse these terms with "pop" psychological ideas or the casual ways nonpsychologists use the same words. For example:

- To a psychologist, people diagnosed with antisocial personality disorder (Unit 5) are not shy or unfriendly but, rather, callous and unfeeling toward others.

- "Learning" in psychological terms refers to much more than learning in school and is divided into many specific kinds of learning such as classical and operant conditioning. You can read more about this in Unit 3.

You should make sure that you understand the specific, scientific meaning of psychological terms. Most of the multiple-choice items on the exam (which determine the majority of your final score) measure your ability to apply psychological terminology.

4

Application is key. The AP Psychology test is designed to measure your knowledge of psychological concepts and ability to apply these concepts. Exam items (especially the free-response questions) usually require you to go beyond defining terms by applying them to a scenario or making connections between different concepts. However, the AP Psychology exam is not designed to measure your writing ability or ability to express your knowledge in creative or unique ways. The measurement goals of this exam are to assess your knowledge of psychological concepts and your ability to apply this knowledge.

5

Use what psychology teaches you about cognition (Unit 2) to improve your study habits. You have been a student for many years, and no doubt you've received advice about how to study and have developed your own study habits. Use what psychology teaches you about cognition to improve your study habits. Studying for the AP Psychology exam is an opportunity for you to modify your study methods based on the research findings about the effectiveness of different encoding and recall techniques. For example:

- Memory research clearly indicates that "distributed practice" (spacing your studying over a span of days or weeks) is much more effective than "massed practice" ("cramming" all your studying just before the test).

- Memory techniques like chunking, mnemonic devices, and context cues can dramatically improve your ability to recall sets of terms and save you hours of study time.

- The information-processing model predicts that focusing on the meaning, context, and application of psychological ideas will increase your ability to recall and use psychological ideas.

- Research indicates that students can (and should) take advantage of the "testing effect" (also known as the "retrieval practice"): you should interrupt your reading and studying with frequent small "tests" of your knowledge. Use the practice questions at the end of each unit to test your knowledge.

AP Psychology Course and Exam Description

Traditional Chapters in College Introductory Psychology Textbooks	AP Psychology Course and Exam Description (2024–2025 CED Revision)
History and Approaches	**Unit 0: Science Practices** (research methods, data interpretation, scientific argumentation infused throughout the curriculum and test)
Research Methods	
Biological Bases of Behavior	**Unit 1: Biological Bases of Behavior** (heredity/environment, nervous system, neurons, brain, sleep, sensation) *15–25%*
States of Consciousness	
Sensation and Perception	**Unit 2: Cognition** (perception, thinking/problem solving, memory (encoding/storing/retrieving), forgetting, intelligence) *15–25%*
Cognition	
Testing and Individual Differences	
Developmental	**Unit 3: Development and Learning** (themes and methods, physical development, gender/sexual orientation, cognitive development, language, social-emotional development, classical conditioning, operant conditioning, social/cognitive and neuro factors in learning) *15–25%*
Learning	
Motivation and Emotion	**Unit 4: Social Psychology and Personality** (attribution theory, person perception, attitude formation, social situations, theories of personality [psychodynamic, humanistic, social-cognitive, and trait], motivation, emotion) *15–25%*
Personality	
Social	
Disorders	**Unit 5: Mental and Physical Health** (health, positive psychology, categorization and treatment of psychological disorders *15–25%*
Treatment	

Because this is a review book, our aim is to emphasize the information you need to understand in order to be successful on the AP Psychology exam. However, some of these theories and ideas are particularly important. (Some are keys necessary for understanding concepts later. We believe that some of these theories and ideas will be emphasized on the exam. Finally, some are just very important for understanding the science of thinking and behavior.) We convey this importance by highlighting this material as **Tips** in the text. Terms that also appear in the College Board's *AP Psychology Course and Exam Description* are set in **bold** in the text. These terms can also be found in the index.

Science Practices

Starting with the 2025 AP Psychology test, the College Board began keying multiple-choice items to one of three science practices in addition to the content area appropriate for that question. We include more information about these science practices in Chapter 19, "Multiple-Choice Test-Taking Tips." Here is a summary of what you should know now about the science practices.

Science Practice 1: Concept Application

This skill simply refers to your ability to USE the concepts, theories, terms, perspectives, and other ideas in the AP Psychology curriculum. All the multiple-choice and free-response questions on the exam will require you to

USE your knowledge rather than just recall it. For instance, you are likely to be asked about concepts as they relate to specific scenarios and to compare concepts with one another. Being able to define the terms in this book is a good first step. Remember, though, that you need to understand how to use and apply these terms, not just repeat their definitions. We always emphasize examples and applications in this book, and you should do the same as you study these terms. Creating your own examples and applications of these terms will help you more on the test than memorizing definitions. About 65% of the multiple-choice items on the test (about 49 of the 75 items) will be keyed as concept application items in addition to being keyed to one of the five content units.

Science Practice 2: Research Methods and Design

This skill refers to your understanding of how psychological researchers design research studies. In this book, we call this content Unit 0, "Science Practices." In that unit, you will learn about the unique research methods psychologists use to try to answer the complex research questions posed by psychological research. About 25% of the multiple-choice items on the test (about 18 of the 75 items) will be keyed as research methods items in addition to being keyed to one of the five content units.

Science Practice 3: Data Interpretation

This skill refers to analyzing quantitative data—numbers! You will learn in Chapter 2 "Research Methods" that psychological researchers usually try to measure psychological variables numerically. Then researchers use statistical methods to analyze what these measurements might mean about thinking and behavior. You will learn about a few basic statistical techniques researchers use in psychology and then you can use the data interpretation multiple-choice questions to measure your ability to use those statistical techniques in specific examples. About 10% of the multiple-choice items on the test (7 or 8 of the 75 items) will be keyed as data interpretation items, in addition to being keyed to one of the five content units.

NOTE

You will find a fourth science practice listed in the *AP Psychology Course and Exam Description*: "Science Practice 4: Argumentation." This skill is measured by only one of the free-response questions, not the multiple-choice questions. You will find more information about argumentation in Chapter 20, "Answering Free-Response Questions."

Practice Questions, Test Tips, and Practice Exams

Multiple-choice practice questions and explanations of the correct answers are provided at the end of each unit other than Unit 0. We recommend that you first review the material in the unit and then close the book and try to answer all the review questions with your book closed. Then open the book to check your answers and carefully review the explanations to make sure of the following:

- If you answered the question right, you got it right for the correct reasons!
- If you got the question wrong, review the explanation for the correct answer and why the incorrect answers are wrong. Then close the book again and write out what you remember about how that concept applied to that question. This will help you encode the correct understanding of that term or idea.

To help you prepare for the exam, we include three sections with detailed information about the exam:

- Overview of the AP Psychology exam: includes details about the structure of the exam, timing, and scoring.
- Multiple-choice test-taking tips: includes an analysis of the kinds of multiple-choice items you will see on the exam and a suggested process you can use to think your way through AP Psychology multiple-choice questions to determine the correct answer.
- Answering the free-response questions: includes descriptions of both free-response questions as well as complete sample questions and answers.

Using Psychology to Study Psychology

Research by cognitive and educational psychologists indicates that the following three principles are the most powerful techniques you can use to make your studying more efficient. This book is designed and organized to help you use these principles. If you read this section carefully and plan how you will use these three ideas, you will learn the content for the AP Psychology exam more quickly. You will also increase the chances that you can recall the ideas when you need them on the exam (and in situations you encounter in your life!)

Distributed Practice

Studies consistently show that spreading out your studying over a period of time is much more effective than "massing" studying just before you have to use the information (in other words, cramming for a test). You should use this finding to plan how to distribute your studying time. You are probably busy with many other activities during the weeks before the AP exam, so you should use the **distributed practice** principle to start thinking and planning now about how to distribute your AP Psychology practice. Studying 15–30 minutes a night for three weeks before the exam will be much more effective than waiting until two days before the test and cramming in all your study time right before the exam. We suggest that you make yourself a schedule based on the table of contents of this book and devote shorter study sessions for each of the units in this book.

Depth of Processing

Encoding the meaning of terms and how those ideas apply in realistic examples is an example of deep processing. As you read about the theories, terms, and perspectives in this book, think about what they mean to you and how they apply to your life. Create and describe your own personal examples of these terms rather than spending time copying down definitions. In this book, we provide multiple examples of the terms and concepts. Information that you deeply process is much more likely to be encoded into your long-term memory. The more you personalize the terms and examples, thinking about how they apply to you and your life, the more likely you are to be able to recall those terms on the exam. Remember, learning is a cognitively active process. The more you involve yourself in the process by thinking about how the terms and theories apply to you and your life, which is called the *self-reference effect*, the better you'll remember what you need to remember. You'll also reduce the overall amount of time you need to study!

Retrieval Practice

Using the principle of **retrieval practice** (also called the *testing effect*) simply means that you stop and test yourself to see what you encoded based on what you just read or studied. Interrupting your studying with frequent small quizzes is very effective. Students who frequently answer questions about the content they are studying are more likely to remember that content, even if they don't answer the questions on that small quiz correctly. This book is designed to help you take advantage of the power of retrieval practice. Each unit ends with practice questions. Treat these practice questions like a minitest after you are done studying the unit. Answer the question WITHOUT looking back at the text or looking ahead at the correct answers. Use the practice questions like a real test, and try to answer them based only on what you can pull out of your long-term memory. Even if you don't feel ready for the quiz at the end of the unit or if you get many of the questions wrong, the experience of taking the test and thinking about your answers will help you learn and remember these ideas long term. In fact, taking the AP exam will even feel easier!

Overview of the AP Psychology Exam

The AP Psychology exam has two parts: a multiple-choice section and a free-response section. You will have 2 hours and 40 minutes to complete the whole test.

The multiple-choice portion of the exam contains 75 four-choice (A to D) questions. You have 90 minutes to complete these 75 multiple-choice questions. The score for the multiple-choice section of the AP exam is based on the number of questions answered correctly. No points are deducted for questions answered incorrectly or left blank. Since there is no guessing penalty, make sure you answer every multiple-choice question on the exam. Chapter 19, "Multiple-Choice Test-Taking Tips," explains important tips for correctly answering AP Psychology multiple-choice questions.

The free-response section of the test consists of two questions: the Article Analysis Question (AAQ) and the Evidence-Based Question (EBQ). You must answer both free-response questions. Unlike many other AP exams, you will not be given a choice of topics (although you will be able to choose to use two of the three available article summaries for the EBQ question). You will have a total of 70 minutes for the free-response portion of the exam: 25 minutes for the AAQ and 45 minutes for the EBQ. Some students find that completing two free-response answers under a specific time limit is challenging. Chapter 20, "Answering Free-Response Questions," provides important tips for answering AP Psychology AAQ and EBQ free-response questions. In addition, when you write about the sample item in Chapter 20, you get experience completing these types of questions within the time limit.

Your overall composite score on the exam will range from 1 to 5 and will take into account your performance on both the multiple-choice and free-response questions. The multiple-choice sections will count for twice as much in the final composite score: the multiple-choice section is weighted 66.7% on the exam and the free-response section is weighted 33.3%. So two-thirds of your score depends on your performance on the multiple-choice section, and the other one-third of your score depends on your writing during the free-response section.

Each year, the percentage of students who earn each score differs slightly. More information on the score distributions from past years is available from College Board (see the College Board website: *www.collegeboard.org/ap*). The graph below documents score distributions from 2014 through 2023.

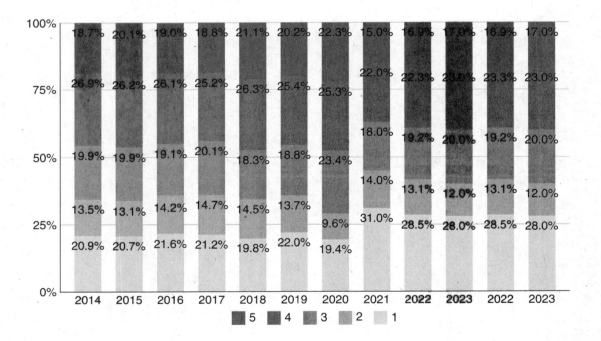

UNIT 0
Science Practices

This first unit focuses on current psychological perspectives and the research methods psychologists use to gather data about human thinking and behavior. You will find the content from this unit in the textbook you use in your AP Psychology class in the history and research methods chapters. Note that the research methods concepts you learn in this unit are important throughout the rest of the curriculum! On the AP test, you'll be asked to apply research methods to answer multiple-choice questions from each unit and in the free-response questions.

History of Psychology

Learning Objectives

In this chapter, you will learn about:

→ Psychological perspectives

Psychological Perspectives

Different contemporary psychologists look at human thought and behavior from different perspectives. Contemporary perspectives can be placed into eight broad categories.

Humanist Perspective

Humanists, including theorists Abraham Maslow (1908–1970) and Carl Rogers (1902–1987), stressed individual choice and free will. This contrasts with the deterministic behaviorists, who theorized that all behaviors are caused by past conditioning. Humanists believe that we choose most of our behaviors and these choices are guided by physiological, emotional, or spiritual needs. A humanistic psychologist might explain that an introverted person may choose to limit social contact with others because he or she finds that social needs are better satisfied by contact with a few close friends rather than large groups. Humanistic theories are not easily tested by the scientific method. Some psychological historians view them as more historical perspectives than current ones. However, some therapists find humanistic ideas helpful in aiding clients to overcome obstacles in their lives.

Psychodynamic Perspective

The psychodynamic perspective continues to be a part of modern psychology, if a controversial one. Psychologists using this perspective believe that the unconscious mind—a part of our mind that we do not have conscious control over or access to—controls much of our thought and action. Psychoanalysts look for impulses or memories pushed into the unconscious mind through repression. This perspective thinks that to understand human thought and behavior, we must examine our unconscious mind through dream analysis, word association, and other psychoanalytic therapy techniques. A psychoanalytic psychologist might explain that an introverted person avoids social situations because of a repressed memory of trauma in childhood involving a social situation, perhaps acute embarrassment or anxiety experienced (but not consciously remembered) at school or a party.

Biopsychology (or Neuroscience) Perspective

Biopsychologists explain human thought and behavior strictly in terms of biological processes. Human cognition and reactions might be caused by the effects of our genes, hormones, and neurotransmitters in the brain or by a combination of all three. A biopsychologist might explain a person's tendency to be extroverted as caused by genes inherited from their parents and the genes' effects on the abundance of certain neurotransmitters in the brain. Biopsychology is a rapidly growing field. Some scientists wonder if the future of psychology might be as a branch of the science of biology.

Evolutionary (or Darwinian) Perspective

Evolutionary psychologists (also sometimes called sociobiologists) examine human thoughts and actions in terms of natural selection. Some psychological traits might be advantageous for survival, and these traits would be passed down from the parents to the next generation. A psychologist using the evolutionary perspective—based on Charles Darwin's (1809–1882) theory of natural selection—might explain a person's tendency to be extroverted as a survival advantage. If a person is outgoing, he or she might make friends and allies. These connections could improve the individual's chances of survival, which increases the person's chances for passing this trait for extroversion down to his or her children. The evolutionary perspective is similar to (and in some ways a subset of) the biopsychology perspective.

Behavioral Perspective

Behaviorists explain human thought and behavior in terms of conditioning. Behaviorists look strictly at observable behaviors and at human and animal responses to different kinds of stimuli. A behaviorist might explain a person's tendency to be extroverted in terms of reward and punishment. Was the person rewarded for being outgoing? Was the person punished for withdrawing from a situation or not interacting with others? A behaviorist would look for environmental conditions that caused an extroverted response in the person (see also Unit 4).

Cognitive Perspective

Cognitive psychologists examine human thought and behavior in terms of how we interpret, process, and remember environmental events. In this perspective, the rules that we use to view the world are important to understanding why we think and behave the way we do. In Unit 3, you will learn about Jean Piaget's (1896–1980) cognitive developmental theory, which focuses on how our cognitions develop in stages as we mature. A cognitive psychologist might explain a person's tendency to be extroverted in terms of how he or she interprets social situations. Does the individual interpret others' offers for conversation as important ways to get to know someone or as important for his or her own life in some way? To a cognitive psychologist, an extroverted person sees the world in such a way that being outgoing makes sense.

Social-Cultural (or Sociocultural) Perspective

Social-cultural psychologists look at how our thoughts and behaviors vary among cultures. They emphasize the influence culture has on the way we think and act. A social-cultural psychologist might explain a person's tendency to be extroverted by examining his or her culture's rules about social interaction. How far apart do people in this culture usually stand when they have a conversation? How often do people touch each other while interacting? How much value does the culture place on being part of a group versus being an individual? These **cultural norms** would be important to a sociocultural psychologist in explaining a person's extroversion.

Biopsychosocial Perspective

This modern perspective acknowledges that human thinking and behavior results from combinations of biological ("bio"), psychological ("psycho"), and social ("social") factors. Psychologists who emphasize the biopsychosocial perspective view other perspectives as too focused on specific influences on thinking and behavior (sometimes called being reductionistic). A biopsychosocial psychologist would agree with a cognitive psychologist about the influence of how we remember and interpret events but would point out that biological and social influences are equally responsible for our decisions. The biopsychosocial perspective might explain extroversion by focusing on the combination of several influences: a genetic tendency for extroversion (similar to the biopsychological explanation), how a person has been conditioned toward extroverted behavior, and how social pressures—such as conformity—influence his or her extroverted behaviors.

Summary

If you ask psychologists which of these perspectives they most agree with, they might say that each perspective has valid explanations depending on the specific situation. This point of view, sometimes called eclectic, claims that no one perspective has all the answers to the variety of human thought and behavior. Psychologists use various perspectives in their work depending on which point of view fits best with the explanation. In the future, some perspectives might be combined, or new perspectives might emerge as research continues.

2

Research Methods

Learning Objectives

In this chapter you will learn about:

→ Experimental method
→ Correlational method
→ Naturalistic observation
→ Case studies

Key Terms

- Hindsight bias
- Confirmation bias
- Overconfidence
- Quantitative research
- Qualitative research
- Hypothesis
- Dependent variable
- Independent variable
- Falsifiable
- Operational definitions
- Replicated
- Sample
- Population

- Representative sample
- Random sampling
- Convenience sampling
- Generalize
- Stratified sampling
- Confounding variables
- Random assignment
- Experimenter bias
- Double-blind study
- Single-blind study
- Social desirability bias
- Experimental group

- Control group
- Placebo method
- Placebo effect
- Positive correlation
- Negative correlation
- Study
- Likert scales
- Directionality problem
- Third variable
- Naturalistic observation
- Structured interview
- Case study

Overview

Psychology is a science, and it is therefore based on research. Although people are often guided effectively by their intuition, sometimes it leads us astray. People have the tendency upon hearing about research findings (and many other things) to think that they knew it all along; this tendency is called **hindsight bias**. After an event occurs, it is relatively easy to explain why it happened. The goal of scientific research, however, is to predict what will happen in advance. Another reason scientific research is important is that people suffer from **confirmation bias** and **overconfidence**. Confirmation bias is the tendency to pay more attention to information that supports our preexisting ideas, and overconfidence is the tendency to be, well, overconfident about the things we believe. An understanding of research methods is fundamental to psychology. In the updated AP exam, more emphasis is put on these methods than ever before.

Sometimes psychologists conduct research to solve practical problems. For instance, psychologists might compare two different methods of teaching children to read to determine which method is better, or they could design and test the efficacy of a program to help people quit smoking. This type of research is known as applied research because it has clear, practical applications. Other psychologists conduct basic research. Basic research explores questions that are of interest to psychologists but are not intended to have immediate, real-world applications. Examples of basic research include studying how people form their attitudes about others and how people in different cultures define intelligence.

Research can also be divided into quantitative and qualitative research. **Quantitative research** uses numerical measures, while **qualitative research** typically uses more complex textual responses and looks for key themes within them.

Hypotheses and Variables

Although some research is purely descriptive, most psychological research is guided by hypotheses. A **hypothesis** expresses a relationship between two variables. Variables, by definition, are things that can vary among the participants in the research. For instance, religion, stress level, and height are variables. According to an experimental hypothesis, the **dependent variable** depends on the **independent variable**. In other words, a change in the independent variable will produce a change in the dependent variable. For instance, consider the hypothesis that watching violent television programs makes people more aggressive. In this hypothesis, watching television violence is the independent variable since the hypothesis suggests that a change in television viewing will result in a change in behavior. In testing a hypothesis, researchers manipulate the independent variable and measure the dependent variable. Hypotheses often grow out of theories. A theory aims to explain some phenomenon and allows researchers to generate testable hypotheses with the hope of collecting data that support the theory. It is essential the hypotheses be **falsifiable**; that is, it must be possible to gather data that would controvert the hypothesis.

Researchers not only need to name the variables they will study but also need to provide **operational definitions** of them. When you operationalize a variable, you explain how you will measure it. For instance, in the hypothesis above, what programs will be considered violent? What behaviors will be considered aggressive? These and many other questions need to be answered before the research commences. The operationalization of the variables raises many issues about the validity and reliability of the research.

Validity and Reliability

Good research is both valid and reliable. Research is valid when it measures what the researcher set out to measure; it is accurate. Research is reliable when it can be **replicated**; it is consistent. If the researcher conducted the same research in the same way, the researcher would get similar results.

Sampling

Before one can begin to investigate a hypothesis, one needs to decide who or what to study. The individuals on which the research will be conducted are called participants (or subjects), and the process by which participants are selected is called sampling. To select a **sample** (the group of participants), one must first identify the **population** from which the sample will be selected. The population includes anyone or anything that could possibly be selected to be in the sample.

The goal in selecting a sample is that it be representative of a larger population. This is called a **representative sample**. If I conduct my research about television violence using only my own psychology students, I cannot say much about how viewing violent television affects other people. My students may not be representative of a larger population. I would be better off specifying a larger and more diverse population, the whole student body of 1,000, for example, and then randomly selecting a sample of 100. The definition of **random sampling** is that every member of the population has an equal chance of being selected. Random selection increases the likelihood that the sample represents the population and that one can **generalize** the findings to the larger population. Using my own students for the research is an example of **convenience sampling**, collecting data from a group of people who are easily accessible to you. Other examples of convenience sampling include using your friends and/or family or your colleagues at work.

Note that psychologists use the term *random* differently than do laypeople. If I choose my sample by standing in front of the library on a Wednesday morning and approaching people in a way that I feel is random, I have not used random sampling. Perhaps, without realizing it, I was less likely to approach people I did not know or people wearing college sweatshirts. Since those individuals would not stand an equal chance of being selected for the study, the selection process is not random. In addition, the method just described would not yield a representative sample of the school's population. Not everybody will walk past the library on Wednesday morning. People who do not will have no chance of being selected for the study and therefore are not part of the population. Random selection is best done using a computer, a table of random numbers, or that tried-and-true method of picking names out of a hat.

Even if I randomly select a sample of 100 people from the school's population of 1,000, clearly the sample will probably not perfectly reflect the composition of the school. For instance, if the school has exactly 500 males and 500 females in it, what are the chances that my random sample will have the same 1:1 ratio? Although we could compute those odds, that's not the point. Clearly, the larger the sample, the more likely it is to represent the population. A sample of all 1,000 students guarantees that it is perfectly representative, and a sample of 1 person guarantees that it is far from representative. So why not use all 1,000 students? The downside of using a large sample is time and money. It is also important to realize that the populations psychologists study are often much larger than 1,000 people. Therefore, for research to use large, but not prohibitively large, samples is considered optimum. Statistics can be used to determine how large a sample should be to represent a population of any particular size, but you won't be expected to know how to do this.

One additional action can be taken to increase the likelihood that a sample will represent the larger population from which it was chosen. **Stratified sampling** is a process that allows a researcher to ensure that the sample represents the population on some criteria. For instance, if I thought that participants of different racial groups might respond differently, I would want to make sure that I represented each race in my sample in the same proportion in which it appears in the overall population. In other words, if 500 of the 1,000 students in a school are white, 300 are Black, and 200 are Latino, in a sample of 100 students I would want to have 50 white students, 30 Black students, and 20 Latino students. To that end, I could first divide the names of potential participants into each of the three racial groups, and then I could choose a random subsample of the desired size from each group.

Experimental Method

Experiments can be divided into laboratory experiments and field experiments. Laboratory experiments are conducted in a lab, which is a highly controlled environment, while field experiments are conducted out in the world. The extent to which laboratory experiments can be controlled is their main advantage. The advantage of field experiments is that they are more realistic.

Psychologists' preferred method of research is the experiment because only through a carefully controlled experiment can one show a causal relationship. An experiment allows the researcher to manipulate the independent variable and control for **confounding variables**. A confounding variable is any difference between the experimental and control conditions, except for the independent variable, that might affect the dependent variable. To show that the violent television programs cause participants' aggression, I need to rule out any other possible cause. An experiment can achieve this goal by randomly assigning participants to conditions and by using various methods of control to eliminate confounding variables.

TIP

Selecting a sample randomly maximizes the chance that the sample will represent the population from which it was drawn and allows researchers to draw generalizations about the population based on their findings about the sample.

TIP

Students often equate all research with experiments. As described in the text, many kinds of research can be conducted, but only experiments can identify cause and effect relationships.

Assignment is the process by which participants are put into a group, whether experimental or control. **Random assignment** means that each participant has an equal chance of being placed into either group. The benefit of random assignment is that it limits the effect of participant-relevant confounding variables. If participants were given the opportunity to choose whether to be in the group watching violent television or not, it is highly unlikely that the two groups would be comprised of similar people. Perhaps violent people prefer violent television and would therefore select the experimental group. Even if one were to assign people to groups based on a seemingly random criterion (for example, when they arrived at the experiment or where they were sitting in the room), the process might open the door to confounding variables. Using random assignment diminishes the chance that participants in the two groups differ in any meaningful way. In other words, it controls for participant-relevant variables.

Note that when we talk about differences between groups, we are referring to the group average. A single, very aggressive subject will not throw off the results of the entire group. The idea behind random assignment is that, in general, the groups will be equivalent.

If one wanted to ensure that the experimental and control groups were equivalent on some criterion (e.g., sex, IQ scores, age), one could use group matching. If one wanted to group match for sex, one would first divide the sample into males and females and then randomly assign half of each group to each condition. Group matching would not result in the same number of males and females within each group. Rather, half of the males and half of the females would be in each of the groups.

Situation-relevant confounding variables can also affect an experiment. For the participants to be equivalent is not enough. The situations that the different groups experience must also be equivalent except for the differences produced by the independent variable. If the experimental group watches violent television in a large lecture hall while the control group watches other programs in a small classroom, their situations are not equivalent. Therefore, any differences found between the groups may possibly be due not to the independent variable, as hypothesized, but rather to the confounding variables. Other situation-relevant variables include the time of day, the weather, and the presence of other people in the room. Making the environments into which the two groups are placed as similar as possible controls for situation-relevant confounding variables.

Experimenter bias is a special kind of situation-relevant confounding variable. Experimenter bias is the unconscious tendency for researchers to treat members of the experimental and control groups differently to increase the chance of confirming the researchers' hypothesis. Note that experimenter bias is not a conscious act. If researchers purposely distort their data, it is called fraud, not experimenter bias. Experimenter bias can be eliminated by using a double-blind procedure. A **double-blind study** occurs when neither the participants nor the researcher are able to affect the outcome of the research. A double-blind study can be accomplished in a number of ways. The most common way is for the researcher to have someone blind to the participants' condition interact with the participants. A **single-blind study** occurs when only the participants do not know to which group they have been assigned; this strategy minimizes the effect of demand characteristics as well as certain kinds of response or participant bias. Demand characteristics are cues about the purpose of the study. Participants use such cues to try to respond appropriately. Response or subject bias is the tendency for participants in a study to behave in certain ways (for example, circle the midpoint on a scale or pick the right-hand option more than the left-hand one). One important kind of response bias, the tendency to try to give answers that reflect well upon oneself, is called **social desirability bias**.

Experiments typically involve at least one **experimental group** and a **control group**. The experimental group is the one that gets the treatment operationalized in the independent variable. The control group gets none of the independent variable. It serves as a basis for comparison. Without a control group, knowing whether changes in the experimental group are due to the experimental treatment or simply to any treatment at all is impossible. In fact, merely selecting a group of people on whom to experiment has been determined to affect the performance of that group, regardless of what is done to those individuals. This finding is known as the Hawthorne effect.

TIP

Random assignment controls for participant-relevant confounding variables. Students sometimes confuse random assignment and random sampling. Although both involve randomization, sampling is the process of choosing the research participants from the population, and it happens before assignment. Assignment is the process of dividing participants into groups (for example, experimental and control), and it cannot be done until after you have identified the sample.

Continuing with the television example, the experimental group would be the participants who view violent television, while the control group would view some other type of television, perhaps a comedy. If I were really designing an experiment, I would have to be much more specific in operationally defining my independent variable. I would need to identify exactly what program(s) each group would watch and for how long. Many experiments involve much more complicated designs. In our example, additional groups would view other types of shows or groups would view differing amounts of violent content.

One important method of control is known as the **placebo method**. Whenever participants in the experimental group are supposed to ingest a drug, participants in the control group are given an inert but otherwise identical substance. This technique allows researchers to separate the physiological effects of the drug from the psychological effects of people thinking they took a drug (called the **placebo effect**).

Sometimes using participants as their own control group is possible, a procedure known as counterbalancing. For instance, if I wanted to see how frustration affected performance on an IQ test, I could have my participants engage in a task unlikely to cause frustration, then test their IQ, and then give them a frustrating task and test their IQs again. However, this procedure creates the possibility of order effects. Participants may do better on the second IQ test simply by virtue of having taken the first IQ test. This problem can be eliminated by using counterbalancing. I can counterbalance by having half the participants do the frustrating task first and half the participants do the not-frustrating task first and then switching.

> **TIP**
> Students sometimes believe that using a control group is the only possible method of control. Remember that although it is an extremely important and obviously named type of control, using control groups is but one of many such methods.

Correlational Method

A correlation expresses a relationship between two variables without ascribing cause. Correlations can be either positive or negative. A **positive correlation** between two things means that the presence of one thing predicts the presence of the other. A **negative correlation** means that the presence of one thing predicts the absence of the other. See Chapter 3 "Statistics" for more information about correlations.

Sometimes psychologists elect not to use the experimental method. In some cases, testing a hypothesis with an experiment is impossible. Suppose, for example, I want to test the hypothesis that retired adults are more likely to vote in national elections than working adults. Clearly, I cannot randomly assign participants to conditions. Some people are retired, and others are working. The assignment of the independent variable, in this case, has been predetermined. As a result, I will never be able to isolate the cause of any difference in voting behavior. It could be that being retired affects people's likelihood to vote, or it could be some other factor that tends to occur with working or retiring (such as a difference in the amount of free time or childcare demands). If I seek to control all other aspects of the research process, as I would in an experiment, I will have conducted an ex post facto (quasi-experimental) **study**.

An even more popular research design is the survey method. The survey method, as common sense suggests, involves asking people to fill out surveys. One common type of item used on surveys are **Likert scales**, which pose a statement and ask people to express their level of agreement/disagreement with the statement. For instance, if I wanted to measure how much you are enjoying your AP Psychology class, I could provide a statement such as "AP Psychology is one of my favorite classes" and ask you to select from several options that range from "strongly disagree" to "strongly agree."

To contrast the survey method with the experimental method, return to the question about whether there is a relationship between watching violence on television and aggressive behavior. The original hypothesis, that watching violent television programs makes people more aggressive, cannot be tested using the survey method, because only an experiment can reveal a cause-effect relationship. However, one could use the survey method to investigate whether there is a relationship between the two variables, watching violence on television and aggressive behavior. In the survey method, neither of the variables is manipulated. Therefore, although two variables are measured, there is no independent or dependent variable. As a result, the researcher cannot conclude that one of the variables causes the other. It may be that watching violent television causes aggression, but it is also possible that aggressive people are drawn to watch violent television. The inability to tell which of the variables came first (also known as temporal precedence) is called the **directionality problem**. It is also possible that a **third variable**—for instance, a genetic predisposition—causes both the love of violent television and one's aggressive behavior. In this case, there is no real relationship between the two variables being studied at all, and the correlation is known as a spurious (false) correlation.

Using the survey method means that one cannot control participant-relevant confounding variables. Some people watch a lot of violent television, and others do not. In all likelihood, these two groups of people would differ in a number of other ways as well. The survey method does not enable the researcher to determine which of these differences cause a difference in violent behavior.

Although controlling situation-relevant confounding variables using the survey method is possible (by bringing all the participants to one place at one time to fill out the survey), it is rarely done. One of the advantages of the survey method is that conducting research by sending surveys for people to fill out at their convenience is easy. However, if people fill out the surveys in different places, at different times of day, by taking different amounts of time, and so on, the research will be plagued by confounding variables. Thus, again, determining what causes a difference in violent behavior becomes impossible. In addition, obtaining a random sample when one sends out a survey is difficult because relatively few people will send it back (low response rate), and these people are unlikely to make up a representative sample.

Naturalistic Observation

Sometimes researchers opt to observe participants in their natural habitats without interacting with them at all. Such unobtrusive observation is called **naturalistic observation**. The goal of naturalistic observation is to get a realistic and rich picture of the participants' behavior. To that end, control is sacrificed.

Qualitative Methods

Although many surveys are comprised of items that participants select from a set of choices, they also can include open-ended questions where participants can write in their responses; this type of data are qualitative. Instead of using a survey, someone collecting qualitative data might conduct an interview with one person or a focus group with a small number of people at the same time. Interviews can vary based on how structured they are. A **structured interview** is like a survey in that there are fixed number of questions asked in a set order. A structured interview can even be completely quantitative if the questions all have a prescribed set of answer choices. However, interviews can also be semistructured or unstructured, allowing more opportunity for the interviewer to react to the participants' responses and obtain a richer, albeit less controlled, set of data.

Another qualitative research method is the **case study**. The case study method is used to get a full, detailed picture of one participant or a small group of participants. For instance, clinical psychologists often use case studies to present information about a person suffering from a particular disorder. Although case studies allow researchers to get the richest possible picture of what they are studying, the focus on a single individual or small group means that the findings cannot be generalized to a larger population.

TIP

Students often confuse the use of surveys to measure the dependent variable in an experiment with the survey method. Although surveys can be used as part of the experimental method, the survey method, as described, is a kind of correlational research in which the researcher does not manipulate the independent variable.

TIP

Students often confuse naturalistic observation with field experiments. Both involve doing research out in the world. However, in naturalistic observation, the researchers do not impact the behavior of the participants at all. In contrast, in field experiments, as in all experiments, the researcher manipulates the independent variable and attempts to eliminate as many confounding variables as possible.

3

Statistics

Learning Objectives

In this chapter you will learn about:

→ Descriptive statistics
→ Correlations
→ Inferential statistics
→ APA Ethical Guidelines

Key Terms

- Central tendency
- Mean
- Median
- Mode
- Bimodal
- Positively skewed
- Negatively skewed
- Range
- Variance
- Standard deviation

- Normal curve
- Percentiles
- Correlation
- Correlation coefficient
- Scatterplot
- Statistically significant
- Effect size
- Replication
- Meta-analysis

- Peer review
- No coercion
- Informed consent
- Deception
- Informed assent
- Confidentiality
- Risk
- Protection from harm
- Debriefing

Overview

Content in this chapter is relevant to one of the skills the College Board identified to be measured on the AP Psychology test. Specifically, in this section you will learn about what the College Board calls Science Practice 3—Data Analysis: understanding and making inferences based on numerical data. As you study the terms and ideas in this chapter, test yourself with the questions at the end of the unit to make sure that you are able to use the statistical terms and processes to analyze data from psychological studies and recognize valid conclusions based on those data.

Descriptive Statistics

Descriptive statistics, as the name suggests, simply describe a set of data. For instance, if you were interested in researching what kinds of pets your schoolmates have, you might summarize that data by creating a frequency distribution that would tell you how many students had dogs, how many had cats, how many had zebras, and so on. Graphing your findings is often helpful. Frequency distributions can be easily turned into line graphs called frequency polygons or bar graphs known as histograms. The y-axis (vertical) always represents frequency. Whatever you are graphing, which in this case is pets, is graphed along the x-axis (horizontal).

You are probably already familiar with at least one group of statistical measures called measures of **central tendency**. Measures of central tendency attempt to mark the center of a distribution. Three common measures of central tendency are the **mean**, **median**, and **mode**. The mean is what we usually refer to as the average of all the scores in a distribution. To compute the mean, you simply add up all the scores in the distribution and divide by the number of scores. The median is the central score in the distribution. To find the median of a distribution, simply write the scores in ascending (or descending) order and then, if there are an odd number of scores, find the middle one. If the distribution contains an even number of scores, the median is the average of the middle two scores. The mode is the score that appears most frequently. A distribution may, however, have more than one mode. A distribution is **bimodal**, for instance, if two scores appear equally frequently and more frequently than any other score.

The mean is the most used measure of central tendency, but its accuracy can be distorted by extreme scores or outliers. Imagine that 19 of your 20 friends drive cars valued at $12,000 but your other friend has a Maserati valued at $120,000. The mean value of your friends' cars is $17,400. However, since that value is more than everyone's car except one person's, you would probably agree that mean is not the best measure of central tendency in this case. When a distribution includes outliers, the median is often used as a better measure of central tendency.

Unless a distribution is symmetrical, it is skewed. Outliers skew distributions. When a distribution includes an extreme score (or group of scores) that is very high, as in the car example above, the distribution is said to be **positively skewed**. When the skew is caused by a particularly low score (or group of scores), the distribution is **negatively skewed**. A positively skewed distribution contains more low scores than high scores; the skew is produced by some aberrantly high score(s). Conversely, a negatively skewed distribution contains more high scores than low scores. In a positively skewed distribution, the mean is higher than the median because the outlier(s) have a much more dramatic effect on the mean than on the median. Of course, the opposite is true in a negatively skewed distribution (see Figure 3.1).

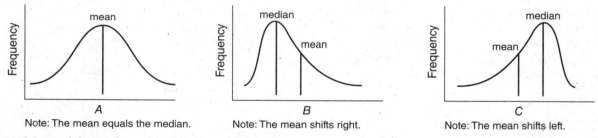

Figure 3.1 (A) Symmetrical distribution; (B) Positively skewed distribution; (C) Negatively skewed distribution

Measures of variability are other types of descriptive statistical measures. Again, you may be familiar with some of these measures, such as the **range**, **variance**, and **standard deviation**. Measures of variability attempt to depict the diversity of the distribution. The range is the distance between the highest and lowest scores in a distribution. The variance and standard deviation are closely related; standard deviation is simply the square root of the variance. Both measures essentially relate the average distance of any score in the distribution from the mean. The higher the variance and standard deviation, the more spread out the distribution.

Sometimes, being able to compare scores from different distributions is important. To do so, you can convert scores from the different distributions into measures called z-scores. These z-scores measure the distance of a score from the mean in units of standard deviation. Scores below the mean have negative z-scores, while scores above the mean have positive z-scores. For instance, if Clarence scored 72 on a test with a mean of 80 and a standard deviation of 8, Clarence's z-score would be -1. If Maria scored 84 on that same test, her z-score would be $+0.5$.

Often, in psychology, you will see reference to the **normal curve**. The normal curve is a theoretical bell-shaped curve for which the area under the curve lying between any two z-scores has been predetermined. Approximately 68 percent of scores in a normal distribution fall within 1 standard deviation of the mean, approximately

95 percent of scores fall within 2 standard deviations of the mean, and almost 99 percent of scores fall within 3 standard deviations of the mean. Knowing that the normal curve is symmetrical and knowing the three **percent-** ages just given will allow you to calculate the approximate percentage of scores falling between any given z-scores. For instance, approximately 47.5 percent (95/2) of scores fall between the z-scores of 0 and $+2$ (see Figure 3.2).

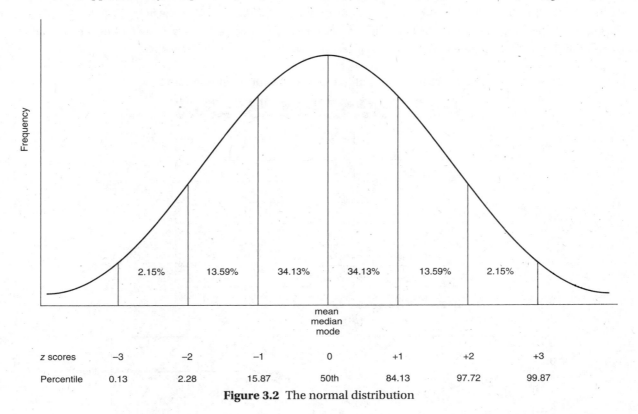

Figure 3.2 The normal distribution

While z-scores measure the distance of a score away from the mean, **percentiles** indicate the distance of a score from 0. Someone who scores in the 90th percentile on a test has scored better than 90 percent of the people who took the test. Similarly, someone who scores at the 38th percentile scored better than only 38 percent of the people who took the test. A clear relationship exists between percentiles and z-scores when dealing with the normal curve. Someone who scores at the 50th percentile has a z-score of 0, and someone who scores at the 98th percentile has an approximate z-score of $+2$.

Correlations

A **correlation** measures the relationship between two variables. As explained in Chapter 2, correlations can be either positive or negative. If two things are positively correlated, the presence of one thing predicts the presence of the other. In contrast, a negative correlation means that the presence of one thing predicts the absence of the other. When no relationship exists between two things, no correlation exists. As an example, one would suspect that a positive correlation exists between studying and earning good grades. Conversely, one would suspect that a negative correlation might occur between cutting classes and earning good grades. Finally, it is likely that there is no correlation between the number of stuffed animals one has and earning good grades.

Correlations may be either strong or weak. The strength of a correlation can be computed by a statistic called the **correlation coefficient**. Correlation coefficients range from -1 to $+1$, where -1 is a perfect negative correlation and $+1$ is a perfect positive correlation. Both -1 and $+1$ denote equally strong correlations. The number 0 denotes the weakest possible correlation—no correlation—which means that knowing something about one variable tells you nothing about the other variable.

A correlation may be graphed using a **scatterplot**. A scatterplot graphs pairs of values, one on the *y*-axis and one on the *x*-axis. For instance, the number of hours a group of people study per week could be plotted on the *x*-axis while their GPAs could be plotted on the *y*-axis. The result would be a series of points called a scatterplot. The closer the points come to falling on a straight line, the stronger the correlation. The line of best fit, or regression line, is the line drawn through the scatter plot that minimizes the distance of all the points from the line. When the line slopes upward, from left to right, it indicates a positive correlation. A downward slope evidences a negative correlation. The scatterplot depicting the dataset given in Table 3.1 is graphed in Figure 3.3.

Table 3.1 The Relationship Between Hours Studied and GPA

Name	Hours Studied	GPA
Teresa	15	3.8
Raoul	17	3.8
Todd	4	1.3
Lucy	11	3.1
Aaron	8	2.4
Pam	12	3.3
Laticia	14	3.9
Greg	9	2.5
Megan	5	0.6

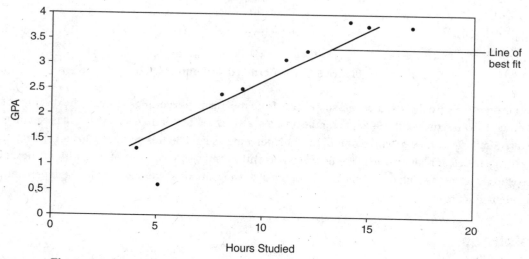

Figure 3.3 Scatterplot showing the correlation between hours studied and GPA

Inferential Statistics

Whereas descriptive statistics provide a way to summarize information about the sample studied, the purpose of inferential statistics is to determine whether findings can be applied to the larger population from which the sample was selected. Remember that one of the primary goals in selecting a sample is that the sample represents the population from which it was picked. If a sample does not represent the larger population, one cannot infer anything about the larger population from the sample. Guaranteeing that a sample is representative of a population is impossible. The extent to which the sample differs from the population is known as sampling error.

Say that you ran an experiment testing the effects of sugar consumption on short-term memory. You randomly assigned your 50 participants to either a control group that was given a sugar-free lollipop or to the experimental group that was given a seemingly identical lollipop that contained sugar. You then tested the participants' ability to recall 15 one-syllable nouns. If the experimental group remembered an average of 7 words and the control group remembered an average of 6.9 words, would you be comfortable concluding that sugar does, in fact, enhance short-term memory? Your gut reaction is probably to say that the 0.1 difference in the example is too small to allow us to draw such a conclusion. What if the experimental group consisted of just one person who recalled all 15 words while the control group contained one person who remembered only 5 words? You would probably be similarly reluctant to draw any conclusions even given this enormous difference in the number of words recalled due to the tiny sample size.

In both cases, you would be correct to be skeptical. The differences between the groups are likely due to sampling error and chance. The purpose of inferential statistics is to help psychologists decide when their findings can be applied to the larger population. Many different inferential statistical tests exist such as t-tests, chi-square tests, and ANOVAs. They all consider both the magnitude of the difference found and the size of the sample. However, what is most important for you to know is that all these tests yield a p-value. The p-value gives the probability that the difference between the groups is due to chance. The smaller the p-value, the more significant the results. Scientists have decided that a p-value of 0.05 is the cutoff for **statistically significant** results. A p-value of 0.05 means that a 5 percent chance exists that the results occurred by chance. A p-value can never equal 0 because we can never be 100 percent certain that results did not happen due to chance. As a result, scientists often try to replicate their results, thus gathering more evidence that their initial findings were not due to chance.

A p-value can also be computed for any correlation coefficient. The stronger the correlation and the larger the sample, the more likely the relationship will be statistically significant, which will be shown by a p-value of 0.05 or less.

In addition to statistical significance, psychologists are interested in practical significance—or how large an effect is. There are a number of different measures of **effect size** that enable psychologists to quantify practical significance. When research is conducted on large samples, it is possible for a finding to be statistically significant (unlikely to happen due to chance) but so small as to be practically unimportant. The converse is true as well; research conducted with small samples may show a large effect but one that we cannot be confident would appear in a larger sample or replication. The most useful findings therefore have low p-values and high effect sizes.

In recent years, many areas of science, including psychology, have been experiencing a **replication** crisis. When we replicate a study, we conduct it again using the same methodology in an attempt to see if the results will be the same. Many efforts at replication have failed, casting doubt on the findings of these studies and leading to a concerted effort to be more cautious in accepting the results of a single study, especially those with very surprising effects. **Meta-analysis** is a type of research that combines the results of many studies on the same topic in order to approximate an average effect. Prior to publication, psychology studies undergo **peer review**, a process by which a paper is read by several others in the field and the is author asked to make revisions in order to ensure high quality publications.

APA Ethical Guidelines

Ethical considerations are a major component in research design. You should know and understand the ethical guidelines established by the APA (American Psychological Association) for human and animal research and be prepared to apply the concepts to specific research designs. Any type of academic research must first propose the study to the ethics board or institutional review board (IRB) at the institution. The IRB reviews research proposals for ethical violations and/or procedural errors. This board ultimately gives researchers permission to go ahead with the research or requires them to revise their procedures.

Animal Research

Groups advocating the ethical treatment of animals are focusing more and more attention on how animals are treated in laboratory experiments. The APA developed strict guidelines about what animals and how animals can be used in psychological research. Ethical psychological studies using animals must meet the following requirements:

- The research must have a clear scientific purpose.
- The research must answer a specific, important scientific question.
- Animals chosen must be best suited to answer the question at hand.
- Researchers must care for and house animals in a humane way.
- Researchers must acquire animal subjects legally. Animals must be purchased from accredited companies. If wild animals must be used, they need to be trapped in a humane manner.
- Researchers must design experimental procedures that employ the least amount of suffering feasible.

Human Research

Research involving human subjects must meet the following standards:

- **No coercion**—Participation should be voluntary.
- **Informed consent**—Participants must know that they are involved in research and give their consent. If the participants are deceived in any way about the nature of the study, the **deception** must not be so extreme as to invalidate the informed consent, and it is ethically preferable to keep deception to a minimum. The research the participants thought they were consenting to must be similar enough to the actual study to give the informed consent meaning. Only adults can consent to be in research; minors should be asked to assent **(informed assent)** and may also be asked to obtain the consent of their parent or guardian.
- **Confidentiality** (or anonymity)—Participants' privacy must be protected. Their identities and actions must not be revealed by the researcher. Participants have anonymity when the researchers do not collect any data that enable the researchers to match a person's responses with his or her name. In some cases, such as interview studies, a researcher cannot promise anonymity but instead guarantees confidentiality, which means the researcher will not identify the source of any of the data.
- **Risk**—Participants cannot be placed at significant mental or physical risk; they must have **protection from harm**. Typically, it is considered permissible for participants to experience temporary discomfort or stress. However, activities that might cause someone long-term mental or physical harm must be avoided. This clause requires interpretation by the review board. Some institutions might allow a level of risk that other boards might not allow. This consideration was highlighted by Stanley Milgram's obedience studies in the 1970s in which participants thought they were causing significant harm or death to other participants (see Chapter 13 "Social Psychology").
- **Debriefing**—After the study, participants should be told the purpose of the study and provided with ways to contact the researchers about the results. When research involves deception, it is particularly important to conduct a thorough debriefing.

UNIT 1
Biological Bases of Behavior

This unit summarizes the structure and function of different parts of the brain (including neural anatomy and processes). The unit includes a brief overview of how the biological systems of genetics and the endocrine system influence thinking and behavior. The unit discusses the application of biological psychology research to the topics of states of consciousness and sensation. You will find the content from this unit in the textbook you use in your AP Psychology class in the biological psychology, states of consciousness, and sensation chapters.

4

Biological Bases of Behavior

Learning Objectives

In this chapter, you will learn about:

→ Genetics
→ Neuroanatomy
→ Nervous system
→ Endocrine system

Key Terms

- Genetic predisposition
- Neurons
- Multiple sclerosis
- Neural transmission
- Resting potential
- Threshold
- Action potential
- All-or-none principle
- Depolarization
- Resting potential
- Excitatory
- Inhibitory
- Dopamine
- Serotonin
- Norepinephrine
- Glutamate
- GABA
- Endorphins
- Substance P
- Acetylcholine
- Alzheimer's disease
- Myasthenia gravis
- Sensory neurons
- Interneurons
- Motor neurons
- Central nervous system

- Peripheral nervous system
- Reflex arcs
- Somatic nervous system
- Autonomic nervous system
- Sympathetic nervous system
- Parasympathetic nervous system
- Endocrine system
- Hormones
- Adrenaline
- Leptin
- Ghrelin
- Melatonin
- Oxytocin
- Lesioning
- Electroencephalogram (EEG)
- Functional MRI (fMRI)
- Medulla
- Cerebellum
- Reticular formation
- Thalamus
- Hypothalamus
- Amygdala

- Hippocampus
- Brain stem
- Cerebral cortex
- Limbic system
- Contralateral hemispheric organization
- Hemispheric specialization
- Split-brain patients
- Corpus callosum
- Lobes
- Association area
- Frontal lobes
- Prefrontal cortex
- Central executive
- Broca's area
- Aphasia
- Wernicke's area
- Motor cortex
- Parietal lobes
- Somatosensory cortex
- Phantom limb syndrome
- Occipital lobes
- Temporal lobes
- Linguistic processing

Overview

The influence of biology (sometimes called the neuroscience or biopsychological perspective) is growing. An understanding of the biological principles relevant to psychology is needed not only for the AP exam but also for any understanding of current psychological thinking.

Genetics

Besides the functioning of the brain and nervous system, another biological factor that affects human thought and behavior is genetics. Most human traits, like body shape, introversion, or temper, result from the combined effects of nature (our genetic code) and nurture (the environment where we grow up and live). The term **genetic predisposition** refers to the increased chance of developing a specific trait or condition due to our genetic code. Psychological researchers attempt to determine how much nature and nurture contribute to human traits.

Basic Genetic Concepts

Every human cell contains 46 chromosomes in 23 pairs. The genetic material that makes up chromosomes is DNA—deoxyribonucleic acid. Certain segments of DNA control the production of specific proteins that control some human traits. These discrete segments are called genes. Genes can be dominant or recessive. If we inherit two recessive genes for a particular trait, that trait is expressed. In any other combination of genes, the dominant trait is expressed. Psychological researchers investigate how different combinations of genes create tendencies for physical and behavioral traits.

Twins

Since identical twins (called monozygotic twins since they develop from one fertilized egg called a zygote) share all the same genetic material, researchers study them in order to examine the influence of genes on human traits. In one famous study, Thomas Bouchard found more than 100 identical twins who were given up for adoption and raised in different families. The study compared hundreds of traits and made conclusions about the relative influences of genetics and the environment on specific traits. For example, the study found a correlation coefficient of 0.69 on the IQ test for identical twins raised apart and a 0.88 for identical twins living together. This shows that the environment has some effect on IQ score since twins raised in the same family have more similar IQs. However, the IQs of twins raised apart are still highly correlated, demonstrating that IQ is also heavily influenced by genetics. Twin studies like this one have been criticized in one important way, however. Even twins raised in separate families obviously share very similar physical appearances. This physical similarity may cause others to treat them in similar ways, creating the same effective psychological environment for both twins. This similarity in environment might explain the high correlations attributed to genetic influence.

Chromosomal Abnormalities

Our sex is determined by our 23rd pair of chromosomes. Males have an X and a Y chromosome, and females have two X chromosomes. Usually, a male will contribute either an X or a Y chromosome to a child. Occasionally, chromosomes will combine (or fail to) in an unusual way, resulting in a chromosomal abnormality. For example, babies with Turner's syndrome are born with only a single X chromosome in the spot usually occupied by the 23rd pair. Turner's syndrome causes some physical characteristics, like short stature, webbed necks, and differences in physical sexual development. Babies born with Klinefelter's syndrome have an extra X chromosome, resulting in an XXY pattern. The effects of this syndrome vary widely, but it usually causes minimal sexual development and personality traits like extreme introversion.

Other chromosomal abnormalities may cause intellectual disability. The most common type is Down syndrome. Babies with Down syndrome are born with an extra chromosome on the 21st pair. Some physical characteristics are indicative of Down syndrome: rounded face, shorter fingers and toes, slanted eyes set far apart, and some degree of intellectual disability.

Neuroanatomy

Neuroanatomy refers to the study of the parts and function of neurons. **Neurons** are individual nerve cells. These cells make up our entire nervous system, from the brain to the neurons that fire when you stub your toe. Every neuron is made up of discrete parts (see Figure 4.1).

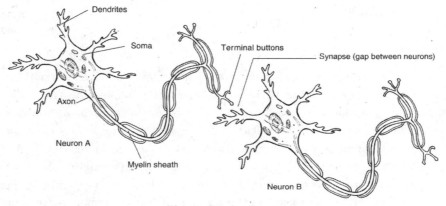

Figure 4.1 A neuron

Dendrites—rootlike parts of the cell that stretch out from the cell body. Dendrites grow to make synaptic connections with other neurons (see "Synapse," below).

Cell body (also called the soma)—contains the nucleus and other parts of the cell needed to sustain its life.

Axon—wirelike structure ending in the terminal buttons that extends from the cell body.

Myelin sheath—a fatty covering around the axon of some neurons that speeds neural impulses. Multiple sclerosis occurs when the myelin sheath deteriorates around neurons, interfering with neural transmission.

Terminal buttons (also called end buttons, terminal branches of axons, and synaptic knobs)—the branched end of the axon that contain neurotransmitters.

Neurotransmitters—chemicals contained in terminal buttons that enable neurons to communicate. Neurotransmitters fit into receptor sites on the dendrites of neurons like a key fits into a lock.

Synapse—the space between the terminal buttons of one neuron and the dendrites of the next neuron.

How a Neuron "Fires"

All of the different parts of the neuron work in sequence when a neuron transmits a message (**neural transmission**). In its resting state (also referred to as **resting potential**), a neuron has an overall slightly negative charge (-70 mV) because mostly negative ions are within the cell and mostly positive ions are surrounding it. The cell membrane of the neuron is selectively permeable and works to maintain this difference in charge. Visualize a two-neuron chain (see Figure 4.1). The reaction begins when the terminal buttons of neuron A are stimulated and release neurotransmitters into the synapse. These neurotransmitters fit into receptor sites on the dendrites of neuron B. If enough neurotransmitters are received (this level is called the **threshold**), the cell membrane of neuron B becomes permeable and positive ions rush into the cell, bringing the charge within the cell to approximately +40 mV. The change in charge spreads down the length of neuron B. This electric message firing is called an **action potential**. It travels quickly: 120 meters per second. When the charge reaches the terminal buttons of neuron B, the buttons release their neurotransmitters into the synapse. The process may begin again if enough neurotransmitters are received by that next cell to pass the threshold. It's important to note that a neuron either fires completely or does not fire; this is called the **all-or-none principle**. If the dendrites of a neuron receive enough neurotransmitters to push the neuron past its threshold, the neuron will fire completely every time. A neuron cannot fire a little or a lot; the impulse is the same every time. This process of neural firing is also called **depolarization** because the cell fires due to the **resting potential** of the cell—its negative charge—becoming "depolarized" when positive ions rush into the cell, changing the overall charge from negative to positive.

TIP

Neural firing is an electrochemical process. Electricity travels within the cell (from the dendrites to the terminal buttons), and chemicals (neurotransmitters) travel between cells in the synapse. Electricity does not jump between the neurons.

Neurotransmitters

You already know that neurotransmitters are chemicals held in the terminal buttons that travel in the synaptic gap between neurons. It is important to understand that different types of neurotransmitters exist. Some neurotransmitters are **excitatory**, meaning that they excite the next cell into firing. Other neurotransmitters are **inhibitory**, meaning that they inhibit the next cell from firing. Each synaptic gap at any time may contain many kinds of inhibitory and excitatory neurotransmitters. The amount and type of neurotransmitters received on the receptor sites of the neuron determine whether it will pass the threshold and fire. Researchers are identifying different types and functions of neurotransmitters every year. This ongoing research makes generalizing about what each neurotransmitter does difficult. However, Table 4.1 indicates some of the more important types and functions of neurotransmitters to psychologists.

Table 4.1 Neurotransmitters Important to Psychologists

Neurotransmitter	Function	Problems Associated with an Excess or a Deficit
Dopamine	Motor movement and alertness	Lack of dopamine is associated with Parkinson's disease; an overabundance is associated with schizophrenia.
Serotonin	Mood control	Lack of serotonin is associated with clinical depression.
Norepinephrine	Alertness, arousal	Lack of norepinephrine is associated with depression.
Glutamate	Excitatory neurotransmitter, involved in memory	Triggers migraines, seizures.
GABA	Important inhibitory neurotransmitter	Internalizes when having seizures and can cause sleep problems.
Endorphins	Pain control	Involved in addictions.
Substance P	Pain perception	Lack of substance P may be associated with a lack of pain perception.
Acetylcholine	Motor movement	Lack of acetylcholine is associated with **Alzheimer's disease**. Acetylcholine is also involved in the disease **Myasthenia gravis**, a condition that causes muscle weakness.

Nervous System

We can sense the world because our nervous system brings information from our senses to our brain. Since a neuron fires in only one direction (from dendrite to terminal buttons), our body needs two sets of wires: one to take information to the brain and one to take instructions back from the brain to the muscles.

Sensory Neurons

Sensory neurons, or afferent neurons, take information from the senses to the brain.

Interneurons

Once information reaches the brain or spinal cord, **interneurons** (also called association neurons) take the messages and send them elsewhere in the brain or on to efferent neurons.

Motor Neurons

Motor neurons, or efferent neurons, take information from the brain to the rest of the body.

Organization of the Nervous System

Our nervous system is divided into different categories based on function. The two main divisions are the **central nervous system** and the **peripheral nervous system**. These are then further subdivided (see Figure 4.2).

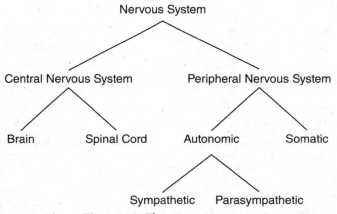

Figure 4.2 The nervous system

Central Nervous System

The central nervous system (CNS) consists of our brain and spinal cord—all the nerves housed within bone (the skull and vertebrae). Information about the structure and function of different parts of the brain is available in a later section. The spinal cord is a bundle of nerves that run through the center of the spine. It transmits information from the rest of the body to the brain.

Typical Peripheral Nervous System Transmission

Let us use an example to demonstrate how sensory information gets to our brain. While on a late-night quest for a snack, you stub your toe on a cast-iron coffee table. Sensory neurons in your toe are activated, and this message is transmitted up a neuron that runs from your toe to the base of your spine (afferent nerves). The message continues up your spinal cord on more afferent nerves until it enters your brain through the brainstem and is transmitted to the brain's sensory cortex (see the section "The Brain"), and you know you have stubbed your poor little toe. Your motor cortex now sends impulses down the spinal cord to the muscles controlling your leg and foot (efferent nerves), causing you to hop up and down holding your damaged limb, muttering under your breath.

Reflexes: An Important Exception

Most sensory information and muscle movements are controlled by the process described above. However, humans have a few reflexes that work differently: **reflex arcs**. Certain reactions occur the moment sensory impulses reach the spinal cord. If you stimulate the correct area just below your kneecap, your leg will jerk without your conscious control. This sensory information is processed by the spine, and the spine tells your leg to move. The information reaches your brain, and you realize your knee has been stimulated but only after this reflex has occurred. Another important reflex occurs in response to intense heat or cold. If we touch an object that is very hot or extremely cold, our spine will send back a message jerking us away from that object. This might help keep us from harming ourselves, so it has adaptive value. (It might help us survive, and therefore this trait is passed on to our children.)

Peripheral Nervous System

The peripheral nervous system (PNS) consists of all the nerves in your body that are not part of the central nervous system—that is, all the nerves not encased in bone. The peripheral nervous system is divided into two categories: the somatic and the autonomic nervous systems.

Somatic Nervous System

The **somatic nervous system** controls our voluntary muscle movements. The motor cortex of the brain sends impulses to the somatic nervous system, which controls the muscles that allow us to move.

Autonomic Nervous System

The **autonomic nervous system** controls the automatic functions of our body—our heart, lungs, internal organs, glands, and so on. These nerves control our responses to stress: the fight-or-flight response that prepares our body to respond to a perceived threat. The autonomic nervous system is divided into two categories: the sympathetic and parasympathetic nervous systems.

Sympathetic Nervous System

The **sympathetic nervous system** mobilizes our body to respond to stress. This part of our nervous system carries messages to the control systems of the organs, glands, and muscles that direct our body's response to stress. This process is sometimes called the fight-or-flight response; it is the warning system of our body. It accelerates some functions (such as heart rate, blood pressure, and respiration) but conserves resources needed for a quick response by slowing down other functions (such as digestion).

Parasympathetic Nervous System

The **parasympathetic nervous system** has the opposite job of the sympathetic system. It carries messages to the stress response system that cause many of our body activities to slow down and return the body to homeostasis (its typical level) after a stress response. Think of the parasympathetic nervous system as the brake pedal that slows down the body's autonomic nervous system.

Endocrine System

Another part of human biology relevant to psychology is the **endocrine system**. This is a system of glands that secrete **hormones** that affect many different biological processes in our bodies. The endocrine system is controlled in the brain by the hypothalamus (discussed more below). The endocrine system is complex, but a few elements of the entire process are especially relevant to psychologists. Table 4.2 includes the basic functions of some of humans' important hormones.

Table 4.2 Basic Functions of Important Hormones in Humans

Hormone	Function
Adrenaline	Activated during the fight-or-flight response in stressful situations. Speeds up bodily processes.
Leptin	Involved in weight regulation. Suppresses hunger (food may be perceived as less appetizing).
Ghrelin	Motivates eating/increases hunger (food may be perceived as more appetizing).
Melatonin	Triggers sleep and wakefulness responses in the brain.
Oxytocin	Promotes good feelings such as trust and bonding.

Adrenal Glands

The adrenal glands produce adrenaline (also known as epinephrine), which signals the rest of the body to prepare for fight or flight. This response was mentioned earlier in connection with the autonomic nervous system—the part of our nervous system that controls involuntary responses, such as heart rate and blood pressure.

Ovaries and Testes

Ovaries and testes produce our sex hormones, estrogen for females and testosterone for males. Research shows that levels of these hormones may partially explain gender differences demonstrated in certain experiments and situations.

The Brain

Possibly the most relevant part of biology to psychologists is the brain. As far as we can tell, the brain controls most of human thought and behavior. Researchers know quite a bit about brain anatomy and function, but many mysteries remain about how the brain functions. Studying how the brain works is challenging because we cannot simply observe brain function the way we might observe a heart beating. To our eyes, a brain thinking looks exactly like a brain not thinking. Researchers are discovering many new details about how the brain works by using experimentation and technology. However, we still have a long way to go before we really understand how the brain controls our thoughts and behavior.

Ways of Studying the Brain

As mentioned previously, the first challenge of brain research is creating a way of detecting brain function. The following describes some of the methods researchers use.

Accidents

In 1848, a railroad worker named Phineas Gage was involved in an accident that damaged the front part of his brain. Gage's doctor took notes documenting the brain damage and how Gage's behavior and personality changed after the accident. Accidents like this give researchers clues about brain function. Gage became highly emotional and impulsive after the accident. Researchers concluded that the parts of the brain damaged in the accident are somehow involved in emotional control.

Phineas Gage

Lesions

Lesioning is the removal or destruction of part of the brain. This, of course, is never done purely for experimental purposes. Sometimes doctors decide that the best treatment for a certain condition involves surgery that will destroy or incapacitate part of the brain. For example, a person may develop a brain tumor that cannot be removed without removing part of the surrounding brain. When these types of surgeries are performed, doctors closely monitor the patient's subsequent behavior for changes. Any time brain tissue is removed (lesioning), researchers can examine behavior changes and try to infer the function of that part of the brain.

A famous historical example of lesioning is the frontal lobotomy. In the past, this surgery was used (many historians say overused) to control mentally ill patients who had no other treatment options. Researchers knew that lesioning part of the frontal lobe would make the patients calm and relieve some serious symptoms. Drug treatments have now replaced frontal lobotomies.

Electroencephalogram

An **electroencephalogram (EEG)** detects brain waves. Researchers can examine what type of waves the brain produces during different stages of consciousness and use this information to generalize about brain function. The EEG is widely used in sleep research to identify the different stages of sleep and dreaming.

Computerized Axial Tomography

A computerized axial tomography (CAT or CT) scan is a sophisticated X ray. The CAT scan uses several X ray cameras that rotate around the brain and combine all the pictures into a detailed three-dimensional picture of the brain's structure. Note that the CAT scan can show only the structure of the brain, not the functions or the activity of different brain structures. A doctor could use a CAT scan to look for a tumor in the brain but would not get any information about how active different parts of the brain are.

Magnetic Resonance Imaging

Magnetic resonance imaging (MRI) is similar to a CAT scan in a way: both scans give you pictures of the brain. The MRI, however, uses different technology to create more detailed images. An MRI uses magnetic fields to measure the density and location of brain material. Since the MRI does not use X rays like the CAT scan does, the patient is not exposed to carcinogenic radiation. Like the CAT scan, the MRI gives doctors information about only the structure of the brain, not the function.

Positron Emission Tomography

A positron emission tomography (PET) scan lets researchers see what areas of the brain are most active during certain tasks. A PET scan measures how much of a certain chemical (e.g., glucose) parts of the brain are using. The more glucose used, the higher the activity. High levels of activity are indicated by warm colors like oranges and reds, while cool colors like blue and green show low activity levels. Different types of scans are used for different chemicals such as neurotransmitters, drugs, and oxygen flow.

Functional MRI

Functional MRI (fMRI) is a technology that combines elements of the MRI and PET scans. An fMRI scan can show details of brain structure with information about blood flow in the brain, tying brain structure to brain activity during cognitive tasks.

Brain Structure and Function

All the different methods of studying the brain give researchers different types of information about brain structure and function. The brain is the most complicated organ in the body. (In some ways, it is the most complex object we know of.) Because of this complexity, we need to divide the brain into separate categories to keep track of the information. Researchers have categorized hundreds of different parts and functions of different parts of the brain. When you study the brain, think about three separate major categories or sections: hindbrain, midbrain, and forebrain. Some evolutionary psychologists organize these categories into two major divisions: the "old brain" (hindbrain and midbrain) and the "new brain" (forebrain).

Hindbrain

The hindbrain consists of structures located on top of the spinal cord. The hindbrain is our life support system; it controls the basic biological functions that keep us alive. Some of the important specific structures within the hindbrain are the medulla, pons, and cerebellum. (Refer to Figure 4.3 for the locations of these structures.)

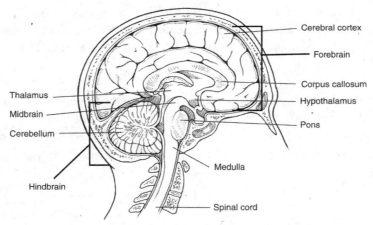

Figure 4.3 The brain

Medulla

The **medulla** is involved in the control of our blood pressure, heart rate, and breathing. It is also known as the medulla oblongata and is located above the spinal cord.

Pons

The pons (located just above the medulla and toward the front) connects the hindbrain with the midbrain and forebrain. It is also involved in the control of facial expressions.

Cerebellum

The **cerebellum** (located on the bottom rear of the brain) looks like a smaller version of our brain stuck onto the underside of our brain. *Cerebellum* means "little brain." The cerebellum coordinates some habitual muscle movements, such as tracking a target with our eyes or moving our fingers when playing the saxophone.

Midbrain

The midbrain is located just above the structures in the hindbrain but still below areas categorized as the forebrain. It is very small in humans, but this area of the brain controls some very important functions. In general, your midbrain coordinates simple movements with sensory information. For example, if you turn your head right now, your midbrain coordinates with muscles in your eyes to keep them focused on this text. Different parts of the midbrain are important in various muscle coordinations. For purposes of the AP test, though, you should remember that this area is between the hindbrain and the forebrain and that it integrates some types of sensory information and muscle movements. One specific structure in the midbrain you should be familiar with is the **reticular formation**. It is a netlike collection of cells throughout the midbrain that controls general body arousal and the ability to focus our attention. If the reticular formation does not function, we fall into a deep coma.

Forebrain

The various areas of the forebrain are very important to psychologists (and to students taking the AP Psychology test). Areas of the forebrain control what we think of as thought and reason. Notice in Figure 4.3 how large the forebrain is in comparison with the other areas. The size of our forebrain makes humans human, and most psychological researchers concentrate their efforts on this area of the brain. Specific areas of interest to us in the forebrain are the **thalamus**, **hypothalamus**, **amygdala**, and **hippocampus**. (The amygdala and hippocampus are not illustrated in Figure 4.3.)

Thalamus

The thalamus is located on top of the **brain stem**. It is responsible for receiving the sensory signals coming up the spinal cord and sending them to the appropriate areas in the rest of the forebrain. (See the specific areas listed in the section "Areas of the Cerebral Cortex" for examples of where some of these messages end up.)

Hypothalamus

The hypothalamus is a small structure right under the thalamus. The small size of the hypothalamus doesn't mean that it is not important. The hypothalamus controls several metabolic functions, including body temperature, sexual arousal (libido), hunger, thirst, and the endocrine system. If you consider yourself a morning person or a night person, the hypothalamus might be involved since it controls our biological rhythms.

Amygdala and Hippocampus

There are two armlike structures surrounding the thalamus. These are called the hippocampus. Structures near the end of each hippocampal arm are called the amygdala. The amygdala is vital to our experiences of emotion, and the hippocampus is vital to our memory system. Memories are not permanently stored in this area of the brain, however. Memories are processed through this area and then sent to other locations in the cerebral cortex for permanent storage. Researchers now know that memories must pass through this area first in order to be encoded because individuals with brain damage in this area are unable to retain new information.

Cerebral Cortex

When most people think of the human brain, they think of and picture the **cerebral cortex**. The gray, wrinkled surface of the brain is actually a thin (0.039-inch [1 mm]) layer of densely packed neurons. This layer covers the rest of the brain, including most of the structures we have described. When we are born, our cerebral cortex is full of neurons (more than we have now, actually), but the neurons are not yet well connected. As we develop and learn,

TIP

These parts of the brain (thalamus, hypothalamus, amygdala, and hippocampus) are grouped together and called the limbic system because they all deal with aspects of emotion and memory. When you study the parts of the brain, grouping structures together according to function should help you remember them.

the dendrites of the neurons in the cerebral cortex grow and connect with other neurons. This process, called pruning, forms the complex neural web you now have in your brain. The surface of the cerebral cortex is wrinkled (the wrinkles are called fissures) to increase the available surface area of the brain. The more wrinkles there are, the more surface area that is contained within our skull. If our cerebral cortex were not wrinkled, our skull would have to be 3 square feet (0.3 sq m) to hold all those neural connections!

Hemispheres

The cerebral cortex is divided into two hemispheres: left and right. The hemispheres look like mirror images of one another, but their similar appearance masks profound differences in function. The left hemisphere gets sensory messages and controls the motor functions of the right half of the body. The right hemisphere gets sensory messages and controls the motor functions of the left half of the body. (The idea that each side of the brain controls the opposite side of the body is called **contralateral hemispheric organization**.) Researchers are currently investigating other differences between the hemispheres, such as the possibility that the left hemisphere may be more active during logic and sequential tasks and the right during spatial and creative tasks. However, these generalizations need to be researched further before conclusions are drawn. This specialization of function in each hemisphere is called **hemispheric specialization**, or brain lateralization. Most of this research in differences between the hemispheres is done by examining **split-brain patients**—patients whose **corpus callosum** (the nerve bundle that connects the two hemispheres, see Figure 4.3) has been cut to treat severe epilepsy. The operation was pioneered by neuropsychologists Roger Sperry (1913–1994) and Michael Gazzaniga (1939–present). Split-brain patients also cannot orally report information presented only to the right hemisphere since the spoken language centers of the brain are usually located in the left hemisphere.

Areas of the Cerebral Cortex

When you study the cerebral cortex, think of it as a collection of different areas and specific cortices. Think of the cerebral cortex as eight different **lobes**, four on each hemisphere: frontal, parietal, temporal, and occipital. Some of the major functions of these parts of the brain that are relevant to the AP test are mentioned here. Any area of the cerebral cortex that is not associated with receiving sensory information or controlling muscle movements is labeled as an **association area**. Although specific functions are not known for each association area, these areas are very active in various human thoughts and behaviors. For example, association areas are thought to be responsible for complex, sophisticated thoughts like judgment and humor.

Frontal Lobes

The **frontal lobes** are large areas of the cerebral cortex located at the top front part of the brain behind the eyes (see Figure 4.4). The anterior or front of the frontal lobe is called the **prefrontal cortex** and is thought to play a critical role in directing thought processes. It is said to act as the brain's **central executive** and is believed to be important in predicting consequences, pursuing goals, maintaining emotional control, and engaging in abstract thought. The story of Phineas Gage mentioned previously exemplifies some of the functions of the prefrontal cortex. Phineas Gage's limbic system was separated from his frontal lobes in an accident. Doctors reported that he lost control of his emotions and became impulsive and animalistic.

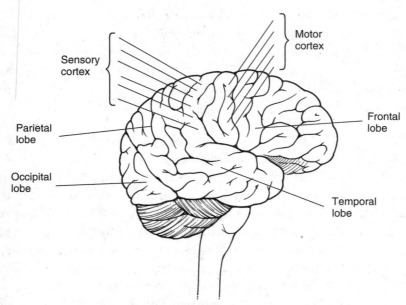

Figure 4.4 The lobes of the cerebral cortex

In most people, the frontal lobe in the left hemisphere contains one of the two special areas responsible for language processing. (Some left-handed people's language centers are in the right hemisphere.) **Broca's area** (named for Paul Broca, 1824–1880) is in the frontal lobe and is responsible for controlling the muscles involved in producing speech. Damage to this area can result in the loss of this ability (a type of **aphasia**). (The other area is **Wernicke's area** [named for Carl Wernicke, 1848–1905] and is located in the temporal lobe—see that section for more information.)

A thin vertical strip at the back of the frontal lobe (farthest from the eyes, see Figure 4.4) is called the **motor cortex**. This part of the cerebral cortex sends signals to our muscles, controlling our voluntary movements. The top of the body is controlled by the neurons at the bottom of this cortex (by the ears), progressing down the body as you go up the cortex. So the top of the motor cortex controls the feet and toes of the body.

Parietal Lobes

The **parietal lobes** are located behind the frontal lobe but still on the top of the brain (see Figure 4.4). The parietal lobes contain the **somatosensory cortex** (also known as the sensory cortex), which is located right behind the motor cortex in the frontal lobe. The sensory cortex is a thin vertical strip that receives incoming touch sensations from the rest of our body. The sensory cortex is organized similarly to the motor cortex. The top of the sensory cortex receives sensations from the bottom of the body, progressing down the cortex to the bottom, which processes signals from our face and head. One fascinating phenomenon that involves the somatosensory cortex is **phantom limb syndrome**: if an individual loses a part of their body, like an arm or hand, the person may still perceive sensations from that lost limb because part of their somatosensory cortex is still "mapped" to the missing body part.

Occipital Lobes

Our **occipital lobes** are at the very back of our brain, farthest from our eyes. This is some-what counterintuitive since one of the major functions of this lobe is to interpret messages from our eyes in our visual cortex. Impulses from the retinas in our eyes are sent to the visual cortex to be interpreted. Impulses from the right half of each retina are processed in the visual cortex in the right occipital lobe. Impulses from the left part of each retina are sent to the visual cortex in our left occipital lobe.

TIP

The term *occipital* looks like the word *optical* to some students. Thinking about this might help you remember the primary function of the occipital lobe!

Temporal Lobes

The **temporal lobes** process sound sensed by our ears. Sound waves are processed by the ears, turned into neural impulses, and interpreted in our auditory cortices. The auditory cortices are not lateralized like the visual cortices are. Sound received by the left ear is processed in the auditory cortices in both hemispheres. The second language area is located in the temporal lobe. (The first was Broca's area in the frontal lobe.) Wernicke's area is involved with **linguistic processing** via both written and spoken speech. Damage to this area would affect our ability to understand language. Our speech might sound fluent but lack the proper syntax and grammatical structure needed for meaningful communication.

Brain Plasticity

Researchers know some of the functions of different areas of the cerebral cortex, but they have also discovered that the brain is somewhat plastic or flexible. Although these cortices and lobes usually perform the functions already mentioned, other parts of the brain can adapt themselves to perform different functions if needed. You already know that the cerebral cortex is made up of a complex network of neurons connected by dendrites that grow to make new connections. Since dendrites grow throughout our lives, if one part of the brain is damaged, dendrites might be able to make new connections in another part of the brain that would be able to take over the functions usually performed by the damaged part of the brain. Dendrites grow most quickly in younger children. Researchers know that younger brains are more plastic and are more likely to compensate for damage.

5

States of Consciousness

Learning Objectives

In this chapter, you will learn about:

→ Drugs
→ The brain
→ Levels of consciousness
→ Sleep
→ Dreams

Key Terms

- Priming
- Blind sight
- Consciousness
- Psychoactive drugs
- Agonists
- Antagonists
- Reuptake
- Tolerance
- Withdrawal
- Caffeine
- Cocaine
- Stimulants

- Alcohol
- Depressants
- Hallucinogens
- Marijuana
- Opiates
- Heroin
- Circadian rhythm
- NREM stage 1
- NREM stage 2
- NREM stage 3
- Restoration of resources

- REM—rapid eye movement
- Paradoxical sleep
- REM rebound
- Insomnia
- Narcolepsy
- Sleep apnea
- Somnambulism
- Activation-synthesis theory
- Consolidation theory

Overview

While you are reading this text, you can probably become aware of your sense of consciousness. Early psychologists such as William James, author of the first psychology textbook, were very interested in consciousness. However, since no tools existed to examine it scientifically, the study of consciousness faded for a time. Currently, consciousness is becoming a more common research area due to more sophisticated brain-imaging tools and an increased emphasis on cognitive psychology.

Levels of Consciousness

Ironically, we experience different levels of consciousness in our daily life without being consciously aware of the experience. While you are reading this text, you might be tapping your pen or moving your leg in time to the music you are listening to. One level of consciousness is controlling your pen or leg, while another level is focused on reading these words. Research demonstrates other more subtle and complex effects of different levels of consciousness. The mere exposure effect (see also Unit 4) occurs when we prefer stimuli we have seen before over novel stimuli, even if we do not consciously remember seeing the old stimuli. For example, a researcher shows a group of research participants a list of nonsense terms for a short period of time. Later, the same group is shown another list of terms and asked which terms they prefer or like best. The mere exposure effect predicts that the group will choose the terms they saw previously, even though the group could not recall the first list of nonsense terms if asked. On some level, the group knows the first list.

A closely related concept is **priming**. Research participants respond more quickly and/or accurately to questions they have seen before, even if they do not remember seeing them. Another fascinating phenomenon that demonstrates levels of consciousness is **blind sight**. Some people who report being blind can nonetheless accurately describe the path of a moving object or accurately grasp objects they say they cannot see! One level of their consciousness is not getting any visual information, while another level is able to "see" as demonstrated by their behavior.

The concept of consciousness consisting of different levels or layers is well established. Not all researchers agree about what the specific levels are, but some of the possible types offered by researchers are shown in Table 5.1.

> **TIP**
>
> According to the psychological definition of consciousness, sleep is a state of consciousness because, while we are asleep, we are less aware of ourselves and our environment than we are when we are in our normal awake state. Other states of consciousness—drug-induced states, daydreaming, and so on—are states of consciousness for similar reasons.

Table 5.1 Levels of Consciousness

Conscious level	The information about yourself and your environment you are currently aware of. Your conscious level right now is probably focusing on these words and their meanings.
Nonconscious level	Body processes controlled by your mind that we are not usually (or ever) aware of. Right now, your nonconscious is controlling your heartbeat, respiration, digestion, and so on.
Preconscious level	Information about yourself or your environment that you are not currently thinking about (not in your conscious level) but you could be. If I asked you to remember your favorite toy as a child, you could bring that preconscious memory into your conscious level.
Subconscious level	Information that we are not consciously aware of but we know must exist due to behavior. The behaviors demonstrated in examples of priming and mere exposure effect suggest some information is accessible to our subconscious level but not to our conscious level.
Unconscious level	Psychodynamic psychologists believe some events and feelings are unacceptable to our conscious mind and are repressed into the unconscious mind. Many psychologists object to this concept as difficult or impossible to prove.

Drugs

Psychoactive drugs are chemicals that change the chemistry of the brain (and the rest of the body) and induce an altered state of consciousness. Some of the behavioral and cognitive changes caused by these drugs are due to physiological processes, but some are due to expectations about the drug. Research shows that people will often exhibit some of the expected effects of the drug if they think they ingested it, even if they did not. (This is similar to the placebo effect.)

All psychoactive drugs change our consciousness through similar physiological processes in the brain. Normally, the brain is protected from harmful chemicals in the bloodstream by thicker walls surrounding the brain's blood vessels. This is called the blood-brain barrier. However, the molecules that make up psychoactive drugs are small enough to pass through the blood-brain barrier. These molecules either mimic or block naturally occurring neurotransmitters in the brain. The drugs that mimic neurotransmitters are called **agonists**. These drugs fit in the receptor sites on a neuron that normally receive the neurotransmitter and function as that neurotransmitter normally would. (See Figure 5.1.) The drugs that block neurotransmitters are called **antagonists**.

These molecules don't fit the receptor sites well enough to substitute for them but do fit well enough to occupy the same space, thereby preventing neurotransmitters or agonists from causing a reaction. (See Figure 5.1.) Other drugs prevent natural neurotransmitters from being reabsorbed back into a neuron, creating an abundance of that neurotransmitter in the synapse. One example of this kind of drug is Prozac, which is called a "selective serotonin **reuptake** inhibitor" because it prevents serotonin from being reabsorbed back into the neuron. No matter what mechanism they use, psychoactive drugs gradually alter the natural levels of neurotransmitters in the brain. In some cases, the brain will produce less of a specific neurotransmitter if the amount of that neurotransmitter is being influenced by a psychoactive drug.

Agonists   Drugs that occupy receptors and activate them.

Antagonists   Drugs that occupy receptors but do not activate them. Antagonists block receptor activation by agonists.

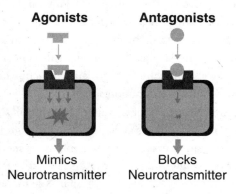

Figure 5.1 Agonists and antogonists

This change causes **tolerance**, a physiological change that produces a need for more of the same drug in order to achieve the same effect. Tolerance will eventually cause **withdrawal** symptoms in users. Withdrawal symptoms vary from drug to drug. They range from the headache I might get if I do not consume any caffeine during the day to the dehydrating and potentially fatal night sweats (sweating profusely during sleep) a heroin addict experiences during withdrawal. Dependence on psychoactive drugs can be either psychological or physical or can be both. Persons psychologically dependent on a drug feel an intense desire for the drug because they are convinced they need it in order to perform or feel a certain way. Persons physically dependent on a substance have a tolerance for the drug, experience withdrawal symptoms without it, and need the drug to avoid the withdrawal symptoms.

Different researchers categorize psychoactive drugs in different ways, but four common categories are stimulants, depressants, hallucinogens, and opiates. Table 5.2 describes the main effects and gives examples of these four categories of psychoactive drugs.

Caffeine, **cocaine**, amphetamines, and nicotine are common **stimulants**. Stimulants speed up body processes, including autonomic nervous system functions such as heart and respiration rates. This dramatic increase is accompanied by a sense of euphoria. The more powerful stimulants, such as cocaine, produce a euphoric rush that may make a

TIP

Alcohol is categorized as a depressant because of its effect on our nervous system, even though some people report feeling more energized after ingesting a small amount of alcohol. This energizing effect is due to expectations about alcohol and because alcohol lowers inhibitions. Similarly, nicotine is a stimulant because it speeds up our nervous system, but some people smoke to relax.

user feel extremely self-confident and invincible. All stimulants produce tolerance, withdrawal effects, and other side effects (such as disturbed sleep, reduced appetite, increased anxiety, and heart problems) to a greater or lesser degree that corresponds with the power of the drug.

Depressants slow down the same body systems that stimulants speed up. Alcohol, barbiturates, and anxiolytics (also called tranquilizers or antianxiety drugs) like Valium are common depressants. Alcohol is by far the most commonly used depressant and psychoactive drug. A euphoria can accompany the depressing effects of depressants, as do tolerance and withdrawal symptoms. In addition, alcohol slows down our reactions and judgment by slowing down brain processes. The inhibition of different brain regions causes behavioral changes. For example, when enough alcohol is ingested to affect the cerebellum, our motor coordination is dramatically affected, eventually making it difficult or impossible for the user even to stand. Because alcohol use is so widespread, more research has been done on alcohol than on any other psychoactive drug.

Hallucinogens (also sometimes called psychedelics) do not necessarily speed up or slow down the body. These drugs cause changes in perceptions of reality, including sensory hallucinations, loss of identity, and vivid fantasies. Common hallucinogens include LSD, peyote, psilocybin mushrooms, and **marijuana**. One notable feature of hallucinogens is their persistence. Some amount of these drugs may remain in the body for weeks. If an individual ingests the hallucinogen again during this time period, the new dose of the chemical is added to the lingering amount, creating more profound and potentially dangerous effects. This effect is sometimes called reverse tolerance because the second dose may be less than the first but cause the same or greater effects. Effects of hallucinogens are less predictable than those of stimulants or depressants.

Opiates such as morphine, **heroin**, methadone, codeine, and fentanyl are all similar in chemical structure to opium, a drug derived from the poppy plant. The opiates all act as agonists for endorphins and thus are powerful painkillers and mood elevators. Opiates cause drowsiness and euphoria associated with elevated endorphin levels. The opiates are some of the most physically addictive drugs because they rapidly change brain chemistry and create tolerance and withdrawal symptoms. Fentanyl, in particular, is so incredibly powerful that even minute quantities mixed in with other drugs can be lethal.

Table 5.2 Types of Psychoactive Drugs

Type of Drug	Main Effect	Examples
Stimulants	Arouse the autonomic nervous system	Caffeine, cocaine, amphetamines, nicotine
Depressants	Slow down the autonomic nervous system	Alcohol, barbiturates, tranquilizers
Hallucinogens	Cause sensory distortions	Marijuana, LSD, peyote, mushrooms, psilocybin
Opiates	Relieve pain, elevate mood	Codeine, morphine, heroin, methadone, fentanyl

Sleep

As a student, sleep is probably a subject near and dear to you. Many studies show that a large percentage of high school and college students are sleep deprived, meaning they do not get as much sleep as their body wants. To a psychologist, referring to being asleep as being unconscious is incorrect. Sleep is one of the states of consciousness.

Sleep Cycle

You may be familiar with the term **circadian rhythm**. During a 24-hour day, our metabolic and thought processes follow a certain pattern. Some of us are more active in the morning than others, some of us get hungry or go to the bathroom at certain times of day, and so on. Part of our circadian rhythm is our sleep cycle. Our sleep cycle is our typical pattern of sleep. Researchers using EEG (electroencephalogram) machines can record how active our brains are during sleep and describe the different stages of sleep we progress through each night. Refer to Figure 5.2 for a graphic representation of the stages of a typical sleep cycle.

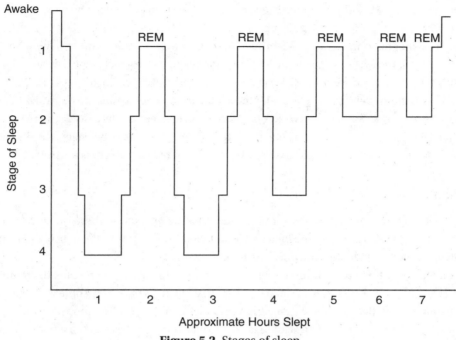

Figure 5.2 Stages of sleep

As you can see in Figure 5.2, sleep is far from being a time of unconsciousness. We cycle through different stages of sleep during the night. Our brain waves and level of awareness change as we cycle through the stages. The period when we are falling asleep is called sleep onset. This is the stage between wakefulness and sleep. Our brain produces alpha waves when we are drowsy but awake. We might experience mild hallucinations (such as falling or rising) before actually falling asleep and entering stage 1. The rest of the stages of sleep are divided into REM sleep (which you will read about later) and non-REM (NREM) sleep stages: **NREM stage 1**, **NREM stage 2**, **NREM stage 3,** and **NREM stage 4**. While we are awake and in stages NREM 1 and NREM 2, our brains produce theta waves, which are relatively high-frequency, low-amplitude waves. However, the theta waves get progressively slower and higher in amplitude as we go from wakefulness and through NREM stage 1 and NREM stage 2. In NREM stage 2, the EEG starts to show sleep spindles, which are short bursts of rapid brain waves. From there, we move into NREM stages 3 and 4, which are sometimes called delta sleep (also called deep or slow-wave sleep) because of the delta waves that exist during these stages. The slower the wave (slow waves are low-frequency waves), the deeper the sleep and the less aware we are of our environment. A person in delta sleep is very difficult to wake up. If you are awakened out of delta sleep, you may be very disoriented and groggy. Delta sleep seems to be very important in replenishing the body's chemical supplies, releasing growth hormones in children and fortifying our immune system. A person deprived of delta sleep will be more susceptible to illness and will feel physically tired. Increasing exercise will increase the amount of time we spend in NREM stages 3 and 4. This finding indicates that one of the functions of sleep (and the different stages in the sleep cycle) is **restoration of resources**: sleep is necessary because our body has to rebuild various resources it used while we were awake and active.

After a period of time in delta sleep, our brain waves start to speed up and we go back through NREM stages 3 and 2. However, as we reach NREM stage 1, our brain produces a period of intense activity, our eyes dart back and forth, and many of our muscles may twitch repeatedly. This is **REM—rapid eye movement**. This sleep stage is sometimes called **paradoxical sleep** since our brain waves appear as active and intense as they do when we are awake. The exact purposes of REM are not clear, but some effects are known. Dreams can occur in any stage of sleep but are far more likely to take place during REM sleep, especially detailed dreams. REM sleep deprivation interferes with memory. Individuals deprived of REM sleep will experience **REM rebound**—experiencing more and longer periods of REM—the next time they are allowed to sleep normally. The more stress we experience during the day, the longer our periods of REM sleep will be.

Notice in Figure 5.2 that not only do we cycle through these approximately 90-minute stages about four to seven times during the night but the cycle itself also varies during the night. As we get closer to morning (or whenever we naturally awaken), we spend more time in NREM stages 1 and 2 and in REM sleep and less in NREM stages 3 and 4. Also, age affects the pattern. Babies not only spend more total time sleeping than we do (up to 18 hours), but they also spend more time in REM sleep. As we age, our total need for sleep declines as does the amount of time we spend in REM sleep. Although research has not answered all the questions about sleep, details about our sleep cycle provide clues as to why we spend so much of our life in this altered state of consciousness.

Sleep Disorders

Many of us will experience a night, or perhaps a series of nights, of sleeplessness. These isolated periods of disruption in our sleep pattern give us an idea of the inconvenience and discomfort true sleep disorders can cause in people's lives. Sleep researchers identify and diagnose several sleep disorders.

Insomnia is far and away the most common sleep disorder, affecting up to 10 percent of the population. An insomniac has persistent problems getting to sleep or staying asleep at night. Most people will experience occasional bouts of insomnia, but diagnosed insomniacs have problems getting to sleep more often than not. Insomnia is usually treated with suggestions for changes in behavior: reducing the intake of caffeine or other stimulants, exercising at appropriate times (not right before bedtime) during the day, and maintaining a consistent sleep pattern. Doctors and researchers encourage insomniacs to use sleeping pills only with caution as they disturb sleep patterns during the night and can prevent truly restful sleep.

Narcolepsy occurs far more rarely than insomnia, occurring in less than 0.001 percent of the population. Narcoleptics suffer from periods of intense sleepiness and may fall asleep at unpredictable and inappropriate times. Narcoleptics may suddenly fall into REM sleep regardless of what they are doing at the time. One of my students suffered from narcolepsy from the time he was a preadolescent up until his graduation from high school. After he was finally diagnosed, he estimated that before his treatment he was drowsy almost his entire day except for two to three hours in the late afternoon. Narcolepsy can be successfully treated with medication and by changing sleep patterns, such as introducing naps at strategic times during the day.

Sleep apnea may be almost as common as insomnia and, in some ways, might be more serious. Apnea causes a person to stop breathing for short periods of time during the night. The body causes the person to wake up slightly and gasp for air, and then sleep continues. This process robs the person of deep sleep and causes tiredness and possible interference with attention and memory. Severe apnea can be fatal. Since these individuals do not remember waking up during the night, apnea frequently goes undiagnosed. Overweight men are at a higher risk for apnea. Apnea can be treated with a respiration machine that provides air for the person as he or she sleeps.

My mother tells me that I experienced night terrors as a child. I would sit up in bed in the middle of the night and scream and move around my room. Night terrors usually affect young children, and most do not remember the episode when they wake up. The exact causes are not known, but night terrors are probably related in some way to **somnambulism** (sleepwalking). They occur more commonly in children, and both phenomena occur during the first few hours of the night in stage 4 sleep. Most people stop having night terrors and episodes of somnambulism as they get older.

Dreams

Dreams are the series of storylike images we experience as we sleep. Some people remember dreams frequently, sometimes more than one per night, while others are not aware of their dreams at all. Some of us even report lucid dreams in which we are aware that we are dreaming and can control the storyline of the dream. Dreams are a difficult research area for psychologists because they rely almost entirely on self-reports. As mentioned previously, researchers know that if people are awakened during or shortly after an REM episode, they often report they were dreaming. Researchers theorize about the purposes and meanings of dreams. However, validating these theories is difficult with the limited access researchers currently have to dreams.

The **activation-synthesis theory** of dreaming looks at dreams first as biological phenomena. Brain imaging proves that our brain is very active during REM sleep. This theory proposes that perhaps dreams are nothing more than the brain's interpretations of what is happening physiologically during REM sleep. Researchers know that our minds are very good at explaining events, even when the events have a purely physiological cause. Split-brain patients sometimes make up elaborate explanations for behaviors caused by their operation. Dreams may be a story made up by a literary part of our mind caused by the intense brain activity during REM sleep. According to this theory, dreams, while interesting, have no more meaning than any other physiological reflex in our body.

The information-processing theory of dreaming suggests that we use dreams to process the events of the day. This theory points out that stress during the day will increase the number and intensity of dreams during the night. Also, most people report their dream content relates somehow to daily concerns. Proponents of information processing theorize that perhaps the brain is dealing with daily stress and information during REM dreams. The function of REM may be to integrate the information processed during the day into our memories. Babies may need more REM sleep than adults because they process so much new information every day.

The information-processing theory of dreaming is closely related to the **consolidation theory** of dreams: one of the functions of dreams might be to help us encode events and information in our short-term memory into our long-term memory.

6

Sensation

Learning Objectives

In this chapter, you will learn about:
- → Energy senses
- → Chemical senses
- → Body position senses

Key Terms

- Transduction
- Sensory adaptation
- Cocktail party effect
- Synesthesia
- Prosopagnosia
- Wavelengths
- Accommodation
- Lens
- Nearsightedness
- Farsightedness
- Retina
- Transduction
- Thalamus
- Photoreceptors
- Cones
- Rods
- Ganglion cells

- Blind spot
- Trichromatic theory
- Afterimages
- Dichromatism
- Monochromatism
- Opponent-process theory
- Amplitude
- Frequency
- Loudness
- Pitch
- Sound localization
- Place theory
- Conduction deafness
- Nerve deafness
- Sensorineural deafness

- Gate control theory
- Taste receptors
- Supertasters
- Nontaster
- Medium taster
- Semicircular canals
- Kinesthesis
- Gustation
- Olfaction
- Vestibular sense
- Sweet
- Sour
- Salty
- Bitter
- Umami
- Oleogustus

Overview

Right now, as you read this, your eyes capture the light reflected off the page or emitted by the screen in front of you. Structures in your eyes change this pattern of light into signals that are sent to your brain and interpreted as language. The sensation of the symbols on the page and the perception of these symbols as words allow you to understand what you are reading. All our senses work in a similar way. In general, our sensory organs receive stimuli. These messages go through a process called **transduction**, which means the signals are transformed into neural impulses. These neural impulses travel first to a part of the brain called the **thalamus** and then on to different cortices of the brain. (You will see later that the sense of smell is the one exception to this rule.)

What we sense and perceive is influenced by many factors, including how long we are exposed to stimuli. For example, you probably felt your socks when you put them on this morning, but you stopped feeling them after a while. You probably stopped perceiving the feeling of your socks on your feet because of a combination of **sensory adaptation** (decreasing responsiveness to stimuli due to constant stimulation) and sensory habituation (our perception of sensations is partially due to how focused we are on them). What we perceive is determined by what sensations activate our senses and by what we focus on perceiving. We can voluntarily attend to stimuli in order to perceive them, as you are doing right now, but paying attention can also be involuntary. If you are talking with a friend and someone across the room says your name, your attention will probably involuntarily switch across the room. (This is sometimes called the **cocktail party effect**.)

These processes are our only way to get information about the outside world. The exact distinction between what is sensation and what is perception is debated by psychologists and philosophers. Some researchers spend their careers studying rare but fascinating differences in how people sense and perceive the world. One example is **synesthesia**, a phenomenon some people experience in which the activation of one sense, like seeing a color, activates another sense, like hearing a specific sound (or vice versa)! **Prosopagnosia**, another rare condition, involves the inability to recognize faces. For our purposes, though, we can think of sensation in more general terms: the activation of our senses (eyes, ears, and so on) and perception as the process of understanding these sensations. We will review the structure and functions of each sensory organ and then explain some concepts involved in perception in Chapter 7, "Perception."

Energy Senses

Vision

Vision is the dominant sense in human beings. Sighted people use vision to gather information about their environment more than any other sense. The process of vision involves several steps.

Step One: Gathering Light

Vision is a complicated process, and you should have a basic understanding of the structures and processes involved for the AP test. First, light is reflected off objects and gathered by the eye. Visible light is a small section of the electromagnetic spectrum that you may have studied in your science classes; the spectrum is made up of waves. **Wavelengths** longer than visible light are infrared waves, microwaves, and radio waves. Wavelengths shorter than visible light include ultraviolet waves and X rays.

The colors we see depend on several factors. Different wavelengths within the visible light spectrum appear as different hues. These hues, in order from longest to shortest wavelengths, are red, orange, yellow, green, blue, indigo, and violet; you probably were taught the acronym *Roy G. Biv* to help you remember this order. When you mix all these light waves together, you get white light or sunlight. Although we think of objects as possessing colors (a red shirt, a blue car), objects appear the color they do because of the wavelengths of light they reflect. For instance, a red object reflects red light and absorbs other colors. Objects appear black because they absorb all colors, and those that appear white reflect all wavelengths of light. However, our perception of color is influenced by more than the length of the wave. Another important factor is the waves's amplitude (height), which dictates its intensity. The higher a wave's amplitude, the more energy it contains and the brighter the color we perceive.

> **Try this:** Hold up one finger and focus on it. Now change your focus and look at the wall behind your finger. Then look at your finger again. You can feel the muscles changing the shape of your lens as you switch your focus. As the light passes through the lens, the image is flipped upside down and inverted. The focused inverted image projects on the **retina**, which is like a screen on the back of your eye. On this screen are specialized neurons that are activated by the different wavelengths of light.

Step Two: Within the Eye

When we look at something, we turn our eyes toward the object and the reflected light coming from it enters our eye. To understand the following descriptions, refer to Figure 6.1 for structures in the eye. The reflected light first enters the eye through the cornea. The cornea provides some protection to the rest of the eye but also plays an important role in focusing the light. Then the light goes through the pupil. The pupil is like the shutter of a camera. The muscles that control the pupil (called the iris) open it (dilate) to let more light in and also make it smaller (contract) to let less light in. Through a process called **accommodation**, light that enters the pupil is focused by the **lens**; the lens is curved and flexible so it can change shape to focus the light on the retina. When the lens cannot adapt enough to focus the light properly, **nearsightedness** or **farsightedness** can result.

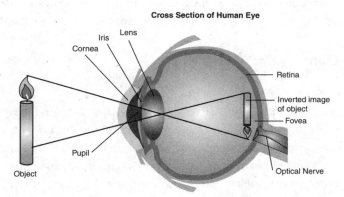

Figure 6.1 Cross section of the eye

Step Three: Transduction

The term **transduction** refers to the translation of incoming stimuli into neural signals. This term applies not only to vision but to all our senses. In vision, transduction occurs when light activates the neurons in the retina. There are several layers of cells in the retina.

The first layer of cells are **photoreceptors** and are directly activated by light. These cells are **cones**, which are cells that are activated by color, and **rods**, which are cells that respond to black and white. These cells are arranged in a pattern on the retina. Rods outnumber cones (the ratio is approximately 20 to 1) and are distributed throughout the retina. Cones are concentrated toward the center of the retina. At the very center of the retina is an indentation called the fovea that contains the highest concentration of cones. If you focus on something, you are focusing the light onto your fovea, and you will see it in color. Your peripheral vision, especially at the extremes, relies on rods and is mostly in black and white. Your peripheral vision may seem to be full color, but controlled experiments prove otherwise. (You can demonstrate this yourself. Focus on a spot in front of you and have a friend hold different colored pens in your peripheral vision. You will find you cannot determine the color of the pens until they get close to the center of your vision.)

If enough rods and cones fire in an area of the retina, they activate the next layer of bipolar cells. If enough bipolar cells fire, the next layer of cells, **ganglion cells**, is activated. The axons of the ganglion cells make up the optic nerve that sends these impulses to a specific region in the thalamus called the lateral geniculate nucleus (LGN). From there, the messages are sent to the visual cortices located in the occipital lobes of the brain. The spot where the optic nerve leaves the retina has no rods or cones, so it is referred to as the **blind spot**. There are more rods and cones than bipolar cells, and there are more bipolar cells than ganglion cells (enabled by a phenomenon called summation), which minimizes the size of the blind spot. The optic nerve is divided into two parts. Impulses from the left side of each retina go to the left hemisphere of the brain. Impulses from the right side of each retina go to the right side of our brain. The spot where the nerves cross each other is called the optic chiasm.

You might have guessed that this is a simplified version of this process. Different factors are involved in why each layer of cells might fire, but this explanation is suitable for our purposes.

Step Four: In the Brain

You might remember that the visual cortex of the brain is located in the occipital lobe. Some researchers say it is at this point that sensation ends and perception begins. Others say some interpretation of images occurs in the layers of cells in the retina. Still others say it occurs in the LGN region of the thalamus. That debate aside, the visual cortex of the brain receives the impulses from the cells of the retina, and the impulses activate feature detectors. Perception researchers David Hubel (1926–2013) and Torsten Wiesel (1924–present) discovered that groups of neurons in the visual cortex respond to different types of visual images. The visual cortex has feature detectors for vertical lines, curves, motion, and many other features of images. What we perceive visually is a combination of these features.

Theories of Color Vision

Trichromatic Theory

Competing theories exist about how and why we see color. The oldest and simplest theory is **trichromatic theory**. This theory hypothesizes that we have three types of cones in the retina and that each type detects a different primary color of light: blue, red, or green. These cones are activated in different combinations to produce all the colors of the visible spectrum. Although this theory has some research support and makes sense intuitively, it cannot explain some visual phenomena, such as **afterimages** and color blindness. If you stare at one color for a while and then look at a white or blank space, you will see a negative color afterimage. If you stare at green, the afterimage will be red, while the afterimage of yellow is blue. Color blindness is similar. Individuals with **dichromatism** cannot see either red/green shades or blue/yellow shades. (The other type of color blindness is **monochromatism**, which causes people to see only shades of gray.) Another theory of color vision is needed to explain these phenomena.

Opponent-Process Theory

The **opponent-process theory** states that the sensory receptors arranged in the retina come in pairs: red/green pairs, yellow/blue pairs, and black/white pairs. If one sensor is stimulated, its pair is inhibited from firing. This theory explains color afterimages well. If you stare at the color red for a while, you fatigue the sensors for red. Then when you switch your gaze and look at a white page, the red sensors won't be able to fire as much as the green ones so you will see a green afterimage. The opponent-process theory also explains color blindness. If color sensors do come in pairs and an individual is missing one pair, he or she should have difficulty seeing those hues. People with dichromatic color blindness have difficulty seeing shades of red and green or of yellow and blue.

> **TIP**
>
> Most researchers agree with a combination of trichromatic and opponent-process theory. Individual cones appear to correspond best to the trichromatic theory, while the opponent processes may occur at other layers of the retina. The important thing to remember is that both concepts are needed to explain color vision fully.

Hearing

Our auditory sense also uses energy in the form of waves, but sound waves are vibrations in the air rather than electromagnetic waves. Sound waves are created by vibrations, which travel through the air and are then collected by our ears. These vibrations then finally go through the process of transduction into neural messages and are sent to the brain. Sound waves, like all waves, have **amplitude** and **frequency**. Amplitude is the height of the wave and determines the **loudness** of the sound, which is measured in decibels. Frequency refers to the length of the waves and determines **pitch**, which is measured in megahertz. High-pitched sounds have high frequencies, and their waves are densely packed together. Low-pitched sounds have low frequencies, and their waves are spaced apart.

Sound waves are collected in your outer ear, or pinna. (Figure 6.2 shows structures in the ear.) The waves travel down the ear canal (also called the auditory canal) until they reach the eardrum or tympanic membrane. This is a thin membrane that vibrates as the sound waves hit it. Think of it as the head of a drum. This membrane is attached to the first in a series of three small bones collectively known as the ossicles. The eardrum connects with the hammer (or malleus), which is connected to the anvil (or incus), which connects to the stirrup (or stapes). The vibration of the eardrum is transmitted by these three bones to the oval window, a membrane very similar to the eardrum. The oval window membrane is attached to the cochlea, a structure shaped like a snail's shell and filled with fluid. As the oval window vibrates, the fluid moves. The floor of the cochlea is the basilar membrane. It is lined with hair cells connected to the organ of Corti, which are neurons activated by movement of the hair cells. When the fluid moves, the hair cells move, and transduction occurs. The organ of Corti fires, and these impulses are transmitted to the brain via the auditory nerve. Have you ever wondered why humans have two ears? When the information from the left and right ears reach the brain, our auditory cortices notes whether the sound was louder in one ear or another. In this way, we can determine approximately where a sound originated; this is called **sound localization**.

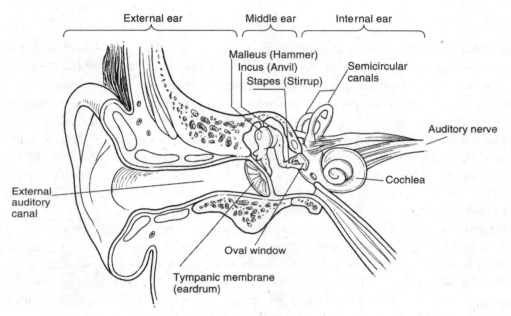

Figure 6.2 Cross section of the ear

Pitch Theories

The description of the hearing process above explains how we hear in general, but how do we hear different pitches or tones? As with color vision, two different theories describe the two processes involved in hearing pitch: place theory and frequency theory.

Place Theory

Place theory holds that the hair cells in the cochlea respond to different frequencies of sound based on where they are located in the cochlea. Some bend in response to high pitches and some to low. We sense pitch because the hair cells move in different places in the cochlea.

Frequency Theory

Research demonstrates that place theory accurately describes how hair cells sense the upper range of pitches but not the lower tones. Lower tones are sensed by the rate at which the cells fire. Frequency theory states that we sense pitch because the hair cells fire at different rates (frequencies) in the cochlea.

> **TIP**
>
> One way to remember amplitude and frequency is to imagine you are watching waves go by. Frequency is how frequently the waves come by. If they speed by quickly, the waves are high in frequency. Amplitude is how tall the waves are. The taller the waves, the more energy and the louder the noise is.

Deafness

An understanding of how hearing works explains hearing problems as well. **Conduction deafness** occurs when something goes wrong with the system of conducting the sound to the cochlea (in the ear canal, eardrum, hammer/anvil/stirrup, or oval window). For example, my mother-in-law has a medical condition that is causing her stirrup to deteriorate slowly. Eventually, she will need surgery to replace that bone to hear well. **Nerve deafness** (or **sensorineural deafness**) occurs when the hair cells in the cochlea are damaged, usually by loud noise. If you have ever been to a concert, football game, or other event loud enough to leave your ears ringing, chances are you came close to or did cause permanent damage to your hearing. Prolonged exposure to noise that is loud can permanently damage the hair cells in your cochlea, and these hair cells do not regenerate. Nerve deafness is much more difficult to treat since no method has been found that will encourage the hair cells to regenerate.

Touch

When our skin is indented, pierced, or experiences a change in temperature, our sense of touch is activated by this energy. We have many different types of nerve endings in every patch of skin, and the exact relationship between these different types of nerve endings and the sense of touch is not completely understood. Some nerve endings respond to pressure, while others respond to temperature. We do know that our brain interprets the amount of indentation (or temperature change) as the intensity of the touch, from a light touch to a hard blow. We also sense placement of the touch by the place on our body where the nerve endings fire. Nerve endings are also more concentrated in different parts of our body. If we want to feel something, we usually use our fingertip, an area of high nerve concentration, rather than the back of our elbow, an area of low nerve concentration. If touch or temperature receptors are stimulated sharply, a different kind of nerve ending called pain receptors will also fire. Pain is a useful response because it warns us of potential dangers.

  Gate control theory helps explain how we experience pain the way we do. This theory explains that some pain messages have a higher priority than others. When a higher-priority message is sent to the brain, the gate swings open for it and swings shut for a lower-priority message, which we will not feel. Of course, this gate is not a physical gate swinging in the nerve; it is just a convenient way to understand how pain messages are sent. When you scratch an itch, the gate swings open for your high-intensity scratching and shuts for the low-intensity itching, and you stop the itching for a short period of time. (Do not worry, though, the itching usually starts again soon!) Endorphins, or pain-killing chemicals in the body, also swing the gate shut. Natural endorphins in the brain, which are chemically similar to opiates like morphine, control pain.

Chemical Senses

Taste (or Gustation)

The nerves involved in the chemical senses respond to chemicals rather than to energy, such as light and sound waves. Chemicals from the food we eat (or whatever else we stick into our mouths) are absorbed by taste buds on our tongue (see Figure 6.3). **Taste receptors** are located on papillae, which are the bumps you can see on your tongue. Taste buds are located all over the tongue and some parts of the inside of the cheeks and roof of the mouth. Humans sense five different types of tastes: sweet, salty, sour, bitter, umami (savory or meaty taste), and oleogutus (taste of fat). Some taste buds respond more intensely to a specific taste and more weakly to others. People differ in their ability to taste food. The more densely packed the taste buds, the more chemicals that are absorbed and the more intensely the food is tasted. You can get an idea of how densely packed taste buds are by looking at the papillae on your tongue. If all the bumps are packed tightly together, you probably taste food intensely. (These individuals are called **supertasters**.) The density of these bumps on the tongue is a trait controlled by genetic predispositions. If the taste buds are spread apart, you are probably a **nontaster** (or **medium taster**). What we think of as the flavor of food is actually a combination of taste and smell.

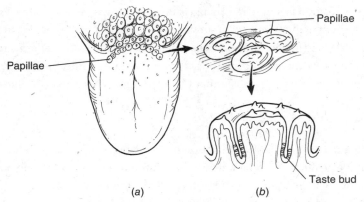

Figure 6.3 Taste sensors

Smell (or Olfaction)

Our sense of smell also depends on chemicals emitted by substances. Molecules of substances, hot chocolate for example, rise into the air. Some of them are drawn into our nose. The molecules settle in a mucous membrane at the top of each nostril and are absorbed by receptor cells located there. The exact types of these receptor cells are not yet known as they are for taste buds. Some researchers estimate that as many as 100 different types of smell receptors may exist. These receptor cells are linked to the olfactory bulb (see Figure 6.4), which gathers the messages from the olfactory receptor cells and sends this information to the brain. Interestingly, the nerve fibers from the olfactory bulb connect to the brain differently than all the other senses do. The impulses from all, except smell, go through the thalamus first before being sent to the cortex. However, information from our sense of smell goes directly to the amygdala (emotional impulses) and then to the hippocampus (memory). This direct connection to the limbic system may explain why smell is such a powerful trigger for memories.

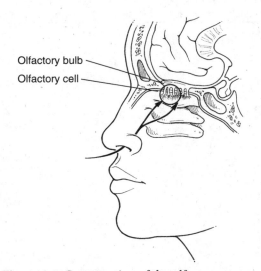

Figure 6.4 Cross section of the olfactory system

Body Position Senses

Vestibular Sense

Our vestibular sense tells us about how our body is oriented in space. Three **semicircular canals** in the inner ear (see Figure 6.2) give the brain feedback about body orientation. The canals are basically tubes partially filled with fluid. When the position of your head changes, the fluid moves in the canals, causing sensors in the canals to move. The movement of these hair cells (similar to the hair cells in the cochlea in our ear) activate neurons, and their impulses go to the brain. You have probably experienced the nausea and dizziness caused when the fluid in these canals is agitated. During an exciting roller-coaster ride, the fluid in the canals might move so much that the brain receives confusing signals about body position. This causes dizziness and nausea.

Kinesthetic Sense

While our vestibular sense keeps track of the overall orientation of our body, our kinesthetic sense (**kinesthesis**) gives us feedback about the position and orientation of specific body parts. Receptors in our muscles and joints send information to our brain about our limbs. This information, combined with visual feedback, lets us keep track of our body. You could probably reach down with one finger and touch your kneecap with a high degree of accuracy because your kinesthetic sense provides information about where your finger is in relation to your kneecap.

Table 6.1 provides a summary of the senses and their associated receptors.

Table 6.1 Senses and Associated Receptors

Energy senses	Vision	Rods, cones (in retina)
	Hearing	Hairlike cells in the cochlea
	Touch	Temperature, pressure, pain nerves (in the skin)
Chemical senses	Taste (**gustation**)	**Sweet**, **sour**, **salty**, **bitter**, **umami**, and **oleogustus** taste buds (in papillae on the tongue)
	Smell (**olfaction**)	Smell receptors connected to the olfactory bulb (in the nose)
Body position senses	**Vestibular sense**	Hairlike cells in the three semicircular canals (in the inner ear)
	Kinesthetic sense	Receptors in muscles and joints

Unit 1 Multiple-Choice Questions

1. Dr. Dahab, a brain researcher, is investigating the connection between certain environmental stimuli and brain processes. Which types of brain scans is he most likely to use?

   (A) MRI and CAT
   (B) CAT and EKG
   (C) PET and EEG
   (D) EKG and CAT

2. Split-brain patients are unable to

   (A) coordinate movements between their major and minor muscle groups.
   (B) speak about information received exclusively in their right hemisphere.
   (C) speak about information received exclusively in their left hemisphere.
   (D) solve abstract problems involving integrating logical (left-hemisphere) and spatial (right-hemisphere) information.

3. Mr. Spam is a 39-year-old male who has been brought into your neurology clinic by his wife. She has become increasingly alarmed by her husband's behavior over the last four months. You recommend a CAT scan to look for tumors in the brain. Which two parts of the brain would you predict are being affected by the tumors?

   List of symptoms: vastly increased appetite, body temperature fluctuations, decreased sexual desire, jerky movements, poor balance when walking and standing, inability to throw objects, and exaggerated efforts to coordinate movements in a task

   (A) Motor cortex and emotion cortex
   (B) Somatosensory cortex and hypothalamus
   (C) Hypothalamus and cerebellum
   (D) Cerebellum and medulla

4. A deer runs into the road while Harry is driving, and he has to swerve and hit the brakes. As he slows to a stop, Harry's heart is pounding and his breathing rate is elevated. Harry's reaction is controlled by the

   (A) peripheral nervous system.
   (B) central nervous system.
   (C) parasympathetic nervous system.
   (D) sympathetic nervous system.

5. What is the principal difference between amplitude and frequency in the context of sound waves?

   (A) Amplitude is the tone or timbre of a sound, whereas frequency is the pitch.
   (B) Amplitude is detected in the cochlea, whereas frequency is detected in the auditory cortex.
   (C) Amplitude is the height of the sound wave, whereas frequency is a measure of how frequently the sound waves pass a given point.
   (D) Both measure qualities of sound, but frequency is a more accurate measure since it measures the shapes of the waves rather than the strength of the waves.

6. What behavior would be difficult without our vestibular sense?

   (A) Integrating what we see and hear
   (B) Writing our name
   (C) Repeating a list of digits
   (D) Walking a straight line with our eyes closed

7. After being in a car accident, Suzy is having difficulty with her vision. Which part of her brain is most likely to have been affected?

   (A) Cerebellum
   (B) Thalamus
   (C) Parietal lobe
   (D) Amygdala

8. Bertrand falls asleep at unusual times, including in the middle of arguments. With which disorder is he most likely to be diagnosed?

(A) Sleep apnea
(B) Insomnia
(C) Narcolepsy
(D) Somnambulism

9. Which of the following provides the best evidence for the influence of heredity as opposed to environment?

(A) Fraternal twins have more similar interests than typical siblings.
(B) Identical twins raised together score less similarly on intelligence tests than identical twins raised separately.
(C) Fraternal twins raised together score more similarly on intelligence tests than fraternal twins raised separately.
(D) Identical twins raised separately tend to resemble their birth parents more than their adoptive parents.

10. How do chemical senses differ from energy senses?

(A) People need to interact more closely with a chemical stimulus sense.
(B) The chemical senses are more important to most people than the energy senses.
(C) More research has focused on chemical senses than on energy senses.
(D) More of the brain is devoted to processing chemical sensation than energy sensation.

11. Eli plays percussion in a band. He's been urged to wear earplugs in order to protect his hearing. Which part of the ear is most likely to be protected by earplugs?

(A) Hair cells
(B) Ossicles
(C) Pinna
(D) Tympanic membrane

12. A drug that blocks the perception of pain is most likely to be

(A) an acetylcholine agonist.
(B) an endorphin agonist.
(C) a serotonin antagonist.
(D) a glutamate antagonist.

Questions 13 through 15 refer to the following.

Dr. Webb is studying what happens when people are deprived of REM sleep. In his university lab, 40 students from his Introduction to Psychology class are randomly assigned either to a control condition in which they are left to sleep without disruption or to a REM deprivation condition in which they are awakened every time an EEG indicates that they are entering REM. The students report to the lab directly after Dr. Webb's class on Monday, and at the next class meeting, they take a quiz on the material taught Monday. The graph below shows the results of the study.

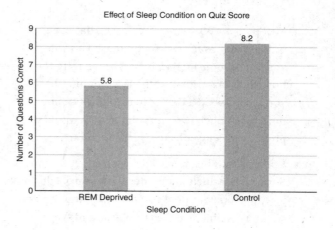

13. The results provide the strongest support for the argument that sleep has a

(A) biological purpose.
(B) cognitive purpose.
(C) social purpose.
(D) psychodynamic purpose.

14. The biggest ethical concern associated with Dr. Webb's study would be

    (A) deception.
    (B) privacy.
    (C) long-lasting harm.
    (D) consent.

15. If Dr. Webb wants to generalize his findings beyond his sample, it would be most valuable for him to

    (A) test these students again later in the semester.
    (B) test students from a class he will teach the following semester.
    (C) test students of different ages from a variety of schools.
    (D) test students from a variety of colleges and classes.

Answer Explanations

1. **(C)** The PET and EEG scans both give information about brain function. (The PET measures brain activity, and the EEG measures brain waves.) The MRI and CAT scans give information about brain structure, not function. An EKG is a medical test for heart function.

2. **(B)** Since the left hemisphere typically controls speech, split-brain patients are usually unable to talk about information exposed to only the right hemisphere. Their muscle coordination is usually normal (possible after a short adjustment period). Their ability to solve abstract problems is not affected.

3. **(C)** A tumor on the hypothalamus would explain the first three symptoms since the hypothalamus controls (at least in part) body temperature, libido, and hunger. The cerebellum coordinates some types of movements, including throwing objects and our sense of balance. The motor cortex controls voluntary muscle movements, but the specific movements described in the question are controlled by the cerebellum. The medulla controls our life-support functions, like heart rate and respiration.

4. **(D)** Harry's reaction is controlled by the sympathetic nervous system. The sympathetic and parasympathetic nervous systems make up the autonomic nervous system, which controls our involuntary actions. The sympathetic nervous system prepares us to react to stressful situations, while the parasympathetic symptom calms us back down after the threat has passed.

5. **(C)** Amplitude is a measure of the height of the wave, creating the volume of the sound. Frequency is the measure of how quickly the waves pass a point, causing the pitch of the sound. The other choices are incorrect distractions.

6. **(D)** Our vestibular sense helps with our sense of balance and orientation in space. Our vestibular sense has little to do with our sense of sight or hearing. Repeating digits would not be affected by the vestibular sense.

7. **(B)** The thalamus is the relay station for all sensory information except for smell. Information coming from the optic nerve is routed to the lateral geniculate nucleus in the thalamus and then on to the occipital lobe of the brain. Suzy is having difficulty with her vision most likely because her thalamus was affected by the car accident.

8. **(C)** Narcolepsy typically involves falling asleep at unusual, often stressful, times. Sleep apnea is characterized by waking up in the middle of the night and struggling to breathe, insomnia is difficulty falling or staying asleep, and somnambulism is sleepwalking.

9. **(D)** Identical twins raised separately tend to resemble their birth parents more than their adoptive parents in many ways, which suggests that genetics plays a stronger role than the family environment. Identical twins share 100 percent of their genetic material, so differences between them are attributed to their environments. Because, on average, fraternal twins share the same amount of genetic material as siblings born at different times, any greater similarity between them must be due to environmental factors. Likewise, given that fraternal twins share an average of 50 percent of their genes, differences between them are likely due to the environment.

10. **(A)** Chemical senses include smell and taste. To smell or taste things, they need to come into contact with our receptors—our olfactory and taste cells. Vision, which is an energy sense, is thought of as humans' dominant sense. Because most humans rely on their vision more than their other senses, more research has been done on vision and more of the brain's real estate is devoted to processing this energy sense.

11. **(A)** Hair cells are the receptors for hearing, which means they are where transduction (the conversion of one form of energy to another) takes place. Although it is not impossible to damage the ossicles (bones in the middle ear) or tympanic membrane (ear drum) with loud noise, this type of hearing loss is usually caused by damage to the hair cells. The pinna, the outer part of the ear, is not damaged by noise.

12. **(B)** Endorphins are the body's natural painkillers. Agonists mimic the effect of other compounds; thus, an endorphin agonist would decrease the perception of pain.

13. **(B)** Memory is a cognitive function. Therefore, the finding that depriving people of REM sleep interferes with the memory of information taught suggests that REM sleep has a cognitive function.

14. **(D)** Given that Dr. Webb is experimenting on his own students, he needs to be especially concerned about their ability to freely consent (or not) to their participation. As he is their professor, they may feel some pressure to agree to be in the study. Dr. Webb would therefore need to make clear that their participation or lack thereof will have no effect on their performance in his class or on their relationship with him outside of the class.

15. **(C)** Although all the replications mentioned would be useful, if Dr. Webb wants to make the argument that REM sleep is important for learning and remembering information in a broader population than college students, choice (C) is the best method.

UNIT 2
Cognition

This unit focuses on some of the most important concepts in an introductory psychology class. These concepts are important because they represent a significant number of questions on the AP Psychology test and because concepts covered in this unit can help you study and learn more effectively. (See "Using Psychology to Study Psychology" in the "AP Psychology Course and Exam Description" section at the beginning of the book.)

7

Perception

Learning Objectives

In this chapter, you will learn about:

- → Thresholds
- → Perceptual theories
- → Principles of visual perception
- → Effects of culture on perception
- → Extrasensory perception

Key Terms

- Placebo effect
- Just-noticeable difference
- Weber's law
- Top-down processing
- Schemata
- Schema
- Perceptual set
- Bottom-up processing

- Figure-ground relationship
- Gestalt psychology
- Proximity
- Similarity
- Continuity
- Closure
- Visual cliff
- Monocular depth cues

- Binocular depth cues
- Linear perspective
- Relative size cue
- Interposition cue
- Texture gradient
- Retinal disparity
- Binocular disparity
- Convergence

Overview

Perception is the process of understanding and interpreting sensations. Psychophysics is the study of the interaction between the sensations we receive and our experience of them. Researchers who study psychophysics try to uncover the rules our minds use to interpret sensations. We will cover some of the basic principles in psychophysics and examine some basic perceptual rules for vision.

Thresholds

Research shows that although our senses are very acute, they do have their limits. The absolute threshold is the smallest amount of stimulus we can detect. For example, the absolute threshold for vision is the smallest amount of light we can detect, which is estimated to be a single candle flame about 30 miles (48 km) away on a perfectly clear, dark night. Most of us could detect a single drop of perfume a room away. Actually, the technical definition of absolute threshold is the minimal amount of stimulus we can detect 50 percent of the time, because researchers try to take into account individual variation in sensitivity and interference from other sensory sources. Stimuli below our absolute threshold are said to be subliminal. Some companies claim to produce subliminal message media that can change unwanted behavior. Psychological research does not support their claim. In fact, a truly subliminal message would not, by definition, affect behavior at all because if a message were truly subliminal, we would not perceive it! Research indicates some messages called subliminal (because they are so faint we do not report perceiving them) can sometimes affect behavior in subtle ways, such as choosing a word at random from a list after the word was presented subliminally. Evidence does not exist, however, that more complex subliminal messages such as "exercise more" or "increase your vocabulary" are effective. If these tapes do change behavior, the change most likely comes from the **placebo effect** rather than from the effect of the subliminal message.

If we can see a single candle 30 miles (48 km) away, would we notice if another candle was lit right next to it? In other words, how much does a stimulus need to change before we notice the difference? The difference threshold defines this change. The difference threshold, sometimes called a **just-noticeable difference**, is the smallest amount of change needed in a stimulus before we detect a change. This threshold is computed by **Weber's law**, which states that the change needed is proportional to the original intensity of the stimulus. The more intense the stimulus, the more it will need to change before we notice a difference. You might notice a change if someone adds a small amount of cayenne pepper to a dish that is typically not very spicy, but you would need to add much more hot pepper to five-alarm chili before anyone would notice a difference. Further, Weber discovered that each sense varies according to a constant but the constants differ among the senses. For example, the constant for hearing is 5 percent. If you listened to a 100-decibel tone, the volume would have to increase to 105 decibels before you noticed that it was any louder. Weber's constant for vision is 8 percent. So 8 candles would need to be added to 100 candles before it looked any brighter.

Perceptual Theories

Psychologists use several theories to describe how we perceive the world.

Signal Detection Theory

Real-world examples of perception are more complicated than controlled laboratory perception experiments. After all, how many times do we get the opportunity to stare at a single candle flame 30 miles (48 km) away on a perfectly clear, dark night? Signal detection theory investigates the effects of the distractions and interference we experience while perceiving the world. This area of research tries to predict what we will perceive among competing stimuli. For example, will the surgeon see the tumor on the CAT scan among all the irrelevant shadows and flaws in the picture? Will the quarterback see the one open receiver in the end zone despite the oncoming lineman? Signal detection theory considers how motivated we are to detect certain stimuli and what we expect to perceive.

> **TIP**
>
> These perceptual theories are not competing with one another. Each theory describes different examples or parts of perception. Sometimes a single example of the interpretation of sensation needs to be explained using all the following theories.

These factors together are called response criteria (also called receiver operating characteristics). For example, I will be more likely to smell a freshly baked rhubarb pie if I am hungry and enjoy the taste of rhubarb. By using factors like response criteria, signal detection theory tries to explain and predict the different perceptual mistakes we make. A false positive is when we think we perceive a stimulus that is not there. For example, you may think you see a friend of yours on a crowded street and end up waving at a total stranger. A false negative is not perceiving a stimulus that is present. You may not notice the directions at the top of a test that instruct you not to write on the test form. In some situations, one type of error is much more serious than the other, and this importance can alter perception. In the surgeon example mentioned previously, a false negative (not seeing a tumor that is present) is a more serious mistake than a false positive (suspecting that a tumor is there), although both mistakes are obviously important.

Top-Down Processing

When we use **top-down processing**, we perceive by filling in gaps in what we sense. For example, try to read the following sentence:

I _ope yo_ _et a 5 on t_ _ A_ e_am.

You should be able to read the sentence as "I hope you get a 5 on the AP exam." You perceived the blanks as the appropriate letters by using the context of the sentence. Top-down processing occurs when you use your background knowledge to fill in gaps in what you perceive. Our experience creates **schemata** (also called **schema**), which are mental representations of how we expect the world to be. Our schemata influence how we perceive the world. Schemata can create a **perceptual set**, which is a predisposition to perceiving something in a certain way. If you have ever seen images in the clouds, you have experienced top-down processing. You use your background knowledge (schemata) to perceive the random shapes of clouds as organized shapes.

In the 1970s, some parent groups were very concerned about backmasking: supposed hidden messages musicians recorded backward in their music. These parent groups would play song lyrics backward and hear messages, usually threatening. Some groups of parents demanded an investigation about the effects of the backmasking. What was happening? Lyrics played backward are basically random noise. However, if you expect to hear a threatening message in the random noise, you probably will, much like expecting to see an image in the clouds. People who listened to the songs played backward and had schemata of this music as dangerous or evil perceived the threatening messages due to top-down processing.

Bottom-Up Processing

Bottom-up processing, also called feature analysis, is the opposite of top-down processing. Instead of using our experience to perceive an object, we use only the features of the object itself to build a complete perception. We start our perception at the bottom with the individual characteristics of the image and put all those characteristics together into our final perception. Bottom-up processing can be hard to imagine because it is such an automatic process. The feature detectors in the visual cortex allow us to perceive basic features of objects, such as horizontal and vertical lines, curves, motion, and so on. Our mind builds the picture from the bottom up using these basic characteristics. We are constantly using both bottom-up and top-down processing as we perceive the world. Top-down processing is faster but more prone to error, while bottom-up processing takes longer but is more accurate.

Principles of Visual Perception

The rules we use for visual perception are too numerous to cover completely in this book. However, some of the basic rules are important to know and understand for the AP Psychology exam. One of the first perceptual decisions our mind must make is the **figure-ground relationship**. What part of a visual image is the figure and what part is the ground or background? Several optical illusions play with this rule. One example is the famous picture of the vase that if looked at one way is a vase but by switching the figure and the ground can be perceived as profiles of two faces looking at each other (see Figure 7.1).

Figure 7.1 Optical illusion

Gestalt Rules

At the beginning of the twentieth century, a group of researchers called the Gestalt psychologists described the principles that govern how we perceive groups of objects. The **Gestalt psychology** points out that we normally perceive images as groups, not as isolated elements.

They thought this process was innate and inevitable. They suggested that the factors illustrated in Figure 7.2 and described in Table 7.1 influence how we will group objects.

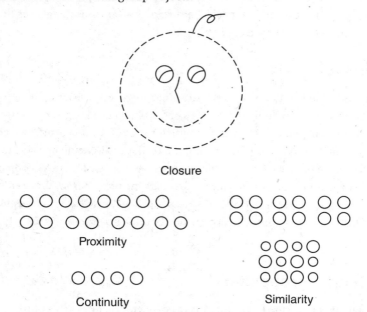

Figure 7.2 Factors for grouping objects according to Gestalt psychology

Table 7.1 Gestalt Principles of Perception

Proximity	Objects that are close together are more likely to be perceived as belonging in the same group.
Similarity	Objects that are similar in appearance are more likely to be perceived as belonging in the same group.
Continuity	Objects that are arranged in a continuous line or curve (such as a trail or a geometric figure) are more likely to be perceived as belonging in the same group.
Closure	Objects that make up a recognizable image are more likely to be perceived as belonging in the same group even if the image contains gaps that the mind needs to fill in; note that this perception is influenced by top-down processing.

Constancy

Every object we see changes minutely from moment to moment due to our changing angle of vision, variations in light, and so on. Our ability to maintain a constant perception of an object despite these changes is called constancy. Table 7.2 describes several types of constancy.

Table 7.2 Types of Perceptual Constancy

Size constancy	Objects closer to our eyes produce bigger images on our retinas, but we take distance into account in our estimations of size. We keep a constant size in mind for an object (if we are familiar with the typical size of the object) and know that it does not grow or shrink in size as it moves closer or farther away.
Shape constancy	Objects viewed from different angles produce different shapes on our retinas, but we know the shape of an object remains constant. For example, the top of a coffee mug viewed from a certain angle produces an elliptical image on our retinas, but we know the top is circular due to shape constancy. Again, this depends on our familiarity with the usual shape of the object.
Brightness constancy	We perceive objects as being a constant color even as the light reflecting off the object changes. For example, we perceive a brick wall as brick red even as the daylight fades and the actual color reflected from the wall turns gray.

Perceived Motion

Another aspect of perception is our ability to gauge motion. Our brains are able to detect how fast images move across our retinas and take into account our own movement. Interestingly, in a number of situations, our brains perceive objects to be moving when, in fact, they are not. A common example of this is the stroboscopic effect, used in movies or flip books. Images in a series of still pictures presented at a certain speed will appear to be moving. Another example you have probably encountered on movie marquees and with holiday lights is the phi phenomenon. A series of lightbulbs turned on and off at a particular rate will appear to be one moving light. A third example is the autokinetic effect. If a spot of light is projected steadily onto the same place on a wall of an otherwise dark room and people are asked to stare at it, they will report seeing it move.

Depth Cues

One of the most important and frequently investigated parts of visual perception is depth. Without depth perception, we would perceive the world as a two-dimensional flat surface and be unable to differentiate between what is near and what is far. This limitation could obviously be dangerous. Researcher Eleanor Gibson used the **visual cliff** experiment to determine when human infants can perceive depth. An infant is placed onto one side of a glass-topped table that creates the impression of a cliff. Actually, the glass extends across the entire table, so the infant cannot possibly fall. Gibson found that an infant old enough to crawl will not crawl across the visual cliff, implying the child has depth perception. Other experiments demonstrate that depth perception develops when we are about three months old. Researchers divide the cues that we use to perceive depth into two categories: **monocular depth cues** (depth cues that do not depend on having two eyes) and **binocular depth cues** (cues that depend on having two eyes).

Visual Cliff

Monocular Cues

If you have taken a drawing class, you have learned monocular depth cues. Artists use these cues to imply depth in their drawings. One of the most common cues is **linear perspective**. If you wanted to draw a railroad track that runs away from the viewer off into the distance, most likely you would start by drawing two lines that converge somewhere toward the top of your paper. If you added a drawing of the train, you might use the **relative size cue**. You would draw the boxcars closer to the viewer as larger than the engine off in the distance. A water tower blocking our view of part of the train would be seen as closer to us due to the **interposition cue**; objects that block the view to other objects must be closer to us. If the train were running through a desert landscape, you might draw the rocks closest to the viewer in detail while the landscape off in the distance would not be as detailed. This cue is called **texture gradient**; we know that we can see details in texture close to us but not far away. Finally, your art teacher might teach you to use shadowing in your picture. By shading part of your picture, you can imply where the light source is and thus imply depth and position of objects.

Binocular Cues

Other cues for depth result from our anatomy. We see the world with two eyes set a certain distance apart, and this feature of our anatomy gives us the ability to perceive depth. The finger trick you read about during the discussion of the anatomy of the eye demonstrates the first binocular cue— **retinal disparity** (also called **binocular disparity**). Each of our eyes will view an object from a slightly different angle. The brain receives both images. It knows that if the object is far away, the images will be similar, but the closer the object is, the more disparity there will be between the images coming from each eye. The other binocular depth cue is **convergence**. As an object gets closer to our face, our eyes must move toward each other to keep focused on the object. The brain receives feedback from the muscles controlling eye movement and knows that the more the eyes converge, the closer the object must be.

Effects of Culture on Perception

One area of psychology cross-cultural researchers are investigating is the effect of culture on perception. Research indicates that some of the perceptual rules psychologists once thought were innate are actually learned. For example, cultures that do not use monocular depth cues (such as linear perspective) in their art do not see depth in pictures using these cues. Also, some optical illusions are not perceived the same way by people from different cultures. For example, below is a representation of the famous Muller-Lyer illusion. Which of the following straight lines, *A* or *B*, appears longer to you?

Line *A* should look longer even though both lines are actually the same length. People who come from noncarpentered cultures that do not often use right angles and corners in their building and architecture are not usually fooled by the Muller-Lyer illusion. Cross-cultural research demonstrates that some basic perceptual sets are learned from our culture.

Extrasensory Perception

Now that you've reviewed the senses and how the brain changes these sensations into perceptions, you can interpret the term extrasensory perception (ESP) in a more specific way than most people can: someone claiming to have "extrasensory perception" is claiming to perceive a sensation "outside" the senses discussed in Unit 1. Psychologists are skeptical of ESP claims primarily because our senses are well understood, and researchers do not find reliable evidence that we can perceive sensations other than through our sight, smell, hearing, taste, touch, and vestibular/balance systems. Researchers who test ESP claims using rigorous experiments, such as double-blind studies, find other more likely explanations for supposed extrasensory phenomena. Usually, ESP claims are better explained by such things as deception, magic tricks, or coincidence.

8

Thinking and Creativity

Learning Objectives

In this chapter, you will learn about:

→ Describing thought
→ Problem-solving
→ Creativity

Key Terms

- Prototypes
- Algorithm
- Heuristic
- Availability heuristic
- Representativeness heuristic

- Gambler's fallacy
- Sunk-cost fallacy
- Mental set
- Functional fixedness
- Framing
- Creativity

- Convergent thinking
- Divergent thinking

Overview

Describing thinking and creativity is one of the most challenging areas in the science of psychology. Researchers focus on carefully defining specific elements of our thinking. These concepts and this research help describe and unpack examples of obstacles to accurate thinking and problem-solving.

Describing Thought

Once we perceive things in the world, we can think about them. Trying to describe thought is problematic. Descriptions are thoughts, so we are attempting to describe thought using thought itself. Forming a global, all-inclusive definition of thought is difficult, but psychologists try to define types or categories of thoughts. Concepts are similar to the schemata mentioned in Chapter 7. We each have cognitive rules we apply to stimuli from our environment that allow us to categorize and think about the objects, people, and ideas we encounter. These rules are concepts. Our concept of "mom" is different from our concept of "dad," which is different from our concept of "a soccer game." We may base our concepts on **prototypes**, or what we think is the most typical example of a particular concept.

Another type of thought, images, are the mental pictures we create in our minds of the outside world. Images can be visual, such as imagining what your cat looks like. However, images can also be auditory, tactile, or olfactory or can be an image of a taste, such as thinking about what hot chocolate tastes like on a very cold day.

Problem-Solving

Many researchers try to study thought by examining the results of thinking. Researchers can ask participants to solve problems and then investigate how the solutions were reached. This research indicates at least two different problem-solving methods we commonly use and some traps to avoid when solving a problem.

Algorithms

One way to solve a problem is to try every possible solution. An **algorithm** is a rule that guarantees the right solution by using a formula or other foolproof method. If you are trying to guess a computer password and you know it is a combination of only two letters, you could use an algorithm and guess pairs of letters in combination until you hit the right one. What if the password is a combination of five letters, not two? Sometimes algorithms are impractical, so a shortcut is needed to solve certain problems.

Heuristics

A **heuristic** is a rule of thumb—a strategy we can use to make a quick but not necessarily accurate judgment in a situation. For example, if you are trying to guess the password mentioned previously, you might begin by guessing actual five-letter words rather than random combinations of letters. The password might be a meaningless combination of letters, but you know that passwords are most often actual words. This heuristic limits the possible combinations dramatically. Two common heuristics, the availability and representativeness heuristics are described in Table 8.1.

Table 8.1 Two Common Heuristics

Availability heuristic	Judging a situation based on examples of similar situations that come to mind initially. This heuristic might lead to incorrect conclusions due to variability in personal experience. For example, a person may judge his or her neighborhood to be more dangerous than others in the city simply because that person is more familiar with violence in his or her neighborhood than in other neighborhoods.
Representativeness heuristic	Judging a situation based on how similar the aspects are to prototypes the person holds in his or her mind. For example, a person might judge a young person more likely to commit suicide because of a prototype of the depressed adolescent when, in fact, suicide rates are not higher in younger populations.

Use of these heuristics is not the only cause of errors in how people reason. Overconfidence is our tendency to overestimate how accurate our judgments are. How confident we are in a judgment is not a good indicator of whether we are right. In studies, most people report extreme confidence in a judgment that turns out to be wrong in a significant number of cases. Two concepts closely related to overconfidence are belief bias and belief perseverance. Both of these concepts involve our tendency not to change our beliefs in the face of contradictory evidence. Belief bias occurs when we make illogical conclusions to confirm our preexisting beliefs. Belief perseverance refers to our tendency to maintain a belief even after the evidence we used to form the belief is contradicted. Overall, these concepts demonstrate that humans are generally more confident in our beliefs than we should be, and we often stick with our beliefs even when presented with evidence that disproves them.

Another example of a limitation of a heuristic is the **gambler's fallacy**: this occurs when we believe that a certain event or outcome is more or less likely to occur because of how often it has recently occurred. A slot machine is not more likely to pay off just because someone has been playing it for an hour. The **sunk-cost fallacy** can also influence our thinking in negative ways. Sometimes we are unwilling to change a course of action because we spent a lot of effort and time trying to make that solution work, even when it becomes clear that the course of action is unlikely to solve the problem.

Impediments to Problem-Solving

Problem-solving research identifies some common mistakes people make while trying to solve problems. **Mental set** (also called rigidity) refers to the tendency to fall into established thought patterns. Most people use their experience to try to solve novel problems. Occasionally, this tendency prevents them from seeing a novel solution. One specific example of rigidity is **functional fixedness**, the inability to see a new use for an object. One of my students recently got his car stuck up to the axles in mud. Our attempts to pull him out failed until another student pointed out we could use the car jack to raise the car and put planks under the tires. Most of us thought of the jack only as a tool to help with a flat tire and didn't consider that it could be helpful in getting a car out of the mud. Another common trap in problem-solving is not breaking the problem into parts. Studies show that good problem solvers identify subgoals, which are smaller and more manageable problems they need to solve in order to solve the whole problem. Tackling the problem in these smaller parts helps good problem solvers be more successful.

Another obstacle to successful problem-solving is confirmation bias. Many studies show that we tend to look for evidence that confirms our beliefs and ignore evidence that contradicts what we think is true. Consequently, we may miss evidence important to finding the correct solution. For example, once teachers become accustomed to the usual quality of their students' work, they may have expectations about whose essays will be strong and whose will be less so. When reading that work, they may be more likely to notice examples that confirm their preexisting beliefs.

Even the way a problem is presented can get in the way of solving it. **Framing** refers to the idea that the same information can be presented in different ways and the method of presentation can drastically change the way we view a problem or an issue. If I tell my students, "The majority of my students have been able to solve this logic problem," they would most likely feel confident and not expect much of a challenge. However, if I tell them, "Almost half of the students in my classes never get the answer to this logic puzzle," they would probably expect a very difficult task. In both cases, I am really telling them that 51 percent of the students can solve the logic problem, but the way I frame the task changes their expectation and possibly their ability to solve the problem. Researchers must be careful about unintentionally framing questions in ways that might influence participants in their studies.

Creativity

If you thought defining thought was tough, try defining **creativity**! The concept itself resists categorization. Again, even though defining this concept is difficult, researchers have investigated definable aspects of creativity. For example, Wolfgang Köhler (1887–1967) documented details of the "aha experience" by observing a group of chimpanzees as they generated original solutions to retrieve bananas that were out of reach. Researchers investigating creative thinking find little correlation between intelligence and creativity. Studies show that although we may agree in general about specific examples that demonstrate creativity, individual criteria for creativity vary widely. Most people's criteria do involve both originality and appropriateness. When judging whether something is creative, we look at whether it is original or novel and if it somehow fits the situation. Some researchers are investigating the distinctions between **convergent thinking**, which is thinking pointed toward one solution, and **divergent thinking**, which is thinking that searches for multiple possible answers to a question. Divergent thinking is more closely associated with creativity. Creative activities usually involve thinking of new ways to use what we are all familiar with or new ways to express emotions or ideas we share. Painting by the numbers is convergent thinking, but we would probably call painting outside the lines and/or mixing your own hues creative and divergent thinking.

9

Memory

Learning Objectives

In this chapter, you will learn about:

→ Three-box/information-processing model
→ Sensory memory
→ Short-term and working memory
→ Long-term memory
→ Levels of processing model
→ Encoding memories
→ Storing memories
→ Retrieval
→ Constructive memory
→ Forgetting

Key Terms

- Three-box/information-processing model
- Levels of processing model
- Multi-store model
- Sensory memory
- Iconic memory
- Echoic memory
- Short-term memory
- Selective attention
- Cocktail party effect
- Inattentional blindness
- Change blindness
- Working memory
- Central executive
- Visuospatial sketchpad
- Auditory loop
- Maintenance rehearsal

- Elaborative rehearsal
- Effortful processing
- Long-term memory
- Storage
- Episodic memory
- Semantic memory
- Procedural memory
- Explicit memories
- Implicit memories
- Prospective memory
- Shallowly encoded
- Deeply encoded
- Long-term potentiation
- Encoding
- Primacy effect
- Recency effect
- Serial position effect
- Serial position curve
- Method of loci
- Spacing effect
- Massed practice

- Chunking
- Mnemonic devices
- Anterograde amnesia
- Retrograde amnesia
- Retrieval
- Recognition
- Recall
- Retrieval cues
- Tip-of-the-tongue phenomenon
- Context-dependent memory
- Mood-congruent memory
- State-dependent memory
- Constructed memory
- Misinformation effect
- Retroactive interference
- Proactive interference

Overview

Several different models, or explanations, of how memory works have emerged from memory research. We will review two of the most important models: the **three-box/information-processing model** and the **levels of processing model**. Neither model is perfect. They describe how memory works in different ways, and each can describe some memory experiences better than others.

Three-Box/Information-Processing Model

The principal model of memory is the three-box model, also called the information-processing model or the **multi-store model**. This model proposes the three stages that information passes through before it is stored (see Figure 9.1).

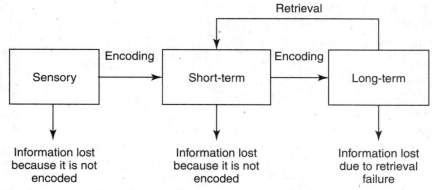

Figure 9.1 Atkinson and Shiffrin three-box/information-processing model

External events are first processed by our sensory memory. Then some information is encoded into our short-term (or working) memory. Some of that information is then encoded into long-term memory.

Sensory Memory

The first stop for external events is **sensory memory**. It is a holding tank for incoming sensory information. All the information your senses are processing right now is held in sensory memory for a very short period of time: less than a second for visual information (**iconic memory**) and 3 to 4 seconds for auditory information (**echoic memory**). Researcher George Sperling demonstrated iconic memory in a series of experiments in which he flashed a grid of nine letters, in three rows and three columns, to participants for 1/20th of a second. The participants in the study were directed to recall either the top, middle, or bottom row immediately after the grid was flashed at them. (Sperling used a high, medium, or low tone to indicate which row they should recall.) The participants could recall any of the three rows perfectly, although they could not report the whole grid, ostensibly because their iconic memory faded before they could type out all the letters. This experiment demonstrated that the entire grid must be held in sensory memory for a split second.

Most of the information in sensory memory is quickly lost. A small fraction is encoded into **short-term memory**. Events are encoded as visual codes (a visual image), acoustic codes (a series of sounds), or semantic codes (a sense of the meaning of the event). What determines which sensory messages get encoded? **Selective attention**. We encode what we are attending to or what is important to us. Try the following exercise. Pay attention to how your feet feel in your socks right now. You feel this now because the sensory messages from your feet are encoded from sensory memory into short-term memory. Why did you not feel your socks before? Because the messages entered sensory memory but were not encoded because you were not selectively attending to them. Sometimes selective attention is not as controlled. You have probably had the experience of speaking with one person at a party but then hearing someone say your name across the room. You were selectively attending to the person you were talking to. However, once a sensory message that you knew was important (like someone saying your name or hearing someone shout "Fire!") entered sensory memory, you switched your attention to that message, and it was encoded into your short-term memory. (This phenomenon is called the **cocktail party effect**.) Selective attention is also related to examples of NOT noticing events. We've all experienced **inattentional blindness**: when we fail to perceive something that was in our visual field (and that our eyes probably sensed) because we weren't paying attention to it and were intensely focused on something else. A closely related experience is **change blindness**: sometimes we do not observe an obvious change in our visual world because we are selectively attending to something else and do not perceive that an object or person changed.

Short-Term and Working Memory

Everything you are thinking at the current moment is held in your short-term memory, and if you are trying to do something with that information, it's in your **working memory**. Short-term memories are also temporary. If we do nothing with them, they usually fade in 10 to 30 seconds. Working memory is your ability to manipulate items in your short-term memory. If you think about the numbers 22 and 9, they are in your short-term memory. However, if I ask you to multiply them, you are using your working memory. Several elements are involved in how our working memory systems manipulate and work with information from our short-term memory. Our working memory systems involve at least three systems:

- The **central executive**—monitors incoming information and determines what other systems should be involved in processing the information.
- The **visuospatial sketchpad**—deals with visual information; this is our "mind's eye" that we use to visualize the world.
- The **auditory loop**—deals with words or numbers.

So as we use our working memory system to process memories, feelings, and other information in our short-term memory, our central executive figures out what the information is and which elements of our working memory system should process them.

Another way to retain information in short-term memory is to rehearse (or repeat) it. When you get a confirmation code, you probably need to repeat it to yourself until you type it in; this is an example of **maintenance rehearsal**. Repetition can hold information in short-term memory, but other strategies are more effective in ensuring short-term memories are encoded into long-term memory. Another type of rehearsal, **elaborative rehearsal**, can be especially beneficial to learning. Elaborative rehearsal is a type of **effortful processing**: it occurs when we focus on putting mental effort into encoding the meaning of a term, an event, a process, and so on. This is closely related to semantic memory, which involves memories related to the significance or meaning of information.

Long-Term Memory

Since memories fade from sensory and short-term memory so quickly, we obviously need a more permanent way to remember events. **Long-term memory** is our permanent **storage**. As far as we know, the capacity of long-term memory is unlimited. No one reports their memory as being full and unable to encode new information. Studies show that once information reaches long-term memory, we will likely remember it for the rest of our lives. However, memories can decay or fade from long-term memory, so it is not truly permanent (see the section "Forgetting"). Long-term memories can be stored in three different formats (see Table 9.1).

Table 9.1 Types of Long-Term Memories

Episodic memory	Memories of specific events, stored in a sequential series of events. Example: Remembering the last time you went on a date.
Semantic memory	General knowledge of the world, stored as facts, meanings, or categories rather than sequentially. Example: What is the difference between the terms *effect* and *affect*?
Procedural memory	Memories of skills and how to perform them. These memories are sequential but might be too complicated to describe in words. Example: How to throw a curveball.

Memories can also be implicit or explicit. **Explicit memories** (also called declarative memories) are what we usually think of first. They are the conscious memories of facts or events we actively tried to remember. When you study this material, you try to form explicit memories about the memory theories. **Implicit memories** (also called nondeclarative memories) are unintentional memories that we might not even realize we have. For example, while you are helping your friend clean her house, you might find that you have implicit memories about how to scrub a floor properly after watching your parents do it for so many years.

Yet another type of memory is **prospective memory**, which is your memory for things you plan to do in the future. Examples would be if you need to take some kind of medication each morning or plug in your laptop every night before bed.

Memory researchers are particularly interested in individuals who demonstrate eidetic, or photographic, memory. Psychologist Alexander Luria studied a patient with eidetic memory who could repeat a list of 70 letters or digits. The patient could even repeat the list backward and recall it up to 15 years later! Luria and other researchers showed that these rare individuals seem to use very powerful and enduring visual images.

TIP

Some people say they have a photographic memory when what they mean is a very good memory. True eidetic memory occurs very rarely. Most of us could enhance our memories through training with mnemonic devices, context, and visual imagery.

Levels of Processing Model

An alternate way to think about memory is the levels of processing model. This theory explains why we remember what we do by examining how deeply the memory was processed or thought about. Memories are neither short-term nor long-term. Instead, they are either shallowly encoded or deeply (elaboratively) encoded. If you simply repeat a fact to yourself several times and then write it on your test as quickly as you can, you have only **shallowly encoded** that fact and you will forget it quickly. However, if you study the context and research the reasons behind the fact, you have **deeply encoded** it and will likely recall it later. According to the levels of processing theory, we remember things we spend more cognitive time and energy processing. This theory explains why we remember stories better than a simple recitation of events and why, in general, we remember questions better than statements. When we get caught up in a story or an intriguing question, we process it deeply and are therefore more likely to remember it.

At the neurological level, researchers focus on a process called **long-term potentiation**. Studies show that neurons can strengthen connections between each other. Through repeated firings, the connection is strengthened, and the receiving neuron becomes more sensitive to the messages from the sending neuron. This strengthened connection might be related to the connections we make in our long-term memory.

Encoding Memories

Encoding is the process by which we put information into our memories, and it can be affected by many factors. One is the order in which the information is presented. In some of the first psychological experiments, Hermann Ebbinghaus (1850–1909) established that the order of items in a list is related to whether or not we will recall them. The **primacy effect** predicts that we are more likely to recall items presented at the beginning of a list. The **recency effect** is demonstrated by our ability to recall the items at the end of a list. Items in the middle are most often forgotten. Together the primacy effect and recency effect demonstrate the **serial position effect** (also called the **serial position curve**). This effect is seen when recall of a list is affected by the order of items in a list.

Some people have created ways to improve our ability to encode a list of items or people. A well-known example is the **method of loci**. This method involves using imagery to associate the things you want to remember with various places. For instance, if I need to go pick up some items at the grocery store, I could imagine them in different places I go to in my house each morning: orange juice dripping off my bed, Oreos in my bathroom sink, broccoli in my coffee pot, and so on.

Probably more important to you as a student is the ability to remember a lot of information for tests. One of the most robust findings in memory research is called the **spacing effect.** Research has consistently demonstrated the benefit of spacing studying out or using what is called distributed practice, as opposed to **massed practice**. Therefore, studying for the AP Psychology exam for 1 hour every day for a week should result in better performance than studying 7 hours the day before.

Our capacity in short-term memory is limited on average to around seven items. (This average was established in a series of famous experiments by George Miller titled "The Magical Number Seven, Plus or Minus Two.") However, this limit can be expanded through a process called **chunking**. If you want to remember a grocery list with 15 items on it, you should chunk, or group, the items into no more than seven groups. Most **mnemonic devices**, which are memory aids, are really examples of chunking. If you memorized the names of the planets by remembering the sentence "My Very Educated Mother Just Served Us Nachos," you chunked the names of the planets into the first letters of the words in one sentence.

Storing Memories

Researchers know some of the brain processes and structures involved in memory, but much of this process is still a mystery. By studying patients with specific brain damage, we know that the hippocampus is important in encoding new memories. However, other brain structures are involved. Individuals with damage to the hippocampus might have **anterograde amnesia** (cannot encode new memories) but can recall events already in memory. They can learn new skills, although they will not remember learning these skills. This indicates that the memory for these skills, or procedural memory, is stored elsewhere in the brain. (Studies on animals indicate that procedural memories are stored in the cerebellum.) People with **retrograde amnesia** have a different problem; they are unable to remember information learned before a trauma to the brain.

Retrieval

The last step in any memory model is **retrieval**, or getting information out of memory so we can use it. There are two different kinds of retrieval: recognition and recall. **Recognition** is the process of matching a current event or fact with one already in memory (e.g., "Have I smelled this smell before?"). **Recall** is retrieving a memory with an external cue (e.g., "What does my Aunt Beki's perfume smell like?"). Both rely on **retrieval cues**, which are stimuli that help people retrieve memories. Studies have identified several factors that influence why we can retrieve some memories and why we forget others.

Context is an important factor in retrieval. Have you ever tried to remember someone's name and start listing things about their appearance or personality until you finally come up with the name? This temporary inability to remember information is sometimes called the **tip-of-the-tongue phenomenon**. One theory that explains why this might work is the semantic network theory. This theory states that our brain might form new memories by connecting their meaning and context with meanings already in memory. Thus, our brain creates a web of inter-connected memories, each one in context tied to hundreds or thousands of other memories. So, by listing traits, you gradually get closer and closer to the name, and you are finally able to retrieve it. **Context-dependent memory** also explains another powerful memory experience we all have. If you ask someone born in the 1990s or earlier where they were during the September 11, 2001, terrorist attack, they are likely to give you a detailed description of exactly what they were doing in those moments. Also called flashbulb memories, these memories are powerful because the importance of the event caused us to encode the context surrounding the event. However, some studies show that flashbulb memories can be inaccurate. Perhaps we tend to construct parts of the memory to fill in gaps in our stories. (See the section "Constructive Memory" that follows.)

The emotional or situational context of a memory can affect retrieval in yet another way. Studies consistently demonstrate the power of **mood-congruent memory** or the greater likelihood of recalling an item when our current mood matches the mood we were in when the event happened. We are likely to recall happy events when we are happy and recall negative events when we are feeling pessimistic. **State-dependent memory** refers to the phenomenon of recalling events encoded while in particular states of consciousness. If you suddenly remember an appointment while you are drowsy and about to go to sleep, you need to write it down. Very possibly, you will not remember it again until you are drowsy and in the same state of consciousness. Alcohol and other drugs affect memory in similar ways.

Constructive Memory

Maybe you have seen media coverage of the "recovered memory" phenomenon. Individuals claim to suddenly remember events they have repressed for years, often during the process of therapy. Parents have been accused of molesting and even killing children based on these recovered memories. Although some of the memories can be corroborated by other means, memory researchers like Elizabeth Loftus have shown that many of these memories may be constructed or false recollections of events. A **constructed memory** (or reconstructed memory) includes false details of a real event or might even be a recollection of an event that never occurred. Studies show that leading questions (questions or statements that purposefully include information or events that never happened—called the **misinformation effect**) can easily influence us to recall false details, and questioners can create an entirely new memory by repeatedly asking insistent questions. Constructed memories feel like accurate memories to the person recalling them. The only way to differentiate between a false and a real memory is through other types of evidence, such as physical evidence or other validated reports of the event. Although some genuine memories may be recalled after being forgotten for years, researchers and therapists are investigating ways to ensure that memories are accurate and that innocent people are not accused of acts they did not commit.

Forgetting

Sometimes, despite our best efforts, we forget important events or facts that we try and want to remember. One cause of forgetting is decay: forgetting because we do not use a memory or connections to a memory for a long period of time. For example, you might memorize the state capitals for a civics test but forget many of them soon after the test because you do not need to recall them. However, your studying was not in vain! Even memories that decay do not seem to disappear completely. Many studies show an important relearning effect. If you have to memorize the capitals again, it will take you less time than it did the first time you studied them.

Another factor that causes forgetting is interference. Sometimes other information in your memory competes with what you are trying to recall. Interference can occur through two processes, as shown in Table 9.2.

Table 9.2 Two Types of Interference

Retroactive interference	Learning new information interferes with the recall of older information. If you study for your psychology class at 3:00 p.m. and for your sociology class at 6:00 p.m., you might have trouble recalling the psychology information on a test the next day.
Proactive interference	Older information learned previously interferes with the recall of information learned more recently. If a researcher reads you a list of items in a certain order, then rereads them differently and asks you to list the items in the new order, the old list proactively interferes with recall of the new list.

TIP

Some students find remembering the difference between retroactive and proactive interference difficult. Focus on which type of information is trying to be recalled. If old information is what you are searching for, retroactive (older) interference most likely applies. If you are searching for newer information, proactive (new) interference might be taking place.

10

Testing and Individual Differences

Learning Objectives

In this chapter, you will learn about:

→ Standardization and norms
→ Reliability and validity
→ Theories of intelligence
→ Intelligence tests
→ Nature vs. nurture: intelligence

Key Terms

- Standardized
- Reliability
- Split-half reliability
- Test-retest reliability
- Validity
- Predictive validity
- Construct validity

- Aptitude tests
- Achievement tests
- Intelligence
- Fluid intelligence
- Crystallized intelligence
- Mental age

- Stanford-Binet IQ
- Chronological age
- Heritability
- Flynn effect

Overview

We all take many standardized tests and receive scores that tell us how we perform. Given the world in which we have grown up, it is almost unimaginable that there ever could have been a time during which people's mental abilities were not measured and tested. Francis Galton was a pioneer in the study of human intelligence and testing. He initiated the use of surveys for collecting data, and he both developed and applied statistics for analyzing that data. In this chapter, we will review what makes for a good test, how to interpret your scores on such tests, and what different kinds of tests exist. Then we will focus on one of the most tested characteristics of all, intelligence.

Standardization and Norms

As a student, you probably take a lot of tests. Although most teachers are experienced with creating tests, psychometricians are psychologists who specialize in making standardized tests. When we say that a test is **standardized**, we mean that the test items have been piloted on a similar population of people as those who are meant to take the test (the standardization sample) and that achievement norms have been established. For standardized tests, like Advanced Placement tests, we want to be confident that scoring a 5 is indicative of a similar level of mastery on each exam.

The purpose of tests is to distinguish among people. Therefore, test questions that virtually everyone answers correctly as well as questions that almost no one can answer correctly are discarded. Such items do not provide information that differentiates among the people taking the test.

Reliability and Validity

In order for us to have any faith in the meaning of a test score, we must believe the test is both reliable and valid. **Reliability** refers to the repeatability or consistency of the test as a means of measurement. For instance, if you were to take a test three times that purportedly determined what career you should pursue and if on each occasion you received radically different recommendations, you might question the reliability of the test. Similarly, if you scored 115, 92, and 133 on three different administrations of the same IQ (intelligence quotient) test, you would have little reason to believe your intelligence had been accurately measured.

The reliability of a test can be measured in several different ways. **Split-half reliability** involves randomly dividing a test into two different sections and then correlating people's performances on the two halves. The closer the correlation coefficient is to +1, the greater the split-half reliability of the test. Many tests are available in several equivalent forms. The correlation between performance on the different forms of the test is known as equivalent-form reliability. Finally, **test-retest reliability** refers to the correlation between a person's score on one administration of the test with the same person's score on a subsequent administration of the test.

A test is valid when it measures what it is supposed to measure. **Validity** is often referred to as the accuracy of a test. A personality test is valid if it truly measures an individual's personality, and the career inventory described above is valid only if it truly measures for which jobs a person is best suited. The latter example should serve to highlight an important point: a test cannot be valid if it is not reliable. If subsequent administrations of the career inventory yield grossly disparate results for the same person, it clearly does not accurately reflect a person's vocational strengths or interests. However, a test may be reliable without being valid. Even if someone's performance on the test repeatedly indicates that he or she should be a chef and thus is reliable, if the person hates to cook, the test is not a valid measure of his or her interest. (See Table 10.1 for a comparison of reliability and validity.)

Just as several different kinds of reliability exist, several different kinds of validity exist. Face validity refers to a superficial measure of accuracy. A test of cake-baking ability has high face validity if you are looking for a chef but has low face validity if you are in the market for a doctor. Face validity is a type of content validity. Content validity refers to how well a measure reflects the entire range of material it is supposed to be testing. If one really wanted to design a test to find a good chef (as opposed to a cake baker), a test that requires someone to create an entrée and whip up a salad dressing in addition to baking a cake would have greater content validity.

> **TIP**
>
> Reliability and validity are important terms for you to know. The psychological meaning ascribed to these two terms may differ somewhat from how they are used by the general population. Reliability refers to a test's consistency, and validity refers to a test's accuracy.

Another kind of validity is criterion-related validity. Tests may have two kinds of criterion-related validity: concurrent and predictive. Concurrent validity measures how much of a characteristic a person has now. For example, is a person a good chef now? **Predictive validity** is a measure of future performance. For example, does a person have the qualities that would enable him or her to become a good chef?

Finally, **construct validity** is thought to be the most meaningful kind of validity. If an independent measure already exists that has been established to identify those who will make fine chefs and love their work, we can correlate prospective chefs' performance on this measure with their performance on any new measure. The higher the correlation, the more construct validity the new measure has. The limitation, of course, is the difficulty in creating any measure that we believe is perfectly valid in the first place.

Table 10.1 Reliability Versus Validity in Archery

Neither reliable nor valid	An archer always misses the target: sometimes shooting too high, sometimes too low, sometimes too far to the left, and sometimes too far to the right.
Reliable but not valid	An archer always misses the target, but the arrows consistently go just over the right side of the top of the target.
Both reliable and valid	An archer always puts the arrow in or near the bull's-eye.

Types of Tests

Two common types of tests are aptitude tests and achievement tests. **Aptitude tests** measure ability or potential, while **achievement tests** measure what one has learned or accomplished. For instance, any intelligence test is supposed to be an aptitude test. These tests are made to express someone's potential, not their current level of achievement. Conversely, most, if not all, the tests you take in school are supposed to be achievement tests. They are meant to indicate how much you have learned in a given subject. However, making a test that exclusively measures one of these qualities is virtually impossible. Whatever one's aptitude for a particular field or skill, one's experience affects it. Someone who has had a lot of schooling will score better on a test of mathematics aptitude than someone who might have an equally great potential to be a mathematician but who has never had any formal training in math. Similarly, two people who have achieved equally in learning biology will not necessarily score the same on an achievement test. If one has far greater test-taking aptitude, she or he will likely outscore the other.

Distinguishing between speed and power tests is also possible. Speed tests generally consist of a large number of questions asked in a short amount of time. The goal of a speed test is to see how quickly a person can solve problems. Therefore, the amount of time allotted should be insufficient to complete the problems. The goal of a power test is to gauge the difficulty level of problems an individual can solve. Power tests consist of items of increasing difficulty levels. Examinees are given sufficient time to work through as many problems as they can since the goal is to determine the ceiling difficulty level, not their problem-solving speed.

Finally, some tests are group tests while others are individual tests. Group tests are administered to many people at a time. Interaction between the examiner and the people taking the test is minimal. Generally, instructions are provided to the group, and then people are given a certain amount of time to complete the various sections of the test. Group tests are less expensive to administer and are thought to be more objective than individual tests. Individual tests involve greater interaction between the examiner and the examinee.

TIP
Even though it is essentially impossible to create a pure aptitude or pure achievement test, tests that purport to measure aptitude seek to measure someone's ability or potential, whereas achievement tests seek to measure how much of a body of material someone has learned.

Theories of Intelligence

Although **intelligence** is a commonly used term, it is an extremely difficult concept to define. Typically, intelligence is defined as the ability to gather and use information in productive ways. However, we will not present any one correct definition of intelligence because nothing that approaches a consensus has been achieved. Rather, we will present brief summaries of some of the most widely known theories of intelligence. Table 10.2 compares three of these theories.

Many psychologists differentiate between fluid intelligence and crystallized intelligence. **Fluid intelligence** refers to our ability to solve abstract problems and pick up new information and skills, while **crystallized intelligence** involves using knowledge accumulated over time. Although fluid intelligence seems to decrease as adults age, research shows that crystallized intelligence holds steady or may even increase. For instance, a 20-year-old may be able to learn a computer language more quickly than a 60-year-old, whereas the older person may well have the advantage on a vocabulary test or an exercise dependent on wisdom.

One fundamental issue of debate is whether intelligence refers to a single ability, a small group of abilities, or a wide variety of abilities. Charles Spearman argued that intelligence could be expressed by a single factor. He used factor analysis, which is a statistical technique that measures the correlations between different items, to conclude that underlying the many different specific abilities, s, that people regard as types of intelligence is a single factor that he named g for general.

Howard Gardner subscribes to the idea of multiple intelligences. Unlike many other researchers, however, the kinds of intelligences that this contemporary researcher has named thus far encompass a large range of human behavior. Three of Gardner's multiple intelligences—linguistic, logical-mathematical, and spatial—fall within the bounds of qualities traditionally labeled as intelligences. To that list Gardner has added musical, bodily-kinesthetic, intrapersonal, interpersonal, and naturalist intelligences. Musical intelligence, as one might suspect, includes the ability to play an instrument or compose a symphony. A dancer or an athlete would have a lot of bodily-kinesthetic intelligence as would a hunter. Intrapersonal intelligence refers to one's ability to understand oneself. People who can persevere without becoming discouraged or who can differentiate between situations in which they will be successful and those that may simply frustrate them have intrapersonal intelligence. Interpersonal intelligence, on the other hand, corresponds to a person's ability to get along with and be sensitive to others. Successful psychologists, teachers, and salespeople typically have a lot of interpersonal intelligence. Finally, naturalist intelligence is found in people gifted at recognizing and organizing the things they encounter in the natural environment. Such people would be successful in fields such as biology and ecology.

Robert Sternberg is another contemporary researcher who has offered a somewhat nontraditional definition of intelligence. Sternberg's triarchic theory holds that three types of intelligence exist. Componential, or analytic, intelligence involves the skills traditionally thought of as reflecting intelligence. Most of what we are asked to do in school involves this type of intelligence: the ability to compare and contrast, explain, and analyze. The second type, experiential or creative intelligence, focuses on people's ability to use their knowledge and experiences in new and innovative ways. Rather than comparing the different definitions of intelligence that others have offered, someone with this type of intelligence might prefer to come up with his or her own theory of what constitutes intelligence. The third kind of intelligence Sternberg discusses is contextual or practical intelligence. People with this type of intelligence are what we consider street-smart; they can apply what they know to real-world situations.

This last aspect of Sternberg's theory, the idea of practical intelligence, raises another important and unresolved issue in the study of intelligence: does intelligence depend on context? The other theories of intelligence discussed above essentially posit that intelligence is an ability, something or some collection of things that one has or does not have. Sternberg, on the other hand, asserts that what is intelligent behavior depends on the context or situation in which it occurs. If intelligence does, indeed, depend on context, devising an intelligence test becomes a particularly difficult task. The most common intelligence tests used (described in the next section) are based on the view of intelligence as ability based.

Recently there has been a lot of discussion of EQ, which is also known as emotional intelligence. One of the main proponents of EQ is Daniel Goleman. EQ roughly corresponds to Gardner's notions of interpersonal and intrapersonal intelligence. Researchers who argue for the importance of EQ point out that the people with the highest IQs are not always the most successful people. They contend that both EQ and IQ are needed to succeed.

Table 10.2 Theories of Intelligence

Spearman	Intelligence can be measured by a single, general ability (*g*).
Gardner	Theory of multiple intelligences—the term "intelligence" should be applied to a wide variety of abilities including kinesthetic, musical, interpersonal, intrapersonal, naturalistic, verbal, spatial, and mathematical.
Sternberg	Triarchic theory of intelligence—people can be intelligent in different ways; they can evidence analytic, practical, and creative intelligence.

Intelligence Tests

Not surprisingly, the ongoing debate over what constitutes intelligence makes constructing an assessment particularly difficult. Two widely used individual tests of intelligence are the Stanford-Binet and the Wechsler.

Alfred Binet was a Frenchman who wanted to design a test that would identify which children needed special attention in schools. His purpose was not to rank or track children but, rather, to improve the children's education by finding a way to tailor it better to their specific needs. Binet came up with the concept of **mental age**, an idea that presupposes that intelligence increases as one gets older. The average 10-year-old child has a mental age of 10.

When this average child grows to age 12, she or he will seem more intelligent and will have a mental age of 12. By using this method, Binet created a test that would identify children who lagged behind most of their peers, who were in step with their peer group, and who were ahead of their peers. Binet created a standardized test using the method described earlier in this unit. He administered questions to a standardization sample and constructed a test that would differentiate among children functioning at different levels.

Lewis Terman, a Stanford professor, used this system to create the measure we know as IQ and the test known as the **Stanford-Binet IQ** test. **IQ** stands for intelligence quotient. A person's IQ score on this test is computed by dividing the person's mental age by his or her **chronological age** and multiplying by 100. Thus, the 10-year-old child described above has an IQ of 100 because $10/10 \times 100 = 100$. A child who has a mental age of 15 at age 10 would have an IQ of 150, $15/10 \times 100 = 150$. A commonly asked question about this system is how it deals with adults. While talking about a mental age of 8 or 11 or 17 makes sense, what does having a mental age of 25 or 33 or 58 mean? To address this problem, Terman assigned all adults an arbitrary age of 20.

David Wechsler used a different way to measure intelligence. Although it does not involve finding a quotient, it is still known as an IQ test. Three different Wechsler tests actually exist. The Wechsler Adult Intelligence Scale (WAIS) is used in testing adults, the Wechsler Intelligence Scale for Children (WISC) is given to children between the ages of 6 and 16, and the Wechsler Preschool and Primary Scale of Intelligence (WPPSI) can be administered to children as young as 4. The Wechsler tests yield IQ scores based on what is known as deviation IQ. The tests are standardized so that the mean is 100, the standard deviation is 15, and the scores form a normal distribution. Remember that in a normal distribution, the percentages of scores that fall under each part of the normal curve are predetermined (see Figure 10.1).

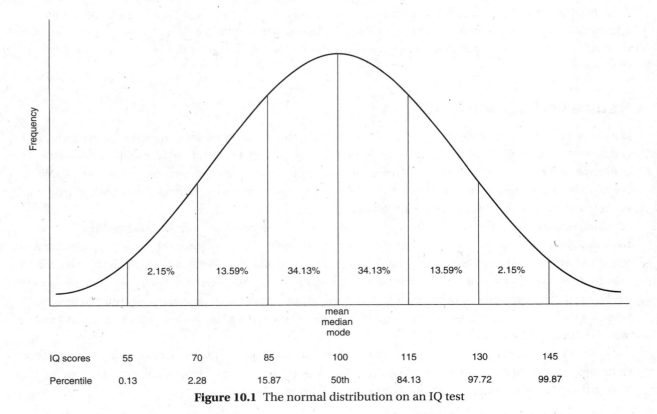

IQ scores	55	70	85	100	115	130	145
Percentile	0.13	2.28	15.87	50th	84.13	97.72	99.87

Figure 10.1 The normal distribution on an IQ test

For instance, approximately 68 percent of scores fall within 1 standard deviation of the mean, approximately 95 percent fall within 2 standard deviations of the mean, and nearly 99 percent of scores fall within 3 standard deviations of the mean. People's scores are determined by how many standard deviations they are away from the mean. Thus, Peter who scores at the 15.87th percentile falls at 1 standard deviation below the mean and is assigned a score of 85, while Juanita who scores at the 97.72nd percentile has scored 2 standard deviations above the mean and has scored 130. Of course, most people do not fall exactly 1 or 2 standard deviations above the mean. However, using such an example would necessitate less obvious mathematical calculations. For more information on the normal curve, you might want to refer to Chapter 3, "Statistics."

Whereas the Stanford-Binet IQ test utilizes a variety of different kinds of questions to yield a single IQ score, the Wechsler tests result in scores on several subscales as well as a total IQ score. For instance, the WAIS has 11 subscales. Six of them are combined to produce a verbal IQ score. Five are used to indicate performance IQ. The kinds of questions used to measure verbal IQ ask people to define words, solve mathematical word problems, and explain ways in which different items are similar. The items on the performance section involve tasks like duplicating a pattern with blocks, correctly ordering pictures so they tell a story, and identifying missing elements in pictures. Differences between a person's score on the verbal and performance sections of this exam can be used to identify learning disabilities.

Bias in Testing

Much discussion has centered on whether widely used IQ tests and the SAT are biased against certain groups. Interestingly, researchers seem to agree that although different races and genders may score differently on these tests, the tests have the same predictive validity for all groups. In other words, SAT scores are equally good predictors of college grades for different genders and for different racial groups. Thus, in a sense, the test is clearly not biased. However, other researchers have argued that both the tests and the college grades are biased in a far more fundamental way. Advantages seem to accrue to the white, middle-class, and upper-class students. The experiences of other cultural groups seem to work to their detriment both on these tests and in college. Writers of the test may assume a level of vocabulary and a range of experiences that members of these groups have not been exposed to. To the extent that the tests are supposed to identify academic potential, they may then be both flawed and biased.

Nature vs. Nurture: Intelligence

One of the most difficult and controversial issues in psychology involves sorting out the relative effects of nature and nurture. Keep in mind that nature refers to the influence of genetics, while nurture stresses the importance of the environment and learning. One of the more hotly contested aspects of the nature-nurture debate is intelligence. Human intelligence is clearly affected by both nature and nurture. Research suggests that both genetic and environmental factors play a role in molding intelligence.

An important term that researchers use in discussing the effects of nature and nurture is heritability. **Heritability** is a measure of how much of a trait's variation is explained by genetic factors. Heritability can range from 0 to 1, where 0 indicates that the environment is totally responsible for differences in the trait and 1 means that all the variation in the trait can be accounted for genetically. Thus, the question can be asked: How heritable is intelligence? That heritability does not apply to an individual but, rather, to a population is important to point out. Whatever the heritability ratio for intelligence, it will not tell us how much of any person's intelligence was determined by nature or by nurture.

Solving this controversy once and for all is essentially impossible because we cannot ethically set up the kind of controlled experiment necessary to provide definitive answers to this question. However, many researchers have studied this issue, and some of their findings are presented below:

- Performance on intelligence tests has been increasing steadily throughout the century, a finding known as the **Flynn effect**. Since the gene pool has remained relatively stable, this finding suggests that environmental factors such as nutrition, education, and, perhaps, television and video games play a role in intelligence.

- Monozygotic (identical) twins, who share 100 percent of their genetic material, score much more similarly on intelligence tests than do dizygotic (fraternal) twins, who have, on average, only 50 percent of their genes in common. Nonetheless, some researchers have suggested that monozygotic twins tend to be treated more similarly than dizygotic twins, thus confounding the effects of nature with those of nurture.
- Research on identical twins separated at birth has found strong correlations in intelligence scores. However, researchers advocating more of an environmental influence point out that usually the twins are placed into similar environments, again making it difficult to sift out the relative effects of nature and nurture. For instance, if each of the twins is placed into a white, middle-class, suburban home, concluding that all their similarities are genetically based does not make sense.
- Psychologists agree that racial differences in IQ scores are explained by differences in environment.
- Participation in government programs such as Head Start, meant to redress some of the disadvantages faced by impoverished groups, has been shown to correlate with higher scores on intelligence tests. However, opponents of such programs assert that these gains are limited and of short duration. Advocates of such interventions respond that expecting the gains to outlast the programs is unreasonable.

After putting the issue of cause aside, when comparing groups of people on any characteristic, keep in mind that differences within groups generally dwarf differences between groups. In other words, within any one group there will be more diversity than between any two groups. Practically speaking, if we find that boys perform better on a certain test than girls do, more of a difference will exist between the highest-scoring boy and the lowest-scoring boy than between the average-scoring boy and the average-scoring girl. Furthermore, knowing that boys generally outperform girls on this test tells us nothing about the performance of any particular girl compared with the performance of any particular boy. Therefore, we need to be careful about how we use information about differences between groups. Essentially, we should not use it. We should ignore it and evaluate each person, regardless of group membership, as an individual.

A CAUTIONARY NOTE

It is often said that we live in a testing society. We like to be able to measure things and assign them a number. Therefore, keeping in mind the limitations and extraordinary labeling power of these instruments is particularly important. As we have discussed, the definition of intelligence (and many other concepts) remains hotly debated and many factors affect people's performances on tests. Thus, we need to take care not to ascribe too great a meaning to a test score. Many schools that used to measure all their students' IQs periodically have abandoned that practice. Schools that used to base admission to programs for exceptional children solely on these tests now frequently gather information in other ways as well. When IQ tests are given, the results remain confidential so as not to create expectations about how people ought to perform. Although well-designed tests can be extremely useful, we must recognize their limitations.

Unit 2 Multiple-Choice Questions

1. If you had sight in only one eye, which of the following depth cues could you NOT use?

   (A) Texture gradient
   (B) Convergence
   (C) Linear perspective
   (D) Interposition

2. You are shown a picture of your grandfather's face, but the eyes and mouth are blocked out. You still recognize it as a picture of your grandfather. Which type of processing best explains this example of perception?

   (A) Bottom-up processing
   (B) Signal detection theory
   (C) Top-down processing
   (D) Opponent-process theory

3. Which of the following sentences best describes the relationship between culture and perception?

   (A) Our perceptual rules are inborn and not affected by culture.
   (B) Perceptual rules are culturally based, so rules that apply to one culture rarely apply to another.
   (C) Most perceptual rules apply in all cultures, but some perceptual rules are learned and vary among cultures.
   (D) Slight variations in sensory apparatuses among cultures create slight differences in perception.

4. Mr. Krohn, a carpenter, is frustrated because he misplaced his hammer and needs to pound in the last nail in the bookcase he is building. He overlooks the fact that he could use the tennis trophy sitting above the workbench to pound in the nail. Which concept best explains why Mr. Krohn overlooked the trophy?

   (A) Representativeness heuristic
   (B) Retrieval
   (C) Functional fixedness
   (D) Belief bias

5. In a perception research lab, you are asked to describe the shape of the top of a box as the box is slowly rotated. Which concept are the researchers most likely investigating?

   (A) Shape constancy
   (B) Feature detectors in the retina
   (C) Placement of rods and cones in the retina
   (D) Binocular depth cues

6. Which of the following is an example of the use of the representativeness heuristic?

   (A) Judging that a young person is more likely to be the instigator of an argument than an older person because you believe younger people are more likely to start fights
   (B) Breaking down a math story problem into smaller, representative parts in order to solve it
   (C) Judging a situation by a rule that is usually, but not always, true
   (D) Solving a problem with a rule that guarantees the right, more representative answer

7. Which of the following is the best example of the use of the availability heuristic?

   (A) Judging a situation by a rule that is usually, but not always, true
   (B) Making a judgment according to past experiences that are most easily recalled
   (C) Judging that a problem should be solved using a formula that guarantees the right answer
   (D) Making a judgment according to what is usually true in your experience

8. Simeon finds that when he crams for a test the night before, he usually does well but is almost completely unable to remember the material he studied a few weeks later. What best explains why this might happen?

   (A) The material he crams only makes it into his short-term memory.
   (B) Cramming the night before usually involves a shallow level of processing.
   (C) After a few weeks, he misremembers because memory is often constructed.
   (D) Simeon is suffering from retrograde amnesia.

9. A friend mentions to you that she heard humans never forget anything; we remember everything that ever happens to us. What concept from memory research most directly contradicts this belief?

   (A) Sensory memory
   (B) Selective attention
   (C) Long-term memory
   (D) Constructive memory

10. Paul takes a test in the army to see if he would make a good pilot. Such a test is a (an)

    (A) standardized test.
    (B) aptitude test.
    (C) intelligence test.
    (D) achievement test.

11. Mrs. Cho is careful to make sure that she fairly represents the whole year's work on the final exam for her American literature class. If Mrs. Cho achieves this goal, her test will have

    (A) test-retest reliability.
    (B) construct validity.
    (C) content validity.
    (D) split-half reliability.

12. Which is the best example of crystallized intelligence?

    (A) Tino uses his exceptional vocabulary to excel at Scrabble.
    (B) Susan quickly learns to use a computerized statistics program for her class.
    (C) Gina is always the first to finish class math tests.
    (D) Arjun changes jobs and adapts to the demands of the new environment.

Questions 13 through 15 refer to the following.

Amelia wants to investigate the hypothesis that the more math classes people have taken, the less likely they are to believe that after a fair coin is tossed 3 times and comes up heads each time, the next coin toss will result in tails. She asks 30 people to report how many math classes they took in high school and college and then to rate the likelihood of the fourth coin toss coming up tails on a scale from 50 percent to 100 percent.

13. The best way for Amelia to display her findings would be with

    (A) a table that lists the number of classes and percent guessed by each person.
    (B) a bar graph that contrasts the percents guessed by people who took 3 or fewer math classes with those who took 4 or more math classes.
    (C) a sentence that states the mean number of math classes and the mean percentage guessed.
    (D) a scatterplot that plots the number of math classes on one axis and the percent guessed on the other.

14. Based on the description of her study, Amelia seems most interested in

    (A) algorithms.
    (B) the sunk-cost fallacy.
    (C) the gambler's fallacy.
    (D) representativeness heuristic.

15. The design of Amelia's study would best be described as

    (A) correlational.
    (B) a case study.
    (C) naturalistic observation.
    (D) experimental.

Answer Explanations

1. **(B)** All the other choices are monocular cues for depth, so they could be used by a person sighted in only one eye. Convergence is a binocular cue and does not work without two functioning eyes. When an object is close to our face and our eyes have to point toward each other slightly, our brain senses this convergence and uses it to help gauge distance.

2. **(C)** Your mind filled in the information from the picture by drawing on your experience. This is top-down processing. The example does not reflect bottom-up processing because information is being filled in instead of an image being built from the elements present. Signal detection theory has to do with what sensations we pay attention to, not filling in missing elements in a picture. Opponent-process theory explains color vision.

3. **(C)** Most perceptual principles apply in all cultures. However, some perceptual sets are learned and do vary, so choices (A) and (B) are incorrect. Sensory apparatuses do not vary among cultures.

4. **(C)** Functional fixedness would explain why Mr. Krohn did not think of another use for the trophy: to use it as a hammer. The representativeness heuristic is a rule of thumb for making a judgment that does not apply well to this example. Retrieval is a step in the memory process. Belief bias is our tendency to stick with a belief even when presented with evidence to the contrary.

5. **(A)** According to shape constancy, we know shapes remain constant even when our viewing angle changes. This experiment would not be investigating feature detectors, because the equipment required to measure the firing of feature detectors is not described. Placement of rods and cones in the retina would not affect perception of the top of the box. Binocular depth cues are probably not the target of the research because the researchers are not asking questions about depth.

6. **(A)** The representativeness heuristic is judging a situation based on how similar the aspects are to prototypes the person holds in his or her mind. If a person has a prototype of young people as aggressive, he or she might use the representativeness heuristic to judge the situation. Breaking down the problem into smaller parts is a problem-solving technique. Judging a situation by a rule that is usually, but not always, true is a description of heuristics in general, not specifically the representativeness heuristic. An algorithm is a rule that guarantees the right answer.

7. **(B)** By using the availability heuristic, we draw on examples that are the most readily recalled. Choice (A) is a good description of heuristics in general but not specifically the availability heuristic. Using a formula or rule that always gets the correct answer is an algorithm, so choice (C) is incorrect. Choice (D) more accurately describes the representativeness heuristic.

8. **(B)** Cramming the night before typically involves relatively superficial forms of processing that make recalling the information later difficult. Choice (A) is incorrect because short-term memory (STM) only lasts 20–30 seconds. So if the information never made it out of the STM, Simeon would forget it long before the test. The idea that we construct our memories could explain some errors in memory like source amnesia but is unlikely to explain the inability to recall a topic at all. Finally, amnesia isn't the same as not remembering something you once learned; it typically involves learning a larger amount of information and is most often due to a brain injury.

9. **(B)** The concept of selective attention contradicts this statement. Selective attention determines what sensations we attend to and encode into short-term memory. Research shows that stimuli not attended to are not remembered, so we do not remember everything that happens to us. Sensory memory, long-term memory, and constructed memories do not obviously contradict the statement.

10. **(B)** Aptitude tests aim to measure someone's ability or potential. In this case, the test is supposed to show whether Paul has the ability to be a pilot. The test may or may not be standardized.

The test is not attempting to measure Paul's intelligence. Since Paul has not yet been trained as a pilot, the test is not an achievement test.

11. **(C)** Mrs. Cho is concerned about the content validity of her test. A test that fairly represents all the material taught in her class has content validity. Validity, in general, measures how well a test measures what it is supposed to measure. For Mrs. Cho's test to have construct validity, we would need to know that the test was successful in differentiating among varying levels of achievement in her class. Reliability is a measure of how consistent the scores are on a test. Test-retest reliability involves giving the same test to the same population on at least two different occasions and measuring the correlation between the sets of scores. Split-half reliability is when one test is divided into two parts and the correlation between people's scores on the two halves is measured.

12. **(A)** Vocabulary tends to increase with age and does not depend on speed; such attributes characterize crystallized intelligence. Choices (B), (C), and (D) are more typically associated with fluid intelligence because they involve speed and learning new things.

13. **(D)** Because the data for both variables Amelia collects will be numerical (more specifically interval), she can plot each variable on an axis and represent each person's pair of scores with a dot—this is called a scatterplot. Scatterplots are typically used to depict correlational relationships like the one Amelia is studying. Such a graph would be a more effective summary of 30 people's scores than a table, so choice (A) is incorrect. The options described in choices (B) and (C) involve a loss of data specificity. For instance, if you know how many math classes people took, you don't want to reduce that information into a group of 3 or fewer versus a group of 4 or more.

14. **(C)** The gambler's fallacy is the belief that after a string of losses (or wins) in a game of chance, one is more likely to experience the opposite outcome to balance out things. Every time you flip a fair coin, you have a 50 percent chance of it landing on heads and a 50 percent chance of it landing on tails. Those probabilities do not change just because your last 3, 5, or 27 flips came up the same way; the gambler's fallacy is the belief that those probabilities do change.

15. **(A)** Because Amelia is not manipulating a variable but, rather, is looking at the relationship between two unmanipulated variables, her study is correlational. A case study is a research method that focuses on one or a small group of participants. Naturalistic observation is when the researcher watches the organisms in a study unobtrusively in order to obtain a realistic picture of what they do. An experimental study involves the manipulation of an independent variable.

UNIT 3

Development and Learning

This unit is an example of applied psychology, meaning that researchers apply psychological research to questions about how humans develop. Developmental psychologists use some unique research methods and study the entire life span, from before we are born to old age. Issues related to physical, cognitive, and social developmental topics are addressed. The learning part of this chapter refers to many kinds of learning, including classical and operant conditioning as well as observational learning. You read earlier about the behaviorist perspective: the view that human thinking and behavior is mostly influenced by classical and operant conditioning. You will learn details about that perspective in this unit.

11

Developmental Psychology

Learning Objectives

In this chapter, you will learn about:

→ Research methods
→ Prenatal influences
→ Motor/sensory development
→ Gender and development
→ Stage theories
→ Cognitive development
→ Language
→ Parenting

Key Terms

- Nature
- Nurture
- Teratogens
- Reflexes
- Rooting reflex
- Sucking reflex
- Grasping reflex
- Moro reflex
- Babinski reflex
- Visual cliff
- Motor skills
- Gross motor skills
- Gender schema
- Discontinuous
- Growth spurt
- Zone of proximal development
- Psychosocial stage theory
- Trust versus mistrust
- Autonomy versus shame and doubt
- Initiative versus guilt
- Industry versus inferiority
- Identity versus role confusion

- Intimacy versus isolation
- Generativity versus stagnation
- Integrity versus despair
- Imaginary audience
- Assimilation
- Accommodation
- Schemata
- Object permanence
- Mental symbols
- Egocentric
- Pretend play
- Theory of mind
- Concepts of conservation
- Formal operational stage
- Abstract reasoning
- Hypothetical thinking
- Concrete operational stage
- Metacognition
- Personal fable
- Phonemes
- Morphemes
- Syntax

- Semantics
- Babbling
- Holophrastic stage
- One-word stage
- Telegraphic speech
- Two-word stage
- Overgeneralization
- Overregularization
- Critical period
- Attachment parenting
- Temperament
- Secure attachments
- Avoidant attachments
- Anxious/ambivalent attachments
- Resistant attachments
- Insecure attachments
- Separation anxiety
- Microsystem
- Mesosystem
- Exosystem
- Macrosystem
- Chronosystem
- Authoritarian parents
- Permissive parents
- Authoritative parents

Overview

In a way, developmental psychology is the most comprehensive topic psychologists attempt to research. Developmental psychologists study how our behaviors and thoughts change over the course of our entire lives, from birth to death (or from conception to cremation). Consequently, developmental psychology involves many concepts traditionally included in other areas of psychology. For example, both personality researchers and developmental psychologists closely examine identical twins for personality similarities and differences. Some psychologists consider developmental psychology to be an applied research topic because developmental psychologists apply research from other areas of psychology to topics involving maturation.

One way to organize the information included in the developmental psychology section is to think about one of the basic controversies: nature versus nurture. This chapter discusses influences on development from **nature** (genetic factors) first and then moves on to theories about **nurture** (environmental factors).

Developmental Psychology Research Methods

Studies in developmental psychology are usually either cross-sectional or longitudinal. Cross-sectional research uses participants of different ages to compare how certain variables may change over the lifespan. For example, a developmental researcher might be interested in how our ability to recall nonsense words changes as we age. The researcher might choose participants from different age groups, such as 5–10, 10–20, 20–30, and 30–40, and then test the recall of a list of nonsense words in each group. Cross-sectional research can produce quick results, but researchers must be careful to avoid the effects of historical events and cultural trends. For example, participants in the 30–40 age group described in the study above might have had very different experiences in school than those in the 5–10 age group are having. Perhaps memorization was emphasized in school for one group and not for the other. When the researcher examines the results, she or he might not know if the differences in recall between the two groups are due to age or different styles of education.

Longitudinal research takes place over a long period of time. Instead of sampling from various age groups as in cross-sectional research, a longitudinal study examines one group of participants over time. For example, a developmental researcher might study how a group of mentally challenged children progress in their ability to learn skills. The researcher would gather the participants and test them at various intervals of their lives (e.g., every three years). Longitudinal studies have the advantage of precisely measuring the effects of development on a specific group. However, they are obviously time-consuming, and the results can take years or decades to develop.

Prenatal Influences

Genetics

In Unit 1, you reviewed basic information about how hereditary traits are passed on from parents to their children. Many developmental psychologists investigate how our genes influence our development. Specifically, researchers might look at identical twins to determine which traits are most influenced by genetic factors (e.g., the Bouchard twin study). Our genes also help determine what abilities we are born with, such as our reflexes and our process of developing motor skills.

Teratogens

Most prenatal influences on our development are strictly genetic (nature) in origin. However, the environment can also have profound influences on us before we are born. Certain chemicals or agents (called **teratogens**) can cause harm if ingested or contracted by the mother. The placenta can filter out many potentially harmful substances, but teratogens pass through this barrier and can affect the fetus in profound ways. One of the most common teratogens is alcohol. Even small amounts of alcohol can change the way the fetal brain develops. Children of alcoholic mothers who drink heavily during pregnancy are at high risk for fetal alcohol syndrome (FAS). Children born with FAS have small, malformed skulls and intellectual disability. Researchers are also investigating a less severe effect of moderate drinking during pregnancy, fetal alcohol effect. These children typically do not show all the symptoms of FAS but may have specific developmental problems later in life, such as learning disabilities or behavioral problems.

Alcohol is certainly not the only teratogen. Unlike alcohol, other psychoactive drugs, like cocaine and heroin, can cause newborns to share their parent's physical drug addiction. The serious withdrawal symptoms associated with these addictions can kill an infant. Some polluting chemicals in the environment can cause abnormal infant development. Certain bacteria and viruses are not screened by the placenta and may be contracted by the fetus.

TIP

These are the reflexes we are born with and lose later in life. Humans have other reflexes (for example, eye blinking in response to a puff of air to the eye) that remain with us throughout our life. Humans lose the reflexes listed in this table as our brain grows and develops.

Motor/Sensory Development

Reflexes

In the past, some philosophers and early psychologists believed that humans are born as blank slates—helpless and without any skills or reflexes. In fact, they believed this lack of reflexes or instinctual behavior was one of the factors that separated humans from animals. Researchers now know that humans are far from blank slates when we are born. All babies exhibit a set of **reflexes**, which are specific, inborn, automatic responses to certain specific stimuli. Some important reflexes humans are born with are listed in Table 11.1.

Table 11.1 Important Reflexes Humans Have at Birth

Rooting reflex	When touched on the cheek, a baby will turn his or her head to the side where he or she felt the touch and seek to put the object into his or her mouth.
Sucking reflex	When an object is placed into the baby's mouth, the infant will suck on it. (The combination of the rooting and sucking reflexes obviously helps babies eat.)
Grasping reflex	If an object is placed into a baby's palm or foot pad, the baby will try to grasp the object with his or her fingers or toes.
Moro reflex	When startled, a baby will fling his or her limbs out and then quickly retract them, making himself or herself as small as possible.
Babinski reflex	When a baby's foot is stroked, he or she will spread the toes.

The Newborn's Senses

In addition to inborn reflexes, humans are also born equipped with our sensory apparatus. Some of the ways that babies sense the world are identical to the way you do, but some differ greatly. Researchers know that babies can hear even before birth. Minutes after birth, a baby will try to turn his or her head toward the mother's voice. Babies have the same basic preferences in taste and smell as we do. Babies love the taste of sugar and respond to a higher concentration of sugar in foods. Preferences in tastes and smells change as we develop (we might learn to like the smell of fish or to hate it), but babies are born with the basic preferences in place. Babies' vision is different from ours in important ways, however. Sight becomes our dominant sense as we age, but when we are born, hearing is the dominant sense due to babies' poor vision. Babies are born almost legally blind. They can see well 8–12 inches in front of them, but everything beyond that range is a blur. Their vision improves quickly as they age, improving to normal vision (barring any vision problems) by the time they are about 12 months old. In addition, babies are born with certain visual preferences. Babies like to look at faces and face-like objects (symmetrical objects and shapes organized in an imitation of a face) more than any other objects. This preference and their ability to focus about 12 inches in front of them make babies well equipped to see their mother as soon as they are born. However, this is a difficult research area because determining what a baby does or does not perceive is tricky to measure or determine. Some researchers develop innovative techniques like the **visual cliff** to measure what babies can perceive visually. The visual cliff experiments involved placing babies who could crawl onto a platform that was partially covered with see-through material (glass or plexiglass). Researchers observed that past a certain age, babies would not crawl on the transparent material, indicating that they could perceive the "cliff" and refuse to crawl over it in order to avoid falling.

Motor Development

Barring developmental difficulties, all humans develop the same basic **motor skills** in the same sequence, especially our **gross motor skills** like the examples described in this section. However, the age we develop them may differ from person to person. Our motor control develops as neurons in our brain connect with one another and become myelinated (see Chapter 4 "Biological Bases of Behavior" for a review of neural anatomy). Research shows that most babies can roll over when they are about 5-1/2 months old, stand at about 8–9 months, and walk by themselves after about 15 months. These ages are very approximate and apply to babies all over the world. Although environment and parental encouragement may have some effect on motor skills, the effect is slight.

Gender and Development

Another area of developmental research focuses on gender issues. Specifically, researchers are interested in how we develop our ideas about what it means to be male and female and in developmental differences between genders.

Different cultures encourage different gender roles, which are behaviors that a culture associates with a gender. Gender roles vary widely among cultures. A behavior considered feminine in one culture, such as holding hands with a friend, might be considered masculine or not gender specific in another. Different psychological perspectives provide different theories that try to explain how gender roles develop.

Biopsychological (Neuropsychological) Theory

Biopsychological psychologists concentrate on the nature element in the nature/nurture combination that produces our gender roles. Children learn (and are often very curious about!) the obvious biological differences between the sexes. However, biopsychologists look for more subtle biological gender differences. For the purposes of this book, going into extensive detail about all the differences between male and female brains is unnecessary. For the AP test, you should know that studies demonstrate that these differences do exist. One of the most significant findings is that, on average, female brains have larger corpus callosums (see Chapter 4 "Biological Bases of Behavior") than male brains. Theoretically, this difference may affect how the right and left hemispheres communicate and coordinate tasks.

Social-Cognitive Theory

Social-cognitive psychologists concentrate on the effects society and our own thoughts about gender have on role development. Social psychologists look at how we react to boys and girls differently. For example, boys are more often encouraged in rough physical play than are girls. These psychologists focus on the internal interpretations we make about the gender messages we get from our environment. For instance, if a girl sees that her little brother is encouraged to wrestle with their father but she is criticized for similar rough play, she may learn that there are different rules governing how boys and girls should play.

Stage Theories

Besides nature versus nurture, one of the other major controversies in developmental psychology is the argument about continuity versus discontinuity. Do we develop continually, at a steady rate from birth to death, or is our development **discontinuous**, happening in fits and starts with some periods of rapid development and some of relatively little change? Biologically, we know our development is somewhat discontinuous. We grow more as an infant and during our adolescent **growth spurt** than at other times in our lives. However, what about psychologically? Do we develop in our thought and behavior continuously or discontinuously?

Psychologist Lev Vygotsky's concept of **zone of proximal development** is one answer to this question of continuity versus discontinuity: a child's zone of proximal development is the range of tasks the child can perform independently and those tasks the child needs assistance with. Teachers/parents can provide "scaffolds" for students to help them accomplish tasks at the upper end of their zone of proximal development, encouraging further cognitive development. Several theorists concluded that we pass through certain stages in the development of certain psychological traits, and their theories attempt to explain these stages. Stage theories are, by definition, discontinuous theories of development.

Erik Erikson

Erik Erikson was a psychodynamic theorist. He thought that our personality was profoundly influenced by our experiences with others, so he created the **psychosocial stage theory**. It consists of eight stages, each stage centering on a specific social conflict (see Table 11.2).

Table 11.2 The Eight Stages of Erikson's Psychosocial Stage Theory

Trust versus Mistrust	Babies' first social experience of the world centers on need fulfillment. Babies learn whether or not they can trust that the world provides for their needs. Erikson thought that babies need to learn that they can trust their caregivers and that their requests (crying, at first) are effective. This sense of trust or mistrust will carry throughout the rest of our lives, according to Erikson.
Autonomy versus Shame and Doubt	In this next stage, toddlers begin to exert their will over their own bodies for the first time. Autonomy is our control over our own body, and Erikson thought that potty training was an early effort at gaining this control. Toddlers should also learn to control temper tantrums during this stage. Children's most popular word during this stage might be "No!," demonstrating their attempt to control themselves and others. If we learn how to control ourselves and our environment in reasonable ways, we develop a healthy will. Erikson believes we can then control our own body and emotional reactions during the rest of the social challenges we will face.
Initiative versus Guilt	In this stage, children's favorite word changes from "No!" to "Why?" If we trust those around us and feel in control of our bodies, we feel a natural curiosity about our surroundings. Children in this stage want to understand the world. We take the initiative in problem solving and ask many (many!) questions. If this initiative is encouraged, we will feel comfortable about expressing our curiosity throughout the rest of the stages. If those around us scold us for our curiosity, we might learn to feel guilty about asking questions and avoid doing so in the future.
Industry versus Inferiority	This stage is the beginning of our formal education. Preschool and kindergarten are mostly about play and entertainment. In the first grade, for the first time we are asked to produce work that is evaluated. We expect to perform as well as our peers at games and schoolwork. If we feel that we are as good at kickball (or math problems, or singing, and so on) as the child at the next desk, we feel competent. If we realize that we are behind or cannot do as well as our peers, which is having an inferiority complex, we may feel anxious about our performance in that area throughout the rest of the stages.
Identity versus Role Confusion	In adolescence, Erikson felt our main social task is to discover what social identity we are most comfortable with. He thought that a person might naturally try out different roles before he or she finds the one that best fits his or her internal sense of self. Adolescents try to fit into groups in order to feel confident in their identities. An adolescent should figure out a stable sense of self before moving on to the next stage or risk having an identity crisis later in life. Other researchers connect this idea with the tendency of adolescents to think about how they are viewed by an **imaginary audience** and overestimate how much other people are thinking about or focusing on them.

(Continued)

Table 11.2 The Eight Stages of Erikson's Psychosocial Stage Theory (Continued)

Intimacy versus Isolation	Young adults who established stable identities then must figure out how to balance their ties and efforts between work (including careers, school, or self-improvement) and relationships with other people. How much time should we spend on ourselves and how much time with our families? What is the difference between a platonic and a romantic relationship? Again, the patterns established in this stage will influence the effort spent on self and others in the future.
Generativity versus Stagnation	Erikson felt that by the time we reach this stage, we are starting to look critically at our life path. We want to make sure that we are creating the type of life that we want for ourselves and our family. We might try to seize control of our lives at this point to ensure that things go as we plan. In this stage, we try to ensure that our lives are going the way we want them to go. If they are not, we may try to change our identities or control those around us to change our lives.
Integrity versus Despair	Toward the end of life, we look back at our accomplishments and decide whether or not we are satisfied with them. Erikson thought that if we can see that our lives were meaningful, we can "step outside" the stress and pressures of society and offer wisdom and insight. If, however, we feel serious regret over how we lived our lives, we may fall into despair over lost opportunities.

Cognitive Development

Jean Piaget

Jean Piaget was working for Alfred Binet, creator of the first intelligence test, when he started to notice interesting behaviors in the children he was interviewing. Piaget noted that children of roughly the same age almost always gave similar answers to some of the questions on the intelligence test, even if the answers were wrong. He hypothesized that this was because they were all thinking in similar ways and these ways of thinking differed from the ways adults think. This hypothesis led to Piaget's theory of cognitive development. Piaget described how children viewed the world through schemata, cognitive rules we use to interpret the world. Typically, we incorporate our experiences into these existing schemata in a process called **assimilation**. Sometimes, information does not fit into or violates our schemata, so we must accommodate and change our schemata. For example, a four-year-old boy named Daniel gets a pair of cowboy boots from his parents for his birthday. He wears his cowboy boots constantly and does not see anyone else wearing cowboy boots. Daniel develops a schema for cowboy boots: only little boys wear boots. Most of his experiences do not violate this schema. He sees other little boys wearing cowboy boots and assimilates this information into his schema. Then Daniel's family takes a trip to Arizona. When he gets off the plane, he sees a huge (huge to a four-year-old, at least) man wearing cowboy boots. Daniel points at the man and starts to laugh hysterically. Why is Daniel causing this scene? His schema has been violated. To Daniel, the large man is dressed like a little boy! After he stops laughing, Daniel will have to accommodate this new information and change his schema to include the fact that adults can wear cowboy boots, too. By the way, this process may repeat itself the first time Daniel sees a woman wearing cowboy boots!

Piaget thinks humans go through this process of schema creation, assimilation, and **accommodation** as we develop cognitively. His cognitive development theory describes how our thinking progresses through four stages.

Sensorimotor Stage (Birth to Approximately Two Years Old)

Babies start experiencing and exploring the world strictly through their senses. Piaget noted that at the beginning of life, behavior is governed by the reflexes we are born with. Soon, we start to develop our first cognitive **schemata** that explain the world we experience through our senses. One of the major challenges of this stage is to develop **object permanence**. Babies at first do not realize that objects continue to exist even when they are out of sensory range. When babies start to look for or somehow acknowledge that objects do exist when they cannot see them, they have object permanence.

Preoperational Stage (Two to Approximately Seven Years Old)

Acquiring the scheme of object permanence prepares a child to start to use **mental symbols** to represent real-world objects. This ability is the beginning of language, the most important cognitive development of this stage. We start speaking our first words and gradually learn to represent the world more completely through language. Although we can refer to the world through symbols during the preoperational stage, we are still limited in the ways we can think about the relationships among objects and the characteristics of objects. Children in this stage are also **egocentric** in their thinking since they cannot look at the world from anyone's perspective but their own. Piaget also thought that children in the preoperational stage developed the ability to imagine what someone else might be thinking and act on those predictions. This leads to the ability to **pretend play**. Modern developmental and cognitive psychologists call the ability to think about and consider the mental states of others the **theory of mind**.

Concrete Operational Stage (Eight to Approximately Twelve Years Old)

During the concrete operational stage, children learn to think more logically about complex relationships among different characteristics of objects. Piaget categorized children as being in the concrete operational stage when they demonstrated knowledge of **concepts of conservation**, the realization that properties of objects remain the same even when their shapes change. These concepts demonstrate how the different aspects of objects are conserved even when their arrangement changes. See Table 11.3 for examples of the concepts.

Table 11.3 Concepts of Conservation

Concept	Description	How to Test
Volume	The volume of a material is conserved even if the material's container or shape changes.	Pour water into differently shaped glasses and ask if the volume of the water increased, decreased, or stayed the same.
Area	Area is conserved even if objects within that area are rearranged. Do these 2 squares have the same amount of shaded area? Do the squares *still* have the same amount of shaded area?	Ask a child to examine two different squares of equal area and rearrange objects within the area in order to determine if children realize the area was conserved.

(*Continued*)

Table 11.3 Concepts of Conservation (Continued)

Concept	Description	How to Test
Number	The number of objects stays the same when the objects are rearranged. Does each row have the same number of circles? → Now does each row have the same number of circles?	Take a few objects, let the child count them, rearrange the objects, and ask the child how many there are now. If the child counts them again, he or she does not understand conservation of number.

Formal Operational Stage (Twelve Through Adulthood)

This final stage of Piaget, the **formal operational stage**, describes adult reasoning. Piaget theorized that not all of us reach formal operations in all areas of thought. Formal operational reasoning is abstract reasoning. Through **abstract reasoning**, we can manipulate objects and contrast ideas in our mind without physically seeing them or having real-world correlates. One example of abstract reasoning is hypothesis testing. A person in Piaget's formal operational stage can reason from a hypothesis. This is known as **hypothetical thinking**. To test for formal operational thought, you might ask a child, "How would you be different if you were born on a planet that had no light?" A child in the preoperational or **concrete operational stage** would have trouble answering the question because no real-world model exists to fall back on. Someone in the formal operational stage would be able to extrapolate from this hypothesis and reason that the beings on that planet might not have eyes, would have no words for color, and might exclusively rely on other senses. Also, in the formal operational stage, we gain the ability to think about the way we think; this is called **metacognition**. We can trace our thought processes and evaluate the effectiveness of how we solved a problem. This new ability to think abstractly can lead some adolescents into a different kind of egocentric thinking: they can develop a **personal fable**, which is a belief that they are unique or different from everyone else, or they can develop an attitude of superiority or invulnerability.

Criticisms of Piaget: Information Processing Model

Many developmental psychologists still value Piaget's insights about the order in which our cognitive skills develop, but most agree that he underestimated children. Many children go through the stages faster and enter them earlier than Piaget predicted. Piaget's error may be due to the way he tested children. Some psychologists wonder if some of his tests relied too heavily on language use, thus biasing the results in favor of older children with more language skills. Other theorists wonder if development does not occur more continuously than Piaget described. Perhaps our cognitive skills develop more continuously and not in discrete stages.

The information processing model is a more continuous alternative to Piaget's stage theory. Information processing points out that our abilities to memorize, interpret, and perceive gradually develop as we age rather than developing in distinct stages. For example, research shows that our attention span gradually increases as we get older. This one continuous change could explain some apparent cognitive differences Piaget attributed to different cognitive stages. Maybe children's inability to understand conservation of number has more to do with their ability to focus for long periods of time than with any developing reasoning ability. Developmental researchers agree that no one has the perfect model to describe cognitive development. Future research will refine our current ideas and create models that more closely describe how our thinking changes as we mature.

Language

For us to conceive of thought without using language is impossible. Your brain is processing the language you are reading right now. If you stop to think about the previous sentence, you think about it using language. Language is intimately connected to cognition. Some psychologists investigate how language works and how we acquire it in an attempt to understand better how we think and behave.

Elements of Language

All languages can be described with **phonemes** and **morphemes**. Phonemes are the smallest units of sound used in a language. English speakers use approximately 44 phonemes. If you have studied another language or if your primary language is not English, you have experience with other phonemes. Native Spanish speakers find the rolled *R* phoneme natural, but many English speakers have difficulty learning how to produce it since it is not used in English. Speakers of other languages have difficulty learning some English phonemes.

A morpheme is the smallest unit of meaningful sound. Morphemes can be words, such as *a* and *but*, or they can be parts of words, such as the prefixes *an-* and *pre-*. So, language consists of phonemes put together to become morphemes, which make up words. These words are then spoken or written in a particular order, called **syntax**. Each language has its own syntax, such as where the verb is usually placed in the sentence. By examining phonemes, morphemes, and syntax (the grammar of a language), psychologists can describe different languages in detail. The meanings of words, and the combinations of words in phrases and sentences, is referred to as **semantics**. Meaning is constructed through the combinations of phonemes, morphemes, and syntax.

Language Acquisition

Many psychologists are particularly interested in how we learn language. Often, developmental psychologists are curious about how our language learning reflects or predicts our cognitive development. These studies show that while babies are learning very different languages, they progress through the same basic stages to master any language. First, if you have ever been around babies, you know that babies babble. This is often cute, and it is the first stage of language acquisition that occurs about four months of age. The **babbling** stage appears to be innate; even babies born completely deaf go through the babbling stage. This babbling represents experimentation with phonemes. They are learning what sounds they can produce. Babies in this stage can produce any phoneme from any language in the world. So, although you may not be able to roll your *R*s, your infant sister can! As language acquisition progresses, we retain the ability to produce phonemes from our primary language (or languages) and lose the ability to make some other phonemes. This is one reason why learning more than one language starting at infancy may be advantageous. Babbling progresses into utterances of words as babies imitate the words they hear caregivers speaking. The time during which babies speak in single words (holophrases) is sometimes called the **holophrastic stage** or **one-word stage**. This usually happens around their first birthday.

The next language acquisition stage occurs at around 18 months and is called the **telegraphic speech** or **two-word stage**. Toddlers combine the words they can say into simple commands. Meaning is usually clear at this stage, but syntax is absent. When your little brother shouts, "No book, movie!" you know that he means, "I do not wish to read a book at this time. I would prefer to watch a movie." Children begin to learn grammar and syntax rules during this stage, sometimes misapplying the rules. For example, they might learn that adding the suffix *-ed* signifies past tense, but they might apply it at inappropriate times, such as, "Marky hitted my head so I throwed the truck at him." Children gradually increase their abilities to combine words in proper syntax if these uses are modeled for them. This misapplication of grammar rules is called **overgeneralization** or **overregularization**.

One important controversy in language acquisition concerns how we acquire language. Behaviorists theorized that language is learned like other learned behaviors: through operant conditioning and shaping. They thought that when children used language correctly, they got rewarded by their parents with a smile or other encouragement, and therefore the children would be more likely to use language correctly in the future. More recently, cognitive psychologists challenged this theory. They point out the amazing number of words and language rules learned by children without explicit instruction by parents. Researcher Noam Chomsky theorized that humans are born with a language acquisition device, the ability to learn a language rapidly as children. (This is also called the nativist theory of language acquisition.) Chomsky pointed to the retarded development of language in cases of children deprived of exposure to language during childhood. He theorized that a **critical period** (a window of opportunity during which we must learn a skill or our development will permanently suffer) for learning language may exist. Most psychologists now agree that we acquire language through some combination of conditioning and an inborn propensity to learn language.

Language and Cognition

If language is central to the way we think, how does it influence what we are able to think about? Psychologist Benjamin Whorf theorized that the language we use might control, and in some ways limit, our thinking. This theory is called the linguistic relativity hypothesis. Many studies demonstrate the effect of labeling on how we think about people, objects, or ideas, but few studies show that the language we speak drastically changes what we can think about.

Parenting

Attachment Theory

The influences discussed so far in this chapter have mostly been genetic or prenatal in nature. After birth, uncountable environmental influences begin to affect how we develop. Some species respond in very predictable ways to environmental stimuli. Biologist Konrad Lorenz established that some infant animals (such as geese) become attached to (imprint on) individuals or even objects they see during a critical period after birth. Certainly, one of the most important aspects of a baby's early environment is the relationship between parent(s) and child. Some research focused on how **attachment parenting**, or the reciprocal relationship between caregiver and child, affects development. Two significant areas of study in this field are contact comfort and secure attachment.

Contact Comfort

In the 1950s, researcher Harry Harlow raised baby monkeys with two artificial wire frame figures made to resemble mother monkeys. One mother figure was fitted with a bottle the infant could eat from, and the other was wrapped in a soft material. Harlow found that infant monkeys when frightened preferred the soft mother figure over the figure that they fed from. When the infants were surprised or stressed, they fled to the soft mother for comfort and protection. Harlow's studies demonstrated the importance of physical comfort in the formation of attachment to parents. As Harlow's infant monkeys developed, he noticed that the monkeys raised by the wire frame mothers became more stressed and frightened than monkeys raised with real mothers when put into new situations. The deprivation of an attachment with a real mother had long-term effects on these monkeys' behavior. Some researchers try to investigate the possible influences of attachment experiences on our later **temperament**—our emotional style or typical way we react to stressful situations.

Secure Attachment

Mary Ainsworth researched the idea of attachment by placing human infants into novel situations. Ainsworth observed infants' reactions when placed into a strange situation: their parents left them alone for a short period of time and then returned. She divided the reactions into three broad categories:

- Infants with **secure attachments** (about 66 percent of the participants) confidently explored the novel environment while the parents were present, were distressed when the parents left, and came to the parents when they returned.
- Infants with **avoidant attachments** (about 21 percent of the participants) resisted being held by the parents and explored the novel environment. The infants did not go to the parents for comfort when they returned after an absence.

- Infants with **anxious/ambivalent attachments** (also called **resistant attachments** or **insecure attachments**, about 12 percent of the participants) had ambivalent reactions to the parents. The infants may have shown extreme stress (**separation anxiety**) when the parents left but resisted being comforted by them when they returned.

Ecological Systems Theory

This theory views human development as a system of relationships that is impacted by our environment. Combinations of relationships across different contexts (like family, school, work, neighborhood, culture, and country) interact to impact our development. The ecological systems theory describes five interrelated systems that influence development:

- **Microsystem:** direct interactions between the child and their immediate surroundings, including their caregivers. For example: interactions between the child and parents.
- **Mesosystem:** our microsystems are not isolated. The mesosystem acknowledges that each of the five ecological systems interact. For example: communication between a child and their parents and teachers, and then parents communicating with teachers and vice versa. These conversations influence one another, and those influences are acknowledged in the mesosystem.
- **Exosystem:** this system involves indirect influences on the child's development. For example, if a parent sacrifices time with the family in order to earn more money, the parent's absence may impact the child's development, and the extra income may indirectly influence the child through increased opportunities for enriching experiences.
- **Macrosystem:** influences of the cultures a child is immersed in will also influence his or her development. For example, if a child is raised in a family and community culture that acknowledges that any career is appropriate for both boys and girls, that openness to gender roles will influence development of children in the community.
- **Chronosystem:** times of transition or change that occur over the chronology or timeline of a child's life that influence development. Biological changes like puberty that occur at specific times in human development are examples of chronosystems.

Parenting Styles

So far, the developmental research and categories described focus on the behaviors of children. Parents' interactions with their children definitely have an influence on the way we develop and can be categorized in similar ways. Developmental psychologist Diana Baumrind researched parent-child interactions and described three overall categories of parenting styles.

Authoritarian parents set strict standards for their children's behavior and apply punishments for violations of these rules. Obedient attitudes are valued more than discussions about the rationale behind the standards. Punishment for undesired behavior is more often used than reinforcement for desired behavior. If your parents are authoritarian and you come home 15 minutes after your curfew, you might be grounded from going out again the rest of the month without explanation or discussion.

Permissive parents do not set clear guidelines for their children. The rules that do exist in the family are constantly changed or are not enforced consistently. Family members may perceive that they can get away with anything at home. If your parents are permissive and you come home 15 minutes after your curfew, your parents' reaction would be unpredictable. They may not notice, may not seem to mind, or may threaten you with a punishment that they never follow through on.

Authoritative parents have set consistent standards for their children's behavior, but the standards are reasonable and explained. The rationale for family rules is discussed with children old enough to understand them. Authoritative parents encourage their children's independence but not past the point of violating rules. They praise as often as they punish. In general, explanations are encouraged in an authoritative house, and the rules are reasonable and consistent. If your parents are authoritative and you come home 15 minutes after your curfew, you already know the consequences of your action. You know what the family rule is for breaking curfew, why the rule exists, and what the consequences are; your parents make sure you suffer the consequences!

Studies show that the authoritative style produces the most desirable and beneficial home environment. Children from authoritative homes are more socially capable and perform better academically on average. The children of permissive parents are more likely to have emotional control problems and are more dependent. Authoritarian parents' children are more likely to distrust others and be withdrawn from peers. These studies indicate another way in which our upbringing influences our development. Researchers agree that parenting style is certainly not the whole or final answer to why we develop the way we do (and the research is correlational, not causational). However, it is a key influence along with genetic makeup, peer relationships, and other environmental influences on thought and behavior.

TIP

Some students confuse the terms *authoritarian* and *authoritative*. Remember that the authoritarian style involves very strict rules without much explanation, while authoritative parents set strict rules but make sure they are reasonable and explained.

12

Learning

Learning Objectives

In this chapter, you will learn about:

→ Classical conditioning
→ Operant conditioning
→ Cognitive learning

Key Terms

- Puberty
- Menopause
- Classical conditioning
- Associative learning
- Unconditioned stimulus (US or UCS)
- Unconditioned response (UR or UCR)
- Conditioned response (CR)
- Conditioned stimulus (CS)
- Acquisition
- Trace conditioning
- Simultaneous conditioning
- Backward conditioning
- Extinction
- Spontaneous recovery
- Generalization
- Discrimination

- Higher-order conditioning
- Taste aversions
- One-trial learning
- Biological preparedness
- Association
- Operant conditioning
- Law of effect
- Reinforcement
- Positive reinforcement
- Negative reinforcement
- Punishment
- Shaping
- Reinforcement discrimination
- Discriminative stimulus
- Primary reinforcers
- Secondary reinforcers
- Generalized reinforcer

- Continuous reinforcement
- Partial-reinforcement effect
- Reinforcement schedules
- Fixed-ratio (FR) schedule
- Variable-ratio (VR) schedule
- Fixed-interval (FI) schedule
- Variable-interval (VI) schedule
- Instinctive drift
- Modeling
- Vicarious learning
- Social learning theory
- Latent learning
- Cognitive map
- Insight learning

Overview

Psychologists differentiate among many different types of learning, several of which we will discuss in this chapter. Learning is commonly defined as a long-lasting change in behavior resulting from experience. Although learning is not the same as behavior, most psychologists accept that learning can best be measured through changes in behavior. Brief changes are not thought to be indicative of learning. Consider, for example, the effects of running a marathon. For a short time afterward, one's behavior might differ radically, but we would not want to attribute this change to the effects of learning. In addition, learning must result from experience rather than from any kind of innate or biological change. Thus, changes in one's behavior as a result of **puberty** or **menopause** are not considered to be due to learning.

Classical Conditioning

Around the turn of the twentieth century, a Russian physiologist named Ivan Pavlov inadvertently discovered a kind of learning while studying digestion in dogs. Pavlov found that the dogs learned to pair the sounds in the environment where they were fed with the food that was given to them and began to salivate simply upon hearing the sounds. As a result, Pavlov deduced the basic principle of **classical conditioning** (also called **associative learning**). People and animals can learn to associate neutral stimuli (e.g., sounds) with stimuli that produce reflexive, involuntary responses (e.g., food) and will learn to respond similarly to the new stimulus as they did to the old one (e.g., salivate).

The original stimulus that elicits a response is known as the **unconditioned stimulus (US or UCS)**. The US is defined as something that elicits a natural, reflexive response. In the classic Pavlovian paradigm, the US is food. Food elicits the natural, involuntary response of salivation. This response is called the **unconditioned response (UR or UCR)**. Through repeated pairings with a neutral stimulus such as a bell, animals will come to associate the two stimuli together. Ultimately, animals will salivate when hearing the bell alone (see Figure 12.1). Once the bell elicits salivation, which is now a **conditioned response (CR)**, the bell is no longer a neutral stimulus but, rather, a **conditioned stimulus (CS)**.

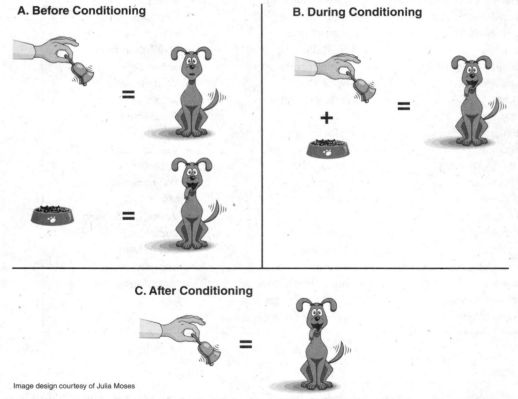

Image design courtesy of Julia Moses

Figure 12.1 Prior to classical conditioning (A), a neutral stimulus like a bell elicits no reaction from a dog, but presenting the dog with food leads it to salivate. During conditioning (B), the bell is paired repeatedly with food, and the dog salivates to this combination. Once conditioning has occurred (C), merely ringing the bell will cause the dog to salivate.

Learning has taken place once the animals respond to the CS without a presentation of the US. This learning is also called **acquisition** since the animals have acquired a new behavior. Many factors affect acquisition. For instance, up to a point, repeated pairings of CSs and USs yield stronger CRs. The order and timing of the CS and US pairings also have an impact on the strength of conditioning. Generally, the most effective method of conditioning is to present the CS first and then to introduce the US while the CS is still evident. Now return to Pavlov's dogs. Acquisition occurs fastest if the bell is rung and, while it is still ringing, the dogs are presented with food. This procedure is known as delayed conditioning. Less effective methods of learning include:

- **Trace conditioning**—Presentation of the CS, followed by a short break, followed by presentation of the US.
- **Simultaneous conditioning**—Presentation of the CS and US at the same time.
- **Backward conditioning**—Presentation of the US first, followed by presentation of the CS. This method is particularly ineffective.

Of course, what can be learned can be unlearned. In psychological terminology, the process of unlearning a behavior is known as **extinction**. In terms of classical conditioning, extinction has taken place when the CS no longer elicits the CR. Extinction is achieved by repeatedly presenting the CS without the US, thus breaking the association between the two. If one rings the bell over and over again and never feeds the dogs, the dogs will ultimately learn not to salivate to the bell.

One fascinating part of this process that has not yet been adequately explained is known as **spontaneous recovery**. Sometimes, after a conditioned response has been extinguished and no further training of the animals has taken place, the response briefly reappears upon presentation of the conditioned stimulus. This phenomenon is known as spontaneous recovery.

Often animals conditioned to respond to a certain stimulus will also respond to similar stimuli, although the response is usually smaller in magnitude. The dogs may salivate to the sounds of a number of bells, not just the one with which they were trained. This tendency to respond to similar CSs is known as **generalization**. Subjects can be trained, however, to tell the difference, or discriminate, among various stimuli. This is called **discrimination**. (Table 12.1 describes the basic conditioning phenomena.) To train the dogs to discriminate among bells, we would repeatedly pair the original bell with presentation of food but would intermix trials where we presented other bells that we did not pair with food.

Table 12.1 Basic Conditioning Phenomena in Pavlov's Work

Conditioning Phenomenon	Pavlov's Dog
Acquisition	The dog learns to salivate to the bell.
Extinction	The dog unlearns the bell-food connection and ceases to salivate to the bell.
Spontaneous recovery	After extinction and a period of rest, the dog salivates when hearing the bell.
Generalization	The dog salivates to other bell-like noises.
Discrimination	The dog learns to salivate only to the sound of a specific bell.

Classical conditioning can also be used with humans. In one famous, albeit ethically questionable, study, John B. Watson and Rosalie Rayner conditioned a little boy named Albert to fear a white rat. Little Albert initially liked the white, fluffy rat. However, by repeatedly pairing it with a loud noise, Watson and Rayner taught Albert to cry when he saw the rat. In this example, the loud noise is the US because it elicits the involuntary, natural response of fear (UR) and, in Albert's case, crying. The rat is a neutral stimulus that becomes the CS, and the CR is Albert crying in response to presentation of the rat alone. Albert also generalized, crying in response to a white rabbit, a man's white beard, and a variety of other white, fluffy things.

This example is an illustration of what is known as aversion conditioning. Whereas Pavlov's dogs were conditioned with something pleasant (food), baby Albert was conditioned to have a negative response to the white rat. Aversive conditioning has been used in several more socially constructive ways. For instance, to stop biting their nails, some people paint them with truly horrible-tasting materials. Nail biting therefore becomes associated with a terrible taste, and the biting should cease.

Once a CS elicits a CR, it is possible, briefly, to use that CS as a US in order to condition a response to a new stimulus. This process is known as **higher-order conditioning** or **second-order conditioning**. By using a dog and a bell as our example, after the dog salivates to the bell (first-order conditioning), the bell can be paired repeatedly with a flash of light. The dog will salivate to the light alone (second-order conditioning) even though the light has never been paired with the food (see Table 12.2).

Table 12.2 First-Order and Second-Order Conditioning

First-Order Conditioning	
Training	Presentation of bell + food = salivation
Acquisition	Presentation of bell = salivation
Second-Order Conditioning (After First-Order Conditioning Has Occurred)	
Training	Presentation of light + bell = salivation
Acquisition	Presentation of light = salivation

Biology and Classical Conditioning

As is evident from its description, classical conditioning can be used only when one wants to pair an involuntary, natural response with something else. Once one has identified such a US, can a subject be taught to pair it equally easily with any CS? Not surprisingly, the answer is no. Research suggests that animals and humans are biologically prepared to make certain connections more easily than others. **Taste aversions** are a classic example of this phenomenon. If you ingest an unusual food or drink and then become nauseous, you may develop an aversion to the food or drink. Learned taste aversions are interesting because they can result in powerful avoidance responses based on a single pairing. In addition, the two events (eating and sickness) are probably separated by at least several hours. Animals, including people, seem biologically prepared to associate strange tastes with feelings of sickness. Clearly, this response is adaptive (helpful for the survival of the species) because it helps us learn to avoid dangerous things in the future. Also interesting is how we seem to learn what, exactly, to avoid. Taste aversions most commonly occur with strong and unusual tastes. The food, the CS, must be salient in order for us to learn to avoid it. Salient stimuli are easily noticeable and therefore create a more powerful conditioned response. Sometimes taste aversions are acquired without good reason. If you were to eat some mozzarella sticks a few hours before falling ill with the stomach flu, you might develop an aversion to that popular American appetizer even though it had nothing to do with your sickness.

John Garcia and Robert Koelling performed a famous experiment illustrating how rats more readily learned to make certain associations than others. This kind of classical conditioning occurs so quickly and so powerfully that it is sometimes called **one-trial learning**. They used four groups of subjects in their experiment and exposed each to a particular combination of CS and US as illustrated in Table 12.3.

Table 12.3 Garcia and Koelling's Experiment Illustrating Biological Preparedness in Classical Conditioning

CS	US	Learned Response
Loud noise	Shock	Fear
Loud noise	Radiation (nausea)	Nothing
Sweet water	Shock	Nothing
Sweet water	Radiation (nausea)	Avoid water

The rats learned to associate noise with shock and unusual-tasting water with nausea. This type of powerful conditioning may occur because of **biological preparedness**: we are biologically predisposed to associate nausea with something we ate or drank. However, the rats were unable to make the connection between noise and nausea and between unusual-tasting water and shock. Again, learning to link loud noise with shock (e.g., thunder and lightning) and unusual-tasting water with nausea seems to be adaptive. The ease with which animals learn taste aversions is known as the Garcia effect.

Operant Conditioning

Whereas classical conditioning is a type of learning based on **association** of stimuli, **operant conditioning** is a kind of learning based on the association of consequences with one's behaviors. Edward Thorndike was one of the first people to research this kind of learning.

Thorndike conducted a series of famous experiments using a cat in a puzzle box. The hungry cat was locked in a cage next to a dish of food. The cat had to get out of the cage to get the food. Thorndike found that the amount of time required for the cat to get out of the box decreased over a series of trials. This amount of time decreased gradually; the cat did not suddenly understand how to get out of the cage. This finding led Thorndike to assert that the cat learned the new behavior without mental activity but, rather, simply connected a stimulus and a response.

Thorndike put forth the **law of effect** that states that if the consequences of a behavior are pleasant, the stimulus-response (S-R) connection will be strengthened and the likelihood of the behavior will increase. However, if the consequences of a behavior are unpleasant, the S-R connection will weaken and the likelihood of the behavior will decrease. He used the term instrumental learning to describe his work because he believed the consequence was instrumental in shaping future behaviors.

B. F. Skinner, who coined the term operant conditioning, is the best-known psychologist to research this form of learning. Skinner invented a special contraption, aptly named a Skinner box, to use in his research of animal learning. A Skinner box usually has a way to deliver food to an animal and a lever to press or disk to peck to get the food. The food is called a reinforcer, and the process of giving the food is called **reinforcement**. Reinforcement is defined by its consequences; anything that makes a behavior more likely to occur is a reinforcer. Two kinds of reinforcement exist. **Positive reinforcement** refers to the addition of something pleasant. **Negative reinforcement** refers to the removal of something unpleasant. For instance, if we give a rat in a Skinner box food when it presses a lever, we are using positive reinforcement. However, if we terminate a loud noise or shock in response to a press of the lever, we are using negative reinforcement. The latter example results in escape learning. Escape learning allows one to terminate an aversive stimulus; avoidance learning, on the other hand, enables one to avoid the unpleasant stimulus altogether. If Sammy creates a ruckus in the English class he hates and is asked to leave, he is evidencing escape learning. An example of avoidance learning would be if Sammy cut English class.

TIP

Students often confuse negative reinforcement and punishment. However, any type of reinforcement results in the behavior being more likely to be repeated. The negative in negative reinforcement refers to the fact that something is taken away. The positive in positive punishment indicates that something is added. In negative reinforcement, the removal of an aversive stimulus is what is doing the reinforcing.

Affecting behavior by using unpleasant consequences is also possible. Such an approach is known as **punishment**. By definition, punishment is anything that makes a behavior less likely. The two types of punishment are known as positive punishment (usually referred to simply as punishment), which is the addition of something unpleasant, and omission training or negative punishment, which is the removal of something pleasant. If we give a rat an electric shock every time it touches the lever, we are using punishment. If we remove the rat's food when it touches the lever, we are using omission training. Both procedures will result in the rat ceasing to touch the bar. Imagine that your parents decided to use operant conditioning principles to modify your behavior. If you did something your parents liked and they wanted to increase the likelihood of your repeating the behavior, your parents could use either of the types of reinforcement described in Table 12.4. On the other hand, if you did something your parents wanted to discourage, they could use either of the types of punishment described in Table 12.5.

Table 12.4 Reinforcement = A Consequence That Increases the Likelihood of a Behavior

Types	Mechanism	Examples
Positive reinforcement	Adds something pleasant	Parent gives child present as reward for cleaning room
Negative reinforcement	Removes something unpleasant	Parent stops yelling when child goes to clean room

Table 12.5 Punishment = A Consequence That Decreases the Likelihood of a Behavior

Types	Mechanism	Examples
Positive punishment	Adds something negative	Parent yells when child comes home after curfew
Omission training (also known as negative punishment)	Removes something pleasant	Parent takes away cell phone when child comes home after curfew

Punishment Versus Reinforcement

Generally, the same ends can be achieved through punishment and reinforcement. If I want students to arrive on time to my class, I can either punish them for lateness or reward them for arriving on time. Punishment is operant conditioning's version of aversive conditioning. Punishment is most effective if it is delivered immediately after the unwanted behavior and if it is harsh. However, harsh punishment may also result in unwanted consequences such as fear and anger.

You might wonder how the rat in the Skinner box learns to push the lever in the first place. Rather than wait for an animal to perform the desired behavior by chance, we usually try to speed up the process by using **shaping**. Shaping reinforces the steps used to reach the desired behavior. First the rat might be reinforced for going to the side of the box with the lever. Then we might reinforce the rat for touching the lever with any part of its body. By rewarding approximations of the desired behavior, we increase the likelihood that the rat will stumble upon the behavior we want.

Animals can also be taught to perform several responses successively in order to get a reward. This process is known as chaining. One famous example of chained behavior involved a rat named Barnabus who learned to run through a veritable obstacle course in order to obtain a food reward. Whereas the goal of shaping is to mold a single behavior (e.g., pressing a bar), the goal in chaining is to link together several separate behaviors into a more complex activity (e.g., running an obstacle course).

The terms acquisition, extinction, spontaneous recovery, discrimination, and generalization can be used in our discussion of operant conditioning, too. Using a rat in a Skinner box as our example (see Table 12.6), acquisition occurs when the rat learns to press the lever to get the reward. Extinction occurs when the rat ceases to press the lever because the reward no longer results from this action. Note that punishing the rat for pushing the lever is not necessary to extinguish the response. Behaviors that are not reinforced will ultimately stop and are said to be on an extinction schedule. Spontaneous recovery would occur if, after having extinguished the bar press response and without providing any further training, the rat began to press the bar again. Generalization would be if the rat began to press other things in the Skinner box or the bar in other boxes. Discrimination (also called **reinforcement discrimination**) would involve teaching the rat to press only a particular bar or to press the bar only under certain conditions (e.g., when a tone is sounded). In this last example, the tone is called a **discriminative stimulus**.

Table 12.6 Basic Conditioning Phenomena in Skinner's Work

Conditioning Phenomenon	Rat in a Skinner Box
Acquisition	The rat learns to press the bar for food.
Extinction	The rat unlearns the bar-food connection and ceases to press the bar.
Spontaneous recovery	After extinction and a period of rest, the rat presses the bar.
Generalization	The rat presses other objects that look like the bar.
Discrimination	The rat learns to press only a particular bar.

Not all reinforcers are food, of course. Psychologists speak of two main types of reinforcers: primary and secondary. **Primary reinforcers** are, in and of themselves, rewarding. They include things like food, water, and rest, whose natural properties are reinforcing. **Secondary reinforcers** are things we have learned to value such as praise or the chance to play a video game. Money is a special kind of secondary reinforcer, called a **generalized reinforcer**, because it can be traded for virtually anything. One practical application of generalized reinforcers is known as a token economy. In a token economy, every time people perform a desired behavior, they are given a token. Periodically, they are allowed to trade their tokens for any one of a variety of reinforcers. Token economies have been used in prisons, mental institutions, and even schools.

> **TIP**
>
> Students sometimes intuit that if there is no consequence to a behavior, its likelihood will be unchanged. Remember that unless behaviors are reinforced, the likelihood of their recurrence decreases.

Intuitively, you probably realize that what functions as a reinforcer for some may not have the same effect on others. Even primary reinforcers, like food, will affect different animals in different ways depending, most notably, on how hungry they are. This idea, that the reinforcing properties of something depend on the situation, is expressed in the Premack principle. It explains that whichever of two activities is preferred can be used to reinforce the activity that is not preferred. For instance, if Peter likes apples but does not like to practice for his piano lesson, his mother could use apples to reinforce practicing the piano. In this case, eating an apple is the preferred activity. However, Peter's brother Mitchell does not like fruit, including apples, but he loves to play the piano. In his case, playing the piano is the preferred activity, and mother can use it to reinforce eating an apple.

Reinforcement Schedules

When you are first teaching a new behavior, rewarding the behavior each time is best. This process is known as **continuous reinforcement**. However, once the behavior has been learned, higher response rates can be obtained using certain partial-reinforcement schedules. In addition, according to the **partial-reinforcement effect**, behaviors will be more resistant to extinction if the animal has not been reinforced continuously.

Reinforcement schedules differ in two ways:

- What determines when reinforcement is delivered—the number of responses made (ratio schedules) or the passage of time (interval schedules).
- The pattern of reinforcement—either constant (fixed schedules) or changing (variable schedules).

A **fixed-ratio (FR) schedule** provides reinforcement after a set number of responses. For example, if a rat in a Skinner box is on an FR-5 schedule, it will be rewarded after the fifth bar press. A **variable-ratio (VR) schedule** also provides reinforcement based on the number of bar presses, but that number varies. A rat on a VR-5 schedule might be rewarded after the second press, the ninth press, the third press, the sixth press, and so on; the average number of presses required to receive a reward is five.

A **fixed-interval (FI) schedule** requires that a certain amount of time elapses before a bar press will result in a reward. In an FI-3-minute schedule, for instance, the rat will be reinforced for the first bar press that occurs after three minutes have passed. A **variable-interval (VI) schedule** varies the amount of time required to elapse before a response will result in reinforcement. In a VI-3-minute schedule, the rat will be reinforced for the first response made after an average time of three minutes (see Table 12.7).

Variable schedules are more resistant to extinction than fixed schedules. Once an animal becomes accustomed to a fixed schedule (being reinforced after x amount of time or y number of responses), a break in the pattern will quickly lead to extinction. However, if the reinforcement schedule has been variable, noticing a break in the pattern is much more difficult. In effect, variable schedules encourage continued responding on the chance that just one more response is needed to get the reward.

Sometimes one is more concerned with encouraging high rates of response rather than resistance to extinction. For instance, someone who employs factory workers to make widgets wants the workers to produce as many widgets as possible. Ratio schedules promote higher rates of response than do interval schedules. It makes sense that when people are reinforced based on the number of responses they make, they will make more responses than if the passage of time is also a necessary precondition for reinforcement as in interval schedules. Factory owners historically paid for piece work; workers were paid for each completed task rather than by the hour and were thus motivated to work as quickly as they could.

Table 12.7 Schedules of Reinforcement

	Ratio	Interval
Fixed	Definition: Reinforcement is delivered after a set number of responses.	Definition: Reinforcement is delivered after a behavior is performed following the passage of a fixed amount of time.
	Example: A restaurant gives you a free meal after the purchase of ten meals.	Example: Going to get lunch at a restaurant that opens promptly at noon.
Variable	Definition: Reinforcement is delivered after a variable number of responses.	Definition: Reinforcement is delivered after a behavior is performed following the passage of a variable amount of time.
	Example: Slot machines pay out on variable ratio schedules. Sometimes it takes just one pull to win, but sometimes it takes hundreds.	Example: Checking for your mail when your letter carrier's schedule is unpredictable.

Biology and Operant Conditioning

Just as limits seem to exist concerning what one can classically condition animals to learn, limits seem to exist concerning what various animals can learn to do through operant conditioning. Researchers have found that animals will not perform certain behaviors that go against their natural inclinations. For instance, rats will not walk backward. In addition, pigs refuse to put disks into a bank-like object and tend, instead, to bury the disks in the ground. The tendency for animals to forgo rewards to pursue their typical patterns of behavior is called **instinctive drift**.

Cognitive Learning

Radical behaviorists like Skinner assert that learning occurs without thought. However, cognitive theorists argue that even classical and operant conditioning have a cognitive component. In classical conditioning, such theorists argue that the subjects respond to the CS because they develop the expectation that it will be followed by the US. In operant conditioning, cognitive psychologists suggest that the subject is cognizant that its responses have certain consequences and can therefore act to maximize their reinforcement.

The Contingency Model of Classical Conditioning

The Pavlovian model of classical conditioning is known as the contiguity model because it postulates that the more times two things are paired, the greater the learning that will take place. Contiguity (togetherness) determines the strength of the response. Robert Rescorla revised the Pavlovian model to take into account a more complex set of circumstances. Suppose that dog 1, Rocco, is presented with a bell paired with food ten times in a row. Dog 2, Sparky, also experiences ten pairings of bell and food. However, intermixed with Sparky's ten trials are five trials in which food is presented without the bell and five more trials in which the bell is rung but no food is presented. Once these training periods are over, which dog will have a stronger salivation response to the bell? Intuitively, you will probably realize that Rocco will, even though a model based purely on contiguity would hypothesize that the two dogs would respond the same since each has experienced ten pairings of bell and food.

Rescorla's model is known as the contingency model of classical conditioning and clearly rests upon a cognitive view of classical conditioning. *A* is contingent upon *B* when *A* depends upon *B* and vice versa. In such a case, the presence of one event reliably predicts the presence of the other. In Rocco's case, the food is contingent upon the presentation of the bell; one does not appear without the other. In Sparky's experience, sometimes the bell rings and no snacks are served, other times snacks appear without the annoying bell, and sometimes they appear together. Sparky learns less because, in her case, the relationship between the CS and US is not as clear. The difference in Rocco's and Sparky's responses strongly suggests that their expectations or thoughts influence their learning.

> **TIP**
>
> Pavlov's contiguity model of classical conditioning holds that the strength of an association between two events is closely linked to the number of times they have been paired. Rescorla's contingency model of classical conditioning reflects more of a cognitive spin, positing that it is necessary for one event to reliably predict another for a strong association between the two to result.

In addition to operant and classical conditioning, cognitive theorists have described a number of additional kinds of learning. These include observational learning, latent learning, abstract learning, and insight learning.

Observational Learning

As you are no doubt aware, people and animals learn many things simply by observing others. Watching children play house, for example, gives us an indication of all they have learned from watching their families and the families of others. Such observational learning is also known as **modeling** or **vicarious learning** and was studied a great deal by Albert Bandura in formulating his **social learning theory**. This type of learning is said to be species specific; it occurs only among members of the same species.

Modeling has two basic components: observation and imitation. By watching his older sister, a young boy may learn how to hit a baseball. First, he observes her playing baseball with the neighborhood children in his backyard. Next, he picks up a bat and tries to imitate her behavior. Observational learning has a clear cognitive component in that a mental representation of the observed behavior must exist to enable the person or animal to imitate it.

A significant body of research indicates that children learn violent behaviors from watching violent television programs and violent adult models. Bandura, Ross, and Ross's (1963) classic Bobo doll experiment illustrated this connection (see Table 12.8). Children were exposed to adults who modeled either aggressive or nonaggressive play with, among other things, an inflatable Bobo doll that would bounce back up after being hit. Later, given the chance to play alone in a room full of toys including poor Bobo, the children who had witnessed the aggressive adult models exhibited strikingly similar aggressive behavior to that which they had observed. The children in the control group were much less likely to act aggressively toward Bobo, particularly in the ways modeled by the adults in the experimental condition.

Latent Learning

Latent learning was studied extensively by Edward Tolman (see Table 12.8). Latent means hidden, and latent learning is learning that becomes obvious only once a reinforcement is given for demonstrating it. Behaviorists had previously asserted that learning is evidenced by gradual changes in behavior, but Tolman conducted a famous experiment illustrating that sometimes learning occurs but is not immediately evidenced. Tolman had three groups of rats run through a maze on a series of trials. One group got a reward each time it completed the maze, and the performance of these rats improved steadily over the trials. Another group of rats never got a reward, and their performance improved only slightly over the course of the trials. A third group of rats was not rewarded during the first half of the trials but was given a reward during the second half of the trials. Not surprisingly, during the first half of the trials, this group's performance was very similar to the group that never got a reward. The interesting finding, however, was that the third group's performance improved dramatically and suddenly once it began to be rewarded for finishing the maze.

Tolman reasoned that these rats must have learned their way around the maze during the first set of trials. Their performance did not improve because they had no reason to run the maze quickly. Tolman credited their dramatic improvement in maze-running time to latent learning. He suggested they had made a mental representation, or **cognitive map**, of the maze during the first half of the trials and evidenced this knowledge once it would earn them a reward.

Abstract Learning

Abstract learning involves understanding concepts such as *tree* or *same* rather than learning simply to press a bar or peck a disk to secure a reward. Some researchers have shown that animals in Skinner boxes seem to be able to understand such concepts. For instance, pigeons have learned to peck pictures they had never seen before if those pictures were of chairs. In other studies, pigeons have been shown a particular shape (e.g., square or triangle) and rewarded in one series of trials when they picked the same shape out of two choices and in another set of trials when they pecked at the different shapes. Such studies suggest that pigeons can understand concepts and are not simply forming S-R connections, as Thorndike and Skinner had argued.

Insight Learning

Wolfgang Köhler is well-known for his studies of **insight learning** in chimpanzees (see Table 12.8). Insight learning occurs when one suddenly realizes how to solve a problem. You have probably had the experience of skipping over a problem on a test only to realize later, in an instant (we hope before you handed in the test), how to solve it.

Köhler argued that learning often happens in this sudden way due to insight rather than because of the gradual strengthening of the S-R connection suggested by the behaviorists. He put chimpanzees into situations and watched how they solved problems. In one study, Köhler suspended a banana from the ceiling well out of reach of the chimpanzees. In the room were several boxes, none of which was high enough to enable the chimpanzees to reach the banana. Köhler found the chimpanzees spent most of their time unproductively rather than slowly working toward a solution. They would run around, jump, and be generally upset about their inability to snag the snack until, suddenly, they would pile the boxes on top of each other, climb up, and grab the banana. Köhler believed that the solution could not occur until the chimpanzees had a cognitive insight about how to solve the problem.

Table 12.8 Famous Cognitive Learning Experiments

Research/Experiment	Major Finding	Take Home Message
Albert Bandura's Bobo doll experiments	Children exposed to an aggressive model imitated the model's behavior.	Aggression can be learned through observation.
Edward Tolman's latent learning experiments	Rats that ran a maze repeatedly evidenced dramatic improvement following the introduction of a reward.	Rats learned their way around the maze, created and stored cognitive maps, and were able to use the maps when needed.
Wolfgang Köhler's insight learning experiments	Chimpanzees solved problems suddenly rather than gradually.	Nonhuman animals are capable of insight.

Unit 3 Multiple-Choice Questions

1. Just before something scary happens in a horror film, they often play scary-sounding music. When I hear the music, I tense up in anticipation of the scary event. In this situation, the music serves as a(n)

    (A) US.
    (B) CS.
    (C) UR.
    (D) CR.

2. Try as you might, you are unable to teach your dog to do a somersault. He will roll around on the ground, but he refuses to execute the gymnastic move you desire because of

    (A) equipotentiality.
    (B) preparedness.
    (C) instinctive drift.
    (D) chaining.

3. When teaching your cat to jump through a hoop, which reinforcement schedule would facilitate the most rapid learning?

    (A) Continuous
    (B) Fixed-ratio
    (C) Variable-ratio
    (D) Fixed-interval

4. Tina likes to play with slugs, but she can find them by the shed only after it rains. On what kind of reinforcement schedule is Tina's slug hunting?

    (A) Continuous
    (B) Fixed-interval
    (C) Fixed-ratio
    (D) Variable-interval

5. Just before the doors of the elevator close, Lola, a coworker you despise, enters the elevator. You immediately leave, mumbling about having forgotten something. Your behavior results in

    (A) positive reinforcement.
    (B) a secondary reinforcer.
    (C) punishment.
    (D) negative reinforcement.

6. Many psychologists believe that children of parents who beat them are likely to beat their own children. One common explanation for this phenomenon is

    (A) modeling.
    (B) latent learning.
    (C) abstract learning.
    (D) instrumental learning.

7. When Tito was young, his parents decided to give him a quarter every day he made his bed. Tito started to make his siblings' beds also and to help with other chores. Behaviorists would say that Tito was experiencing

    (A) internal motivation.
    (B) spontaneous recovery.
    (C) acquisition.
    (D) generalization.

8. Before his parents will read him a bedtime story, Charley has to brush his teeth, put on his pajamas, kiss his grandmother good night, and put away his toys. This example illustrates

    (A) shaping.
    (B) acquisition.
    (C) generalization.
    (D) chaining.

9. Which of the following is an example of positive reinforcement?

    (A) Buying a child a video game after she throws a tantrum
    (B) Going inside to escape a thunderstorm
    (C) Assigning a student detention for fighting
    (D) Getting a cavity filled at the dentist to halt a toothache

10. Lily keeps poking Jared in Mr. Clayton's third-grade class. Mr. Clayton tells Jared to ignore Lily. Mr. Clayton is hoping that ignoring Lily's behavior will

   (A) punish her.
   (B) extinguish the behavior.
   (C) negatively reinforce the behavior.
   (D) cause Lily to generalize.

11. You read in your philosophy class textbook that humans are born tabula rasa or as blank slates. As a student of psychology, which of the following responses would you have?

   (A) The statement is incorrect. Humans may be born without reflexes and instincts, but we are born with the ability to learn them.
   (B) The statement is correct. Humans are born without instincts or other mechanisms in place to help us survive.
   (C) The statement is correct. Humans are born with a certain number of neurons, but most develop later as we learn.
   (D) The statement is incorrect. Humans are born with a set of reflexes that help us survive.

12. You have a cousin named Holden who flunked out of three expensive private schools and was arrested for wandering the streets of New York using his parents' credit card. Holden is intelligent but cannot seem to get motivated toward any career. What conflict would the psychosocial stage theory say Holden is struggling with?

   (A) Autonomy versus authority
   (B) Identity versus role confusion
   (C) Integrity versus despair
   (D) Industry versus inferiority

Questions 13 through 15 refer to the following.

Professor Spencer is interested in how children over-generalize grammatical rules and at what age these types of errors decrease. He partners with an elementary school and sits in during show and tell in first- and third-grade classrooms for the month of March. During that time, he records all overgeneralization errors students make.

13. How would you describe Professor Spencer's research design?

   (A) Field experiment
   (B) Case study
   (C) Cross-sectional
   (D) Naturalistic observation

14. What would you expect Professor Spencer to find?

   (A) No overgeneralization errors in any of the classrooms.
   (B) Many overgeneralization errors in all of the classrooms
   (C) More overgeneralization errors in the first-grade classrooms
   (D) More overgeneralization errors in the third-grade classrooms

15. Should Professor Spencer get IRB approval for his study?

   (A) No, it's just a typical classroom activity.
   (B) No, the students are too young to consent.
   (C) Yes, there's a dangerous level of deception involved.
   (D) Yes, all research with humans should be reviewed.

Answer Explanations

1. **(B)** The music before a scary event in a horror movie serves as a CS. It is something we associate with a fear-inducing event (the US). In this example, preparing to be scared is the CR and the fear caused by the event in the movie is the UR.

2. **(C)** Instinctive drift limits your pet's gymnastic abilities. Instinctively, your dog will perform certain behaviors and will drift toward these rather than learning behaviors that go against his nature. Equipotentiality is the opposite position that asserts that any animal can be conditioned to do anything. Preparedness refers to a biological predisposition to learn some things more quickly than others. Preparedness explains why teaching a dog to fetch a stick is easier than teaching it to do a somersault. Chaining is when one has to perform a number of discrete steps in order to secure a reward.

3. **(A)** When teaching your cat to jump through a hoop, continuous reinforcement would result in the most rapid learning. New behaviors are learned most quickly when they are rewarded every time. However, once the skill has been learned, partial reinforcement schedules—which all the other choices are examples of—will make the behaviors more resistant to extinction.

4. **(D)** Tina's slug hunting is rewarded on a variable-interval schedule. The passage of time is a key element in when she is reinforced because the slugs appear only after it rains. Since rain does not fall on a fixed schedule (e.g., every third day), she is on a VI schedule. If she were on a continuous schedule, Tina would find slugs whenever she looked. If the slugs appeared every three days, Tina would be on a fixed-interval schedule. If she needed to turn over three rocks to find a slug, she would be on a fixed-ratio schedule.

5. **(D)** Exiting the elevator to avoid Lola is negative reinforcement. Your behavior, leaving the elevator, is reinforced by the removal of an aversive stimulus (Lola). Remember that reinforcement (including negative reinforcement) always increases the likelihood of a behavior as opposed to punishment, which decreases the likelihood of a behavior.

6. **(A)** Many psychologists believe that children of parents who beat them are likely to beat their own children. One common explanation for this phenomenon is modeling. Modeling, or observational learning, is the idea that people or animals can learn from watching and copying the behavior of others.

7. **(D)** Tito's new bed-making and chore-doing regime indicates that he is generalizing. Just as a rat will press other levers in other cages, Tito is performing more chores in an attempt to maximize his rewards. Behaviorists minimize the role of internal motivation; they believe that the environment motivates. Spontaneous recovery would be correct if Tito began making his bed again after his parents had stopped rewarding him and he had returned to his slovenly ways. Acquisition occurred when Tito initially learned to make his bed to earn a quarter.

8. **(D)** Charley needs to chain together a series of behaviors in order to get a reward (the bedtime story). Shaping is reinforcing approximations of a desired behavior, usually in an effort to teach it. Acquisition, in operant conditioning, is the learning of a behavior. Generalization is when one performs similar behaviors to those that will result in reinforcement.

9. **(A)** Buying a child a video game after she throws a tantrum is an example of positively reinforcing a behavior you probably do not want (the tantrum). This example raises an important point: the word *positive* in positive reinforcement refers to the addition of a reinforcer and not to the goodness or badness of the act that is being reinforced. Going inside to escape a thunderstorm and getting a cavity filled at the dentist to halt a toothache are both examples of negative reinforcement (removing something unpleasant). Assigning a student detention for fighting is an example of punishment (adding something unpleasant).

10. **(B)** Mr. Clayton is hoping that ignoring Lily's behavior will extinguish the behavior. Something that is not reinforced is put onto an extinction schedule.

11. **(D)** Humans are born with reflexes that help us nurse and find our mother. We are born with all the neurons we will ever have. We can observe the behavior of babies and infer what reflexes and abilities babies have.

12. **(B)** Holden's inability to stay in school and decide about goals indicates a search for identity according to Erikson.

13. **(C)** Because Professor Spencer is contrasting two groups of children at different ages, his design is cross-sectional. The study cannot be considered a field experiment because, although it's in the field, it's not an experiment—no variable is manipulated by the experimenter. Spencer is studying too large a group and in insufficient depth to be a case study. Finally, the study would not be termed naturalistic observation both because the students will realize they are being observed and because Spencer is interested in only a very specific behavior.

14. **(C)** Overgeneralization errors—such as regularizing irregular verbs by saying, for example, "I goed" instead of "I went"—occur more commonly in younger children and typically decrease with age and experience.

15. **(D)** Generally speaking, all research using human participants should be reviewed. Although Professor Spencer's study doesn't sound especially dangerous and does not involve a lot of deception, it is always preferable to have a qualified group of people not associated with the study look it over with the goal of protecting the participants. Although show and tell is a typical classroom activity, the introduction of the professor into the classroom and the fact that he is recording information for research purposes is enough reason to ask for an IRB review. The students are, in fact, too young to consent to participate in the study. Part of the IRB's job would be to decide whether to require parental consent and/or assent from the children.

UNIT 4

Social Psychology, Personality, Motivation, and Emotion

This unit looks at some of the main factors that shape human behavior. Social psychologists emphasize the role of the situation in affecting behavior, while the study of personality focuses more on thoughts and behaviors that are shaped over time and that become enduring aspects of people. The study of motivation explores what drives people to what they do, while the topic of emotion examines how people experience and express their feelings. Some of the most well-known and influential psychological research studies and theories are described and discussed in this unit. You will find content from this unit in the social psychology, personality, motivation, and emotion chapters in the textbook you use for your AP Psychology class.

13

Social Psychology

Learning Objectives

In this unit, you will learn about:

→ Attribution theory
→ Attitude formation and change
→ Compliance strategies
→ Stereotypes, prejudice, and discrimination
→ The psychology of social situations
→ Group dynamics

Key Terms

- Prosocial behavior
- Social influence theory
- Attribution theory
- Dispositional attribution
- Person attribution
- Situation attribution
- Self-fulfilling prophecy
- Situational variables
- Fundamental attribution error
- Actor-observer bias
- False-consensus effect
- Self-serving bias
- Just-world phenomenon
- Attitude
- Mere exposure effect
- Elaboration likelihood model
- Central route

- Peripheral route
- Persuasion
- Cognitive dissonance theory
- Foot-in-the-door technique
- Door-in-the-face technique
- Social reciprocity norm
- Social norms
- Social responsibility norm
- Norms of reciprocity
- Social traps
- Stereotypes
- Prejudice
- Implicit attitude
- Ethnocentrism
- Multiculturalism
- Individualistic cultures
- Collectivist cultures
- Discrimination

- Out-group homogeneity bias
- In-group bias
- Superordinate goal
- Social facilitation
- Upward social comparison
- Downward social comparison
- Relative deprivation theory
- Conformity
- Normative social influence
- Informational social influence
- Obedience studies
- Bystander effect
- Social loafing
- Group polarization
- Groupthink
- Deindividuation

Overview

Social psychology is a broad field devoted to studying the way that people relate to others. Our discussion will focus on the development and expression of attitudes, people's attributions about their own behavior and that of others, the reasons why people engage in both antisocial and **prosocial behavior**, and how the presence and actions of others influence the way people behave.

A major influence on the first two areas we will discuss, attitude formation and attribution theory, is social cognition. This field applies many of the concepts you learned about in the field of cognition, such as memory and biases, to help explain how people think about themselves and others. The basic idea behind social cognition is that, as people go through their daily lives, they act like scientists, constantly gathering data and making predictions about what will happen next so that they can act accordingly. Another key concept is **social influence theory**, the idea that how people feel and act is affected by the other people around them. Many examples of this idea will be presented in this chapter.

Attribution Theory

Attribution theory is an area of study within the field of social cognition. Attribution theory tries to explain how people determine the cause of what they observe. For instance, if your friend Charley told you he got a perfect score on his math test, you might find yourself thinking that Charley is very good at math. In that case, you have made a **dispositional attribution** or **person attribution**. Alternatively, you might attribute Charley's success to a situational factor, such as an easy test; in that case, you make a **situation attribution**. Attributions can also be stable or unstable. If you infer that Charley has always been a math whiz, you have made both a person attribution and a stable attribution, also called a person-stable attribution. On the other hand, if you think that Charley studied a lot for this one test, you have made a person-unstable attribution. Similarly, if you believe that Ms. Mahoney, Charley's math teacher, is an easy teacher, you have made a situation-stable attribution. If you think that Ms. Mahoney is a tough teacher who happened to give one easy test, you have made a situation-unstable attribution.

Harold Kelley put forth a theory that explains the kinds of attributions people make based on three types of information: consistency, distinctiveness, and consensus. Consistency refers to how similarly the individual acts in the same situation over time. How does Charley usually do on his math tests? Distinctiveness refers to how similar this situation is to other situations in which we have watched Charley. Does Charley do well on all math tests? Has he evidenced an aptitude for math in other ways? Consensus asks us to consider how others in the same situation have responded. Did many people get a perfect score on the math test?

Consensus is a particularly important piece of information to use when determining whether to make a person or situation attribution. If Charley is the only one to earn such a good score on the math test, we seem to have learned something about Charley. Conversely, if everyone earned a high score on the test, we would suspect that something in the situation contributed to that outcome. Consistency, on the other hand, is extremely useful when determining whether to make a stable or an unstable attribution. If Charley always aces his math tests, then it seems more likely that Charley is particularly skilled at math rather than he happened to study hard for this one test. Similarly, if everyone always does well on Ms. Mahoney's tests, we would be likely to make the situation-stable attribution that she is an easy teacher. However, if Charley usually scores low in Ms. Mahoney's class, we will be more likely to make a situation-unstable attribution such as this particular test was easy.

People often have certain ideas or prejudices about other people before they even meet them. These preconceived ideas can obviously affect the way someone acts toward another person. Even more interesting is the idea that the expectations we have of others can influence the way those others behave. Such a phenomenon is called a **self-fulfilling prophecy**. For instance, if Jon is repeatedly told that Chet, whom he has never met, is really funny, when Jon does finally meet Chet, he may treat Chet in such a way as to elicit the humorous behavior he expects.

A classic study involving self-fulfilling prophecies was Robert Rosenthal and Lenore Jacobson's (1968) Pygmalion in the Classroom experiment (see Table 13.2). They administered a test to elementary school children that supposedly would identify those children who were on the verge of significant academic growth. In reality, the test was a standard IQ test. These researchers then randomly selected a group of children from the population who took the test, and they informed the teachers that these students were ripe for such intellectual progress. Of course, since the children were selected randomly, they did not differ from any other group of children in the school. At the end of the year, the researchers returned to take another measure of the students' IQ and found that the scores of the identified children had increased more than the scores of their classmates. In some way, the teachers' expectations that these students would bloom intellectually over the year actually caused the students to outperform their peers.

Attributional Biases

Although people are quite good at sifting through all the data that bombards them and then making attributions, you will probably not be surprised to learn that errors are not uncommon. Moreover, people tend to make the same kinds of errors. A few typical biases are the fundamental attribution error, false-consensus effect, self-serving bias, and the just-world belief.

When looking at the behavior of others, people tend to overestimate the importance of dispositional factors and underestimate the role of **situational variables**. This tendency is known as the **fundamental attribution error**. Say that you go to a party where you are introduced to Claude, a young man you have never met before. Although you attempt to engage Claude in conversation, he is unresponsive. He looks past you and, soon after, seizes upon an excuse to leave. Most people would conclude that Claude is an unfriendly person. Few consider that something in the situation may have contributed to Claude's behavior. Perhaps Claude just had a terrible fight with his girlfriend, Isabelle. Maybe on the way to the party he had a minor car accident. The point is that people systematically seem to overestimate the role of dispositional factors in influencing another person's actions.

Interestingly, people do not evidence this same tendency in explaining their own behaviors. Claude knows that he is sometimes extremely outgoing and warm. Since people get to view themselves in countless situations, they are more likely to make situational attributions about themselves than about others. Everyone has been shy and aloof at times, and everyone has been friendly. Thus, people are more likely to say that their own behavior depends upon the situation; this phenomenon is known as the **actor-observer bias**. Whereas the fundamental attribution error focuses on how we explain others' behavior, the actor-observer bias explains both the actor's tendency to attribute behavior to situational factors and the observer's tendency to attribute behavior to dispositional factors.

One caveat must be added to our discussion of the fundamental attribution error. The fundamental attribution was named *fundamental* because it was believed to be so widespread. However, many cross-cultural psychologists have argued that the fundamental attribution error is far less likely to occur in collectivist cultures than in individualistic cultures. In an individualistic culture, like the American culture, the importance and uniqueness of the individual is stressed. In more collectivist cultures, like Japanese culture, a person's link to various groups such as family or company is stressed. Cross-cultural research suggests that people in collectivist cultures are less likely to commit the fundamental attribution error, perhaps because they are more attuned to the ways that different situations influence their own behavior.

The tendency for people to overestimate the number of people who agree with them is called the **false-consensus effect**. For instance, if Jamal dislikes horror movies, he is likely to think that most other people share his aversion. Conversely, Sabrina, who loves a good horror flick, overestimates the number of people who share her passion.

TIP

Students often confuse self-serving bias and self-fulfilling prophecies, ostensibly because they both contain the word *self*. Self-serving bias is the tendency to overstate one's role in a positive venture and underestimate it in a failure. Thus, people serve themselves by making themselves look good. Self-fulfilling prophecies, on the other hand, explain how people's ideas about others can shape the behavior of those others.

Self-serving bias is the tendency to take more credit for good outcomes than for bad ones. For instance, a basketball coach would be more likely to emphasize her or his role in the team's championship win than in their heartbreaking first-round tournament loss.

Researchers have found that people evidence a bias toward thinking that bad things happen to bad people. This belief in a just world, known simply as the **just-world phenomenon** or just-world bias, in which misfortunes befall people who deserve them, can be seen in the tendency to blame victims. For example, people believe that others are unemployed because they are lazy. If the world is just in this manner, then, assuming we view ourselves as good people, we need not fear bad things happening to ourselves.

Attitude Formation and Change

One focus of social psychology is attitude formation and change. An **attitude** is a set of beliefs and feelings. We have attitudes about many different aspects of our environment such as groups of people, particular events, and places. Attitudes are evaluative, meaning that our feelings toward such things are necessarily positive or negative.

A great deal of research focuses on ways to affect people's attitudes. In fact, the entire field of advertising is devoted to just this purpose. How can people be encouraged to develop a favorable attitude toward a particular brand of potato chips? Having been the target audience for many such attempts, you are no doubt familiar with a plethora of strategies used to promote favorable opinions toward a product.

The **mere exposure effect** states that the more one is exposed to something, the more one will come to like it. Therefore, in the world of advertising, more is better. When you walk into the supermarket, you will be more likely to buy the brand of potato chips you have seen advertised thousands of times rather than one that you have never heard of before.

According to the **elaboration likelihood model**, persuasive messages can be processed through either the **central route** or the **peripheral route**. The central route to **persuasion** involves deeply processing the content of the message; what about this potato chip is so much better than all the others? The peripheral route, on the other hand, involves other aspects of the message, including the characteristics of the person imparting the message (the communicator).

Certain characteristics of the communicator have been found to influence the effectiveness of a message. Attractive people, famous people, and experts are among the most persuasive communicators. As a result, professional athletes and movie stars often have second careers making commercials. Certain characteristics of the audience also affect how effective a message will be. Some research suggests that more educated people are less likely to be persuaded by advertisements. Finally, the way the message is presented can also influence how persuasive it is. Research has found that when dealing with a relatively uninformed audience, presenting a one-sided message is best. However, when attempting to influence a more sophisticated audience, communication that acknowledges and then refutes opposing arguments will be more effective. Some research suggests that messages that arouse fear are effective. However, too much fear can cause people to react negatively to the message itself.

Relationship Between Attitudes and Behavior

Although you might think that knowing people's attitudes would tell you a great deal about their behavior, research has found that the relationship between attitudes and behaviors is far from perfect. In 1934, Richard LaPiere conducted an early study that illustrated this difference (see Table 13.2). In the United States in the 1930s, prejudice and discrimination against Chinese people were pervasive. LaPiere traveled throughout the West Coast, visiting many hotels and restaurants with a Chinese couple to see how they would be treated. On only one occasion were they treated poorly due to their race. A short time later, LaPiere contacted all the establishments they had visited and asked about their attitudes toward Chinese patrons. Over 90 percent of the respondents said that they would not serve Chinese people. This finding illustrates that attitudes do not perfectly predict behaviors.

Sometimes if you can change people's behavior, you can change their attitudes. **Cognitive dissonance theory** is based on the idea that people are motivated to have consistent attitudes and behaviors. When they do not, they experience unpleasant mental tension or dissonance. For example, suppose Amira thinks that studying is only for losers. If she then studies for 10 hours for her chemistry test, she will experience cognitive dissonance. Since she cannot, at this point, change her behavior (she has already studied for 10 hours), the only way to reduce this dissonance is to change her attitude and decide that studying does not necessarily make someone a loser. Note that this change in attitude happens without conscious awareness.

Leon Festinger and James Carlsmith conducted a classic experiment about cognitive dissonance in the late 1950s (see Table 13.2). Their participants performed a boring task and were then asked to lie and tell the next subject (actually a confederate of the experimenter) that they had enjoyed the task. In one condition, subjects were paid $1 to lie, and in the other condition, they were paid $20 to lie. Afterward, the participants' attitudes toward the task were measured. Contrary to what reinforcement theory would predict, those subjects who were paid $1 were found to have significantly more positive attitudes toward the experiment than those who were paid $20. According to Festinger and Carlsmith, having already said that the boring task was interesting, the subjects were experiencing dissonance. However, those subjects that were paid $20 experienced relatively little dissonance; they lied because they had been paid $20. On the other hand, those subjects who were paid only $1 lacked sufficient external motivation to lie. Therefore, to reduce the dissonance, they changed their attitudes and said that they actually did enjoy the experiment.

> **TIP**
>
> **Attitudes do not perfectly predict behaviors. What people say they would do and what they would actually do often differ.**

Compliance Strategies

Often people use certain strategies to get others to comply with their wishes (see Table 13.1). Such compliance strategies have also been the focus of much psychological research. Suppose you need to borrow $20 from a friend. Would you be better off asking him or her for $20 right away, asking the friend first for $5 and then following up this request with another for the additional $15, or asking him or her for $100 and, after the friend refuses, asking for $20? The **foot-in-the-door technique** suggests that if you can get people to agree to a small request, they will become more likely to agree to a follow-up request that is larger. Thus, once your friend agrees to lend you $5, he or she becomes more likely to lend you the additional funds. After all, the friend is clearly willing to lend you money. The **door-in-the-face technique** argues that after people refuse a large request, they will look more favorably upon a follow-up request that seems, in comparison, much more reasonable. After flat-out refusing to lend you $100, your friend might feel bad. The least he or she could do is lend you $20.

Another common strategy involves using the **social reciprocity norm** (also known as **norms of reciprocity**). People tend to think that when someone does something nice for them, they ought to do something nice in return. Norms are our sense of what is typical and therefore expected in certain circumstances. Norms of reciprocity are at work when you feel compelled to send money to the charity that sent you free return address labels or when you cast your vote in the student election for the candidate who handed out those delicious chocolate chip cookies.

Social norms can influence people in other ways as well. Research has shown that social norms can be used to get people to recycle more, to drink less, and to vote in elections. As social beings, humans neem naturally influenced by what they think others are doing. A related concept is the **social responsibility norm**, the belief that we all should do what we can to make the world and our society a better place. **Social traps** are situations that tend to undermine these efforts. A social trap is a situation in which the betterment of society requires us all to make some kind of sacrifice but our individual contribution is so small that people often choose to act in their own immediate interest instead of in the larger societal interest. Consumption of environmental resources illustrates this point well. It would be better for all of us to conserve more energy—to drive less, to use less heat/air-conditioning, to compost—but people often choose not to do these things, in part, because our personal consumption is such a tiny part of the problem. However, if a lot of people act in this way, we create a social trap that's bad for everyone.

Table 13.1 Compliance Strategies

Foot-in-the-door technique	A small request is followed by a larger request.	First ask for a little time to review by asking questions in class. After your teacher says yes, ask if the test could be postponed by one day.
Door-in-the-face technique	An unrealistically large request is followed by a smaller request.	First ask if the test could be postponed by one week. After your teacher says no, ask if the test could be postponed by one day.
Norms of reciprocity	People have the tendency to feel obligated to reciprocate kind behavior.	First bring your teacher his or her favorite snack. Then ask if the test could be postponed by one day.

Stereotypes, Prejudice, and Discrimination

We all have ideas about what members of different groups are like, and these expectations may influence the way we interact with members of those groups. We call these ideas **stereotypes**. Stereotypes may be either negative or positive and can be applied to virtually any group of people (e.g., racial, ethnic, geographic). For instance, people often stereotype New Yorkers as pushy, unfriendly, and rude and Californians as easygoing and attractive. Some cognitive psychologists have suggested that stereotypes are basically schemata about groups. People who distinguish between stereotypes and group schemata argue that the former are more rigid and more difficult to change than the latter.

Prejudice is an undeserved, usually negative, attitude toward a group of people. Stereotyping can lead to prejudice when negative stereotypes (those rude New Yorkers) are applied uncritically to all members of a group (she is from New York, therefore she must be rude) and a negative attitude results. Attitudes can be either explicit or implicit. An explicit attitude is something someone is conscious of, while an **implicit attitude** is something that may influence someone's behavior without their being aware of it. Implicit attitudes are more difficult to detect. However, implicit attitudes toward a number of social groups can be tested with something called the implicit attitudes test (IAT), which can be found online.

Ethnocentrism, the belief that one's culture (e.g., ethnic, racial) is superior to others, is a specific kind of prejudice. People become so used to their own cultures that they see them as the norm and use them as the standard by which to judge other cultures. Many people look down upon others who don't dress the same, eat the same foods, or worship in the same way that they do. The opposite belief is known as **multiculturalism**; it involves a recognition of the contribution of many different groups in society, making us richer as a result. One type of cultural difference psychologists study is that between **individualistic cultures** and **collectivist cultures**. The United States and other Western nations tend to embrace individualism—the importance of standing out and pursuing what's best for the individual. Collectivist cultures put more value on the well-being of a group and are more likely to believe it can be important to subvert one's personal beliefs or values to do what's good for the group.

Prejudice is an attitude, but **discrimination** involves an action. When one discriminates, one acts on one's prejudices. If I dislike New Yorkers, I am prejudiced, but if I refuse to hire New Yorkers to work in my company, I am engaging in discrimination. Unfortunately, stereotypes, prejudice, and discrimination all reinforce one another. People's beliefs and attitudes influence each other and guide people's behavior. In addition, when people act in discriminatory ways, they are motivated to strengthen their prejudices and stereotypes to justify their behavior (see Figure 13.1).

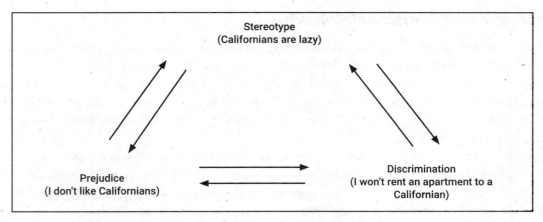

Figure 13.1 The vicious cycle of stereotyping, prejudice, and discrimination

People tend to see members of their own group, the *in-group*, as more diverse than members of other groups, the *out-groups*. This phenomenon is often referred to as **out-group homogeneity bias**. For example, as a New Yorker myself, I know that although some New Yorkers are indeed pushy and rude, most are not. I know many well-mannered and deferential New Yorkers as well as short New Yorkers, tall New Yorkers, honest New Yorkers, and dishonest New Yorkers. Although we all have extensive experience with the members of our own groups, we lack that degree of familiarity with other groups and therefore tend to see them as more similar. In addition, researchers have documented a preference for members of one's own group, a kind of **in-group bias**. In-group bias is thought to stem from people's belief that they themselves are good people. Therefore, the people with whom they share group membership are thought to be good as well.

Origin of Stereotypes and Prejudice

Many different theories attempt to explain how people become prejudiced. Some psychologists have suggested that people naturally and inevitably magnify differences between their own group and others as a function of the cognitive process of categorization. By considering the in-group bias discussed above, this idea suggests that people cannot avoid forming stereotypes.

Social learning theorists stress that stereotypes and prejudice are often learned through modeling. Children raised by parents who express prejudices may be more likely to embrace such prejudices themselves. Conversely, this theory suggests that prejudices could be unlearned by exposure to different models.

Combating Prejudice

One theory about how to reduce prejudice is known as the contact theory. The contact theory, as its name suggests, states that contact between hostile groups will reduce animosity but only if the groups are made to work toward a goal that benefits all and necessitates the participation of all. Such a goal is called a **superordinate goal**.

Muzafer Sherif's (1966) camp study (also known as the Robbers Cave study) illustrates both how easily out-group bias can be created and how superordinate goals can be used to unite formerly antagonistic groups (see Table 13.2). He conducted a series of studies at a summer camp. Sherif first divided the campers into two groups and arranged for them to compete in a series of activities. This competition was sufficient to create negative feelings between the groups. Once such prejudices had been established, Sherif staged several camp emergencies that required the groups to cooperate. The superordinate goal of solving the crises effectively improved relations between the groups.

A number of educational researchers have attempted to use the contact theory to reduce prejudices among members of different groups in school. One goal of most cooperative learning activities is to bring members of different social groups into contact with one another as they work toward a superordinate goal, the assigned task.

Aggression and Antisocial Behavior

Another major area of study for social psychologists is aggression and antisocial behavior. Psychologists distinguish between two types of aggression: instrumental aggression and hostile aggression. Instrumental aggression is when the aggressive act is intended to secure a particular end. For example, if Bobby wants to hold the doll that Carol is holding and he kicks her and grabs the doll, Bobby has engaged in instrumental aggression. Hostile aggression, on the other hand, has no such clear purpose. If Bobby is simply angry or upset and therefore kicks Carol, his aggression is hostile aggression.

Many theories exist about the cause of human aggression. Freud linked aggression to Thanatos, the death instinct. Sociobiologists suggest that the expression of aggression is adaptive under certain circumstances. One of the most influential theories, however, is known as the frustration-aggression hypothesis. This hypothesis holds that the feeling of frustration makes aggression more likely. Considerable experimental evidence supports it. Another common theory is that the exposure to aggressive models makes people aggressive as illustrated by Bandura, Ross, and Ross's (1963) classic Bobo doll experiment. (See the "Observational Learning" section in Chapter 12 for more information.)

Prosocial Behavior

Although social psychologists have devoted a lot of time and effort to studying antisocial behavior, they have also studied the factors that make people more likely to help one another. Such helping behavior is termed prosocial behavior. Much of the research in this area has focused on bystander intervention, the conditions under which people nearby are more and are less likely to help someone in trouble.

The vicious murder of Kitty Genovese in Kew Gardens, New York, committed within view of at least 38 witnesses, none of whom intervened, led John Darley and Bibb Latane to explore how people decided whether or not to help others in distress (see Table 13.2). Counterintuitively, the larger the number of people who witness an emergency situation, the less likely any one is to intervene. This finding is known as the bystander effect. One explanation for this phenomenon is called diffusion of responsibility. The larger the group of people who witness a problem, the less responsible any one individual feels to help. People tend to assume that someone else will take action, so they need not do so. Another factor contributing to the bystander effect is known as pluralistic ignorance. People seem to decide what constitutes appropriate behavior in a situation by looking to others. Thus, if no one in a classroom seems worried by the black smoke coming through the vent, each individual concludes that taking no action is the proper thing to do.

Attraction

Social psychologists also study what factors increase the chance that people will like one another. A significant body of research indicates that we like others who are similar to us, people with whom we come into frequent contact, and those who return our positive feelings. These three factors are often referred to as similarity, proximity, and reciprocal liking. Although conventional wisdom holds that opposites attract, psychological research indicates that we are drawn to people who are similar to us, those who share our attitudes, backgrounds, and interests. Proximity means nearness. As is suggested by the mere exposure effect, the greater the exposure one has to another person, the more one generally comes to like that person. In addition, only by talking to someone can one identify the similarities that will draw the pair closer together. Finally, every reader has probably had the misfortune to experience that liking someone who scorns you is not enjoyable. Thus, the more someone likes you, the more you will probably like that person.

Not surprisingly, people are also attracted to others who are physically attractive. In fact, the benefits of being nice-looking extend well beyond the realm of attraction. Research has demonstrated that good-looking people are perceived as having all sorts of positive attributes, including better personalities and greater job competence.

Psychologists have also devoted tremendous time and attention to the concept of love. Although research seems to indicate that the emotion of love qualitatively differs from liking and a number of theories about love have been proposed, the subject has proved difficult to explain adequately.

A term often employed as part of liking and loving studies is self-disclosure. One self-discloses when one shares a piece of personal information with another. Close relationships with friends and lovers are often built through a process of self-disclosure. On the path to intimacy, one person shares a detail of his or her life and the other reciprocates by exposing a facet of his or her own.

The Psychology of Social Situations

A major area of research in social psychology is how an individual's behavior can be affected by another's actions or even merely by another person's presence. Several studies have illustrated that people perform tasks better in front of an audience than they do when they are alone. They yell louder, run faster, and reel in a fishing rod more quickly. This phenomenon, that the presence of others improves task performance, is known as **social facilitation**. Later studies, however, found that when the task being observed was a difficult one rather than a simple, well-practiced skill, being watched by others actually hurt performance, a finding known as social impairment.

People also have the tendency to compare themselves to others. **Upward social comparison** is when we compare ourselves to people doing better than we are, while **downward social comparison** is when we compare ourselves to people doing worse than we are. **Relative deprivation theory** explains that people tend to feel less satisfied with their lives when they engage in a lot of upward social comparison. Even if you make a good salary and have a perfectly good lifestyle, it's hard to feel satisfied if you compare yourself to Elon Musk and Taylor Swift.

Conformity has been an area of much research as well. Conformity is the tendency of people to go along with the views or actions of others. People conform to the behavior of groups for two reasons. **Normative social influence** is when people conform for social reasons—to belong to the group. On the other hand, **informational social influence** leads to conformity because people think the group knows best. So, if you wear jeans and hoodies to school instead of your favorite pink and orange fluorescent jumpsuit because you want to fit in with everyone else, you are experiencing normative social influence. However, if you wear the jumpsuit because you're in a midnight running club and other members wear bright clothes to limit the danger of getting mowed down in traffic, you are experiencing informational social influence.

Solomon Asch (1951) conducted one of the most interesting conformity experiments (see Table 13.2). He brought participants into a room of confederates and asked them to make a series of simple perceptual judgments. Asch showed the participants three vertical lines of varying sizes and asked them to indicate which one was the same length as a different target line. All members of the group gave their answers aloud, and the participant was always the last person to speak. All of the trials had a clear, correct answer. However, in some trials, all of the confederates gave the same, obviously incorrect judgment. Asch was interested in what the participants would do. Would they conform to a judgment they knew to be wrong or would they differ from the group? Asch found that in approximately one-third of the cases when the confederates gave an incorrect answer, the participants conformed. Furthermore, approximately 70 percent of the participants conformed in at least one of the trials. In general, studies have suggested that conformity is most likely to occur when a group's opinion is unanimous. Although it would seem that the larger the group, the greater conformity that would be expressed, studies have shown that groups larger than three (in addition to the participant) do not significantly increase the tendency to conform.

Although conformity involves following a group without being explicitly told to do so, **obedience studies** have focused on participants' willingness to do what another asks them to do. Stanley Milgram (1974) conducted the classic obedience studies (see Table 13.2). His participants were told that they were taking part in a study about teaching and learning, and they were assigned to play the part of teacher. The learner, of course, was a confederate. As teacher, each participant's job was to give the learner an electric shock for every incorrect response. The participant sat behind a panel of buttons, each labeled with the number of volts, beginning at 15 and increasing by increments of 15 up to 450. The levels of shock were also described in words ranging from *mild* up to

XXX—severe shock. In reality, no shocks were delivered; the confederate pretended to be shocked. As the level of the shocks increased, the confederate screamed in pain, said he suffered from a heart condition, and eventually fell silent. Milgram was interested in how far participants would go before refusing to deliver any more shocks. The experimenter watched the participant and, if questioned, gave only a few stock answers, such as "Please continue." Contrary to the predictions of psychologists who Milgram polled prior to the experiment, over 60 percent of the participants obeyed the experimenter and delivered all the possible shocks.

Milgram replicated his study with a number of interesting twists. He found that he could decrease participants' compliance by bringing them into closer contact with the confederates. Participants who could see the learners gave fewer shocks than participants who could only hear the learners. The lowest shock rates of all were administered by participants who had to force the learner's hand onto the shock plate. However, even in that last condition, approximately 30 percent delivered all of the shocks. When the experimenter left in the middle of the experiment and was replaced by an assistant, obedience also decreased. Finally, when other confederates were present in the room and they objected to the shocks, the percentage of participants who quit in the middle of the experiment skyrocketed.

One final note about the Milgram experiment bears mentioning. It has been severely criticized on ethical grounds, and such an experiment would surely not receive the approval of an institutional review board (IRB) today. When debriefed, many participants learned that had the shocks been real, they would have killed the learner. Understandably, some people were profoundly disturbed by this insight.

Table 13.2 Famous Social Psychology Experiments

Experimenter	Topic	Major Finding
LaPiere	Attitudes	Attitudes don't always predict behavior; establishments that served a Chinese couple later reported they would refuse such a couple service.
Festinger and Carlsmith	Cognitive dissonance	Changing one's behavior can lead to a change in attitudes; people who described a boring task as interesting for $1 in compensation later reported liking the task more than people who were paid $20.
Rosenthal and Jacobson	Self-fulfilling prophecy	One person's attitudes can elicit a change in another person's behavior; teachers' positive expectations led to increases in students' IQ scores.
Sherif	Superordinate goals	Intergroup prejudice can be reduced through working toward superordinate goals; campers in unfriendly, competing groups came to have more positive feelings about one another after working together to solve several camp-wide problems.
Darley and Latane	**Bystander effect**	The more people who witness an emergency, the less likely any one person is to help; in one study, college students who thought they were the only person to overhear a peer have a seizure were more likely to help than students who thought others heard the seizure too.
Asch	Conformity	People are loathe to contradict the opinions of a group; 70 percent of people reported at least one obviously incorrect answer.
Milgram	Obedience	People tend to obey authority figures; 60 percent of participants thought they delivered the maximum possible level of shock.
Zimbardo	Roles, deindividuation	Roles are powerful and can lead to deindividuation; college students role-playing prisoners and guards acted in surprisingly negative and hostile ways.

Group Dynamics

We are all members of many different groups. The students in your school are a group, a baseball team is a group, and the lawyers at a particular firm are a group. Some groups are more cohesive than others and exert more pressure on their members. All groups have norms, which are rules about how group members should act. For example, the lawyers at the firm mentioned above may have rules governing appropriate work dress. Within groups is often a set of specific roles. On a baseball team, for instance, the players have different, well-defined roles, such as pitcher, shortstop, and center fielder.

Sometimes people take advantage of being part of a group by **social loafing**. Social loafing is the phenomenon when individuals do not put in as much effort when acting as part of a group as they do when acting alone. One explanation for this effect is that when alone, an individual's efforts are more easily discernible than when in a group. Thus, as part of a group, a person may be less motivated to put on an impressive performance. In addition, being part of a group may encourage members to take advantage of the opportunity to reap the rewards of the group effort without taxing themselves unnecessarily.

Group polarization is the tendency of a group to make more extreme decisions than the group members would make individually. Studies about group polarization usually have participants give their opinions individually, then group them to discuss their decisions, and then have the group make a decision. Explanations for group polarization include the idea that in a group, individuals may be exposed to new, persuasive arguments they had not thought of themselves and that the responsibility for an extreme decision in a group is diffused across the group's many members.

Groupthink, a term coined by Irving Janis, describes the tendency for some groups to make bad decisions. Groupthink occurs when group members suppress their reservations about the ideas supported by the group. As a result, a kind of false unanimity is encouraged, and flaws in the group's decisions may be overlooked. Highly cohesive groups involved in making risky decisions seem to be at particular risk for groupthink. Sometimes people get swept up by a group and do things they never would have done if on their own, such as looting or rioting. This loss of self-restraint occurs when group members feel anonymous and aroused, and this phenomenon is known as **deindividuation**.

One famous experiment that showed not only how such conditions can cause people to deindividuate but also the effect of roles and the situation in general is Philip Zimbardo's prison experiment (see Table 13.2). Zimbardo assigned a group of Stanford students to play the role of either prison guard or prisoner. All were dressed in uniforms, and the prisoners were assigned numbers. The prisoners were locked up in the basement of the psychology building, and the guards were put in charge of their treatment. The students took to their assigned roles perhaps too well, and the experiment had to end early because of the cruel treatment the guards were inflicting on the prisoners.

14

Personality

Learning Objectives

In this chapter, you will learn about:

→ Psychodynamic theories of personality
→ Humanistic theories of personality
→ Trait theories
→ Social cognitive theories

Key Terms

- Psychodynamic theory
- Unconscious processes
- Preconscious
- Conscious
- Id
- Ego
- Superego
- Instincts
- Defense mechanisms
- Repression
- Denial
- Displacement
- Projection
- Reaction formation
- Regression

- Rationalization
- Intellectualization
- Sublimation
- Projective tests
- Humanistic psychology
- Self-concept
- Self-esteem
- Self-actualize
- Unconditional positive regard
- Big Five
- Agreeableness
- Openness to experience
- Extroversion
- Conscientiousness

- Emotional stability
- Reciprocal determinism
- Self-efficacy
- Internal locus of control
- External locus of control
- Explanatory style
- Optimistic explanatory style
- Pessimistic explanatory style
- Personality inventories

Overview

Personality is a term we use all the time. When we describe people to others, we try to convey a sense of what their personalities are like. Psychologists define personality as the unique attitudes, behaviors, and emotions that characterize a person. As you might expect, psychologists from each of the different perspectives have different ideas about how an individual's personality is created. However, some ideas about personality do not fit neatly into any one school of thought. An example is the concept of Type A and Type B personalities. Type A people tend to feel a sense of time pressure and are easily angered. They are competitive and ambitious; they work hard and play hard. Interestingly, research has shown that Type A people are at a higher risk for heart disease than the general population. Type B individuals, on the other hand, tend to be relaxed and easygoing. However, these types do not fall on opposite ends of a continuum; some people fit into neither type.

Psychodynamic Theories of Personality

One of the main takeaways from the field of social psychology is the power of the situation to influence individuals' behavior. However, another related field of study focuses on personality—one's characteristic thoughts, feelings, and actions. In the pages that follow, we will describe some of the main theories of personality. The **psychodynamic theory** of personality has its roots in Sigmund Freud's psychoanalytic theory. Freud believed that much of people's behavior is controlled by **unconscious processes**. We do not have access to the thoughts in our unconscious. In fact, Freud asserted that we spend tremendous amounts of psychic energy to keep threatening thoughts in the unconscious. Freud contrasted the unconscious mind with the **preconscious** and the **conscious**. The conscious mind contains everything we are thinking about at any one moment, while the preconscious contains everything that we could potentially summon to conscious awareness with ease. For instance, as you read these words, I hope you are not thinking about your plans for the upcoming weekend; these thoughts were in your preconscious. However, now that I have mentioned these plans, you have brought them into your conscious mind.

Freud posited that the personality consists of three parts: the **id**, the **ego**, and the **superego** (see Table 14.1). The id is in the unconscious and contains **instincts** and psychic energy.

Table 14.1 Freud's Parts of the Mind

Id	Follows the pleasure principle	Exists from birth
Ego	Follows the reality principle	Emerges around ages 2 or 3
Superego	Acts as a conscience	Develops around age 5

The id is propelled by the pleasure principle; it wants immediate gratification. The id exists entirely in the unconscious mind. Babies are propelled solely by their ids. They cry whenever they desire something without regard to the external world around them. The next part of the personality to develop is the ego. The ego follows the reality principle, which means its job is to negotiate between the desires of the id and the limitations of the environment. The ego is partly in the conscious mind and partly in the unconscious mind. The last part of the personality to develop is the superego. Like the ego, the superego operates on both the conscious and unconscious levels. Around the age of five, children begin to develop a conscience and to think about what is right and wrong. This sense of conscience, according to Freud, is their superego. The ego often acts as a mediator between the id and the superego. As you cram for that midterm, the id tells you to go to sleep because you are tired or to go to that party because it will be fun. The superego tells you to study because it is the right thing to do. The ego makes some kind of a compromise. You will study for two hours, drop by the party, and then go to sleep.

Part of the ego's job is to protect the conscious mind from the threatening thoughts buried in the unconscious. The ego uses **defense mechanisms** to help protect the conscious mind. Assume that Muffy, captain of the high school cheerleading squad, decides to leave her boyfriend of two years, Biff, the star wide receiver of the football team, for Alvin, the star of the school's chess team. Needless to say, Biff is devastated, but his ego can choose from a great variety of defense mechanisms with which to protect him. Some of these defense mechanisms are **repression**, **denial**, **displacement**, **projection**, **reaction formation**, **regression**, **rationalization**, **intellectualization**, and **sublimation**.

 TIP

Students sometimes confuse the terms *conscious* and *conscience*. Freudian theory puts great emphasis on the contents of the unconscious as opposed to the conscious. We are aware of what is in our conscious mind but unaware of what is in our unconscious. The conscience, on the other hand, is our sense of right and wrong. It is typically associated with the superego in Freudian theory.

Repression
- Blocking thoughts out from conscious awareness.
- When asked how he feels about the breakup with Muffy, Biff replies, "Who? Oh, yeah, I haven't thought about her in a while."

Denial

- Not accepting the ego-threatening truth.
- Biff continues to act as if he and Muffy are still together. He waits by her locker, calls her every night, and plans their future dates.

Displacement

- Redirecting one's feelings toward another person or object. When people displace negative emotions like anger, they often displace them onto people who are less threatening than the source of the emotion. For instance, a child who is angry at his or her teacher would be more likely to displace the anger onto a classmate than onto the teacher.
- Biff could displace his feelings of anger and resentment onto his little brother, pet hamster, or football.

Projection

- Believing that the feelings one has toward someone else are actually held by the other person and directed at oneself.
- Biff insists that Muffy still cares for him.

Reaction Formation

- Expressing the opposite of how one truly feels.
- Biff claims he loathes Muffy.

Regression

- Returning to an earlier, comforting form of behavior.
- Biff begins to sleep with his favorite childhood stuffed animal, Fuzzy Kitten.

Rationalization

- Coming up with a beneficial result of an undesirable occurrence.
- Biff believes that he can now find a better girlfriend. Muffy is not really all that pretty, smart, and fun to be with.

Intellectualization

- Undertaking an academic, unemotional study of a topic.
- Biff embarks on an in-depth research project about failed teen romances.

Sublimation

- Channeling one's frustration toward a different goal. Sublimation is viewed as a particularly healthy defense mechanism.
- Biff devotes himself to writing poetry and publishes a small volume before he graduates high school.

> **TIP**
>
> Students frequently confuse displacement and projection. In displacement, person A has feelings about person B but redirects those feelings onto a third person or an object. In projection, person A has feelings toward person B but believes, instead, that person B has those feelings toward him or her (person A).

One psychodynamic theorist, Carl Jung, proposed that the unconscious consists of two different parts: the personal unconscious and the collective unconscious. Jung believed that an individual's personal unconscious contains painful or threatening memories and thoughts the person does not wish to confront; he termed these complexes. Jung contrasted the personal unconscious with the collective unconscious. The collective unconscious is passed down through the species and, according to Jung, explains certain similarities we see among cultures. The collective unconscious contains archetypes that Jung defined as universal concepts we all share as part of the human species. For example, the shadow represents the evil side of personality, and the persona is people's creation of a public image. Jung suggested that the widespread existence of certain fears, such as fear of the dark, and the importance of the circle in many cultures provide evidence for archetypes.

Alfred Adler is called an ego psychologist because he downplayed the importance of the unconscious and focused on the conscious role of the ego. Adler believed that people are motivated by the fear of failure, which he termed inferiority, and the desire to achieve, which he called superiority. Adler is also known for his work about the importance of birth order in shaping personality.

Psychodynamic theorists may use **projective tests** to try to delve into the unconscious. These tests involve asking people to interpret ambiguous stimuli. For instance, the Rorschach inkblot test involves showing people a series of inkblots and asking them to describe what they see. The thematic apperception test (TAT) consists of several cards, each of which contains a picture of a person or people in an ambiguous situation. People are asked to describe what is happening in the pictures. Since both the inkblots and TAT cards are ambiguous, psychodynamic theorists reason that people's interpretations reflect their unconscious thoughts. People are thought to project their unconscious thoughts onto the ambiguous stimuli. For instance, someone who is struggling with his or her unconscious aggressive impulses may be more likely to describe violent themes. Scoring projective tests, however, is a complicated process. For instance, the Rorschach test looks not only at the content people describe but also the way they hold and turn the card and whether they focus on the whole inkblot or just a portion of it. Many people believe that projective tests are particularly unreliable given that they rely so extensively on therapists' interpretations.

Humanistic Theories of Personality

Many of the models of personality already discussed are deterministic. Determinism is the belief that what happens is dictated by what has happened in the past. According to psychoanalysts, personality is determined by what happened to an individual in his or her early childhood (largely during the psychosexual stages). Behaviorists assert that personality is similarly determined by the environment in which one has been raised. Neither theory supports the existence of free will, which is an individual's ability to choose his or her own destiny. Free will is an idea that has been embraced by **humanistic psychology**. This perspective is often referred to as the third force because it arose in opposition to the determinism so central to both psychoanalytic and behaviorist models.

Humanistic theories of personality view people as innately good and able to determine their own destinies through the exercise of free will. These psychologists stress the importance of people's subjective experience and feelings. They focus on the importance of a person's **self-concept** and **self-esteem**. Self-concept is a person's global feeling about himself or herself. Self-concept develops through a person's involvement with others, especially parents. Someone with a positive self-concept is likely to have high self-esteem.

One of the most influential humanistic psychologists was Carl Rogers. He believed that people are motivated to reach their full potential or **self-actualize**. Rogers created self-theory. He believed that although people are innately good, they require certain things from their interactions with others, most importantly **unconditional positive regard**, to self-actualize. Unconditional positive regard is a kind of blanket acceptance. Parents who make their children feel as if they are loved no matter what provide unconditional positive regard. However, parents who make their children feel as if they will be loved only if they earn high grades or have the right kind of friends send their children the message that their love is conditional. Rogers believed that people must feel accepted to make strides toward self-actualization. Humanistic theories of personality are criticized for putting forth an overly optimistic theory of human nature. If people are innately good and striving to do their best, it is difficult to explain the number and range of truly terrible acts that people commit.

Trait Theories

Trait theorists believe that we can describe people's personalities by specifying their main characteristics, or traits. These characteristics (for example, honesty, laziness, ambition) are thought to be stable and to motivate behavior in keeping with the trait. In other words, when we describe someone as friendly, we mean that the person acts in a friendly manner across different situations and times.

Some trait theorists believe that the same basic set of traits can be used to describe all people's personalities. Such a belief characterizes a nomothetic approach. For instance, Hans Eysenck believed that by classifying all people along an introversion-extroversion scale and along a stable-unstable scale, we could describe their personalities. Raymond Cattell developed the 16 PF (personality factor) test to measure what he believed were the 16 basic traits present in all people, albeit to different degrees.

More recently, Paul Costa and Robert McCrae have proposed that personality can be described using the **Big Five** personality traits: extroversion, **agreeableness**, conscientiousness, **openness to experience**, and emotional stability (or neuroticism). **Extroversion** refers to how outgoing or shy someone is. Agreeableness has to do with how easy to get along with someone is. People high on the **conscientiousness** dimension tend to be hardworking, responsible, and organized. Openness to new experiences is related to one's creativity, curiosity, and willingness to try new things. Finally, **emotional stability** has to do with how consistent one's mood is.

One might wonder how psychologists can reduce the vast number of different terms we use to describe people to either 16 or five basic traits. Factor analysis is a statistical technique used to accomplish this feat. Factor analysis allows researchers to use correlations among traits to see which traits cluster together as factors. If a strong correlation is found among punctuality, diligence, and neatness, for example, one could argue that these traits represent a common factor that we could name conscientiousness.

Other trait theorists, called idiographic theorists, assert that using the same set of terms to classify all people is impossible. Rather, they argue, each person needs to be seen in terms of what few traits best characterize his or her unique self. For example, although honesty may be a very important trait in describing one person, it may not be at all important in describing someone else.

Gordon Allport believed that although there were common traits useful in describing all people, a full understanding of someone's personality was impossible without looking at his or her personal traits. Allport differentiated among three different types of personal traits. He suggested that a small number of people are so profoundly influenced by one trait that it plays a pivotal role in virtually everything they do. He referred to such traits as cardinal dispositions. Allport posited that there are two other types of dispositions, central and secondary, that can be used to describe personality. As their names indicate, central dispositions have a larger influence on personality than secondary dispositions. Central dispositions are more often apparent and describe more significant aspects of personality.

The main criticism of trait theories is that they underestimate the importance of the situation. Nobody is always conscientious or unfailingly friendly. Therefore, critics assert, to describe someone's personality, we need to take the context into consideration.

> **TIP**
> Today, the most popular trait theory contends that personality can be described with the Big Five traits of extroversion, agreeableness, conscientiousness, openness, and emotional stability.

Social Cognitive Theories

Many models of personality meld together behaviorists' emphasis on the importance of the environment with cognitive psychologists' focus on patterns of thought. Such models are referred to as social-cognitive or cognitive behavioral models.

Albert Bandura suggested that personality is created by an interaction among the person (traits), the environment, and the person's behavior. His model is based on the idea of **reciprocal determinism**, also known as triadic reciprocality. These terms essentially mean that each of these three factors influences both of the other two in a constant, looplike fashion. Look at an example. Brad is a friendly person. This personality trait influences Brad's behavior in that he talks to a lot of people. It influences the environment into which he puts himself in that he goes to a lot of parties. Brad's loquacious behavior affects his environment in that it makes the parties even more party-like. In addition, Brad's talkativeness reinforces his friendliness; the more he talks, the more friendly Brad thinks he is. Finally, the environment of the party reinforces Brad's outgoing nature and encourages him to strike up conversations with many people.

Bandura also posited that personality is affected by people's sense of **self-efficacy**. People with high self-efficacy are optimistic about their own ability to get things done, whereas people with low self-efficacy feel a sense of powerlessness. Bandura theorized that people's sense of self-efficacy has a powerful effect on their actions. For example, assume two students of equal abilities and knowledge are taking a test. The one with higher self-efficacy would expect to do better and therefore might act in ways to make that true (e.g., spend more time on the test questions).

Some of the ideas put forth by social-cognitive theorists, including Bandura's concept of self-efficacy, are almost like traits that describe an individual's characteristic way of thinking. A final example is Julian Rotter's concept of locus of control. A person can be described as having either an internal or an external locus of control. People with an **internal locus of control** feel as if they are responsible for what happens to them. For instance, they tend to believe that hard work will lead to success. Conversely, people with an **external locus of control** generally believe that luck and other forces outside of their own control determine their destinies. A person's locus of control can have a large effect on how a person thinks and acts, thus impacting his or her personality. Several positive outcomes have been found to be associated with having an internal locus of control. As compared with externals, internals tend to be healthier, to be more politically active, and to do better in school. Of course, these findings are based on correlational research, so we can't conclude that locus of control causes such differences.

We can also differentiate people by their **explanatory style**—the kind of attributions they make about the things that happen to them. Some people have an **optimistic explanatory style**, which leads them to make internal, global, and stable attributions for good things that happen to them and external, specific, and unstable attributions for bad experiences. People with a **pessimistic explanatory style** make the opposite types of attributions. For example, imagine you get a good test grade. If you have an optimistic explanatory style, you will attribute that to something internal, like you are a good student. You will also attribute that score to something general. like you are smart, as opposed to something specific, like you are just good at this particular topic. Finally, you will attribute that good test grade to something stable, like you will do well on other exams as well.

A common way to gather data about personality is to use **personality inventories**. Personality inventories are essentially questionnaires that ask people to provide information about themselves. Many kinds of psychologists, such as humanistic psychologists, trait theorists, and cognitive behavioral psychologists, might use self-report inventories as one means by which to gather data about someone. These kinds of tests are often referred to as objective personality tests since people's scores are determined simply by their answers and are thus unlikely to be affected by evaluator bias. An interview, on the other hand, is a subjective assessment. Although such subjectivity decreases reliability and opens the door to bias, some believe that subjective measures yield richer and more valid data.

The Minnesota Multiphasic Personality Inventory (MMPI-2) is one of the most widely used self-report instruments. A potential problem with such inventories is that people may not be completely honest in answering the questions. Some tests have "lie scales" built in to try to detect when people are not being honest. Radical behaviorists would reject all the above methods, arguing instead that the only way to measure people's personality is to observe their behavior. Again, several other kinds of psychologists, particularly cognitive behavioral ones, would use observations of a person's behavior as one way to gather data.

People are naturally curious about what various personality assessments will say about them. Unfortunately, this curiosity makes people susceptible to being deceived. Research has demonstrated that people have the tendency to see themselves in vague, stock descriptions of personality. This phenomenon, called the Barnum effect, is named after the famous circus owner P. T. Barnum, who once said, "There's a sucker born every minute." Astrologers, psychics, and fortune tellers take advantage of the Barnum effect in their work. Personality has proved difficult to define, much less measure. So be skeptical when confronted with people who offer you quick, pat descriptions of your life or future.

15

Motivation and Emotion

Learning Objectives

In this chapter, you will learn about:

→ Theories of motivation
→ Hunger motivation
→ Sexual motivation
→ Social motivation
→ Theories about emotion
→ Nonverbal expressions of emotion

Key Terms

- Instincts
- Drive reduction theory
- Homeostasis
- Arousal theory
- Boredom susceptibility
- Optimal level of arousal
- Yerkes-Dodson law
- Incentives

- Self-determination theory
- Hypothalamus
- Ghrelin
- Leptin
- Sexual orientation
- Twin studies
- Extrinsic motivations
- Intrinsic motivations
- Lewin's motivational conflicts theory

- Approach-approach conflict
- Avoidance-avoidance conflict
- Approach-avoidance conflict
- Facial feedback hypothesis
- Cognitive appraisal
- Cognitive label
- Display rules

Overview

I often ask students at the beginning of my psychology class why they wanted to take this course. One of the most common replies is "Because I wanted to figure out why people do what they do." Motivation theories address this question directly. Motivations are feelings or ideas that cause us to act toward a goal. Some motivations are obvious and conscious, but others are more subtle. In this chapter, we will review the connections between physiology and motivation, general motivation theories, and specific examples of motivation in hunger and sex. Finally, we will review the psychological research and theories about emotion and stress that are closely related to motivation theory.

Theories of Motivation

If you have pets, you know that different animals are born with **instincts**, which are automatic behaviors performed in response to specific stimuli. Your cat did not have to learn how to clean itself; it was born with this instinct. When Charles Darwin's theory of natural selection was published, many psychologists unsuccessfully tried to explain all human behaviors through instincts. Many ethologists and researchers who study animal behavior in a natural environment examine the role evolution is thought to play in human thought and behavior. They look for the evolutionary advantages of persistent human behaviors. While psychologists debate whether humans are born with any instincts, they agree that our behavior is also motivated by other biological and psychological factors.

Drive Reduction Theory

One early theory about how our physiology motivates us was **drive reduction theory**, the theory that our behavior is motivated by biological needs. A need is one of our requirements for survival, such as food, water, or shelter. A drive is our impulse to act in a way that satisfies this need. If, for example, you wake up late and skip breakfast, your body has a need for food that is not satisfied. This need creates a drive, hunger, and this drive causes you to get a candy bar from the vending machine to satisfy the need. Our body seeks **homeostasis**, which is a balanced internal state. When we are out of homeostasis, we have a need that creates a drive. Drives can be categorized in two ways: primary drives and secondary drives. Primary drives are biological needs, like thirst. Secondary drives are learned drives. For instance, we learn that resources like money can get us food and water to satisfy our primary drives. However, drive reduction theory cannot explain all our motivations. Sometimes we are motivated to perform behaviors that do not seem connected with any need or drive, primary or secondary. One of my cousins has always been motivated by speed and excitement. He made sure his first car was faster than anyone else's, he went into the Air Force for the opportunity to fly the fastest planes in the world, and he liked to drag race motorcycles in amateur races. These activities can be risky and seem to violate biological explanations for motivation. Why does anyone go skydiving or ride a roller coaster? Where do these motivations come from?

Arousal (or Sensation-Seeking) Theory

Some motivations that seem to violate biological theories of motivation can be explained by **arousal theory** (or sensation-seeking theory), which states that we seek an optimum level of excitement or arousal. This arousal level can be measured by different physiological tests. Each of us has a different need for excitement or arousal, and we are motivated by activities that will help us achieve this level. Some people are thrill seekers who are especially susceptible to becoming bored (**boredom susceptibility**). People with high optimum levels of arousal might be drawn to high-excitement behaviors, while the rest of us are satisfied with less exciting and less risky activities. In general, most of us perform best with an **optimal level of arousal**, although this varies with different activities. We might perform well at an easy task with a very high level of arousal, but the same high level of arousal would prevent us from performing well on a difficult task. (This concept is similar to social facilitation, described in Chapter 13 "Social Psychology.") This relationship is called the **Yerkes-Dodson law** after the researchers who first investigated the concept in animals and is graphed in Figure 15.1.

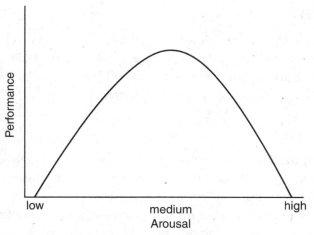

Figure 15.1 The Yerkes-Dodson law

Another theory of motivation, which is similar in some ways to the arousal theory, is the opponent-process theory of motivation. This theory is often used to explain addictive behaviors. The theory states that people are usually at a normal, or baseline, state. We might perform an act that moves us from the baseline state, such as smoking a cigarette. These acts may be initially pleasurable (because nicotine is a stimulant and it makes us feel a good "buzz"). However, the theory states that we eventually feel an opponent process, meaning a motivation to return to our baseline, neutral state. Smokers may tire of the jittery feeling they get when smoking and try to reduce the number of cigarettes they smoke. With physically addictive substances, though, we also experience withdrawal (see Chapter 5 "States of Consciousness"), and the discomfort of the withdrawal state moves us away from our neutral baseline. A smoker might feel uncomfortable without nicotine in her or his system. So, this state creates a motivation to return to the baseline state of feeling all right, creating a desire to smoke more cigarettes to return to a state of feeling normal.

Incentive Theory

Sometimes behavior is not pushed by a need; it is pulled by a desire. **Incentives** are stimuli that we are drawn to due to learning. We learn to associate some stimuli with rewards and others with punishment, and we are motivated to seek the rewards. For example, you may learn that studying with friends is fun but does not produce the desired results around test time, so you are motivated to study alone to get the reward of a good test score.

Self-Determination Theory

The **self-determination theory** of motivation grew out of research on intrinsic (rewards we get internally) motivations for behavior. Researchers have long known that intrinsic motivations are an important element of our overall psychological health and sense of well-being. Self-determination research indicates that three elements are related to intrinsic motivations involved in what they call self-determination: autonomy, competence, and relatedness. Autonomy is the belief that we have the power to make choices that are important to us. Competence is the belief that we have the skills and knowledge needed to accomplish tasks important to us. Relatedness is our ability to form relationships with others who are important to us. Self-determination theory predicts that this combination of elements impacts our ability to be self-determined and work toward goals we want to achieve.

Hunger Motivation

Some human behaviors appear to be deceptively simple. Why do we become hungry? Our bodies need food! However, we know the relationship is not that simple. Some people eat even when their body has enough food, and some people do not eat when their body needs nourishment. Even a seemingly simple motivation such as hunger involves several biological, psychological, and social factors.

Biological Basis of Hunger

Several biological cues create a feeling of hunger. Researchers inserted balloons into participants' stomachs. By inflating and deflating the balloons, they were able to determine that we report feeling hungry when our stomach is empty and contracts and report feeling full when our stomach feels full.

Our brain also plays a role in the feeling of hunger. The hypothalamus monitors and helps to control body chemistry (including the ratio of glucose and insulin) and makes us feel hungry when we need to eat. Electric stimulation of animals' brains indicates that different parts of the **hypothalamus** act in opposition to controlling hunger. The lateral hypothalamus (hunger center), when stimulated, causes the animal to eat. Destruction of this area inhibits hunger, and the animal will starve to death unless forced to eat. Another part of the hypothalamus, the ventromedial hypothalamus (satiety center), causes the animal to stop eating when it is stimulated. If this area is destroyed, the animal will eat and gain more and more weight unless it is deprived of food. If the hypothalamus functions normally, these two areas oppose each other and signal impulses to eat and stop eating at appropriate times.

Hormones also play a role in hunger. Two of the most important are leptin and ghrelin. **Ghrelin** influences short-term hunger; it's produced in the stomach and communicates hunger to the brain. On the other hand, leptin has more of a long-term influence. **Leptin** is produced by fat cells and signals the brain that you have sufficient stored energy and thus are not hungry.

Set-point theory describes how the hypothalamus might decide what impulse to send. This theory states that the hypothalamus wants to maintain a certain optimum body weight. When we drop below that weight, the hypothalamus tells us we should eat and lowers our metabolic rate—how quickly our body uses energy. The hypothalamus tells us to stop eating when that set point is reached and raises our metabolic rate to burn any excess food. Not all researchers agree that we have a set point for weight, however. They might point to psychological factors and believe that weight maintenance has more to do with learning and cognition than with the hypothalamus. In addition, the brain monitors the levels of insulin (released by the liver) and glucose, and this balance also influences our perception of hunger.

Psychological Factors in Hunger Motivation

So far, our drive to eat appears to be governed strictly by our physiology. However, some of the reasons we get hungry have little to do with our brain and body chemistry. For example, research indicates that some of us (called externals) are more motivated to eat by external food cues, such as attractiveness or availability of food. Others (called internals) are less affected by the presence and presentation of food and respond more often to internal hunger cues. Everyone responds to both types of cues but to greater or lesser extents. These and other factors in eating might be learned. The Garcia effect, in particular, can drastically affect what foods make us hungry. You can probably think of a particular food that brings back unpleasant memories of being sick. If you eat hot dogs and then happen to get nauseous, hot dogs will probably be unappetizing to you even if you know the hot dogs did not cause your sickness. This is caused by the Garcia effect and occurs whenever nausea is paired with either food or drink. (See Chapter 12 "Learning" for more information about learned taste aversions and other examples of classical conditioning.)

Culture and background affect our food preferences. The foods we are raised with are most likely the foods we find most appetizing, although new preferences are acquired. Where I live in Nebraska, we eat a traditional Czechoslovakian sandwich called a *runza*, which is spiced beef and cabbage inside a bread pocket. Some of my friends who now live in other parts of the country have cravings for *runza*, but I am willing to bet that it sounds quite unappetizing to some of you reading this. We usually prefer foods our family, region, and culture prefer because those are the foods we learned to like.

Eating Disorders

Research into hunger motivations has at least one very important practical application—eating disorders (see Table 15.1). Many researchers seek to apply what we know about hunger and eating to treat individuals with harmful eating patterns.

Table 15.1 The Two Most Common Eating Disorders

Bulimia	People with bulimia eat large amounts of food in a short period of time (binging) and then get rid of the food (purging) by vomiting, exercising excessively, or using laxatives. Bulimics are obsessed with food and their weight. The majority of people with bulimia are women.
Anorexia nervosa	People with anorexia starve themselves to below 85 percent of their normal body weight and refuse to eat due to their obsession with weight. The vast majority of people with anorexia are women.

Many researchers are investigating the causes of eating disorders. Different cultures have drastically different rates of eating disorders, possibly due to the emphasis on body weight in the particular culture. Eating disorder rates are highest in the United States, possibly for this reason. Research also identifies a family history of eating disorders as a risk factor, indicating a potential genetic component. Researchers agree that eating disorders are influenced by a complex set of factors and are not merely a lack of willpower about food.

TIP

The key difference between a person with anorexia and a person with bulimia is their weight. People who suffer from both disorders tend to be obsessed with food, and some people with anorexia even binge and purge. However, those with anorexia are at least 15 percent below the typical weight of someone their age and size, while the weight of those with bulimia tends to be average or even slightly above.

Sexual Motivation

Sexual motivations are vital for the continuation of any species. One of the primary tasks for most living organisms is reproduction. Since humans are one of the most complex living organisms, our sexual motivations are correspondingly complex. Like hunger, sex is motivated by both biological and psychological factors.

Sexual Response Cycle

The famous lab studies done by William Masters and Virginia Johnson documented the sexual response cycle in men and women. Our sexual response progresses through four stages, as described in Table 15.2.

Table 15.2 The Four Stages of the Sexual Response Cycle in Humans

Initial excitement	Genital areas become engorged with blood; penis becomes erect; clitoris swells; respiration and heart rate increase.
Plateau phase	Respiration and heart rate continue at an elevated level; genitals secrete fluids in preparation for coitus.
Orgasm	Rhythmic genital contractions that may help conception, respiration, and heart rate increase further; males ejaculate, often accompanied by a pleasurable euphoria.
Resolution phase	Respiration and heart rate return to normal resting states. Male systems experience a refractory period—a time period that must elapse before another orgasm. However, female systems do not have a similar refractory period and can repeat the cycle immediately.

Psychological Factors in Sexual Motivation

Unlike many animals, our sexual desire is not motivated strictly by hormones. Many studies demonstrate that sexual motivation is controlled largely by psychological rather than biological sources. Sexual desire can be present even when the capability to have sex is lost. Accident victims who lose the ability to have sex still have sexual desires. Erotic material can inspire sexual feelings and physiological responses in people, including elevated levels of hormones. The interaction between our physiology and psychology creates the myriad of sexual desires we see in society and ourselves.

Sexual Orientation

As attention to LGBTQ+ issues increases, so does research about sexuality. Researchers (like Alfred Kinsey, who documented the variety of human sexual behaviors in the famous Kinsey Reports from the 1940s and 1950s) have been able to dispel some common myths about sexuality. Studies show that gay and lesbian **sexual orientation** is not related to traumatic childhood experiences, parenting styles, the quality of relationships with parents, masculinity or femininity, or the sexual orientation of our parents. Although some researchers believe environmental influences probably affect sexual orientation, these factors have not yet been identified.

Researchers have identified possible biological influences, however. Some studies indicate that specific brain structures might differ in size in brains of gay people when compared with the same structures in heterosexual people. **Twin studies** indicate a genetic influence on sexual orientation since a twin is much more likely to be gay if his or her identical twin is gay. Some researchers theorize that hormones in the womb might change brain structure and influence sexual orientation. Since 3 to 10 percent (estimates vary) of the population worldwide identifies as gay, lesbian, bisexual, transgender, or queer, research in this area will certainly continue, and the causes of sexual orientation will become clearer.

Social Motivation

So far, we have described the research regarding the motivations behind some relatively simple human behaviors such as eating and sex. What motivates the more complicated behaviors, such as taking the AP Psychology exam? Your attitudes and goals, the society you live in, and the people you surround yourself with also affect what you are motivated to do.

Achievement Motivation

Achievement motivation is one theory that tries to explain the motivations behind these more complex behaviors. Achievement motivation examines our desires to master complex tasks and knowledge and to reach personal goals. Humans (and some other animals) seem to be motivated to figure out our world and master skills, sometimes regardless of the benefits of the skills or knowledge.

Studies in achievement motivation find that some people have high achievement motivation and consistently feel motivated to challenge themselves more than do other people. They always set the bar a little higher and seek greater challenges. Obviously, this varies not only from person to person but also from activity to activity. Not many people are motivated to achieve in every aspect of life, which is fortunate because we don't have time to pursue every possible interest. However, studies that measure achievement motivation do indicate a higher-than-average achievement motivation in some people.

Extrinsic/Intrinsic Motivation

Another way to think about the social factors that influence motivation is by dividing them into extrinsic and intrinsic motivations. **Extrinsic motivations** are rewards that we get for accomplishments from outside ourselves (for example, grades, salary, and so on). **Intrinsic motivations** are rewards we get internally, such as enjoyment or satisfaction. Think about your own motives regarding the AP Psychology exam. Are you internally or externally motivated or both? Are you taking the test to get the grade and possible college credit (external) or are you internally motivated to gain the knowledge and challenge yourself by taking a difficult test? Knowing what type of motivation an individual responds best to can give managers and other leaders insight into what strategies will be most effective. Psychologists working with people managing work groups (in government, business, or other areas) might test or evaluate group members for intrinsic or extrinsic motivation and try to alter group policies accordingly. Studies show that if we want an advantageous behavior to continue, intrinsic motivation is most effective. Extrinsic motivations are very effective for a short period of time. Inevitably, though, the extrinsic motivations end and so will the desired behavior unless some intrinsic motivation continues to motivate the behavior.

> **TIP**
>
> Achievement motivation is different from optimum arousal. Achievement motivation involves meeting personal goals and acquiring new knowledge or skills. Optimum arousal indicates the general level of arousal a person is motivated to seek, whether or not the arousal is productive in meeting a goal. The concepts might overlap in a person. (For example, a person with high achievement motivation might also have a high optimum level of arousal.) However, the concepts refer to different aspects of motivation.

Management Theory

Some research into how managers behave is closely related to extrinsic/intrinsic motivation. Studies of management styles show two basic attitudes that affect how managers do their jobs (see Table 15.3).

Table 15.3 Two Theories of Management Style

Theory X	Managers believe that employees will work only if rewarded with benefits or threatened with punishment.
Theory Y	Managers believe that employees are internally motivated to do good work and policies should encourage this internal motive.

Cross-cultural studies show the benefits of moving from a theory X attitude about employees to a theory Y attitude. Some companies hire consultants from other countries to teach their managers how to promote intrinsic motivation in employees.

When Motives Conflict

Sometimes what you want to do in a situation is clear to you. At other times, though, you no doubt find yourself conflicted about what choice to make. **Lewin's motivational conflicts theory** discusses four major types of motivational conflicts. The first, named an **approach-approach conflict**, occurs when you must choose between two desirable outcomes. For instance, imagine that for spring break one of your friends invites you to spend the week in Puerto Rico and another asks you to go to San Francisco. Assuming that both choices appeal to you, you have a conflict because you can do only one. Another type of conflict, an **avoidance-avoidance conflict**, occurs when you must choose between two unattractive outcomes. If, one weekend, your parents were to give you a choice between staying home and cleaning out the garage or going on a family trip to visit some distant relatives, you might experience an avoidance-avoidance conflict. An **approach-avoidance conflict** exists when one event or goal has both attractive and unattractive features. If you were lactose intolerant, an ice cream cone would present such a conflict; the taste of the ice cream is appealing but its effects on you are not. Finally, people experience multiple approach-avoidance conflicts. In these, you must choose between two or more things, each of which has both desirable and undesirable features. You may well face such a conflict in choosing which college to attend. Of the schools at which you have been accepted, University A is the best academically, but you do not like its location. University B is close to your family and boyfriend or girlfriend, but you would like to go someplace with better weather. University C has the best psychology department (hopefully one of your favorite subjects!), but you visit the campus and find it less than attractive.

Theories About Emotion

Our emotional state is closely related to our motivation. In fact, imagining one without the other is difficult. Can you imagine wanting to do a behavior without an accompanying feeling about the action? Emotion influences motivation, and motivation influences emotion. Psychologists investigate emotional states and create theories that try to explain our emotional experiences.

What Comes First—The Emotion or the Physiological Change?

One of the earliest theories about emotion was put forth by William James and Carl Lange. They theorized that we feel emotion because of biological changes caused by stress. So, when the big bad wolf jumps out of the woods, Little Red Riding Hood's heart races, and this physiological change causes her to feel afraid. The **facial feedback hypothesis** is a related idea that suggests that we infer our emotions from our facial expressions. Thus, if I smile, I will feel happy, and if I frown, I will feel sad.

Walter Cannon and Philip Bard doubted this order of events. They demonstrated that similar physiological changes correspond with drastically different emotional states. When Little Red Riding Hood's heart races, how does she know if she feels afraid, in love, embarrassed, or merely joyful? They theorized that the biological change and the cognitive awareness of the emotional state occur simultaneously. Cannon thought the thalamus is responsible for both the biological change and the cognitive awareness of emotions. Cannon believed that when the thalamus receives information about our environment, it sends signals simultaneously to our cortex and to our autonomic nervous system, creating the awareness of emotion and the physiological change at the same time. Recent research shows Cannon overestimated the role of the thalamus in this process. Many other brain structures, such as the amygdala, are also involved.

TIP

The James-Lange theory is mentioned for historical purposes. Current theories about emotion demonstrate that although biological changes are involved in emotions, they are not the sole cause of them.

Two-Factor Theory

Stanley Schachter's two-factor theory explains emotional experiences in a more complete way than either the James-Lange or Cannon-Bard theories do. Schachter pointed out that both our physical responses and our **cognitive appraisal** of them (our mental interpretations) combine to cause any particular emotional response. So, to continue the previous example, Little Red Riding Hood's emotional response depends on both her heart racing and her **cognitive label** of the event as being scary. Schachter showed that people who are already physiologically aroused experience more intense emotions than unaroused people when both groups are exposed to the same stimuli. For example, if your heart rate is already elevated after jogging, you will report being more frightened by a sudden surprise than if you get a surprise while in a resting state. Two-factor theory demonstrates that emotion depends on the interaction between two factors, biology and cognition.

Nonverbal Expressions of Emotion

Many psychologists researching emotions find that the ways we express emotion nonverbally (through facial expressions, and so on) are universal. No matter what culture we grew up in, we are likely to use the same facial expressions for basic emotions like happiness, sadness, anger, disgust, surprise, and fear. Researchers establish this by showing pictures of people experiencing these emotions to people from different cultures and asking them to label the emotions. Most people from cultures around the world can label these facial expressions very accurately. This area of research (sometimes called sociobiology) indicates that the facial expressions we make for basic emotions may be an innate part of our physiological makeup. On the other hand, researchers have documented some differences in how people express emotion. One cause is thought to be different cultural **display rules**. For instance, in individualistic cultures it may be more acceptable to express greater happiness when defeating others in a race than it would be in more collectivist cultures.

Unit 4 Multiple-Choice Questions

1. How would the drive reduction theory explain a person accepting a new job with a higher salary but that requires more work and responsibility?

   (A) Money is a more powerful incentive for this individual than free time.
   (B) This person seeks a higher activity level and takes the job in order to satisfy this drive.
   (C) For this person, money is a higher-level need than free time.
   (D) The person takes the job to satisfy the secondary drive of increased salary.

2. What is the principal difference between how achievement motivation theory and arousal theory explain human motivation?

   (A) Achievement motivation is a specific example of arousal motivation.
   (B) Arousal theory describes the optimum level of general arousal an individual seeks, while achievement motivation describes what type of goals the individual is motivated to achieve.
   (C) Arousal theory describes motivation by referring to stages in our responses to stress (the general adaptation syndrome), while achievement motivation is not used to describe motivation due to stress.
   (D) A person with a low optimum level of arousal according to arousal theory would have a high achievement motivation.

3. Which of the following are reasons why intrinsic motivation might be more advantageous than extrinsic motivation?

   (A) Intrinsic motivation might be more enduring since extrinsic motivations are usually temporary.
   (B) Intrinsic motivations are easier and more convenient to provide.
   (C) Intrinsic motivations are higher on Maslow's hierarchy of needs, so we are motivated to meet them before extrinsic needs.
   (D) Intrinsic motivations are more likely to be primary drives. Extrinsic motivations are secondary drives.

4. Cettina fills out a personality inventory several times over the course of one year. The results of each administration of the test are extremely different. Cettina's situation suggests that this personality inventory may not be

   (A) reliable.
   (B) standardized.
   (C) normed.
   (D) projective.

5. Juan has a huge crush on Sally, but he never admits it. Instead, he tells all who will listen that Sally is really "into him." Psychoanalysts would see Juan's bragging as an example of

   (A) displacement.
   (B) projection
   (C) sublimation.
   (D) denial.

6. Which of the following suggestions is most likely to reduce the hostility felt between antagonistic groups?

   (A) Force the groups to spend a lot of time together
   (B) Encourage the groups to avoid each other as much as possible
   (C) Give the groups a task that cannot be solved unless they work together
   (D) Set up a program in which speakers attempt to persuade the groups to get along

7. On Monday, Tanya asked her teacher to postpone Tuesday's test until Friday. After her teacher flatly refused, Tanya asked the teacher to push the test back one day, to Wednesday. Tanya is using the compliance strategy known as

   (A) door-in-the-face.
   (B) norms of reciprocity.
   (C) compromise.
   (D) strategic bargaining.

8. Your new neighbor seems to know everything about ancient Greece that your social studies teacher says during the first week of school. You conclude that she is brilliant. You do not consider that she might already have learned about ancient Greece in her old school. You are evidencing

(A) the self-fulfilling prophecy effect.
(B) pluralistic ignorance.
(C) confirmation bias.
(D) the fundamental attribution error.

9. Janine has always hated the color orange. However, once she became a student at Princeton, she began to wear a lot of orange Princeton Tiger clothing. The discomfort caused by her long-standing dislike of the color orange and her current ownership of so much orange-and-black-striped clothing is known as

(A) cognitive dissonance.
(B) contradictory concepts.
(C) conflicting motives.
(D) opposing cognitions.

10. After your school's football team has a big win, students in the halls can be heard saying "We are awesome." The next week, after the team loses to the last-place team in the league, the same students lament that "They were terrible." The difference in these comments illustrates

(A) the fundamental attribution error.
(B) self-serving bias.
(C) the self-fulfilling prophecy effect.
(D) the false consensus effect.

11. Which of the following is the best example of prejudice?

(A) Billy will not let girls play on his hockey team.
(B) Santiago dislikes cheerleaders.
(C) Athena says she can run faster than anybody on the playground.
(D) Mr. Tamp calls on boys more often than girls.

12. On their second date, Megan confides in Francisco that she still loves to watch *Aladdin*. He, in turn, tells her that he still cries when he watches *Bambi*. These two young lovers will be brought closer together through this process of

(A) self-disclosure.
(B) deindividuation.
(C) in-group bias.
(D) open communication.

13. On the first day of class, Mr. Simpson divides his class into four competing groups. On the fifth day of school, Jody is sent to the principal for kicking members of the other groups. Mr. Simpson can be faulted for encouraging the creation of

(A) group polarization.
(B) deindividuation.
(C) out-group bias.
(D) superordinate goals.

Questions 14 and 15 refer to the following.

Coach Price believes her varsity basketball team isn't trying hard enough at its practices. As evidence, she shows them the table below that includes the free throw percentages for the starting five players across the last few practices as opposed to the last few games.

	Average Percent of Free Throws Made in Practices	Average Percent of Free Throws Made in Games
Cathy	65	75
LaTonia	70	72
Tina	56	60
Thalia	64	76
Deb	51	68

14. What might explain the phenomenon noticed by Coach Price?

    (A) Social facilitation
    (B) Groupthink
    (C) Conformity
    (D) Group polarization

15. Which of the following values is larger in the distribution of free throws taken during practices than in the distribution of free throws taken during games?

    (A) Median
    (B) Range
    (C) Mean
    (D) Mode

Answer Explanations

1. **(D)** Money is a secondary drive people learn to associate with primary drives. Choice (A) refers to incentive theory, choice (B) refers to arousal theory, and choice (C) refers to the hierarchy of needs.

2. **(B)** Arousal theory says that humans are motivated to seek a certain level of arousal. Achievement motivation theory describes how we are motivated to meet goals and master our environment. The rest of the choices describe the theories incorrectly.

3. **(A)** An intrinsically motivated person motivates himself or herself with internal rewards like satisfaction. Extrinsic motivators like money are usually temporary, and the individual may lose motivation for the task when the motivator stops or does not increase. Intrinsic motivators are not easier to provide. In fact, inspiring people to become intrinsically motivated may be more difficult. Intrinsic/extrinsic motivation does not relate to Maslow's hierarchy or to primary and secondary drives.

4. **(A)** A test that does not yield consistent results is not reliable. Such a test may still have been standardized and normed, both of which mean that it has been pretested on a large population and structured so that certain percentages of people answer each question in certain ways. Projective tests are used by psychoanalysts to try to see what is in a person's unconscious.

5. **(B)** Juan is projecting. Instead of acknowledging the feelings he has toward Sally, he views Sally as having those feelings toward him. Were Juan to displace his feelings, he would express love for someone else or something else. Juan could sublimate by directing his energies toward honing his ice hockey skills or writing poetry. Finally, were Juan to deny his crush, when asked about it, he would continue to deny it.

6. **(C)** A task that requires groups to cooperate is an example of a superordinate goal. Such superordinate goals are effective in breaking down hostility between groups. Contact between antagonistic groups without superordinate goals is less successful, and simply avoiding members of the other group is unlikely to decrease the intergroup hostility. Although guest speakers may be able to influence the group members' attitudes, they will be less effective than the use of superordinate goals.

7. **(A)** Tanya made a large request and, when refused, came back with a smaller, more reasonable sounding request. This compliance strategy is known as door-in-the-face. Had Tanya brought her teacher an apple and then made her request, she would have been attempting to capitalize on norms of reciprocity, the idea that one good turn deserves another. Although Tanya is, in fact, attempting to broker a compromise and engage in some bargaining, the strategy she used has a more specific, psychological name.

8. **(D)** Your failure to consider the role of situational factors in explaining your new neighbor's knowledge of ancient Greece is known as the fundamental attribution error. The self-fulfilling prophecy effect is when one person's expectations affect another person's behavior. Pluralistic ignorance is the tendency to look to others for hints about how one is supposed to act in certain situations. Confirmation bias is the tendency to focus on information that supports one's initial ideas.

9. **(A)** Janine is experiencing cognitive dissonance. The combination of her hatred of the color orange and her ownership of a lot of orange clothing results in a tension called cognitive dissonance. It will motivate her to reduce the tension by either changing her opinion of orange or radically altering her wardrobe. All of the other terms are made up.

10. **(B)** The students in the school are evidencing self-serving bias, which is the tendency to take more credit for good outcomes than bad ones. When the football team wins, they want to identify with them and therefore say "We are awesome." When that same team loses, the students distance themselves from the players, explaining that "They were terrible." Fundamental attribution error is a different attributional bias. It explains

that people overestimate the role of personal factors when explaining other people's behavior. The self-fulfilling prophecy effect is the finding that people's expectations about others can influence the behavior of those others. The false consensus effect is another example of an attributional bias. It says that people overestimate the number of people who share their beliefs.

11. **(B)** A prejudice is an attitude, while discrimination involves an action. Santiago has a negative attitude or prejudice toward cheerleaders. Billy and Mr. Tamp are engaging in discrimination by acting differently toward different groups of people. Athena may be either really fast or overconfident, but she is not evidencing a prejudice.

12. **(A)** Self-disclosure is the process by which two people become closer by sharing intimate details about themselves. Deindividuation is when people in a group lose their self-restraint due to arousal and anonymity. In-group bias is the preference that people show for members of their own groups. Open communication, although healthy in a relationship, does not describe this specific exchange.

13. **(C)** By dividing his students into groups, Mr. Simpson fostered the development of in-group and out-group bias, the belief that members of one's own group are superior to members of other groups. Although Jody's aggressive behavior cannot be fully explained by Mr. Simpson's grouping, the fact that he attacks only members of other groups suggests that out-group bias may play a

role. Group polarization is the tendency of groups to take more extreme positions than those taken by their individual members. Since Jody acts alone and not as part of a group, his aggression cannot be seen as an example of deindividuation. Superordinate goals are helpful in reducing conflict between groups by making the groups' success contingent upon their cooperation.

14. **(A)** Social facilitation is when people perform a well-practiced task better when other people are present. The varsity players are good free throw shooters, and the presence of other people is likely to improve their performance. Groupthink is the tendency of groups to make poor decisions under conditions of high pressure because people are afraid to speak up and oppose what appears to be the group consensus. Conformity is when individuals change their behavior to fit in with a group. Group polarization is when groups make more extreme decisions than their members would have made separately.

15. **(B)** The range is the highest score minus the lowest score: 19 (70 – 51) for free throws made in practice and 16 (76 – 60) for free throws made during games. The median (middle number when ordered from high to low or vice versa) and mean (numerical average) are both higher in the game distribution. Neither distribution has a mode—the most commonly occurring value—because each value appears only once in each distribution.

UNIT 5

Mental and Physical Health

This unit addresses psychological disorders and treatment of mental health issues as well as their opposite: psychological health. Although there are many types of psychologists, including social psychologists, developmental psychologists, and cognitive psychologists, the largest group of psychologists are clinicians. Clinical psychologists are concerned with how psychological disorders are defined and diagnosed and with what treatments are recommended for these disorders. You will find most of the content from this unit in two chapters in the textbook you use for your AP Psychology class: psychological disorders and treatment.

16

Health Psychology

Learning Objectives

In this chapter, you will learn about:

→ Stress
→ Positive psychology

Key Terms

- Eustress
- Distress
- Stressors
- General adaptation syndrome (GAS)
- Alarm reaction
- Resistance
- Exhaustion
- Hypertension
- Immune suppression

- Tend-and-befriend theory
- Emotion-focused coping
- Positive psychology
- Happiness
- Subjective well-being
- Virtues
- Wisdom
- Courage

- Humanity
- Justice
- Temperance
- Transcendence
- Well-being
- Gratitude
- Resilience
- Post-traumatic growth

Overview

Health is an important area of interest for psychologists. Psychological factors can affect physical factors as well as mental ones, and psychologists study how to encourage people to live healthy lives, manage stress, grow emotionally, and deal with mental illness.

Stress

You may have noticed that many of the examples used to describe emotional theories involved stressful experiences. Stress and emotion are intimately connected concepts. Psychologists study stress not only to further our understanding of motivation and emotion but also to help us with problems caused by stress. Stress can be positive and motivating (**eustress**) as well as negative and debilitating (**distress**). The term stress can refer to either certain life events (**stressors**) or how we react to these changes in the environment (stress reactions). Studies try to describe our reactions to stress and identify factors that influence how we react to stressors.

Measuring Stress

Psychologists Thomas Holmes and Richard Rahe designed one of the first instruments to measure stress. Their social readjustment rating scale (SRRS) measured stress using life change units (LCUs). A person taking the SRRS reported changes in her or his life, such as selling a home or changing jobs. Different changes in life were assigned different LCUs; making a career change would be counted as more LCUs than moving to a new apartment. Any major life change increases the score on the SRRS. An event usually considered to be positive, like getting married, counts for as many or more LCUs as a negative event like being fired. A person who scored very high on the SRRS is more likely to have stress-related diseases than a person with a low score. Other researchers have designed more sophisticated measures of stress that take into account individual perceptions of how stressful events are and whether the stresses are pleasant or unpleasant. These more precise measures of stress show an even higher correlation with disease than the original stress measures did.

General Adaptation Syndrome

Hans Selye's **general adaptation syndrome (GAS)** describes the general response humans and other animals have to a stressful event. Our response pattern to many different physical and emotional stressors is very consistent. Table 16.1 shows the stages described by Selye's GAS theory.

Table 16.1 Stages Described by General Adaptation Syndrome

Alarm reaction	Our heart rate increases, and blood is diverted away from other body functions to muscles that are needed to react. Our body readies itself to meet the challenge through activation of the sympathetic nervous system.
Resistance	Our body remains physiologically ready (high heart rate, and so on). Hormones are released to maintain this state of readiness. If the resistance stage lasts too long, our body can deplete its resources.
Exhaustion	Our parasympathetic nervous system returns our physiological state to normal. We can be more vulnerable to disease in this stage, especially if our resources were depleted by an extended resistance stage.

Selye's model explains some of the documented problems associated with extended periods of stress. Excessive stress can contribute to both physical diseases, such as some forms of ulcers and heart conditions, and emotional difficulties, such as depression. Our bodies can remain ready for a challenge for only so long before our resources are depleted, making us vulnerable to disease due to exhaustion. Prolonged or chronic stress can cause **hypertension** (high blood pressure) and **immune suppression** through decreasing the body's ability to produce white blood cells to fight off infection.

Managing Stress

Psychological researchers also investigate other methods people use to manage stress in their lives. Researchers are exploring two more recent techniques:

- **Tend-and-befriend theory**—Some people successfully manage stress by actively seeking ways to tend to their own self-care needs and attend to the needs of friends and family members. These meaningful social connection activities with others can help reduce stress.
- **Emotion-focused coping**—Some people use specific stress management techniques such as meditation/mindfulness exercises, breathing techniques, or combining these stress management techniques with medications prescribed by clinical psychologists.

Perceived Control

Various studies show that a perceived lack of control over events exacerbates the harmful effects of stress. Rats given control over the duration of electric shocks are less likely to get ulcers than rats without this control even if both groups of rats receive the same amount of shocks overall. A patient given control over the flow of morphine will report better pain control than a patient given mandated levels of morphine even though both patients get the same amount of morphine overall. Control over events tends to lessen stress, while a perceived lack of control generally makes the event more stressful.

Positive Psychology

The field of **positive psychology** emerged in the 1990s to counter what some saw as the overly negative focus of psychology on human error, weakness, and sickness. Positive psychology shares the optimistic focus of humanistic psychology but is committed to supporting its theories with empirical evidence from research studies. This area of research includes a variety of interests. In general, though, positive psychology researchers investigate how humans can flourish, maximize their potential, achieve **happiness**, and improve the quality of our lives. One area studied by positive psychologists is **subjective well-being**, which is a sense of how satisfied a person is with their life overall.

Positive psychology researchers investigate how aspects of personality they call character strengths or virtues can be measured and how using these strengths relates to life satisfaction and achievement. These researchers identify six core **virtues** that seem to be valued across all major religions and philosophies: wisdom, courage, humanity, justice, temperance, and transcendence. **Wisdom** is associated not with having learned a lot of information but with being able to use that information creatively, being open-minded, and retaining curiosity. **Courage** is described as including persistence and integrity as well as bravery. **Humanity** requires an appreciation of, kindness toward, and interest in others. The virtue of **justice** involves striving to be a socially responsible citizen of our world and actively striving to improve the world. The word **temperance** means moderation, and this virtue eschews excess and encourages self-control. Finally, **transcendence** involves seeing beyond oneself and valuing one's connection with the world, including nature, beauty, and hope for the future.

Another positive psychology research area is **well-being** and **gratitude**. Well-being refers to our perception of how effectively we function in our personal lives and our role in the groups to which we belong. Well-being is an overall perception of the quality of our lives. Some research indicates a relationship between well-being and gratitude. Practicing gratitude (by expressing thankfulness toward others verbally or in writing) is associated with increases in our perceptions of happiness and satisfaction in life (increases in well-being). One recommended practice involves keeping a gratitude journal in which a person would record things for which they are thankful.

Another important positive psychology research area is **resilience**. Studies indicate that some people are more able to adapt effectively when faced with trauma and extreme stress and that some people experience post-traumatic growth after these intensely negative experiences. These researchers investigate factors related to why some people are more resilient when they experience tragedy and what all of us can do to gain more resilience.

Still, positive psychologists acknowledge that bad things happen. However, even in these situations, they stay focused on how people can flourish. One concept positive psychologists talk about with regard to stress and difficult situations is **post-traumatic growth**, which is the ability to construct a meaningful experience in response to a period of trauma.

17

Psychological Disorders

Learning Objectives

In this chapter, you will learn about:

→ Defining psychological disorders
→ Categories of disorders
→ The advantage and disadvantages of diagnostic labels

Key Terms

- Disfunction
- Distress
- Deviance
- *Diagnostic and Statistical Manual of Mental Disorders* (DSM)
- Adverse childhood experiences (ACEs)
- Maladaptive learned associations
- Sociocultural perspective
- Racism
- Sexism
- Ageism
- Discrimination
- Biological perspective
- Biopsychosocial view
- Diathesis-stress model
- Stressors
- Eclectic
- Psychoanalytic/ psychodynamic perspective
- Humanistic perspective

- Behavioral perspective
- Cognitive perspective
- Sociocultural perspective
- Biological/biomedical perspective
- Autism spectrum disorder
- Attention-deficit/ hyperactivity disorder (ADHD)
- Anxiety disorders
- Specific phobia
- Arachnophobia
- Agoraphobia
- Social anxiety disorder
- Taijin kyofusho
- Generalized anxiety disorder
- Panic disorder
- Panic attacks
- Ataque de nervios
- Acrophobia
- Dissociation
- Dissociative amnesia

- Dissociative identity disorder
- Dissociative disorders
- Major depressive disorder
- Persistent depressive disorder
- Learned helplessness
- Bipolar disorder
- Bipolar I disorder
- Bipolar II disorder
- Mania
- Schizophrenia spectrum disorders
- Disorganized thinking
- Disorganized speech
- Disorganized motor behavior
- Delusions
- Delusions of persecution
- Delusions of grandeur
- Hallucinations
- Word salad
- Flat affect
- Schizophrenia

- Catatonia
- Positive symptoms
- Negative symptoms
- Catatonic stupor
- Dopamine hypothesis
- Cluster A
- Paranoid
- Schizoid
- Schizotypal personality disorders
- Cluster B
- Borderline personality disorders

- Antisocial personality disorder
- Narcissistic personality disorder
- Histrionic personality disorder
- Cluster C
- Avoidant personality disorder
- Dependent personality disorder
- Obsessive-compulsive personality disorder

- Obsessive-compulsive disorder (OCD)
- Obsessions
- Hoarding disorder
- Post-traumatic stress disorder (PTSD)
- Flashbacks
- Anorexia nervosa
- Bulimia
- Substance-related and addictive disorders

Overview

Psychological disorders may manifest in a person's behavior and/or thoughts. The field of psychological disorders (or abnormal psychology) encompasses the study of relatively common problems such as depression, substance abuse, and learning difficulties as well as the study of fairly rare, and particularly severe, disorders such as bipolar disorder and schizophrenia.

Defining Psychological Disorders

To identify a psychological disorder, we must first define it. This task is surprisingly difficult. Disorders are often characterized by causing dysfunction, by resulting in distress, and as being deviant (different) from what is typical. A few examples may help illustrate these ideas:

- **Dysfunction**—Someone who has a fear of open spaces (agoraphobia) and is thus unable to leave their home will likely have trouble functioning in terms of employment and social relationships.
- **Distress**—A disorder like depression is distressing both to the people who suffer from it and their loved ones.
- **Deviance**—Behavior or feelings that are deviant are unusual, which means they are not shared by many members of the population. In the United States, having visions is atypical, whereas in some other cultures it occurs more commonly. Thus, in the United States, having visions is likely to be seen as a symptom of a psychological disorder.

Another important point is that the term insane, which is often used by laypeople to describe psychological disorders in general, is not a medical term. Rather, insanity is a legal term. The reason behind the legal definition of insanity is to differentiate between those people who can be held entirely responsible for their crimes (the sane) and those people who, because of a psychological disorder, cannot be held fully responsible for their actions. When defendants plead not guilty by reason of insanity (NGRI), they are asking that the court acquit them due to psychological factors.

An important question is how psychologists determine whether or not someone has a psychological disorder. To do so, psychologists use resources developed through practice and periodically updated. The World Health Organization (WHO) created the **International Classification of Mental Disorders (ICD)** for this purpose, and the American Psychiatric Association uses the *Diagnostic and Statistical Manual of Mental Disorders* (DSM). The DSM, as its name suggests, provides a way for psychologists to diagnose their patients. The DSM-5, which is the most recent edition, contains the symptoms of everything currently considered to be a psychological disorder.

These resources do not include much discussion of the causes (also called etiologies) or treatments of the various disorders, because adherents to each of the psychological perspectives disagree (see Table 17.1). For example, psychodynamic theorists, who were discussed in Chapter 14 "Personality," locate the cause of psychological disturbances in unconscious conflicts often caused by **adverse childhood experiences (ACEs)**. However, behaviorists assert that psychological problems result from the person's history of reinforcement. Cognitive theorists locate the source of psychological disorders in **maladaptive learned associations**, while humanistic psychologists view the root of such disorders in a person's feelings, self-esteem, and self-concept. The **sociocultural perspective** holds that social ills such as **racism**, **sexism**, **ageism**, and poverty, and the **discrimination** that result from these prejudices, lie at the heart of psychological disorders. Finally, the biomedical model (or **biological perspective**) sees psychological disorders as caused by biological factors such as hormonal or neurotransmitter imbalances or by differences in brain structure. Biomedical psychologists believe that many psychological disorders are associated with genetic abnormalities that may lead to the physiological abnormalities described above. However, the differences do not have to occur at the genetic level.

Many psychologists believe that disorders are caused by the interaction of different factors. For example, the **biopsychosocial view** is that problems likely result from the interplay of biological, psychological, and social factors. Another theory is the **diathesis-stress model**. According to this model, environmental **stressors** can provide circumstances under which a biological predisposition for illness can express itself. This theory helps explain why even people with identical genetic makeups. For example, monozygotic (identical) twins do not always suffer from the same disorders.

Psychologists who do not subscribe strictly to one perspective or another are known as **eclectic**. This means that they accept and use ideas from a number of different perspectives.

Table 17.1 Different Perspectives on the Causes of Psychological Disorders

Perspective	Cause of Disorder
Psychodynamic	Internal, unconscious conflicts
Humanistic	Failure to strive toward one's potential or being out of touch with one's feelings
Behavioral	Reinforcement history, the environment
Cognitive	Irrational, dysfunctional thoughts or ways of thinking
Sociocultural	Dysfunctional society
Biological/biomedical	Genetic predispositions, neurotransmitter imbalances

Categories of Disorders

The DSM-5 lists hundreds of different psychological disorders, most of which lie beyond the scope of your introductory course. We will deal with the disorders you are most likely to encounter on the AP Psychology exam.

After a short explanation of each type of disorder, we will briefly discuss how psychologists from a few of the various perspectives might view the cause of some of the disorders within the category. Keep in mind that many psychologists do not strictly adhere to any one perspective.

Neurocognitive Disorders

One example of the kinds of disorders in the DSM-5 is neurodevelopmental disorders. Some of these developmental disorders deal with deviations from typical social development. Children with **autism spectrum disorder** seek out less social and emotional contact than do other children and are less likely to seek out parental support when distressed. In addition, people with autism spectrum disorder tend to be hypersensitive to sensory stimulation. They often exhibit intense interest in objects not viewed as interesting by most people (e.g., rubber bands) and often engage in simple, repetitive behaviors (e.g., flipping things).

Other neurodevelopmental disorders involve difficulties in terms of developing skills. **Attention-deficit/ hyperactivity disorder (ADHD)** is one example. A child with ADHD may have difficulty paying attention or sitting still. People with ADHD are not incapable of focusing; in fact, they hyperfocus on things of interest to them. Children with ADHD may spend hours working on building a Lego creation but be unable to follow their parents' request to get dressed, brush their teeth, and bring their backpack downstairs. This disorder is diagnosed more frequently in boys. Critics suggest that the more active behavior typical of young boys (regardless of whether the cause of ADHD is biological, environmental, or a combination of the two) results in an overdiagnosis of this problem. On the other hand, the case can be made that ADHD is underdiagnosed in girls who may sit quietly in their classrooms but nonetheless struggle to focus on the teachers' lessons.

The DSM-5 also discusses neurocognitive disorders, the most well-known of which may be Alzheimer's disease. Alzheimer's is a form of dementia, a deterioration of cognitive abilities, often seen most dramatically in memory. The DSM-5 includes a diagnosis for both major and mild forms of neurocognitive disorders.

Anxiety Disorders

Anxiety disorders, as their name suggests, share a common symptom of anxiety. We will discuss three anxiety disorders: phobias, generalized anxiety disorder, and panic disorder.

A simple or **specific phobia** is an intense unwarranted fear of a situation or an object such as claustrophobia (fear of enclosed spaces) or **arachnophobia** (fear of spiders). Another type of phobia is **agoraphobia**. Agoraphobia is a fear of open, public spaces. People with severe agoraphobia may be afraid to venture out of their homes at all. Phobias are classified as anxiety disorders because contact with the feared object or situation results in anxiety. **Social anxiety disorder**, formerly known as social phobia, is a fear of a situation in which one could embarrass oneself in public, such as when eating in a restaurant or giving a lecture. Sociocultural impacts on disorders can be evidenced by the presence of certain issues that manifest only or in particular ways in certain cultures. For instance, **taijin kyofusho** is overwhelmingly diagnosed in Japanese people. It is a type of social anxiety that involves concern that one's body is displeasing to others. A person who suffers from **generalized anxiety disorder**, often referred to as GAD, experiences constant, low-level anxiety. Such a person constantly feels nervous and out of sorts. On the other hand, someone with **panic disorder** suffers from acute episodes of intense anxiety without any apparent provocation. **Panic attacks** tend to increase in frequency, and people often suffer additional anxiety due to anticipating the attacks. In Caribbean cultures, similar symptoms are labeled as **ataque de nervios**.

Theories About the Cause of Anxiety Disorders

We will follow the discussion of psychological disorders with a brief description of how adherents from several perspectives view the etiology of such disorders. Because many introductory psychology texts do not deal with the etiology of specific disorders, we will be selective and focus on the information most likely to appear on the AP exam.

Psychodynamic theorists see psychological disorders as caused by unresolved, unconscious conflicts. Anxiety is viewed as the result of conflicts among the desires of the id, ego, and superego. For instance, a young woman's repressed sexual attraction to her father may cause a conflict between her id, which desires the father, and her superego, which forbids such a relationship. Anxiety disorders could be the outward manifestation of this internal conflict.

Behaviorists believe all behaviors are learned. Therefore, they assert that anxiety disorders are learned. Consider **acrophobia**, the fear of heights, as an example. Behaviorists would say that someone who has acrophobia learned the fear response. This learning could happen through classical conditioning, operant conditioning, or some type of cognitive learning. (See Chapter 12 "Learning" for more information about basic learning principles.) Suppose three-year-old Pablo went with his family to visit the Space Needle in Seattle, Washington. While on the observation deck, Pablo got separated from his family and was found hours later crying hysterically in the gift shop. Ever since then, Pablo has been terrified of heights. In this example, behaviorists would say that Pablo learned through classical conditioning to associate heights with the fear that resulted from losing his family.

Cognitive theorists believe that disorders result from dysfunctional ways of thinking. Therefore, they would attribute an anxiety disorder to an unhealthy and irrational way of thinking and/or specific irrational thoughts. For instance, someone with GAD may have an unrealistically high standard for his or her own behavior. Because the person believes, irrationally, that he or she must always excel at everything he or she does, the person feels constant anxiety stemming from the impossibility of meeting this goal.

Somatic Symptom and Related Disorders

The DSM-5 renamed somatoform disorders as somatic symptom and related disorders. The number of these disorders included in the DSM-5 has been reduced and reflects a growing sense that an absence of an identified medical cause is not necessarily indicative of a psychological problem.

Somatic symptom disorders occur when a person manifests a psychological problem through a physiological symptom. In other words, such a person experiences a physical problem in the absence of any identifiable physical cause. An example of such a disorder is conversion disorder. People who have conversion disorder report the existence of a severe physical problem such as paralysis or blindness, and they will, in fact, be unable to move their arms or see. However, again, no biological reason for such problems can be identified.

Theories About the Cause of Somatic Symptom Disorders

Psychodynamic theorists would assert that somatic symptom disorders are merely outward manifestations of unresolved unconscious conflicts. Behaviorists would say that people with somatic symptom disorders are being reinforced for their behavior. For instance, someone experiencing blindness due to conversion disorder may avoid unpleasant tasks like working.

Dissociative Disorders

Dissociative disorders involve a disruption in conscious processes; **dissociation** involves a break or separation from memories and thoughts or even a sense of who the person is. Dissociative amnesia and dissociative identity disorder (DID) are classified as dissociative disorders. **Dissociative amnesia** is when a person cannot remember things and no physiological basis for the disruption in memory can be identified. Biologically induced amnesia is called organic amnesia.

Dissociative identity disorder, formerly known as multiple personality disorder, is when a person has several personalities rather than one integrated personality. Someone with DID can have any number of personalities. The different personalities can represent many different ages and both sexes. Often, two of the personalities will be the opposite of each other. People with DID commonly have a history of sexual abuse or some other terrible childhood trauma.

Theories About the Cause of Dissociative Disorders

Psychodynamic theorists believe that **dissociative disorders** result when an extremely traumatic event has been so thoroughly repressed that a split in consciousness results. Behaviorists posit that people who have experienced trauma simply find not thinking about it to be rewarding, thus producing amnesia or, in extreme cases, DID.

Interestingly, cases of DID are rare outside of the United States, where the number increased dramatically in the last century as cases became more publicized. Coupled with the growing belief on the part of many psychologists that people do not engage in repression, these facts have led many to question whether DID is a legitimate psychological disorder. Critics suggest that some people diagnosed with DID may have been led to role-play the disorder inadvertently as a result of their therapists' questions (e.g., "Is there a part of you that feels differently?") and media portrayals.

Depressive Disorders

Someone with a mood or affective disorder experiences extreme or inappropriate emotions. **Major depressive disorder**, also known as unipolar depression, is the most common mood disorder and is often referred to as the common cold of all psychological disorders. Although we all feel unhappy now and again, most of us do not suffer from major depressive disorder. The DSM-5 outlines the symptoms that must be present for such a diagnosis. One key factor is the length of the depressive episode. People who are clinically depressed remain unhappy for more than two weeks in the absence of a clear reason. Other common symptoms of depression include loss of appetite, fatigue, change in sleeping patterns, lack of interest in typically enjoyable activities, and feelings of worthlessness. **Persistent depressive disorder** is diagnosed when the depression is long-lasting but not as severe. Finally, some people experience depression but only during certain times of the year, usually winter when there is less sunlight. Seasonal affective disorder (SAD) is the resulting diagnosis. SAD is often treated with light therapy.

Theories About the Cause of Depressive Disorders

Psychodynamic theorists may view depression as the product of anger directed inward or an overly punitive super-ego. Learning theorists view the mood disorder as bringing about some kind of reinforcement such as attention or sympathy.

Aaron Beck, a cognitive theorist, believed that depression results from unreasonably negative ideas that people have about themselves, their world, and their futures. Beck calls these three components the cognitive triad. Another way that cognitive psychologists look at the cause of depression is by exploring the kind of attributions that people make about their experiences. An attribution is an explanation of cause. For instance, if Jonas fails a math test, he may attribute his failure to lack of studying, stupidity, his teacher, or a host of other causes. Pessimistic attributional styles seem more likely to promote depression. Jonas may attribute his failure to an internal (I am bad at math) or an external (The class is difficult) cause. He may attribute his failure to a global (I am bad at all subjects) or a specific (I have trouble with trigonometry) cause. Finally, Jonas may attribute his failure to a stable (I will always be bad at math) or to an unstable (I had a bad day) cause. People who tend to make internal, global, and stable attributions for bad events are more likely to be depressed. Often, these same people tend to make external, specific, and unstable attributions when good things happen to them.

Many theories about the cause of depression combine a cognitive and a behavioral component. An example of these social-cognitive or cognitive behavioral theories is Martin Seligman's idea of **learned helplessness**. Seligman conducted an experiment in which dogs received electric shocks. One group of dogs was able to terminate the shock by pressing a button with their noses, whereas the helpless group had no way to stop the shocks. In a second phase of the experiment, both groups of dogs were put in a situation in which they could easily escape electric shocks by moving to another part of the experimental chamber. While the dogs that were able to stop the shock in the first phase of the experiment quickly learned to move to the area where they would not be shocked, the other group of dogs just hunkered down and endured the shocks. Seligman suggested that due to their lack of ability to control their fate in the first phase of the experiment, these dogs had learned to act helpless.

Seligman further posited that humans, too, might suffer from learned helplessness. Depression has been found to correlate positively with feelings of learned helplessness. Learned helplessness is when one's prior experiences have caused that person to view himself or herself as unable to control aspects of the future that are controllable. This belief may result in passivity and depression. When undesirable things occur, that individual feels unable to improve the situation and therefore becomes depressed.

A growing body of evidence suggests that a biological component to affective disorders exists. Low levels of serotonin, a neurotransmitter, have been linked with major depressive disorder. People who suffer from bipolar disorder have more receptors for acetylcholine, also a neurotransmitter, in their brains and skin. Other researchers have suggested that low levels of norepinephrine are associated with depression. Both unipolar depression and bipolar disorder often respond to somatic therapies (see Chapter 18 "Treatment of Psychological Disorders").

This suggests that these disorders are caused, at least partially, by biological factors. In addition, both major depressive disorder and bipolar disorder seem to run in families, a finding that can also be interpreted as indicative of a genetic component to their etiologies.

Bipolar and Related Disorders

Unlike unipolar depression, **bipolar disorder**, formerly known as manic depression, usually involves both depressed and manic episodes. The depressed episodes involve all the symptoms discussed above. People experience manic episodes in different ways, but they usually involve feelings of high energy. Some sufferers feel a heightened sense of confidence and power, while others simply feel anxious and irritable. Even though some people feel an inflated sense of well-being during the manic period, they usually engage in excessively risky and poorly thought-out behavior that ultimately has negative consequences for them. Psychologists now distinguish between **bipolar I disorder** and **bipolar II disorder**. The major difference is that bipolar II involves at least one episode of hypomania, which is a less extreme level of **mania** than in bipolar I. A small number of people appear to experience mania without depression.

Schizophrenia Spectrum Disorders

Schizophrenia spectrum disorders are probably the most severe and debilitating of the psychological disorders. They tend to strike people who are entering young adulthood. The fundamental symptom of schizophrenia is disordered, distorted thinking often demonstrated through delusions, hallucinations, **disorganized thinking**, **disorganized speech**, and/or **disorganized motor behavior**.

    Delusions are beliefs that have no basis in reality. If I believed that I was going to win a Nobel Prize in literature for writing this book, I would be experiencing a delusion. Common delusions include:

- **Delusions of persecution**—the belief that people are out to get you.
- **Delusions of grandeur**—the belief that you enjoy greater power and influence than you do, that you are the president of the United States or a Nobel Prize–winning author.

    Hallucinations are perceptions in the absence of any sensory stimulation. If I keep thinking I see newspaper headlines, "Weseley Wins Nobel," and hordes of autograph seekers outside my window, then I am suffering from hallucinations.

    Schizophrenics often evidence some odd uses of language. They may make up their own words (neologisms) or string together a series of nonsense words that rhyme (clang associations). As a result, it may be difficult to understand what they are trying to communicate, and the resultant speech has been described as **word salad**. In addition, people with schizophrenia often evidence inappropriate affect. For instance, they might laugh in response to hearing someone has died. Alternatively, they may consistently have essentially no emotional response at all (**flat affect**).

    Some schizophrenics suffer from **catatonia**, a motor problem. They may remain motionless in strange postures for hours at a time, move jerkily and quickly for no apparent reason, or alternate between the two. When motionless, catatonic schizophrenics usually evidence waxy flexibility. That is, they allow their body to be moved into any alternative shape and will then hold that new pose.

    Schizophrenic symptoms are often divided into two types: positive and negative. **Positive symptoms** refer to excesses in behavior, thought, or mood such as neologisms and hallucinations, whereas **negative symptoms** correspond to deficits such as flat affect or **catatonic stupor**.

TIP

People often confuse schizophrenia with DID. Schizophrenics *do not* have split personalities. *Schism* does mean "break," but the break referred to in the term schizophrenia is a break from reality and not a break within a person's consciousness.

Theories About the Cause of Schizophrenic Disorders

One of the most popular ideas about the cause of schizophrenia is biological and is called the **dopamine hypothesis**. The basic idea behind the dopamine hypothesis is that high levels of dopamine seem to be associated with schizophrenia. The evidence for this link includes the findings detailed below:

- Antipsychotic drugs used to treat schizophrenia result in lower dopamine levels and a decrease in the disordered thought and behavior that is the hallmark of schizophrenia. However, extensive use of these drugs may also cause negative side effects such as muscle tremors and stiffness, a problem known as tardive dyskinesia.
- Parkinson's disease, characterized by muscle stiffness and tremors not unlike tardive dyskinesia, is treated with a drug called L-Dopa that acts to increase dopamine levels. When given in excess, L-Dopa causes schizophrenic-like distortions in thought.

More evidence suggests a biological basis for schizophrenia as well. Enlarged brain ventricles are associated with schizophrenia, as are brain asymmetries. Furthermore, a genetic predisposition seems to exist for schizophrenia. People who are related to schizophrenics suffer from the disorder at an increased rate, and the closer the relationship is, the higher the incidence of the disorder. The incidence of schizophrenia in the general population is 1 in 100, but it rises to nearly 1 in 2 among identical twins whose co-twins are schizophrenic. As is the case with most disorders, several genes have been identified that seem to play a role in predisposing people to schizophrenia. Some research has suggested that negative symptoms are linked to genetic factors, whereas positive symptoms tend to be related to abnormalities in dopamine levels.

Not surprisingly, not all psychologists agree that schizophrenia has a biological basis. Some people believe that certain kinds of environments may cause or increase the likelihood of developing schizophrenia. One commonly suggested cognitive behavioral cause is the existence of double binds. A double bind is when a person is given contradictory messages. If Sally's parents demand she get perfect grades and spend her free time studying but also constantly ask her why she doesn't have more friends, Sally is experiencing a double bind. People who live in environments full of such conflicting messages may develop distorted ways of thinking due to the impossibility of rationally resolving their experiences.

Personality Disorders

Personality disorders are well-established, maladaptive ways of behaving that negatively affect people's ability to function. Personality disorders typically manifest in early adulthood or adolescence and remain throughout people's lives. They are divided into three types or clusters.

Cluster A is associated with suspicious or eccentric behaviors and includes **paranoid**, **schizoid**, and **schizotypal personality disorders**. People who suffer from these disorders tend to be suspicious and distant from others.

Cluster B is marked by impulsive or emotional, dramatic, and erratic tendencies and includes antisocial, histrionic, narcissistic, and **borderline personality disorders**. People with **antisocial personality disorder** have little regard for other people's feelings. They view the world as a hostile place where people need to look out for themselves. Not surprisingly, criminals seem to manifest a high incidence of antisocial personality disorder. Borderline personality disorder can result in unstable social relationships; people who suffer from it can fear abandonment and switch back and forth between how they feel about and act toward others. **Narcissistic personality disorder** involves seeing oneself as the center of the universe (*narcissism* means "self-love"), and **histrionic personality disorder** connotes overly dramatic behavior (histrionics).

TIP

Although your vocabulary will generally help you figure out what psychological terms mean, sometimes it will mislead you. For instance, many students incorrectly assume that people who suffer from antisocial personality disorder are merely unfriendly. In reality, as explained above, people with antisocial personality disorder are insensitive to others and thus often act in ways that bring pain to others.

Anxiety is the hallmark of **Cluster C**, which includes avoidant, dependent, and obsessive-compulsive personality disorders. People with **avoidant personality disorder** are plagued by feelings of inadequacy, which can lead them to avoid social situations and be very sensitive to criticism. People with **dependent personality disorder** rely too much on the attention and help of others. Those who suffer from **obsessive-compulsive personality disorder** may be overly concerned with certain thoughts and behaviors and may have a tendency toward perfectionism.

Obsessive-Compulsive and Related Disorders

Obsessive-compulsive disorder (OCD) is when persistent, unwanted thoughts (**obsessions**) cause someone to feel the need (**compulsion**) to engage in a particular action. For instance, a common obsession concerns cleanliness. A man experiencing this obsession compulsion might be plagued with constant worries that his environment is dirty and full of germs. These thoughts might drive him to wash his hands and shower repeatedly, even to the extent that he is able to do virtually nothing else. Obsessions result in anxiety, and this anxiety is reduced when the person performs the compulsive behavior. For this reason, OCD used to be classified as an anxiety disorder. However, the DSM-5 has created a separate classification for OCD and related disorders, including **hoarding disorder** and body dysmorphic disorder (an obsession with perceived defects related to one's appearance).

Post-traumatic stress disorder (PTSD) is one example of this type of disorder included in the AP Psychology curriculum. PTSD usually involves **flashbacks** or nightmares following a person's involvement in or observation of an extremely troubling event such as a war or natural disaster. Memories of the event cause anxiety.

Paraphilic Disorders

Paraphilias, or psychosexual disorders, are marked by the sexual attraction to an object, a person, or an activity not usually seen as sexual. For instance, attraction to children is called pedophilia, to animals is called zoophilia, and to objects, such as shoes, is called fetishism. Someone who becomes sexually aroused by watching others engage in some kind of sexual behavior is a voyeur, someone who is aroused by having pain inflicted upon him or her is a masochist, and someone who is aroused by inflicting pain on someone else is a sadist.

Interestingly, the incidence of paraphilias is much higher in men than in women.

Feeding and Eating Disorders

Feeding and eating disorders are another kind of psychological problem classified in the DSM-5. The relevant disorders we most often hear about include **anorexia nervosa**, **bulimia**, and binge-eating disorder. The basic symptoms that result in a diagnosis of anorexia nervosa are being at significantly low weight for one's age and size, an intense fear of fat and food, and a distorted body image. Anorexia nervosa, which predominates in girls and young women, is essentially a form of self-starvation. Bulimia shares similar features with anorexia nervosa such as a fear of food and fat and a distorted body image. However, bulimics do not lose as much of their body weight. Bulimia commonly involves a binge-purge cycle in which sufferers eat large quantities of food and then attempt to purge the food from their bodies by throwing up or using laxatives. Binge-eating disorder is thought to be the most commonly occurring eating disorder in the United States. It involves eating very large quantities of food in a short time while experiencing feelings of loss of control.

Substance-Related and Addictive Disorders

Another category of psychological disorders involves the use of substances such as alcohol and drugs. Use of such substances does not automatically mean one would be classified as having a disorder. **Substance-related and addictive disorders** is a diagnosis made when the use of such substances or behaviors, like gambling, regularly negatively affects a person's life.

> ## A CAUTIONARY NOTE
>
> The DSM provides psychologists with an invaluable tool by enabling them to diagnose their clients. However, keep in mind that diagnostic labels are not always correct and tend to outlast their usefulness.

The Advantages and Disadvantages of Diagnostic Labels

In 1978, David Rosenhan conducted a study in which he and several associates sought admission to a number of mental hospitals. All claimed that they had been hearing voices; that was the sole symptom they reported. All were admitted to the institutions as suffering from schizophrenia. At that time, they ceased reporting any unusual symptoms and behaved as they normally did. None of the researchers were exposed as imposters, and all ultimately left the institutions with the diagnosis of schizophrenia in remission. While in the institutions, the researchers' every behavior was interpreted as a sign of their disorder. The Rosenhan study, while flawed and widely critiqued, raises several important issues:

1. Should people who were once diagnosed with a psychological problem carry that diagnosis for the rest of their lives?
2. To what extent are disorders the product of a particular environment, and to what extent do they inhere in the individual?
3. What is the level of institutional care available if the imposters could go undetected for a period of days and, in some cases, weeks?

18

Treatment of Psychological Disorders

Learning Objectives

In this chapter, you will learn about:

→ Types of therapy
→ Kinds of therapists

Key Terms

- Patients
- Clients
- Psychodynamic therapy
- Hypnosis
- Free associate
- Dream interpretation
- Person-centered therapy
- Unconditional positive regard
- Active listening
- Applied behavior analysis (ABA)
- Counterconditioning
- Systematic desensitization
- Anxiety or fear hierarchy

- Exposure therapies
- Aversive therapy
- Token economy
- Cognitive restructuring
- Maladaptive thinking
- Cognitive triad
- Cognitive behavioral therapy (CBT)
- Rational emotive behavior therapy
- Psychoactive medications
- Psychotropic medications
- Antipsychotic medications
- Tardive dyskinesia
- Antidepressants

- Lithium
- Antianxiety drugs
- Biofeedback
- Transcranial magnetic stimulation (TMS)
- Electroconvulsive therapy (ECT)
- Psychosurgery
- Prefrontal lobotomy
- Respecting people's rights and dignity
- Fidelity
- Cultural humility
- Nonmaleficence
- Therapeutic alliance
- Evidence-based interventions

Overview

Just as there are many different views about the cause of mental disorders, many different beliefs exist about the appropriate way to treat psychological illness. All the methods of treatment, however, share a common purpose: to alter the client's behavior, thoughts, and/or feelings.

Types of Therapy

Clearly, people's beliefs about effective treatment are grounded in their ideas about the cause of the problem. Psychodynamic, humanistic, behavioral, and cognitive psychologists share a belief in the power of psychotherapy to treat mental disorders (see Table 18.1). On the other hand, psychologists who subscribe to a biomedical model assert that such problems require somatic treatments such as drugs. Psychotherapies, except for behavioral treatments, largely consist of talking to a psychologist. Behaviorists, as you know, believe that psychological problems result from the contingencies of reinforcement to which a person has been exposed. Therefore, behavioral therapy focuses on changing these contingencies.

Psychologists with a biomedical orientation generally refer to the people who come to them for help as **patients**. Other therapists, humanistic therapists in particular, prefer the term **clients**. In discussing the various types of therapy, we will follow these conventions.

Psychodynamic Therapy

Psychodynamic therapy grew out of Sigmund Freud's psychoanalytic approach. Psychoanalysis is a therapeutic technique developed by Sigmund Freud. A patient undergoing traditional psychoanalysis will usually lie on a couch while the therapist sits in a chair out of the patient's line of vision.

Psychodynamic theorists view the cause of disorders as unconscious conflicts. As a result, their focus is on identifying the underlying cause of the problem. Psychodynamic clinicians believe that other methods of therapy may succeed in ridding a client of a particular symptom but do not address the true problem. As a result, psychoanalysts assert that patients will suffer from symptom substitution. Symptom substitution is when, after a person has been successfully treated for one psychological disorder, that person begins to experience a new psychological problem. Psychodynamic therapists argue that a person's symptoms are the outward manifestations of deeper problems that can be cured only through analysis. Often, this approach entails a lengthy, and therefore expensive, course of therapy.

To delve into the unconscious minds of his patients, Freud developed several techniques including hypnosis, free association, and dream analysis. **Hypnosis** is an altered state of consciousness. When in this state, traditional psychoanalysts believe that people are less likely to repress troubling thoughts and can even recover childhood memories about early trauma. However, research has supported only the ability of hypnosis to aid in pain control and decrease anxiety.

More commonly, psychodynamic theorists might ask patients to **free associate**—to say whatever comes to mind without thinking. This technique is based on the idea that we all constantly censor what we say, thereby allowing us to hide some of our thoughts from ourselves. If we force ourselves to say whatever pops into our minds, we are more likely to reveal clues about what is really bothering us by eluding the ego's defenses. When psychodynamic clinicians use **dream interpretation**, they ask their patients to describe their dreams. Again, since the ego's defenses are relaxed during sleep, they hope the dreams will help the therapist see what is at the root of the patient's problem.

All three of these techniques rely heavily on the interpretations of the therapists and are criticized for their inherent subjectivity. In dream analysis, what the patient reports is called the manifest content of the dream. What is really of interest to the analyst is the latent or hidden content. The latent content of the dream is revealed only because of the therapist's interpretive work.

Sometimes patients may disagree with their therapists' interpretations. Psychodynamic theorists may see such objections as signs of resistance. Since analysis can be a painful process of coming to terms with deeply repressed, troubling thoughts, people are thought to try to protect themselves through resistance. In fact, a particularly strongly voiced disagreement to a therapist's suggestion is often viewed as an indication that the analyst is closing in on the source of the problem.

One final aspect of psychodynamic treatment involves transference. Transference is when, during therapy, patients begin to have strong feelings toward their therapists. Patients may think they are in love with their therapists, may view their therapists as parental figures, or may seethe with hatred toward their therapists. Psychodynamic psychologists believe that, in the process of therapy, patients often redirect strong emotions felt toward people with whom they have had troubling relationships (often their parents) onto their therapists. Analysts try to interpret their patients' transference as a further technique to reveal the source of the problem.

Psychodynamic treatments and the humanistic therapies that will be discussed in the next section are sometimes referred to as insight therapies. Insight therapies highlight the importance of the patients/clients gaining an understanding of their problems.

Humanistic Therapies

Humanistic therapies focus on helping people to understand and accept themselves and strive to self-actualize. Self-actualization means to reach one's highest potential. Humanistic psychologists view it as a powerful motivational goal. Humanistic therapists operate from the belief that people are innately good and possess free will. A belief that people have free will means that they can control their own destinies. Determinism is the opposite belief. It holds that people have no influence over what happens to them and that their choices are predetermined by forces outside of their control. Humanistic psychologists' belief in human goodness and free will leads these psychologists to assert that if people are supported and helped to recognize their goals, they will move toward self-fulfillment.

One of the best-known humanistic therapists is Carl Rogers. Rogers created **person-centered therapy**, also known as client-centered therapy. This therapeutic method hinges on the therapist providing the client with what Rogers termed **unconditional positive regard**. Unconditional positive regard is blanket acceptance and support of a person regardless of what the person says or does. Rogers believed that unconditional positive regard is essential to healthy development. People who have not experienced it may come to see themselves in the negative ways that others have made them feel. By providing unconditional positive regard, humanistic therapists seek to help their clients accept and take responsibility for themselves.

In stark contrast to the cognitive therapies to be discussed later, client-centered therapy—and humanistic therapies in general—are nondirective. In other words, Rogerian therapists do not tell their clients what to do but, rather, seek to help the clients choose a course of action for themselves. Often, client-centered therapists say very little. They encourage the clients to talk a lot about how they feel and sometimes mirror back those feelings to help clarify the feelings for the client. ("So, what I'm hearing you say is. . . .") This technique is known as **active listening**.

Another type of humanistic therapy is Gestalt therapy, developed by Fritz Perls. As we discussed in Chapter 7 "Perception," Gestalt psychologists emphasize the importance of the whole. These therapists encourage their clients to get in touch with their whole selves. For example, Gestalt therapists encourage their clients to explore feelings that they may not be aware of and emphasize the importance of body position and seemingly minute actions. These therapists want their clients to integrate all of their actions, feelings, and thoughts into a harmonious whole. Gestalt therapists also stress the importance of the present because one can best appreciate the totality of an experience as it occurs.

Existential therapies are humanistic therapies that focus on helping clients achieve a subjectively meaningful perception of their lives. Existential therapists see clients' difficulties as caused by the clients having lost or failed to develop a sense of purpose for their lives. Therefore, these therapists seek to support clients and help them formulate a vision of their lives as worthwhile.

Behavioral Therapies

Behaviorists believe that all behavior is learned. In Chapter 12 "Learning," we discussed various ways that people learn, including classical conditioning, operant conditioning, and modeling. Behaviorists base their therapies on these same learning principles. One behavioral approach, most used to help people with developmental disorders like autism spectrum disorder, is known as **applied behavior analysis (ABA)**. Therapists trained in ABA set up systems of reinforcement to help teach their clients how to be successful in the world. Behavioral therapies have also been shown to be effective in treating anxiety disorders. One technique is **counterconditioning**, a kind of classical conditioning in which an unpleasant conditioned response is replaced with a pleasant one. For instance, suppose Graham is afraid of going to the doctor and cries hysterically as soon as he enters the doctor's office. His mother might attempt to replace the conditioned response of crying with contentment by bringing Graham's favorite snacks and toys with them every time they go to the office.

One behaviorist method of treatment involving counterconditioning has had considerable success in helping people with anxiety disorders, especially phobias. It was developed by Joseph Wolpe and is called **systematic desensitization**. This process involves teaching the client to replace the feelings of anxiety with relaxation. The first step in systematic desensitization is teaching the client to relax. A variety of techniques can be used such as breathing exercises and meditation. Next the therapist and client work together to construct what is called an **anxiety or fear hierarchy**. An anxiety hierarchy is a rank-ordered list of what the client fears, starting with the least frightening and ending with the most frightening. In the process of in vivo desensitization, the client confronts the actual feared objects or situations, while in covert desensitization, the client imagines the fear-inducing stimuli.

Imagine that Penelope has gone to a therapist for help with her arachnophobia (fear of spiders) and that she elects to try covert desensitization. At the bottom of Penelope's anxiety hierarchy is looking at a photograph of a small spider in a magazine while at the top is allowing several harmless spiders to crawl all over her (see Figure 18.1). Other possible steps in the anxiety hierarchy include Penelope imagining herself engaging in behaviors such as looking at a live spider in a tank, touching a live spider while wearing gloves, and allowing one small, harmless spider to crawl on her leg. Once Penelope has learned some relaxation techniques and constructed an anxiety hierarchy with the therapist, she can begin to use counterconditioning to replace her fear of spiders with relaxation.

The therapist will ask Penelope to relax and then will ask her to imagine the first step on the anxiety hierarchy. In this case, she imagines looking at a picture of a small spider in a magazine. When Penelope can accomplish this task without feeling fear, the therapist will ask her to imagine the second step on the anxiety hierarchy. Penelope will continue to climb up the hierarchy until she feels anxious. As soon as she experiences anxiety, the therapist will tell her to take a step back down on the hierarchy until she feels calm again. This process will continue throughout Penelope's sessions with the therapist until she feels no anxiety, even when reaching the top of the hierarchy. This process is effective because learning through classical conditioning is strengthened by repeated pairings. Thus, the more times relaxation is paired with the feared stimuli, the stronger the relaxation response becomes.

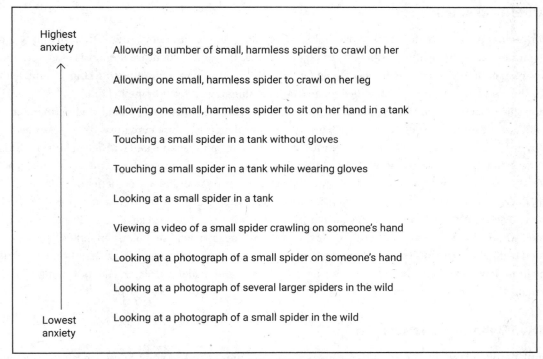

Highest
anxiety

Allowing a number of small, harmless spiders to crawl on her

Allowing one small, harmless spider to crawl on her leg

Allowing one small, harmless spider to sit on her hand in a tank

Touching a small spider in a tank without gloves

Touching a small spider in a tank while wearing gloves

Looking at a small spider in a tank

Viewing a video of a small spider crawling on someone's hand

Looking at a photograph of a small spider on someone's hand

Looking at a photograph of several larger spiders in the wild

Lowest
anxiety

Looking at a photograph of a small spider in the wild

Figure 18.1 Penelope's anxiety hierarchy

Another method of treating anxiety disorders that uses classical conditioning techniques is called flooding. Flooding, like systematic desensitization, can be in vivo or covert. Unlike the gradual process of systematic desensitization, flooding involves having the client address the most frightening scenario first. As one might expect, this technique produces tremendous anxiety. The idea, however, is that if clients face their fears and do not back down, they will soon realize that their fears are, in fact, irrational. In Penelope's case, if she were to begin by imagining that large spiders were crawling on her but that nothing bad was happening as a result, her fear would soon be extinguished.

Alternatively, Penelope's therapist could try to cure the phobia by using modeling. Modeling, as you will recall from Unit 3, is a process through which one person learns by observing and then imitating the behavior of another. Unlike the other techniques described in this section, modeling is a melding of cognitive and behavioral ideas. However, discussing it with systematic desensitization and flooding makes sense because all three are **exposure therapies**; all involve some degree of contact with the feared stimuli. Modeling could be used to treat Penelope's phobia by having her watch someone else interact calmly and without ill effect with various spiders and then asking her to reenact what she witnessed. Modeling can also be used to help people with a host of other difficulties, as well.

Another way that classical conditioning techniques can be used to treat people is called **aversive therapy**. This process involves pairing a habit a person wishes to break, such as smoking or bed-wetting, with an unpleasant stimulus such as electric shock or nausea. Operant conditioning can also be used as a method of treatment. This process involves using the principles developed by B. F. Skinner, such as reinforcement and punishment, to modify a person's behavior. One form of instrumental conditioning used in mental institutions, schools, and even in some people's homes is called a **token economy**. In a token economy, desired behaviors are identified and rewarded with tokens. The tokens can then be exchanged for various objects or privileges.

Cognitive Therapies

As cognitive therapists locate the cause of psychological problems in the way people think, their methods of therapy concentrate on changing these unhealthy thought patterns. The goal of cognitive therapy is often referred to as **cognitive restructuring**, which involves challenging people's patterns of **maladaptive thinking**. Cognitive therapy is often quite combative as therapists challenge the irrational thinking patterns of their clients.

An example of an unhealthy way of thinking is to attribute all failures to internal, global, and permanent aspects of the self. Assume Josephine fails a psychology test. She can explain this failure in many ways. A pessimistic and unhealthy attributional style would involve her thinking that she is bad at school and will fail all tests in all subjects all the time. With a healthier attributional style, Josephine would view the cause of the failure as external (the test was difficult), specific (this topic was particularly difficult), and temporary (she will do better next time).

Aaron Beck created cognitive therapy; a process most often employed in the treatment of depression. This method involves trying to get clients to engage in pursuits that will bring them success. This will alleviate the depression while also identifying and challenging the irrational ideas that cause their unhappiness. Beck explains depression using the **cognitive triad**: people's beliefs about themselves, their worlds, and their futures. People suffering from depression often have irrationally negative beliefs about all three of these areas. Cognitive therapy aims to make these beliefs more positive.

Cognitive Behavioral Therapies

One popular group of therapies combines the ideas and techniques of both cognitive and behavioral psychologists. This approach to therapy is known as **cognitive behavioral therapy (CBT)**. An example of a specific type of CBT is **rational emotive behavior therapy** (also known as REBT and sometimes referred to as RET). REBT was developed by Albert Ellis. Therapists employing REBT look to expose and confront the dysfunctional thoughts of their clients. For instance, someone suffering from a social phobia might voice concern over being publicly embarrassed when giving a class presentation. By using REBT, a therapist would question both the likelihood of such embarrassment occurring and the impact that would result. The therapist's goal would be to show the client that not only is his or her failure an unlikely occurrence but also that, even if it did occur, it would not be such a big deal. REBT focuses not just on how and what clients think but also on what they do. Often, clients are given homework assignments in which they are asked to engage in the behaviors they fear, thus demonstrating that the cataclysmic outcome they expect does not actually occur.

Group Therapy

Psychotherapy can involve groups of people in addition to one-on-one client-therapist interactions. Therapists running groups can have any of the orientations described above or can be eclectic, as described earlier. One common use of group therapy is in treating families. This form of treatment is known as family therapy. Since a client's problems do not occur in a vacuum, many therapists find meeting with the whole family helpful in revealing the patterns of interaction among family members and altering the behavior of the whole family rather than just one member.

Sometimes group therapy involves meeting with several people experiencing similar difficulties. Such an approach is less expensive for the clients and offers them the insight and feedback of their peers in addition to that of the therapist. Self-help groups such as Alcoholics Anonymous (AA) are a form of group therapy that does not involve a therapist at all.

Table 18.1 Summary of Types of Psychotherapy

Perspective	Specific Example	Key Concept/Techniques
Psychodynamic	Psychodynamic therapy	Free association, dream analysis
Humanistic	Client-centered therapy	Unconditional positive regard
Behaviorist	Systematic desensitization	Relaxation, anxiety hierarchy, counterconditioning
Cognitive	Cognitive	Challenging negative beliefs about the cognitive triad
Cognitive behavioral	Rational emotive behavior therapy	Challenging illogical ways of thinking and assigning behavioral homework

Somatic Therapies

Psychologists with a biomedical (biological) orientation, as mentioned earlier, see the cause of psychological disorders in organic causes. These include imbalances in neurotransmitters or hormones, structural abnormalities in the brain, or genetic predispositions that might underlie the other two. Therefore, these psychologists advocate the use of somatic therapies—therapies that produce bodily changes.

The most common type of somatic therapy is drug therapy or psychopharmacology, also known as chemotherapy (see Table 18.2). **Psychoactive medications**, or **psychotropic medications**, treat many kinds of psychological problems, ranging from anxiety disorders to mood disorders to schizophrenia. The more severe a disorder, the more likely that drugs will be used to treat it. Schizophrenia, for example, is almost always treated with drugs. A shortcoming of most kinds of psychotherapy is its limited use in dealing with patients unable to express themselves coherently. Since disordered thought is the primary symptom of schizophrenia, people suffering from this disorder overwhelmingly have difficulty communicating with others, thus rendering psychotherapy of limited use.

Schizophrenia is generally treated with **antipsychotic medications** such as Thorazine or Haldol. These drugs generally function by blocking the receptor sites for dopamine. Their effectiveness therefore provides support for the dopamine hypothesis described in Chapter 17 "Psychological Disorders." An unfortunate side effect of antipsychotic medication is **tardive dyskinesia**—Parkinsonian-like, chronic muscle tremors.

Mood disorders often respond well to chemotherapy. The three most common kinds of drugs used to treat unipolar depression are tricyclic **antidepressants**, monoamine oxidase (MAO) inhibitors, and serotonin selective reuptake inhibitor drugs or SSRIs (most notably Prozac). All tend to increase the activity of serotonin, although tricyclics and MAO inhibitors seem to have wider effects. **Lithium**, a metal, is often used to treat the manic phase of bipolar disorder.

Anxiety disorders are also often treated with **antianxiety drugs**. Essentially, these drugs act by depressing the activity of the central nervous system, thus making people feel more relaxed. Two main types of antianxiety drugs are barbiturates, such as Miltown, and benzodiazepines, including Xanax and Valium. Table 18.2 lists the most common kinds of drugs used to treat many of the disorders discussed in in this unit.

Table 18.2 Chemotherapy

Type of Disorder	Type of Drug(s)
Anxiety disorders	Barbiturates, benzodiazepines
Unipolar depression	Monoamine oxidase (MAO) inhibitors, tricyclic antidepressants, serotonin selective reuptake inhibitors
Bipolar disorder	Lithium
Schizophrenia	Antipsychotics (neuroleptics)

Biofeedback is a type of therapy most commonly used in the treatment of anxiety and depression. During biofeedback, a patient is taught to recognize and then control various physiological responses such as breathing, heart rate, or even brain activity (neurofeedback) without medication. **Transcranial magnetic stimulation (TMS)** employs magnets to alter brain activity and is mainly used in the treatment of depression. Another approach targeted at changing brain activity is **electroconvulsive therapy (ECT)**. In bilateral ECT, electric current is passed through both hemispheres of the brain. Unilateral ECT involves running current through only one hemisphere. Bilateral ECT, although generally more effective, also has more significant negative side effects, most notably loss of memory. The electric shock causes patients to experience a brief seizure. Prior to administering ECT, patients are given a muscle relaxant to reduce the effects of the seizure. Usually, following the seizure, patients briefly lose consciousness. ECT is a less common treatment than chemotherapy. It is used, most often, for severe cases of depression after other methods have failed. Although the means by which ECT works are not completely understood, one theory suggests that the benefits are the result of a change in the brain's blood flow patterns.

The most intrusive and rarest form of somatic therapy is **psychosurgery**. Psychosurgery involves the purposeful destruction of part of the brain to alter a person's behavior. Clearly, such a procedure is used only as a last resort and only on people suffering to a great extent. An early, and unfortunately widespread, form of psychosurgery was the **prefrontal lobotomy**. This operation involved cutting the main neurons leading to the frontal lobe of the brain. Although this procedure often calmed the behavior of patients, it reduced their level of functioning and awareness to a vegetative state. Even today, when surgical procedures have grown much more precise, debate remains over the risks of psychosurgery, and such procedures are done as a last resort.

Eclectic Therapies

If you asked a therapist which of the preceding orientations they use, you might hear something like, "It depends. I use what works." Many therapists do not exclusively use one type of therapy. Therapeutic orientations can be combined in effective ways. For example, cognitive behavioral therapies combine some of the techniques you read about in the cognitive therapies and behavioral therapies sections. Research indicates that cognitive behavioral therapies can be particularly effective for some anxiety and some mood disorders. For example, to treat an anxiety disorder, a therapist might combine a behavioral intervention, such as systematic desensitization, with talk therapy that helps the client understand his or her unrealistic cognitions about the source of the anxiety.

Somatic cognitive therapy is another very common combination eclectic therapy. Many therapists combine drug therapy along with cognitive talk therapy for mood and other disorders. For example, a person diagnosed with unipolar depression might receive a prescription for one of the serotonin selective reuptake inhibitor (SSRI) drugs, such as Prozac or Zoloft, while going through cognitive talk therapy to explore negative cognitions that might be contributing to his or her depression.

Kinds of Therapists

In addition to the different orientations discussed above, therapists have various levels and kinds of training.

- Psychiatrists are medical doctors and are therefore the only therapists permitted to prescribe medication in most U.S. states. Not surprisingly, because of their backgrounds, psychiatrists often favor a biomedical model of mental illness and are often less extensively trained in psychotherapy.
- Clinical psychologists earn doctoral degrees (PhDs) that require four or more years of study. Part of their training involves an internship during which they are overseen by a more experienced professional. Clinical psychologists usually deal with people who are suffering from problems more severe than everyday difficulties with work or family.
- Counseling therapists or counseling psychotherapists typically have some kind of graduate degree in psychology. Their training also includes an internship overseen by a more experienced professional.

Examples of counseling therapists include school psychologists as well as marriage and family therapists. Counseling therapists generally help people whose problems are less severe than those problems that bring people to clinical psychologists.

Regardless of their training, clinicians are guided by principles established by the APA. These guidelines emphasize the importance of **respecting people's rights and dignity**, acting with **fidelity, integrity cultural humility**, and nonmaleficence (the medical obligation not to harm).

HOW EFFECTIVE IS THERAPY?

Although therapy is clearly not always successful and many people recover from a variety of disorders without any intervention, a number of studies have documented that therapy is generally effective. The success of the treatment process is also clearly affected by the relationship between client and therapist—the **therapeutic alliance**. Therefore, a person who has a bad experience with therapy with one therapist at one time might respond more positively to another practitioner in another situation. **Evidence-based interventions** have been demonstrated to work through research, but even these approaches will not be effective for everyone all the time. The challenges of treating psychological disorders are a testament to the complexity of the human brain, but psychologists continually strive to develop better treatments to improve the human experience.

Unit 5 Multiple-Choice Questions

1. Juan hears voices that tell him to kill people. Juan is experiencing

   (A) delusions.
   (B) obsessions.
   (C) anxiety.
   (D) hallucinations.

2. Linda's neighbors describe her as typically shy and mild mannered. She seems to be a devoted wife and mother to her husband and three children. Unbeknownst to these neighbors, Linda sometimes dresses up in flashy, revealing clothing and goes to bars to pick up strange men. At such times, she is boisterous and overbearing. She tells everyone she meets that her name is Jen. At other times, when she is upset, Linda slips into child-like behavior and responds only to the name Sally. Linda is suffering from a

   (A) schizophrenic disorder.
   (B) mood disorder.
   (C) dissociative disorder.
   (D) somatic symptom disorder.

3. "I am the most important person in the world" is a statement that might characterize the views of someone with which of the following personality disorders?

   (A) Schizoid
   (B) Narcissistic
   (C) Histrionic
   (D) Dependent

4. Women in the United States have a higher rate of depression than do men. Which kind of psychologist would be most likely to explain this higher incidence in terms of the pressures and prejudices that women suffer?

   (A) Humanistic
   (B) Psychodynamic
   (C) Sociocultural
   (D) Behavioral

5. Anand is unable to move his right arm. He has been to scores of physicians seeking a cure, but none have been able to find any physiological reason for his paralysis. Anand may be suffering from

   (A) conversion disorder.
   (B) dissociative amnesia.
   (C) GAD.
   (D) SAD.

6. Reni is sexually aroused by shoes. Reni might be diagnosed as having

   (A) pedophilia.
   (B) fetishism.
   (C) sadism.
   (D) exhibitionism.

7. Coretta's therapist says little during their sessions and never makes any recommendations about what Coretta ought to do. What kind of therapy does Coretta's therapist most likely practice?

   (A) Humanistic
   (B) Behavioral
   (C) Cognitive
   (D) Biomedical

8. When Shannon lost her job, she found herself devoting more time to her family and friends. What is the best way to describe this response?

   (A) Fight-or-flight
   (B) Dysfunctional
   (C) Eclectic
   (D) Tend or befriend

9. At his last appointment with his therapist, Ivan explained that since he lost his job he has felt completely worthless and depressed. Which of the following statements would a strictly cognitive therapist be most likely to say?

    (A) "Tell me about your recent dreams."
    (B) "I'm going to give you a homework assignment to do three things that you used to enjoy."
    (C) "That's ridiculous; no one is completely worthless."
    (D) "So, you're feeling very down."

10. Jeb has been working for the same company for three years. Although his responsibilities have increased, his salary has not. Every time he resolves to talk with his supervisor about a raise, he loses his nerve. In therapy, Dr. Flores and her assistant demonstrate how Jeb might go about asking for a raise. Then the assistant pretends to be Jeb's boss, and Jeb practices asking for a raise. This process most closely resembles

    (A) REBT.
    (B) existential therapy.
    (C) modeling.
    (D) free association.

11. One difference between psychodynamic and cognitive modes of treatment is that cognitive therapists

    (A) say little during sessions.
    (B) emphasize the primacy of behavior.
    (C) focus on the present.
    (D) view repressed thoughts about one's childhood as the root of most problems.

12. Which method of therapy is most eclectic?

    (A) Psychodynamic
    (B) Client centered
    (C) Aversive conditioning
    (D) Cognitive behavioral

Questions 13 through 15 refer to the following.

A sample of 60 people diagnosed with major depressive disorder are randomly assigned to receive cognitive behavioral therapy (CBT), drug therapy, or a control group given a placebo. Before the study, they are given a standard measure of psychological distress (on which a score of 1 indicates little distress and 10 indicates tremendous distress). They complete the measure again 3 months after beginning their assigned therapy. Their mean ratings, divided by condition, are seen in the table below.

	Control	CBT	Medication
Baseline	7.2	7.4	7.0
After 3 months	5.8	4.2	3.7

13. Which conclusion is best supported by the data?

    (A) Everyone improved so there is no evidence that either treatment is superior to the control.
    (B) The treatments had a negative effect on the sample.
    (C) The group given medication improved significantly more than both other groups.
    (D) Both treatment groups experienced a similar level of improvement.

14. What phenomenon is illustrated by the change in distress in the control group?

    (A) Regression to the mean
    (B) Statistical significance
    (C) Negative correlation
    (D) Placebo effect

15. Why is it preferable to randomly assign people to treatments rather than let them choose what they prefer?

    (A) Psychologists have important medical expertise so they should do the assignment.
    (B) People may choose treatments without considering all the important factors.
    (C) Random samples better represent populations.
    (D) Random assignment enables researchers to show cause-effect relationships.

Answer Explanations

1. **(D)** Perceiving sensory stimulation when none exists defines a hallucination. Delusions are irrational thoughts but do not involve a belief in the existence of sensory stimulation. Obsessions are persistent, unwanted thoughts.

2. **(C)** Linda is suffering from dissociative identity disorder, a type of dissociative disorder.

3. **(B)** Narcissism is the love of oneself. People who view themselves as the focus of the world would most likely be classified as having narcissistic personality disorder.

4. **(C)** Sociocultural psychologists believe that mental illness is mainly caused by certain negative aspects of society such as sexism and poverty.

5. **(A)** Anand's symptoms suggest he has conversion disorder, a type of somatoform or somatic symptom disorder in which no physical cause can be found for a physical complaint. The hallmark of dissociative amnesia is difficulty remembering things that are potentially disturbing and that cannot be explained by a physical trauma. GAD is generalized anxiety disorder, which is a constant, low-level sense of nervous tension. SAD, or seasonal affective disorder, is a type of mood disorder in which people become depressed during prolonged periods of bad weather.

6. **(B)** Paraphilias involve sexual arousal and interest in people, objects, or situations not generally considered arousing. More specifically, Reni has a fetish since he is aroused by an object. Pedophilia is a sexual attraction to children. Sadism is when one is aroused by inflicting pain on others. Exhibitionism is when one is aroused by exposing himself or herself to others.

7. **(A)** Coretta's therapist is nondirective and therefore is most likely to have a humanistic orientation. An example of such a therapy is Carl Rogers's client-centered therapy.

8. **(D)** Tend and befriend is one way people deal with stressful situations like losing a job; it involves bolstering one's social connections and relationships with others. Fight-or-flight is another common response to stressful situations, but it involves either fighting against or fleeing from the cause of the stress, which is not what this example describes.

9. **(C)** Cognitive therapy is often somewhat confrontational as cognitive psychologists attempt to change the irrational ways their clients think. A common problem that cognitive psychologists fight is depressed people's tendency to globalize and internalize negative thoughts. This is evidenced by Ivan's assertion that he is completely worthless. The statement in choice (A) would more likely be made by a psychoanalytic or psychodynamic therapist. They suggest that the roots of many problems are laid in childhood, and they stress the importance of the unconscious mind to which dreams are clues. The statement in choice (B) would most likely be made by a behaviorist as it stresses the importance of behavior. The statement in choice (D) reflects humanistic psychologists' belief in being nondirective and reflecting back what their clients say.

10. **(C)** Modeling consists of observation and imitation. Jeb first watches someone model how to ask for a raise, and then he practices that skill himself.

11. **(C)** Psychoanalysis stresses the importance of early childhood experience. Psychoanalysts spend a lot of time exploring patients' early lives. Cognitive therapists focus on helping their clients deal with the present. Neither type of therapist is particularly reticent; humanistic therapists are. Neither psychoanalysts nor cognitive therapists emphasize the importance of behavior; that focus characterizes behaviorists. Psychoanalysts, not cognitive psychologists, do see repressed thoughts from childhood as the root of most adult problems.

12. **(D)** Eclectic therapies incorporate aspects of several different models rather than strictly adhering to one theoretical orientation. By virtue of combining cognitive and behavioral methods, cognitive-behavioral therapies are more eclectic than the others listed.

13. **(D)** Choice (A) is incorrect because although everyone improved, both treatment groups improved nearly twice as much as the control group. Seeing as the treatment groups improved similarly, choice (C) is incorrect. Given that all groups improved, choice (B) is incorrect.

14. **(A)** Whenever we feel or do unusually well or unusually poorly, it is likely that later measurements will be less extreme, that they will regress to the mean. Within the context of the question, people are more likely to seek help with their depression when it is very severe. For instance, someone who would usually report being at a 5 on the scale is more likely to go for treatment at a moment in time they are feeling at a 7 or 8 rather than staying at a 5. Therefore, that person may feel better a few months later even without treatment because the natural course of life is that, over time, things tend to drift back toward the mean.

15. **(D)** Random assignment is one of the hallmarks of an experiment. The goal of random assignment is to eliminate differences among the groups so that a difference in groups at the end can be ascribed to the independent variable. When people are divided into groups based on their own preferences or a researcher's preferences, the possibility that the assignment has been affected by extraneous factors is introduced. Choice (C) is incorrect because although random samples are used to better represent populations, random sampling is a different process than the random assignment of participation to groups.

19

Multiple-Choice Test-Taking Tips

Overview

Two-thirds of your test grade depends on your performance on the multiple-choice questions. During the AP Psychology test, you will answer the multiple-choice section first, and then you will answer the free-response questions. You will have 90 minutes to answer the 75 multiple-choice questions. The multiple-choice questions are designed to measure your ability to APPLY the psychological terms, concepts, theories, and perspectives you learned in the course (and this book). Don't be surprised if you have trouble answering one or more of the questions. They are designed to be challenging, so just do your best on that item and move on! If you have time after finishing the questions, you can look back at items you had trouble with and think about them a bit more. Make sure you answer all the items, even if you have to guess. The purpose of this chapter is to provide some test-taking strategies we think will help you with this section of the exam.

Test-Taking Strategies

Sometimes You Don't Even Need the Answer Choices!

Once you've prepared for this test, you'll see that in order to answer many of the questions, you don't even need to look at the answer choices. In fact, it's a good test-taking strategy to try to answer multiple-choice questions BEFORE you look at the choices. That way, once you look at the answer choices, you have a good sense of what you are looking for.

For example, consider the following question:

EXAMPLE

Tiger is extremely concerned about whether there is a meaning to life. She likes going to the library to look through philosophy textbooks to read summaries of ancient philosophies and religious ideas about whether life has preexisting meaning or whether we create meanings in our own lives. According to Piaget, Tiger is in which of the following stages of cognitive development?

If you remember Piaget's stages of cognitive development, you are probably already guessing that Tiger is in the formal operations stage without checking the answer choices. In this case, you would then answer this question easily, because the answer choices are:

(A) Sensorimotor
(B) Preoperations
(C) Concrete operations
(D) Formal operations

Here's another example:

EXAMPLE

A psychologist who subscribes to the biomedical perspective would be most likely to emphasize the importance of which of the following?

In this case, the answer is slightly less obvious. You probably realize that it will have to do with concepts such as genetics, nature, and/or neurochemicals. Once you identify these potential answers, selecting the answer is, again, fairly obvious. The choices are:

(A) The environment
(B) Hormones and neurotransmitters
(C) Repressed impulses
(D) Attributional style

The correct answer is choice (B), as hormones and neurotransmitters are examples of the kind of neurochemicals that biomedical psychologists believe influence thought and behavior.

Read All the Answer Choices

Always read all the answer choices before making your final selection. Even though it is helpful to imagine what the answer might be without reading the answer choices, it is essential that you read and carefully consider all the choices presented. Occasionally, particularly on the more difficult questions, one of the answer choices will seem like the correct answer but another answer will be more correct. Remember, you are choosing the BEST answer on the AP Psychology multiple-choice questions.

Narrow Down the Possible Answers

Sometimes the questions on the exam are more difficult than the examples above, and you will not be able to identify the correct answer before reading the answer choices. That is the beauty of the multiple-choice format: even if you are not sure you completely understand the concept in the question, you should be able to narrow down the possible answers by using what you do know about psychology. As mentioned above, you should always carefully read each of the answer choices. When you decide a choice is incorrect, cross it out. You will be able to use this method often to identify the correct answer by the process of elimination.

When I Don't Know the Answer, Should I Guess?

Some tests include a "guessing penalty" to discourage students from guessing on multiple-choice questions. (Past versions of the AP Psychology exam included a guessing penalty.) However, there is no guessing penalty on the current AP Psychology exam. The score for the multiple-choice section is based on the number of questions answered correctly, and no points are deducted for questions answered incorrectly or left blank. Since there is no penalty for guessing on the exam, you should answer each of the multiple-choice questions, even if you feel like you are guessing.

Don't Get Bogged Down

If you come to a question you find difficult, do not spend an inordinate amount of time on it. Remember that this is a timed test; there is no sense in spending a long time worrying about one question if that will prevent you from spending time on the questions at the end of the test. After you read a question and look at the answer choices, make your best guess and move on. If you doubt your answer, mark the question as one that you want to review later so that you can come back and think about it again if you have time left.

Remember Your Research Methods

About 18 of the 75 multiple-choice items will measure not just your content knowledge from the five units but also your ability to apply what you learned from this book in Chapter 2 "Research Methods." (See the explanation of this skill in the "Science Practice 2: Research Methods and Design" section below.) Often these multiple-choice questions will be stimulus questions: you will read a paragraph and/or a graph or data table, usually summarizing a research study, and then you'll answer several multiple-choice questions about that stimulus. Here are some common concepts from Chapter 2 "Research Methods" you will want to make sure you know how to apply:

- Experimental vs. nonexperimental research methods: Some multiple-choice questions will ask you to identify what research method psychologists used in a study. One of the first steps is to figure out whether the research method is an experiment or not. You can usually spot an experiment because the research involves comparing at least two groups: participants might be randomly assigned to a group or there may be preexisting groups (which we describe as a quasi-experiment). As you look at the stimulus for these multiple-choice questions, try to first identify if the researchers are measuring something between two or more groups. If so, it's probably an experiment!

- Correlation vs. causation: Confusing correlation and causation is a common error, so the authors of the AP exam are likely to include multiple-choice items that measure whether you understand the difference. Remember what you learned in Chapter 2 "Research Methods": a correlation is simply a relationship between two things, but it doesn't mean that one variable causes a change in the other variable. The only way to figure out CAUSE is to do an experiment. (An experiment is needed because you are keeping all other variables the same while changing one variable—the independent variable—and measuring the impact on the other variable—the dependent variable.) So if you determine that the research summarized in a stimulus item isn't an experiment, then the researchers shouldn't be making causal claims. You can usually tell what kind of a claim a researcher is making by the words they use. If a researcher says that one variable caused, impacted, influenced, determined, affected, or changed another variable, that's a causal claim and needs to be supported by experimental evidence. If a researcher says that one variable is related to, correlated with, or predicts another variable, that researcher is talking about a correlational relationship.

- Measures of central tendency: As you learned in Chapter 3 "Statistics," you don't need to know many statistics for the AP Psychology exam. However, some of the common statistics you'll be asked to interpret (especially on stimulus items) are the measures of central tendency: mean, median, and mode. You probably learned these in a math class a long time ago. Make sure, though, that you have the definitions clear and can apply them to a simple list of data quickly so that you can be confident on these multiple-choice questions and not second-guess yourself. Some multiple-choice questions might ask you why you would use the median rather than the mean. This is usually because there is an outlier in the set of data: a variable that is much smaller or much larger than the rest of the data and that pulls the mean so far that it doesn't represent the average of the data well. In these cases, the median is a better measure of central tendency to use.

- Alignment between evidence and a hypothesis: Sometimes a multiple-choice question will ask you whether a researcher's evidence supports or doesn't support the person's conclusion or hypothesis. Reading carefully will often get you the right answer: you just have to see if the evidence in the stimulus points in the same direction as the researcher's conclusions. Sometimes the question is measuring if you understand the difference between correlation and causation (see "Correlation vs. causation" above).

Guess Smart

When you are not sure of the answer to a question and therefore are trying to eliminate incorrect choices, a few other suggestions about how to make good guesses on multiple-choice tests may help you.

1. **USE YOUR COMMON SENSE.** Don't get so caught up thinking about what you learned that you forget to think clearly about the question. For example, consider the following question:

   What is the likely correlation between the amount of time students spend studying psychology and their scores on the AP Psychology Exam?

   (A) –0.80
   (B) –0.25
   (C) 0.62
   (D) 0.97

Assuming you remember that "0" represents no correlation and that "1" represents a perfect positive correlation, your common sense can help you choose the answer. Since you would expect a positive relationship between studying and exam scores, you should be able to eliminate choices (A) and (B), so you are choosing between answers (C) and (D). Answer (D), 0.97, seems too strong. Clearly some of the variation in how people do on a test is related to factors other than time spent studying (for example, prior knowledge, quality of their AP teacher, how rested they are, and test anxiety). Therefore, when you use your common sense, you will choose (C) as the correct answer (and you would get this item right!).

2. **USE YOUR KNOWLEDGE OF THE PSYCHOLOGICAL PERSPECTIVES.** Sometimes language used in the stem of the question can give you a clue about the right answer. Each psychological perspective uses its own vocabulary terms, and the correct answer choice will frequently use language specific to the perspective indicated by the stem of the question. For example, consider the following question:

   How would a behaviorist like B. F. Skinner explain how people learn table manners?

   (A) Table manners are learned by interpreting events we have observed.
   (B) Table manners are learned as a result of reinforcement and punishment.
   (C) Table manners are controlled by brain chemistry and evolutionary forces.
   (D) Table manners are learned by remembering and thinking about past social events.

Notice that the stem of this question gives you a hint that the correct answer must be one that a behaviorist would agree with, so you know that you are looking for an answer that uses behaviorist terms. Options (A) and (D) use cognitive psychological terms (observing, remembering, thinking). Option (C) uses biopsychological language (chemistry and evolution). Only option (B) uses terms from the behavioral perspective (reinforcement and punishment), so it must be the right answer (and it is!).

3. **AVOID EXTREME ANSWER CHOICES.** Choices that contain words like *all* or *never* or *everyone* are not likely to be correct. Multiple-choice items on the AP Psychology exam are very carefully written, so you are not likely to encounter many items that include these extreme answer choices. Be on the lookout for them just in case.

4. **BE WARY OF ANSWER CHOICES THAT ARE VERY SIMILAR TO ONE ANOTHER.** Remember that you are looking for the *best* answer. If some of the answers are so similar that one cannot be better than the other, neither of those choices can be the correct answer.

Budget Your Time

Although most students find that they have enough time on the multiple-choice section of the exam, you should make sure not to spend an undue amount of time on any of the questions. Wear a watch (not a smart watch!) during the exam, and make sure to note the time the multiple-choice section begins and when it is scheduled to end. Since you have 90 minutes to answer 75 multiple-choice questions, you have slightly over 1 minute to answer each question (1 minute and 12 seconds to be precise!). Read each question, and use the techniques we suggest in this chapter to make sure you can move through the multiple-choice items at about 1 per minute. If you find yourself confused on an item, mark it so that you can review it later, guess at an answer, and move on. If you are debating between answer choices, choose your best guess at an answer and mark that item for review too so that you can come back to it later.

All These Tips Are Interesting, but How Many Questions Do I Need to Get Right to Pass the Exam?

Each AP Psychology exam is slightly different regarding the number of multiple-choice questions you need to pass. Assuming that your free-response question answers are average (remember that they determine one-third of your grade), if you get about 50 of the 75 multiple-choice items correct, you set yourself up to receive most likely a 3, 4, or 5 on the AP Psychology exam.

Finally, Remember to Apply Some of What You've Learned About Psychology to How You Study for the Multiple-Choice Section

- It's better to space out your studying over many days than it is to cram for the same amount of time right before the exam.
- Studying is important, but so is sleep. You will think more clearly if you are well rested.
- According to the Yerkes-Dodson law (see Chapter 15 "Motivation and Emotion"), a moderate level of anxiety/arousal will help you perform well on the test. You don't want to be so anxious that you can't focus, but you will want to "psych" yourself up for the test and use a moderate level of anxiety in a useful way.
- In cognitive psychology research (see Chapter 9 "Memory"), retrieval practice consistently produces the best studying results. Use the resources in this book and your textbook to quiz yourself frequently. Remember that quizzing yourself means answering questions under testing conditions: close the book, don't use your computer or your phone, and commit to answering the items as best you can. Then open the book and look up the correct answer to figure out which items you got wrong or right. Also, you can use the blank paper technique: after you read a section of this book or your textbook, close the book, get out a blank sheet of paper (or start a blank document on your computer or phone), and write down everything you can remember about what you just read. All these retrieval practice techniques help you realize what you learned and what you need to review. Another effective technique is to try to answer the practice questions at the end of the unit BEFORE you read the unit. You may not get many of the questions right. However, thinking about those questions and answers will provide context that you can use to encode the new information you learn from the reading.

Skills

The AP Psychology curriculum from the College Board includes four skills the exam authors use to write multiple-choice items (skills 1, 2, and 3) and free-response questions (skill 4). The psychology teachers and professors who write the multiple-choice items key each item to skill 1, 2, or 3 and to a content area (one of the five units in the AP Psychology curriculum).

Science Practice 1: Concept Application

This skill simply refers to your ability to USE the concepts, theories, terms, perspectives, and other ideas in the AP Psychology curriculum. All the multiple-choice questions will require you to USE what you know about that idea in the context of a specific scenario, comparing that concept with another concept or identifying which idea is the most useful for answering a specific question. Being able to define the terms in this book is a good first step. However, to answer the multiple-choice items correctly, you will need to understand how to use and apply these terms, not just repeat their definitions. About 65 percent of the multiple-choice items on the test (about 49 of the 75 items) will be keyed as concept application items in addition to being keyed to one of the five content units.

Science Practice 2: Research Methods and Design

This skill refers to your understanding of how psychological researchers design research studies. In this book, we call this content Chapter 2 "Research Methods." About 25 percent of the multiple-choice items on the test (about 18 of the 75 items) will be keyed as research methods items in addition to being keyed to one of the five content units.

Science Practice 3: Data Interpretation

This skill refers to analyzing quantitative data—numbers! You learned in Chapter 2 "Research Methods" that psychological researchers usually try to measure psychological variables numerically. You learned a few basic statistical techniques researchers use in psychology, and you will use that knowledge on the data interpretation multiple-choice questions. About 10 percent of the multiple-choice items on the test (7 or 8 of the 75 items) will be keyed as data interpretation items in addition to being keyed to one of the five content units.

Science Practice 4: Argumentation

This skill refers to your ability to create psychological arguments or claims based on evidence and then support your argument or claim using that evidence and your reasoning and writing skills. None of the multiple-choice items are keyed to this skill: the only place where your argumentation skill is measured is on the free-response Evidence-Based Question (EBQ). The EBQ question is explained in Chapter 20 "Answering Free-Response Questions".

20

Answering Free-Response Questions

Overview

Beginning with the 2025 AP Psychology exam, the free-response section of the exam consists of two free-response questions:

- **Question 1 is the Article Analysis Question (AAQ).** You will read a summary of a research study and identify several elements related to the research methods, variables, data analysis, and ethical considerations of that research study. You will also write about how this research relates to specific psychological theories or terms. You have 25 minutes to write the AAQ (including 10 minutes to read the research summary). Students can earn up to 7 points for the AAQ.
- **Question 2 is the Evidence-Based Question (EBQ).** For this question, you will read three summaries of research studies (or articles about a research topic). You will choose two of these studies to focus on for the rest of the question. Then you will write a claim based on the research presented in these two summaries. This claim will be a conclusion related to the research in the two summaries that can be supported with evidence from those sources. After writing the claim, you will identify one piece of evidence from one of the sources you chose. (Remember to cite the source by referencing the research summary or article!) Then you will explain how that evidence supports your claim using a term, theory, and/or concept from psychology. You will then repeat this process with the second source you chose. (Identify and cite a piece of evidence and then explain how that evidence supports your claim.) You have 45 minutes for the EBQ (including 15 minutes to read through the three sources). Students can earn up to 7 points for the EBQ.

This may seem like a lot! After you review the practice AAQ and EBQ in this chapter, you will feel very prepared to answer these free-response questions! Notice that these questions have a few things in common that will help you prepare:

- They both rely heavily on your knowledge of Chapter 2 "Research Methods." If you can apply the ideas in that chapter related to research methods, experimental design, operational definitions of variables, and basic statistical analysis, you already know most of what you need to know for both the AAQ and the EBQ!
- Both questions provide time for you to read through the research summaries. At first it may seem overwhelming to have to read through one summary for the AAQ and three summaries for the EBQ. The summaries, though, will not be very long or technical, and you already know what you need to focus on while you read:
  - For the AAQ, you will have six specific questions to answer about the summary, so you can focus on those specific questions as you read.
  - For the EBQ, you know that you only really need to read two of the summaries in detail. (You are asked to choose evidence from two of the summaries, not all three.) After you figure out your claim, all you need to do is pick an appropriate piece of evidence from each summary and then use your knowledge of psychological concepts to explain how that evidence supports your claim. Do that twice, and you're done!

- In the AAQ and EBQ, the people scoring your answer are judging your response based on how well you explain the psychological research in the sources and how well you use your knowledge of psychology to answer the questions. They are NOT judging your writing skills or ability to organize a long essay. You will be writing short, clear explanations in response to specific questions, not composing a long essay!

The rest of this chapter is devoted to explaining details about the AAQ and the EBQ. Read through the explanation and the sample answers (and how they are scored). Based on this summary, you should know exactly what to expect on this part of the exam and should feel confident about earning the full 7 points for each of these free-response questions!

Article Analysis Question (AAQ)

The purpose of the AAQ is to measure how well you can apply six research methods concepts to a summary of a research study. The source document (see below) will explain the overall goal and context of the study (introduction), details about the subjects in the study (participants), how the researchers gathered the data (method), and the resulting data and the researchers' conclusions based on the data (results and discussion).

When you answer an AAQ, your first task is obviously to use your 10-minute reading period to read through the summary. As you read, remember that you are looking for six specific things that you will write about later. You will need to do the following:

(A) **Identify the research method.** You are most likely to find this in the method section, but it may also be mentioned in the introduction.

(B) **Explain how the dependent variable is operationally defined.** You are most likely to find this in the method section.

(C) **Interpret basic statistics from a study.** You will need to interpret basic statistical information from the study, such as explaining the importance of differences between means, interpreting a correlation, or other statistical information. You are most likely to find this information in the results and discussion section.

(D) **Identify an ethical issue related to the study.** You are most likely to find this ethical issue in the method section.

(E) **Discuss whether the findings of a study might be generalizable.** You need to read carefully about the research participants described in the method section as you think about whether the study is generalizable.

(F) **Explain how the findings of a study support or do not support the hypothesis.** This is an "overall" question, and it's the only question worth up to 2 points. You'll need to think about the question the researchers wanted to answer and whether their method and results justify the conclusion they made.

The best way to study for the AAQ is to practice reading summaries of research studies and make sure you can identify these six elements. The following pages include an example of a unique research summary, a sample student answer for each question, and an explanation of how an AP Psychology reader would use the rubric to score that sample student answer. Note that this research summary and sample student answer are written specifically for this book. You can find a different example in the College Board's *AP Psychology Course and Exam Description*.

Sample AAQ and Scored Answer

When you start the AAQ section on the AP Psychology exam, the first thing you will see will be the research summary you will use to answer the questions. Spend 10 minutes reading through the research summary below. You may want to take notes about what you find regarding:

(A) The research method
(B) How the dependent variable is operationally defined
(C) Basic statistics from the study
(D) An ethical issue related to the study
(E) Whether the findings of the study might be generalizable
(F) How the findings of the study support or do not support the hypothesis

Sample Research Summary (Source)

Introduction
Parents, teachers, and others commonly believe that praising children for their intelligence can lead to higher self-esteem and increased motivation to tackle challenging academic tasks. Several systems in schools, such as high-ability learner and "gifted" programs, assume that it is useful for students and families if younger students are identified early in their school careers as being capable of advanced coursework so that they can be tracked into appropriate classes. However, other research indicates that this early identification can influence student self-perception in harmful ways. Emphasizing that students' success may be caused by their "natural intelligence" rather than how hard they try can lead young learners to believe that they shouldn't have to put effort into academic tasks, and when they later must try hard, they may conclude that they just aren't naturally good or talented at that task. This research study attempted to determine the impact of praising young students for how hard they tried (effort) rather than their intelligence after a specific task. Researchers believed that it may be more useful to praise effort rather than intelligence to convince students that if they try hard they can succeed.

Participants
The participants in this study were 128 fifth-grade students. 70 of the students identified as girls, and 58 of the students identified as boys. 49% of the students were selected from a school in a small midwestern city, and 51% of them went to a school in a large city in the northeast. The race/ethnicity distribution of the students is shown:

White	50%
Black/African American	19%
Hispanic/Latino	31%

Method

After obtaining informed consent from these students' parents, teachers, and administrators as well as assent from the students, students were asked to solve three groups of problems from the Raven's Progressive Matrices instrument. Students were randomly assigned to two groups, which determined what kind of feedback they received after their answers to the Raven's Progressive Matrices were scored. All the students were told that they did well on the test, solving at least 80% of the problems correctly. Then students were told:

- Group 1 praise for intelligence: "You must be smart at these problems."
- Group 2 praise for effort: "You must have worked hard at these problems."

After receiving the feedback, students were asked what kind of problems they wanted to work on next. Students could choose from two groups of problems:

- Performance goal options—Students who selected one of these three statements were categorized as having performance goals: "Problems that aren't too hard, so I don't get many wrong," or "Problems that are pretty easy, so I'll do well," or "Problems that I'm pretty good at, so I can show that I'm smart."
- Learning goal option—Students who selected this option were categorized as having a learning goal: "Problems that I'll learn a lot from, even if I won't look so smart."

Results and Discussion

Overall, data from the study indicates that students who were praised for their intelligence, rather than their effort, were more likely to choose future tasks that would make others perceive them as more intelligent. Students who were praised for their effort were more likely to choose tasks that would help them learn new things.

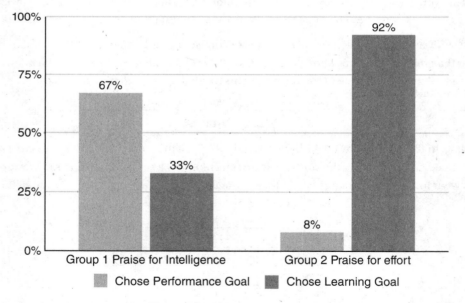

Specifically, the data indicated that students who received the Group 1 praise for intelligence feedback were far more likely to choose performance goal options than effort goal options. In this group, 67% of the students chose performance goals.

In contrast, students who received the Group 2 praise for effort feedback were more likely to choose effort goal options. In this group, 92% of the students chose learning goals rather than performance goals.

Data from all the groups supported the researchers' hypothesis that children who are praised for intelligence when they succeed are likely to choose goals that will reinforce the perception that they are "bright" rather than choosing goals that might help them learn and increase their skills. These findings did not differ among any of the groups tested: students from all gender, race/ethnicity, and large/small school groups showed the same patterns.

Researchers concluded that the feedback students received after their performance may influence their self-perception and this self-perception may influence the future behavior of these students. If a student is praised for their intelligence, this may lead to a student placing value on the perception of others regarding their intelligence and being motivated toward performance goals that they believe will lead to others continuing to perceive them as bright or gifted. Since the goal of most educators (and, hopefully, parents) is to motivate young people to challenge themselves in ways that increase their learning, it may be more valuable to provide effort praise for students (especially younger students). When students hear statements that emphasize effort like "You must have worked hard at these problems," it may lead them to attribute their success to their own efforts, rather than natural intelligence or ability. Since students can control how much effort they put into academic tasks, effort praise may empower younger learners, leading them to strive toward learning goals that will result in increased learning and skills. Emphasizing effort may empower young learners and increase their confidence that they are in control of whether they can successfully complete tasks since they are in control of how much effort they put into the tasks.

Adapted from Mueller, C. M., & Dweck, C. S. (1998). Praise for intelligence can undermine children's motivation and performance. *Journal of Personality and Social Psychology*, 75(1), 33–52. https://doi.org/10.1037/0022-3514.75.1.33

Answering the AAQ Questions

After the 10-minute reading period, you'll start answering the AAQ questions about the research summary. Remember that you aren't writing an overall essay: each of these AAQ questions is its own short-answer question. Write your answer in complete sentences in the space provided, read through your answer to make sure it expresses what you want to say, add anything that you think might help a reader understand exactly what you mean, and then move on to the next question.

In this next section, read through the sample student answer to each of the AAQ questions, the summary of the scoring guide (rubric), and then decide how many points YOU think the sample student answer should score. Then go on and read the explanation for how we think the sample student answer should be scored. This process should help you understand what you need to write in order to convince your reader that you know how to apply these concepts (and get you 7 points!).

AAQ Part (A): Research Method

(A) Identify the research method used in the study.

Sample Student Answer

This study used the experimental research method. I know it was an experiment because there were two groups. One group got one kind of praise, and the other group got a different kind of praise.

Scoring Guide

To get a point for (A), students need to correctly identify the research method used in the study.

> This response earns 1 point because the student correctly identified the method used in the study as an experiment.

AAQ Part (B): How the Dependent Variable Is Operationally Defined

> (B) State the operational definition of learning motivation in the study.

Sample Student Answer

> In this study, the researchers measured learning motivation by checking to see what kind of future problems students chose. Some students chose the performance goal option, and some chose the learning goal option. That choice is the operational definition of learning motivation.

Scoring Guide

To get a point for (B), students need to explain the measurable definition of the variable identified in this study. In this case, that variable is learning motivation.

> This response would score 1 point because the student correctly identifies how learning motivation is measured (operationally defined) in the study (through the participants' choice of the type of future problem to solve).

AAQ Part (C): Basic Statistics from the Study

> (C) Describe the meaning of the differences in results for the praise for intelligence and for the praise for effort groups.

Sample Student Answer

> According to data from the study, the students who were praised for their effort were much more likely to choose the learning goal than the performance goal: 92% of these students chose the learning goal. Students who were praised for their intelligence were more likely to choose the performance goal: 67% of these students chose the performance goal.

Scoring Guide

To get a point for (C), students need to accurately explain the relevant statistic within the context of the study.

> This response would score 1 point because the student accurately identified the statistic—the percentage of students in each group who chose each kind of goal—and explained that difference in the context of the study.

AAQ Part (D): An Ethical Issue Related to the Study

> (D) Identify at least one ethical guideline applied by the researchers.

Sample Student Answer

> In this study, one of the potential ethical problems might be whether the students might be harmed in the long term because of the kind of praise they received during the study. They got informed consent from the parents and that's good, but what if some students end up changing their learning motivation permanently because of the praise? Did they debrief later with the students?

Scoring Guide

To get a point for (D), students need to identify at least one relevant ethical consideration about the study.

> This response would score 1 point because the student actually identified more than one ethical element of the study: the student mentioned informed consent and the possibility of long-term harm.

AAQ Part (E): Whether the Findings of the Study Might be Generalizable

> (E) Explain the extent to which the research findings may or may not be generalizable using specific and relevant evidence from the study.

Sample Student Answer

> This study is probably generalizable because the researchers were pretty careful about the students they chose. They got a pretty big group (128 kids), and they chose them from two different kinds of schools: a small, midwestern school and a large, East Coast school. So these results can probably be generalized to all young students.

Scoring Guide

To get a point for (E), students need to explain why they think the results of the study are or are not generalizable using relevant evidence from the research summary.

> This response would score 1 point because the student used relevant evidence—the number of students and the kinds of schools the students were selected from—to explain why they think this participant sample convinces them that the findings are generalizable.

AAQ Part (F): How the Findings of the Study Support or Do Not Support the Hypothesis

> (F) Explain how at least one of the research findings supports or refutes the researchers' hypothesis about the impact of praise for intelligence or effort.

Sample Student Answer

> These findings definitely support what the researchers wanted to figure out in this study. In the introduction, the summary states that the researchers wanted to figure out what the impact is for praising students for how hard they tried versus praising students for their intelligence. They definitely did that. Their results show that praising kids for their effort leads them to choose tasks that they might actually learn from, and praising them for their intelligence just leads them to choose tasks that will increase the perception of how smart they are.

Scoring Guide

In (F), students can get 1 point for using appropriate evidence but not having a complete explanation. Students can get 2 points for using appropriate evidence AND including a complete argument/explanation for how that evidence shows that the hypothesis is or is not supported.

> This response would score 2 points because the student used relevant evidence—the results that show the impact for praise vs. effort. They use this evidence to show how the study supported the researchers' hypothesis: that the kind of praise has an impact on future learning choices.

This sample student would score 7 points on the AAQ item—the maximum number of points possible.

Evidence-Based Question (EBQ)

The second free-response you will get to answer on the AP Psychology test is EBQ. The purpose of the EBQ is to measure whether you can make a claim based on research summaries, find evidence for that claim, and develop an argument for your claim using that evidence. Argumentation is listed in the AP Psychology curriculum as one of the science practice skills (Argumentation, Science Practice 4), and this EBQ is the only place on the AP Psychology exam that measures the argumentation skill.

For the free-response EBQ, you will first see three research summaries and get a 15-minute reading period to review the three sources. One thing to remember during your reading period is that you will only use TWO of these sources. (You can use all three, but you can earn all 7 points by using just two of the sources.) So, you may want to quickly review the research summaries, decide which two you want to use, and then spend the rest of your 15 minutes closely examining those two research summaries.

After the reading period is over, you will have 45 minutes to answer the EBQ. Remember, you aren't writing one longer overall essay: each of these parts of the EBQ is its own short-answer question. Write your answer in complete sentences in the space provided, read through your answer to make sure it expresses your complete thought, add anything that you think might help a reader understand exactly what you mean, and then move on to the next question.

Here are the different parts of the EBQ you will answer:

- Part A: Write a psychological claim related to the research in the summaries. This claim is probably one sentence that states your conclusion about what you saw in the summaries. You will defend this claim using evidence in the rest of the EBQ. For example, if the research summaries are all about how humans treat other people they view as either attractive or unattractive, you might write a claim like "Humans who are perceived as physically attractive are generally treated more favorably than people who aren't perceived as physically attractive."

- Part B (i): Part B of the EBQ has two parts. In this first part, you will write about one specific piece of evidence from one of the research summaries that supports your claim. Make sure you CITE THE SOURCE for the evidence you use—the research summary from which you got the evidence. To cite the source, all you have to do is write "(Source A)" after the evidence to let the reader know you got the evidence from research summary Source A. For example, one of your sources, Source A, might provide evidence that people who are considered attractive are more likely to get a job offer based on a face-to-face interview.

- Part B (ii): This is the second question in Part B. For this question, you need to explain how the evidence you included in Part B (i) supports your claim. This is the argument you are making: you are telling your reader how the evidence supports the claim, using a psychological term, perspective, or theory. You can earn up to 2 points for this part of the question: 1 point for using the evidence to support your claim or 2 points for using the evidence AND a psychological term, perspective, or theory. For example, you might use the evidence about face-to-face interviews from Source A and the psychological principle of just-world phenomenon to argue that people who are considered attractive are more likely to be treated better because people tend to think that we get what we deserve, so attractive people might be given some advantages just because they are attractive.

- Part C (i) and Part C (ii): These last two parts of the question are just a repeat of Part B (i) and Part B (ii)! All you need to do to earn the points for these parts (up to 3 more points) is to repeat what you did in Part B but use a different source.

One thing you should notice about this free-response question is that you don't have to apply psychological knowledge until you get to Part B (ii) and Part C (ii) of the question! You should be able to earn 5 of the 7 possible points just by reading carefully, making a reasonable claim, and using/citing evidence from two of the sources. If you apply your psychological knowledge in Part B (ii) and Part C (ii), you should score 7 points!

Answering the EBQ Questions

After the 15-minute reading period, you'll get to start answering the EBQ questions about the research summary. Remember that you aren't writing an overall essay: each of these EBQ questions is its own short-answer question. Write your answer in complete sentences in the space provided, read through your answer to make sure it expresses your thought clearly and completely, add anything that you think might help a reader understand exactly what you mean, and then move on to the next question.

In this next section, read through the sample student answer to each of the EBQ questions, the summary of the scoring guide (rubric), and then decide how many points YOU think the sample student answer should score. Then go on and read the explanation for how we think the sample student answer should be scored. This process should help you understand what you need to write to convince your reader that you know how to apply these concepts (and get you 7 points!).

Here are the three sources for this sample EBQ question. Start a timer, and spend 15 minutes reading through these sources. Remember that you will use only two of them in your answer, so you may want to quickly review the research summaries, decide which two you want to use, and then spend the rest of your 15 minutes closely examining those two research summaries.

Source A

Introduction
Researchers investigated whether students used different learning techniques and tested whether these techniques correlated with exam scores. The goal of the study was to find relationships between specific studying techniques and success on course exams.

Participants
Students enrolled in introductory psychology/human development courses at a midwestern college were asked if they wanted to participate in the study. 318 students volunteered to participate. 235 of the participants identified as female, and 83 identified as male. 68% of respondents were first-year students, 16% were second-year students, 10% were third-year students, and 6 had been in college more than 3 years.

Method
Volunteer college students participated in a survey designed to gather information about their studying techniques. Survey items asked about these techniques as well as participants' high school GPAs and ACT scores. College course instructors provided scores from the introductory psychology/human development course exams.

Results and Discussion

Study Technique	Introduction to Human Development Mean Frequency of Use	Introduction to Psychology Mean Frequency of Use
Practice testing	4.67	4.23
Self-explanation	4.64	4.6
Keyword mnemonic	4.62	4.57
Rereading	4.55	4.48
Imagery for text	4.47	4.52
Distributed practice	4.13	4.09
Interleaved practice	4.09	3.98
Highlighting/underlining	3.49	3.71
Elaborative interrogation	3.21	3.23
Summarization	2.6	2.47

College students reported using several techniques frequently, such as practice testing, self-explanation, and keyword mnemonics. The studying technique most associated with success on exams in both courses was practice testing. Common practice-testing techniques used by students involved participating in in-class quizzes, out of class quizzes or other tests included with textbook materials, or self-made quizzes. Several other studying techniques were also associated with higher test scores, such as distributed practice and keyword mnemonics. However, when high school GPA and ACT scores were included in the analysis, the predictive power of the use of studying techniques was reduced.

Adapted from Bartoszewski, B. L., & Gurung, R. A. R. (2015). Comparing the relationship of learning techniques and exam score. *Scholarship of Teaching and Learning in Psychology*, 1(3), 219–228. https://doi.org/10.1037/stl0000036

Source B

Introduction

Researchers investigated different testing procedures in order to determine whether altering testing techniques are associated with transferring learning across contexts. Specifically, the researchers wanted to know if test-enhanced learning (taking a test on material already covered in class) was more effective than other common studying techniques, such as restudying (rereading textbook material or notes).

Participants

48 undergraduate psychology students participated in the research. Researchers used a within-subjects design, meaning that the same participants experienced the different experimental conditions. All participants were students at a large midwestern university.

Method

Three experiments related to test-enhanced learning and transfer were conducted. The experiments focused on how repeated testing and studying impacted long-term retention and transfer of information. In experiment 1, outcomes were measured with a final test that had the same questions as the tests students took earlier in the study. In experiment 2, new inferential questions were added to the final test. In experiment 3, new inferential questions were also added to the final test, but these new questions were drawn from a different knowledge domain than the original test items. In each of the experiments, participants read six passages containing four facts and four concepts each. The final tests were developed based on these facts and concepts. In experiments 2 and 3, inferential questions were developed for the final exam that measured student recall of the original facts and concepts in the same knowledge domain (experiment 2) or a different knowledge domain (experiment 3).

Results and Discussion

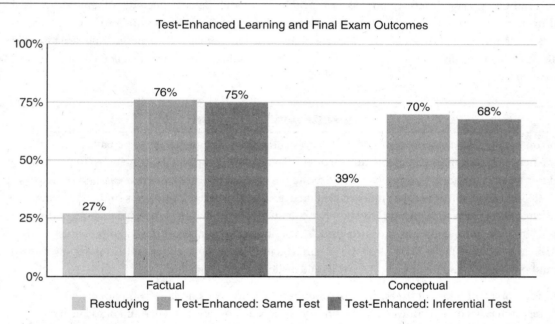

Test-Enhanced Learning and Final Exam Outcomes

Data indicate that repeated testing caused increased retention of the tested knowledge and transfer to each of the final exams in each of the three experiments. The results in Figure 1 indicate that both test-enhanced studying techniques were associated with higher final test results than the restudying technique on both the factual and conceptual tests.

   Researchers concluded that test-enhanced learning is an effective way for students to study specific knowledge as well as increase their ability to transfer/apply that knowledge across different conceptual contexts.

Adapted from Butler, A. C. (2010). Repeated testing produces superior transfer of learning relative to repeated studying. *Journal of Experimental Psychology: Learning, Memory, and Cognition*, 36(5), 1118–1133. https://doi.org/10.1037/a0019902

Source C

<table>
<tr><td align="center">

Introduction

</td></tr>
<tr><td>

The purpose of this systematic review was to thoroughly analyze current research about retrieval practice (defined as events when students attempt to recall and reconstruct knowledge from long-term memory during learning) and summarize the overall impact of retrieval practice on learning. Retrieval practice is an increasingly popular topic in teaching and learning literature, and this review of the literature was designed to provide an empirically based overview of the state of research in the field.

</td></tr>
<tr><td align="center">

Method

</td></tr>
<tr><td>

In contrast with previous literature reviews of the impact of retrieval practice, this systematic review uses narrow, focused criteria to select studies for review. This study included only studies that took place in actual classrooms, and the retrieval practice intervention took place with individual students in person (not remote or virtual learning). The researchers reviewed over 2,000 abstracts of studies of retrieval practice and used this specific selection criteria to identify 50 experiments from 37 studies that met these standards for experimental designs. These 37 studies represent data from over 5,000 participants and resulted in 49 effect sizes that could be combined for the final conclusions.

</td></tr>
<tr><td align="center">

Results and Discussion

</td></tr>
<tr><td>

Based on statistical analysis of the 49 effect sizes from the studies included in the systematic review, the researchers conclude that current literature about retrieval practice support the conclusion that retrieval practice improves learning across a variety of contexts: across education levels, content areas, and course designs, the deliberate inclusion of retrieval practice in course designs and practice increases student learning. The researchers note, however, that very few studies included in this review are based on data from participants from non-WEIRD (Western, Educated, Industrialized, Rich, and Democratic) countries. Commonalities across the 50 experiments included in the review lead the researchers to eight overall recommendations for future research. The authors recommend that more research should be done to investigate:

1. The impact of different time delays between retrieval practice and later summative tests. More granular research is needed to unravel how the time delay between retrieval practice and outcome measures impact student ability to retrieve and use information.
2. How feedback (from teachers or peers) impacts the effectiveness of retrieval practice. After students use retrieval practice, immediate or delayed feedback may modify how students re-encode information, which may impact their ability to recall and use the information later.
3. The various ways retrieval practice is used in actual classrooms. Classroom contexts vary widely, meaning that the ways teachers and students use retrieval practice also vary widely. Future research should investigate this variety of ways retrieval practice are incorporated into learning.
4. How incentives, such as grading practices, impact students' willingness to use retrieval practice (and whether these incentives impact how students use retrieval practice).
5. Whether retrieval practice should be incorporated differently in courses that were neither science nor math. Most of the studies included in the systematic review utilized math and science courses, and future research should investigate the use of retrieval practice in humanities courses.
6. The impact of student age on the effectiveness of retrieval practice. Retrieval practice was effective across age groups represented in the 37 studies, but future research should focus specifically on why the impact on K–12 and undergraduate classes seems to be less than retrieval practice with older (graduate and postgraduate) students.

</td></tr>
</table>

7. Whether retrieval practice operates in online and asynchronous learning contexts in the same way as in person instruction. This systematic review focused exclusively on in-person classes, and future research could determine if online learning contexts are similar or different regarding the impact and use of retrieval practice.

8. If studies involving more diverse participant groups would reveal similar or different patterns of impact of retrieval practice. Since the vast majority of the participants in the 37 studies reviewed were from western, industrialized, comparatively wealthy, and democratic countries, more research should be done elsewhere in the world in order to investigate the generalizability of retrieval practice findings.

Adapted from Agarwal, P. K., Nunes, L. D., & Blunt, J. R. (2021). Retrieval practice consistently benefits student learning: A systematic review of applied research in schools and classrooms. *Educational Psychology Review*, 33(4), 1409–1453. https://doi.org/10.1007/s10648-021-09595-9

EBQ Question

Using the sources provided, develop and justify an argument about the most effective studying techniques students should use.

Part A: Propose a specific and defensible claim based in psychological science that responds to the question.

Sample Student Answer:

Part A: Retrieval practice is an effective way for students to study information because it helps make sure they can recall the information later when they need it.

Scoring Guide:

To earn the point for Part A, students just need to propose a claim that is relevant to the question (in this case, "Using the sources provided, develop and justify an argument about the most effective studying techniques students should use.").

This sample response would score 1 point because it is a claim relevant to the question.

EBQ Question Part B (i):

Use one piece of evidence from one of the sources.

Part B (i): Support your claim using at least one piece of specific and relevant evidence from one of the sources.

Sample Student Answer:

In Source A, researchers found that one of the most frequently used techniques was practice testing, and this method was most associated with success on exams in both courses. Practice testing is a kind of retrieval practice.

Scoring Guide:

To earn the point for Part B (i), students need to describe one relevant piece of evidence and cite the source.

This sample response would score 1 point because the evidence is correctly cited and it is relevant to the claim about retrieval practice.

EBQ Question Part B (ii):

Explain how the evidence supports your claim using a psychological concept.

Part B (ii): Explain how the evidence from Part B (i) supports your claim using a psychological perspective, theory, concept, or research finding learned in AP Psychology.

Sample Student Answer:

The finding about practice testing (retrieval practice) in Source A makes sense because of deep processing. We know that information that is deeply processed is more likely to be moved into long-term memory (because more connections are made to it). Practice testing/ retrieval practice is a kind of deep processing, so it helps students remember the information better.

Scoring Guide:

To earn the 2 points for Part B (ii), students need to explain how the piece of evidence they chose supports their claim, using at least one relevant psychological concept in the explanation.

This sample response would score 2 points because it is a correct interpretation of the evidence from Source A and the student uses a psychological concept (deep processing) correctly to explain the evidence and its relationship to the claim.

EBQ Question Part C (i):

Use another piece of evidence from another one of the sources.

Part C (i): Support your claim using an additional piece of specific and relevant evidence from a different source than the one that was used in Part B (i).

Sample Student Answer:

In Source B, the results showed that repeated testing (a kind of retrieval practice) caused better long-term memory of the tested knowledge and transfer to the final exams in the three experiments. Both test-enhanced studying techniques helped students with their final test results more than the restudying technique.

Scoring Guide:

To earn the point for Part C (i), students need to describe one relevant piece of evidence and cite the source.

This sample response would score 1 point because the evidence is correctly cited and it is relevant to the claim about retrieval practice.

EBQ Question Part C (ii):

Explain how the evidence supports your claim using a psychological concept.

Part C (ii): Explain how the evidence from Part C (i) supports your claim using a psychological perspective, theory, concept, or research finding learned in AP Psychology.

Sample Student Answer:

This evidence about repeated testing being more effective than just restudying makes sense because of semantic encoding. Encoding the meaning of something (semantic encoding) helps us remember it better than just encoding the sight or sound of something. Semantic encoding, needed for repeated testing, is a more powerful form of encoding, so it's a better studying technique than restudying.

Scoring Guide:

To earn the 2 points for Part C (ii), students need to explain how the piece of evidence they chose supports their claim, using at least one relevant psychological concept in the explanation.

This sample response would score 2 points because it is a correct interpretation of the evidence from Source B and the student uses a psychological concept (semantic encoding) correctly to explain the evidence and its relationship to the claim.

Practice Tests

ANSWER SHEET
Practice Test 1

1. Ⓐ Ⓑ Ⓒ Ⓓ
2. Ⓐ Ⓑ Ⓒ Ⓓ
3. Ⓐ Ⓑ Ⓒ Ⓓ
4. Ⓐ Ⓑ Ⓒ Ⓓ
5. Ⓐ Ⓑ Ⓒ Ⓓ
6. Ⓐ Ⓑ Ⓒ Ⓓ
7. Ⓐ Ⓑ Ⓒ Ⓓ
8. Ⓐ Ⓑ Ⓒ Ⓓ
9. Ⓐ Ⓑ Ⓒ Ⓓ
10. Ⓐ Ⓑ Ⓒ Ⓓ
11. Ⓐ Ⓑ Ⓒ Ⓓ
12. Ⓐ Ⓑ Ⓒ Ⓓ
13. Ⓐ Ⓑ Ⓒ Ⓓ
14. Ⓐ Ⓑ Ⓒ Ⓓ
15. Ⓐ Ⓑ Ⓒ Ⓓ
16. Ⓐ Ⓑ Ⓒ Ⓓ
17. Ⓐ Ⓑ Ⓒ Ⓓ
18. Ⓐ Ⓑ Ⓒ Ⓓ
19. Ⓐ Ⓑ Ⓒ Ⓓ

20. Ⓐ Ⓑ Ⓒ Ⓓ
21. Ⓐ Ⓑ Ⓒ Ⓓ
22. Ⓐ Ⓑ Ⓒ Ⓓ
23. Ⓐ Ⓑ Ⓒ Ⓓ
24. Ⓐ Ⓑ Ⓒ Ⓓ
25. Ⓐ Ⓑ Ⓒ Ⓓ
26. Ⓐ Ⓑ Ⓒ Ⓓ
27. Ⓐ Ⓑ Ⓒ Ⓓ
28. Ⓐ Ⓑ Ⓒ Ⓓ
29. Ⓐ Ⓑ Ⓒ Ⓓ
30. Ⓐ Ⓑ Ⓒ Ⓓ
31. Ⓐ Ⓑ Ⓒ Ⓓ
32. Ⓐ Ⓑ Ⓒ Ⓓ
33. Ⓐ Ⓑ Ⓒ Ⓓ
34. Ⓐ Ⓑ Ⓒ Ⓓ
35. Ⓐ Ⓑ Ⓒ Ⓓ
36. Ⓐ Ⓑ Ⓒ Ⓓ
37. Ⓐ Ⓑ Ⓒ Ⓓ
38. Ⓐ Ⓑ Ⓒ Ⓓ

39. Ⓐ Ⓑ Ⓒ Ⓓ
40. Ⓐ Ⓑ Ⓒ Ⓓ
41. Ⓐ Ⓑ Ⓒ Ⓓ
42. Ⓐ Ⓑ Ⓒ Ⓓ
43. Ⓐ Ⓑ Ⓒ Ⓓ
44. Ⓐ Ⓑ Ⓒ Ⓓ
45. Ⓐ Ⓑ Ⓒ Ⓓ
46. Ⓐ Ⓑ Ⓒ Ⓓ
47. Ⓐ Ⓑ Ⓒ Ⓓ
48. Ⓐ Ⓑ Ⓒ Ⓓ
49. Ⓐ Ⓑ Ⓒ Ⓓ
50. Ⓐ Ⓑ Ⓒ Ⓓ
51. Ⓐ Ⓑ Ⓒ Ⓓ
52. Ⓐ Ⓑ Ⓒ Ⓓ
53. Ⓐ Ⓑ Ⓒ Ⓓ
54. Ⓐ Ⓑ Ⓒ Ⓓ
55. Ⓐ Ⓑ Ⓒ Ⓓ
56. Ⓐ Ⓑ Ⓒ Ⓓ
57. Ⓐ Ⓑ Ⓒ Ⓓ

58. Ⓐ Ⓑ Ⓒ Ⓓ
59. Ⓐ Ⓑ Ⓒ Ⓓ
60. Ⓐ Ⓑ Ⓒ Ⓓ
61. Ⓐ Ⓑ Ⓒ Ⓓ
62. Ⓐ Ⓑ Ⓒ Ⓓ
63. Ⓐ Ⓑ Ⓒ Ⓓ
64. Ⓐ Ⓑ Ⓒ Ⓓ
65. Ⓐ Ⓑ Ⓒ Ⓓ
66. Ⓐ Ⓑ Ⓒ Ⓓ
67. Ⓐ Ⓑ Ⓒ Ⓓ
68. Ⓐ Ⓑ Ⓒ Ⓓ
69. Ⓐ Ⓑ Ⓒ Ⓓ
70. Ⓐ Ⓑ Ⓒ Ⓓ
71. Ⓐ Ⓑ Ⓒ Ⓓ
72. Ⓐ Ⓑ Ⓒ Ⓓ
73. Ⓐ Ⓑ Ⓒ Ⓓ
74. Ⓐ Ⓑ Ⓒ Ⓓ
75. Ⓐ Ⓑ Ⓒ Ⓓ

Practice Test 1

Section I: Multiple-Choice Questions

90 MINUTES

> **DIRECTIONS:** Each of the questions or incomplete statements below is followed by four suggested answers or completions. Select the one that is best in each case.

1. After finishing work on a big English project, Leo's room is a mess. His parents are furious and, without letting him explain, prohibit him from using his car or his cell phone for a month. Using this information, which parenting style are Leo's parents most likely using?

    (A) Authoritative
    (B) Indulgent
    (C) Neglectful
    (D) Authoritarian

2. Calinda is usually a hardworking, frugal single mother of two. Sometimes, however, she says her name is Meelo, a pop star, and instead of working she goes on spending sprees at local boutiques. On other occasions, she has been known to say that she is an eight-year-old boy named Curtis. Calinda's symptoms are most typical of

    (A) conversion disorder.
    (B) dissociative identity disorder.
    (C) schizophrenia.
    (D) post-traumatic stress disorder.

3. If Marie Curie, James Madison, and Mahatma Gandhi had all taken an intelligence test and scored poorly, most people would doubt that the test was

    (A) projective.
    (B) standardized.
    (C) valid.
    (D) normed.

4. Saluja decides she wants to try hanging out with a new group of friends. She used to be on the debate team but now tries out for the spring musical. Which of Erikson's stages is she most likely to be in?

    (A) Identity versus role confusion
    (B) Intimacy versus isolation
    (C) Autonomy versus shame and doubt
    (D) Initiative versus guilt

5. Daniel is learning that five pennies spread out on his desk are the same number of coins as five pennies in a pile. According to Piaget, how old is Daniel likely to be?

    (A) 1 year
    (B) 2 years
    (C) 4 years
    (D) 8 years

6. Your knowledge of skills such as how to tie your shoes or ride a bicycle is thought to be stored in which part of the brain?

    (A) Hippocampus
    (B) Cerebral cortex
    (C) Medulla
    (D) Cerebellum

7. Zach is leaving for college and wants to teach his parents how to program their DVR before he goes. What reinforcement schedule would be the most effective to teach them this new skill?

   (A) Continuous reinforcement
   (B) Fixed ratio
   (C) Fixed interval
   (D) Variable ratio

8. Mr. Kan is making soup. After tasting it, he decides it needs more salt and slowly adds some until he can first detect that the soup is saltier than it was before. The amount of salt Mr. Kan needs to add depends on his

   (A) absolute threshold.
   (B) perceptual set.
   (C) difference threshold.
   (D) olfactory sensitivity.

9. Three-year-old Emma went to see a New York Yankees game in Yankee Stadium. From her seat in the bleachers, the players looked like tiny men. As she walked toward the field, the players seemed to grow in size, as if by magic. Emma's belief that the men grew larger is best explained by

   (A) damage to her fovea.
   (B) place theory.
   (C) her inability to use binocular cues.
   (D) the fact that she is still developing size constancy.

10. Infants teach their parents to hold them a lot by crying whenever they are put down. When they are picked up, the babies stop crying. The parents are learning to pick up their babies via

    (A) insight learning.
    (B) positive reinforcement.
    (C) negative reinforcement.
    (D) latent learning.

11. Which of the following sentences illustrates overgeneralization?

    (A) Toby is the fastest boy in the world.
    (B) Psychology majors are kind people.
    (C) Dani goes to the store.
    (D) Only human beings have the ability to use language.

12. What theory suggests that using the term "girls" to refer to women might affect the way those people think about women?

    (A) Linguistic relativity hypothesis
    (B) Social learning theory
    (C) Nativist theory of language
    (D) Signal detection theory

13. Jenna invited Mari to a Ben Folds concert. Mari loves Ben Folds but loathes Jenna. What type of conflict is Mari experiencing?

    (A) Approach-approach
    (B) Avoidance-avoidance
    (C) Approach-avoidance
    (D) Multiple approach-avoidance

14. Mohammed is trying to develop a test that will predict how great someone's potential is to be a prizefighter. This type of test would be best described as a(n)

    (A) power test.
    (B) speed test.
    (C) achievement test.
    (D) aptitude test.

15. A man calls Janie soliciting money for a charity that fights AIDS. He asks if they can count on Janie to contribute $100. Having never contributed to this charity before, Janie is taken aback by the amount and refuses. The representative of the charity then asks if Janie would be willing to make a $25 donation. What technique is the man representing the charity using?

    (A) Door-in-the-face
    (B) Lowballing
    (C) Norms of reciprocity
    (D) Self-fulfilling prophecy

16. Elsa hates her boss, but in order to be successful at work, she goes out of her way to be nice to him. According to cognitive dissonance theory, Elsa's behavior is likely to

    (A) make her resent her boss.
    (B) lead her to displace her hostility onto others.
    (C) cause her to work below her potential.
    (D) result in more positive feelings about her boss.

17. Keela's car breaks down. A woman driving by would be most likely to help her

    (A) if the weather is bad.
    (B) if they are on a highly trafficked road.
    (C) if the driver is a highly religious woman.
    (D) if they are on a desolate country road.

18. Which of the following people demonstrates the most achievement motivation?

    (A) Joey is a carpenter who is anxious to find a life partner with whom to settle down.
    (B) Paula wants to make enough money as a doctor that she can work part-time and still support herself comfortably.
    (C) Nino works in an office supply store. He frequently volunteers to come in early or stay late and prides himself on being a good worker.
    (D) Luther is in high school. He studies constantly because his parents give him $10 for every A he brings home, and Luther is saving up to buy a car.

19. In the past when Nuara's computer wouldn't print, she remedied the situation by restarting the computer. One day, Nuara's printer came unplugged. Instead of checking the connections, however, she repeatedly restarted the computer. Nuara's behavior can best be explained by

    (A) proactive interference.
    (B) functional fixedness.
    (C) belief bias.
    (D) mental set.

20. Paul stared out the window as the train he was on raced through the countryside. He noticed that the telephone poles near the tracks seemed to fly by while the houses in the distance seemed to move slowly. This apparent difference in speed of movement is known as

    (A) texture gradient.
    (B) motion parallax.
    (C) stroboscopic motion.
    (D) the phi phenomenon.

21. Sabrina finds a strong negative correlation between hours spent meditating and reported stress levels. Her findings indicate that

    (A) if a person meditates daily, she or he will not experience any stress.
    (B) people who meditate a lot tend to have higher stress levels.
    (C) meditation lowers stress levels in humans.
    (D) people with low stress levels meditate more than people with high stress levels.

22. In which of the following groups would you expect to find the greatest standard deviation in IQ scores?

    (A) The graduating class of Princeton University
    (B) A special program for children who suffer from severe intellectual disabilities
    (C) Elementary school students in a large public school system
    (D) The entering class of an elite preparatory school in India

23. Gonzo raised his hand to answer his teacher's question. Which part of his nervous system most directly allowed him to perform this behavior?

    (A) Parasympathetic
    (B) Somatic
    (C) Autonomic
    (D) Sympathetic

24. Five-year-old Olivia has never been outside of her neighborhood in New York City. While walking home from school one day, Olivia saw a cow standing in the middle of a cement ball field. To recognize the cow, Olivia most likely had to rely on

(A) signal detection theory.
(B) perceptual set.
(C) bottom-up processing.
(D) difference threshold.

25. After staring at a painting of a red and yellow parrot in a birdcage for a full minute, Saju turns his gaze to an empty birdcage painted on a white wall. What will he see in the empty cage?

(A) The red and yellow parrot
(B) A red and green parrot
(C) A green and blue parrot
(D) A blue and yellow parrot

26. Roscoe works for a nasty and abusive boss but tells everyone what a wonderful woman she is. Psychoanalysts would say that Roscoe is using which of the following defense mechanisms?

(A) Displacement
(B) Reaction formation
(C) Projection
(D) Sublimation

27. Research suggests that genetic and other biological factors play the greatest role in causing

(A) simple phobias.
(B) agoraphobia.
(C) dissociative identity disorder.
(D) bipolar disorder.

28. Armand is the president of his local chapter of the National Rifle Association (NRA). He incorrectly believes that only a tiny fringe element of Americans favor stronger gun control laws. Armand's mistake is best explained by

(A) deindividuation.
(B) the just-world bias.
(C) norms of reciprocity.
(D) the false consensus effect.

29. Dr. Lupin challenges her depressed clients' beliefs that their lives are hopeless and without purpose, and she gives them homework assignments in which the clients are required to engage in the activities that used to bring them joy. What type of therapy is Dr. Lupin using?

(A) Existential
(B) Rational emotive behavior therapy
(C) Gestalt
(D) Psychoanalytic

30. If Artie always seems to act competitively, even in situations where others do not, people are likely to make what kind of attribution about the cause of Artie's competitiveness?

(A) Fundamental
(B) Situation-stable
(C) Situation-unstable
(D) Person-stable

31. Tom is a Type A individual who is seeking short-term, focused psychotherapy to help him make his lifestyle healthier. With what kind of therapist do you think Tom would be happiest?

(A) Behaviorist
(B) Psychodynamic
(C) Sociocultural
(D) Humanistic

32. Isabella fondly remembers the first time she went skydiving. This information is an example of

(A) declarative memory.
(B) semantic memory.
(C) implicit memory.
(D) eidetic memory.

33. Which of the following is an example of observational learning?

(A) A girl learns to howl by watching wolves on a television show.
(B) A parrot learns to say "mama" by listening to its owner.
(C) A student learns to type through the process of trial and error.
(D) A kitten learns to chase birds by copying its mother.

34. Which of the following is an example of discrimination?

    (A) Jessica continues to talk during class even after being publicly reprimanded by the teacher.
    (B) Melissa has learned to dig for earthworms only after it rains.
    (C) Franz always bounces the basketball three times before shooting a free throw.
    (D) After his father yells at and punishes him, Helmut winces when he hears a man yell on television.

35. Which of the following cognitive tendencies is most closely related to the problem of experimenter bias?

    (A) The availability heuristic
    (B) Functional fixedness
    (C) The representative heuristic
    (D) Confirmation bias

36. Banu scored 130 on the WISC. What is his z-score, and approximately what percentile is he in?

    (A) −2, 2nd
    (B) 0, 50th
    (C) 2, 90th
    (D) 2, 98th

37. Which of the following is a positive symptom of schizophrenia?

    (A) Flat affect
    (B) Greater sensitivity toward others
    (C) Catatonia
    (D) Hallucinations

38. One possible explanation for group polarization is

    (A) out-group bias.
    (B) self-fulfilling prophecy.
    (C) self-serving bias.
    (D) diffusion of responsibility.

39. Neural transmission is often described as an electrochemical process. Which of the following is most directly involved in the electrical aspect?

    (A) The synapse
    (B) Terminal buttons
    (C) Hormones
    (D) Myelin

Questions 40 and 41 refer to the following.

Whenever Marva has a difficult day at work, she slams her car door and screams at her children as soon as she enters her house. The children now cringe whenever they hear the sound of a car door slamming.

40. The learning process described would best be labeled as

    (A) classical conditioning.
    (B) instrumental learning.
    (C) observational learning.
    (D) operant conditioning.

41. The fact that the children now cringe when they hear any car door slam is an example of

    (A) acquisition.
    (B) generalization.
    (C) spontaneous recovery.
    (D) discrimination.

42. A low level of glucose in Sam's bloodstream is most likely to make him want to

    (A) engage in risky behavior.
    (B) pursue a romantic interest.
    (C) eat a meal.
    (D) study to improve his grades.

43. Julie is more alert in the morning, and her brother Jack is more alert in the afternoon. This difference stems from a difference in the siblings'

    (A) sleep cycles.
    (B) circadian rhythms.
    (C) daily activities.
    (D) personalities.

44. To treat Zoe's anorexia nervosa, her doctors put her on intravenous feeding tubes, tried to change her irrational belief that she was too fat, and discussed how her early family relationships may have contributed to her current problems. This approach would best be classified as

    (A) cognitive behavioral.
    (B) biological.
    (C) psychodynamic.
    (D) eclectic.

45. After Suzy decided to go to the prom with Dylan, Max was unconsciously furious. Max then channeled all his energies into his artwork. Which defense mechanism was Max using?

    (A) Displacement
    (B) Sublimation
    (C) Rationalization
    (D) Repression

46. Daniel is a toddler who lags behind his peers in terms of speech development. He avoids eye contact with people and resists alterations to his routine. Daniel is most likely to be diagnosed with

    (A) Down syndrome.
    (B) fetal alcohol syndrome.
    (C) intellectual disability.
    (D) autism spectrum disorder.

47. The fact that people's ears are located on opposite sides of their heads is most adaptive because it helps us

    (A) sense a greater range of frequencies.
    (B) gauge the intensity of a stimulus.
    (C) identify the origin of a sound.
    (D) respond to noises behind us.

48. One month before finals, Conrad makes a study schedule and begins to review his notes. Two weeks before finals, Conrad is studying for hours each day to prepare. Right after finals at the start of summer vacation, Conrad comes down with the flu. Which of the following theories best explains this chain of events?

    (A) Selye's general adaptation syndrome
    (B) Yerkes-Dodson law
    (C) Thorndike's law of effect
    (D) Festinger's cognitive dissonance theory

49. Due to brain damage, 10-year-old Genna underwent surgery to remove nearly the entire right hemisphere of her brain. Which of the following observations the day after the operation best illustrates the brain's plasticity?

    (A) Genna was able to understand what was said to her.
    (B) Genna was able to speak.
    (C) Genna was able to move her left hand.
    (D) Genna was able to move her right leg.

50. Tired after a long, hard day at school, Cyrus decides to take a nap. An hour later, his dad wakes him to let him know it's time for dinner. Cyrus feels worse than when he went to bed and can hardly drag himself to the table. An EEG of Cyrus right before he was awoken would most likely have shown a preponderance of

    (A) alpha waves.
    (B) delta waves.
    (C) sleep spindles.
    (D) K complex waves.

Questions 51 and 52 refer to the following.

Alain and Bilal believe that clean-shaven men appear more trustworthy than men with facial hair. They take a photo of a middle-aged man and create two versions: one with no facial hair and the other with a beard and mustache. Alain and Bilal show the photo to 120 students who take AP Psychology in their high school and ask them to rate how likely they would be (from 1 to 10) to give the man $10 if he told them he had lost his wallet and needed train fare to get home.

51. In this study, the version of the photo people see is

    (A) the independent variable.
    (B) the control condition.
    (C) a placebo.
    (D) the dependent variable.

52. Which of the following would be a complaint related to the study's validity?

    (A) Most high school students don't have beards and mustaches.
    (B) Students might respond differently depending on whether they know a lot of people with facial hair.
    (C) Even the same person's ratings might change based on things going on in their lives at the moment.
    (D) Willingness to give someone $10 may not reflect the belief that the person is trustworthy.

Questions 53 through 55 refer to the following.

Alexa surveys the members of her school's award-winning mock trial team about their latest victory. She asks them how skilled they think the opposing team was on a scale from 1 (unskilled) to 7 (exceptionally skilled) and then asks them to select a reason for their victory from the following set of choices: (1) we were the better team, (2) the judge liked us, (3) this was our best case, or (4) we just lucked out. The table below includes the data from the study.

	Skill Rating of Opponents	Reason for Victory
Mya	4	1
Cathy	5	1
Skye	5	3
Tad	4	1
Garrick	5	2
Benji	1	1
Ming	6	1
Paulina	6	1
Levi	5	3
Sebastian	5	1

53. What is the median skill rating given to the opposing team?

    (A) 1
    (B) 4
    (C) 5
    (D) 6

54. How would you describe the distribution of scores?

    (A) Negatively skewed
    (B) Symmetrical
    (C) Bimodal
    (D) Positively skewed

55. What psychological phenomenon might contribute to the team's explanations of their victory?

    (A) False consensus effect
    (B) Self-fulfilling prophecy
    (C) Self-serving bias
    (D) Groupthink

Questions 56 and 57 refer to the following.

Marie is a volunteer in a study about how music affects brain activity. While undergoing a PET scan, Marie is exposed to various types of music meant to evoke feelings of fear, joy, and sadness.

56. On what part of the brain are the researchers most likely focused?

(A) Pons
(B) Reticular formation
(C) Frontal lobe
(D) Amygdala

57. Which of the following would indicate high activity to the researchers?

(A) High-amplitude waves
(B) High-frequency waves
(C) Bright, warm colors
(D) Dark, cool colors

Questions 58 through 60 refer to the following.

Sylvia is interested in how many of her college peers are using cannabis now that use has been legalized in many U.S. states, including the one in which her college is located. She starts by posting signs in the student center asking for volunteers to participate in short, confidential interviews. Six students agree, and Sylvia asks them about how often they ingest cannabis, in what form, and what effects it has on them.

58. Which effect would be most surprising to find?

(A) Mild hallucinations
(B) Intense feelings of joy
(C) Sleepiness
(D) Relaxation

59. For the data on the effects of the drug, what statistic would be most useful for Sylvia to report?

(A) Mean
(B) Median
(C) Mode
(D) p-value

60. Which ethical concern should Sylvia be most concerned with?

(A) Long-lasting harm
(B) Consent
(C) Deception
(D) Privacy

Questions 61 through 63 refer to the following.

The Wechsler Intelligence Scale for Children (WISC) is a commonly used, standardized measure of IQ.

61. Ten-year-old Cal scores a 115 on the Weschler Intelligence Scale for Children (WISC). What is his z-score?

(A) −2
(B) −1
(C) 0
(D) 1

62. What is Cal's approximate percentile score?

(A) 34
(B) 50
(C) 68
(D) 84

63. The WISC could best be described as a(n)

(A) aptitude test.
(B) projective test.
(C) speed test.
(D) achievement test.

Questions 64 and 65 refer to the following.

Professor Pan brings his students to his university lab to observe a study where parents try to coax their newly crawling infants to cross a clear glass "bridge" connecting two tables. Of 10 infants they observe, only one will cross the bridge.

64. Not crossing the bridge could be called the

(A) mean response.
(B) independent variable.
(C) modal response.
(D) dependent variable.

65. The research described is primarily focused on

(A) depth perception.
(B) intelligence.
(C) motor behavior.
(D) obedience.

Questions 66 through 68 refer to the following.

Jeni is curious about whether teens who report high levels of anxiety are more or less likely to have trouble paying attention in school. She surveys students in one of her clubs at school and graphs the data as shown below.

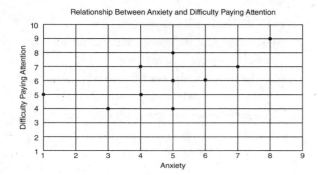

Relationship Between Anxiety and Difficulty Paying Attention

66. What kind of graph did Jeni use to display her data?

(A) A histogram
(B) A pie chart
(C) A scatterplot
(D) A bar chart

67. Which of the following is true based on the graph?

(A) The variables appear to be negatively related.
(B) The relationship between the variables appears curvilinear.
(C) The data appear skewed.
(D) There appears to be a positive relationship between the variables.

68. Which variable has a greater range?

(A) The range of the two is the same.
(B) The range of anxiety scores is greater.
(C) The range of attention-paying scores is greater.
(D) The graph does not include enough information to answer this question.

Questions 69 and 70 refer to the following.

Paolo is school phobic. Paolo's therapist has taught him relaxation techniques, and they have discussed the various aspects of being in school that cause Paolo anxiety. During each meeting with his therapist, Paolo begins by relaxing, and then his therapist guides him through imagining situations that cause him increasing anxiety while he attempts to stay calm. The goal of the therapy is to replace Paolo's anxious feelings with feelings of calm.

69. What type of approach is Paolo's therapist using?

(A) Behavioral
(B) Psychodynamic
(C) Eclectic
(D) Humanistic

70. The therapeutic approach described most closely resembles

(A) flooding.
(B) person-centered therapy.
(C) mindfulness.
(D) systematic desensitization.

Questions 71 through 73 refer to the following.

Adrian believes that using scientific language (jargon) in describing a research study will make people feel more convinced by the study's results. She gives students in her chemistry class a description with complicated jargon and students in her English class a description of the same study but without the jargon. After students read a description of the study, Adrian gives them a survey that asks them to rate how convincing the results were on a 10-point scale.

71. Adrian could minimize experimenter bias if she

(A) did not tell the students what her hypothesis was.
(B) used a control group.
(C) recorded one set of instructions for all the students.
(D) greeted each participant so they all felt important.

72. Which of the following increases the likelihood of confounding variables in Adrian's study?

    (A) Some people like English more than chemistry and vice versa.
    (B) She did not select her sample randomly from the school's population.
    (C) She didn't randomly assign her participants to the different conditions.
    (D) She selected a dependent variable that is difficult to measure.

73. What value will Adrian need to compute in order to assess whether or not any differences between groups she finds are due to chance?

    (A) *r*-value
    (B) *p*-value
    (C) Median
    (D) Mean

Questions 74 and 75 refer to the following.

Nate wants to see whether athletic performance will improve more when athletes receive praise as opposed to when they receive criticism. He partners with a college track coach, and they randomly assign runners to receive either praise or criticism after their runs that week. At the end of the week, the runners' new times are compared to their times from the beginning of the week and the amount each group improved is graphed below.

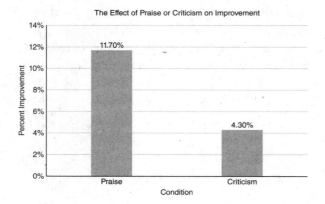

74. What would an IRB likely decide about the risk involved in this study?

    (A) Risk is minimal because the students are used to being coached for running.
    (B) Risk is minimal as long as all members of the team are required to participate.
    (C) Risk is more than minimal because injuries can happen when running.
    (D) Risk is more than minimal because the study is an experiment.

75. What is true based on the results depicted in the graph?

    (A) Criticism makes performance worse.
    (B) Both groups improved, but the praised runners improved more.
    (C) The runners who were praised ran faster than the runners who were criticized.
    (D) A combination of praise and criticism works best.

STOP   If there is still time remaining, you may review your answers.

Section II: Free-Response Questions

70 MINUTES

> **DIRECTIONS:** You have 70 minutes to answer the TWO questions that follow. Your answer should present an argument rather than a list of facts. Make sure to incorporate psychological terminology into your answers whenever possible.

Question 1: Article Analysis Question (AAQ)

Note that the text of the question below is adapted from the *AP Psychology Course and Exam Description*.

Your response to the question should be provided in six parts: A, B, C, D, E, and F. Write the response to each part of the question in complete sentences. Use appropriate psychological terminology in your response.

Using the source provided, respond to all parts of the question.

(A) Identify the research method used in the study.

(B) State the operational definition of personality in this research study.

(C) Describe the meaning of the *r*-values found between the variables described in the graphs.

(D) Identify at least one ethical guideline applied by the researchers.

(E) Explain the extent to which the research findings may or may not be generalizable using specific and relevant evidence from the study.

(F) Explain how at least one of the research findings supports or refutes the researchers' hypothesis that there is a relationship between personality and physiological reaction to stress.

Introduction
In this large-scale health psychology study, researchers gathered data about the relationship between personalities and responses to stress. It is commonly thought that some people respond to stress in more healthy ways than others and that this healthy stress response might be related to differences in personality. This study sought to investigate that claim thoroughly with careful psychological and physiological data collection.

Participants
Data for this study was gathered from the Dutch Famine Birth Cohort. This established database consists of 2,414 men and women who were born in the Netherlands in the 1940s. Participants in this cohort are often asked to provide health and psychological data, which are stored in an anonymous database. Participants sign informed consent each time they provide data to be added to the database, and security measures are in place so that no individual's data can be tied to their name or other identifying information.
352 individuals in the cohort responded to a request from the managers of the database to contribute data about their cortisol and cardiovascular reactions to high levels of psychological stress.

Method

The 352 participants in this current analysis reported to participating hospitals or other health centers to participate in a protocol that involved measuring physiological stress responses while experiencing psychological stress tests. Physiological reactions were assessed in two ways:

- Cortisol levels via saliva samples (higher levels of cortisol indicate high levels of physiological arousal)
- Heart rate measurements (measured through standard blood pressure and heart rate tests)

The stress tests consisted of three tasks:

- Stroop task: A computer-based word-reading task in which the color of the word on the screen interfered with reading the word. Participants were told that they were being timed and that speed was essential. Psychological stress was increased by an auditory alarm that would sound when responses exceeded a designated time limit and/or participants made errors.
- Mirror-tracing task: Participants were directed to trace a star pattern in a mirror image, flipping their visual perception left/right. Participants were again told that speed was important, and an alarm sounded when participants made an error.
- Speech task: A videotape was made of participants giving a speech imagining being accused of committing a crime (being pickpockets). They had 3 minutes to defend themselves and were told that the number of times they repeated themselves and any hesitations would count against them. Participants thought that their persuasiveness would be judged by a team of communication experts.

Earlier in their involvement in the Dutch Famine Birth Cohort, these 352 participants took a version of the Big Five personality test (The Big Five Inventory). This personality test measures personality across five traits: extraversion, agreeableness, openness, conscientiousness, and neuroticism.

All elements of this study were approved by the local medical ethics committee and carried out in accordance with the Declaration of Helsinki. All participants signed informed consent forms.

Results and Discussion

Researchers completed analyses to check for associations between physiological reactions to stress and personality traits.

The table below includes data about physiological reaction to the stressful information. These findings indicate that the stressful situations included in the study did indeed raise participants' physiological stress levels.

	Average Cortisol nmol/L	Average Heart Rate bpm
Baseline	4.70	73.63
Stress	6.32	81.87

The main analysis in this study consisted of checking relationships between high or low levels of each of the Big Five personality traits and physiological reaction to stress. The most important findings were uncovered regarding one of the Big Five personality traits: neuroticism.

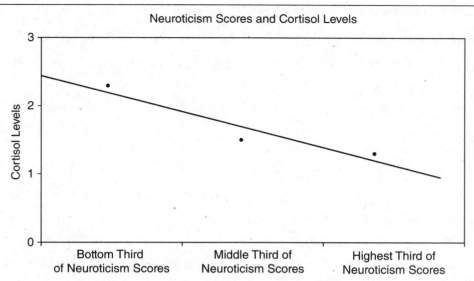

Figure 1: Neuroticism Scores and Cortisol Levels

Figure 1 shows a relationship between neuroticism levels and physiological reaction to stress. The *r*-value for this relationship is $r = -0.5$.

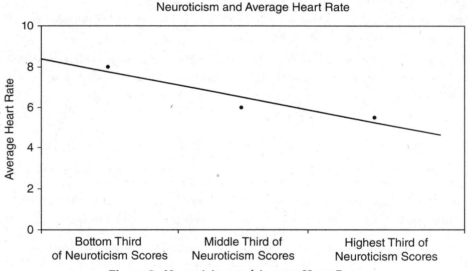

Figure 2: Neuroticism and Average Heart Rate

Figure 2 shows the relationship between neuroticism levels and average heart rate. The *r*-value for this relationship is $r = -0.38$.

These findings reveal that individuals who score high on the neuroticism trait on the Big Five personality test are less likely to react strongly in a physiological way to stress. This finding helps explain why some individuals are able to mask stress responses such as sweating or hesitations in their speech, potentially helping future researchers investigating why some people are more able to deceive others or conceal deceit.

Adapted from Bibbey, A., Carroll, D., Roseboom, T. J., Phillips, A. C., & de Rooij, S. R. (2013). Personality and physiological reactions to acute psychological stress. *International Journal of Psychophysiology, 90*, 28–36. 10.1016/j.ijpsycho.2012.10.018

Question 2: Evidence-Based Question (EBQ)

Note that the text of the question below is adapted from the *AP Psychology Course and Exam Description*.

This question has three parts: Part A, Part B, and Part C. Use the three sources provided to answer all parts of the question.

For Part B and Part C, you must cite the source that you used to answer the question. You can do this in two different ways:

- Parenthetical Citation: For example: "... (Source A)"
- Embedded Citation: For example: "According to Source A,..."

Write the response to each part of the question in complete sentences. Use appropriate psychological terminology.

Using the sources provided, develop and justify an argument about how teachers can help students be more motivated and engaged.

(A) Propose a specific and defensible claim based in psychological science that responds to the question.

(B) (i) Support your claim using at least one piece of specific and relevant evidence from one of the sources.

(ii) Explain how the evidence from Part B (i) supports your claim using a psychological perspective, theory, concept, or research finding learned in AP Psychology.

(C) (i) Support your claim using an additional piece of specific and relevant evidence from a different source than the one that was used in Part B (i).

(ii) Explain how the evidence from Part C (i) supports your claim using a different psychological perspective, theory, concept, or research finding learned in AP Psychology than the one that was used in Part B (ii).

Source A

Introduction
Researchers investigated factors related to student motivation in college. They were interested in factors that increased or decreased student motivation during college classes, including whether an explanation about the goals and objectives of the lesson might influence how motivated students felt during the college class.

Participants
Researchers recruited 136 college students (108 women, 28 men) from an introductory educational psychology class at a large midwestern university. All participants were enrolled in the teacher certification program and preparing to be teachers. Students received extra credit for participating.

Method

Researchers created a purposefully dull lesson by making very plain slides and delivering the lesson in a monotonous style that didn't include any interactive elements or engaging visuals. The dull lesson covered the following topics: correlation coefficient, scatterplots, correlation and prediction, and correlation/causation. Researchers pilot tested the lesson with a small group of students who reported that the lesson was very dull (an average rating of 2.17 on a scale of 1 = not at all interesting to 7 = extremely interesting).

Students were randomly divided into two groups. One group was told that this lecture might not feel fun but also why and how this lecture would help them in the future. The second group did not receive any message before the boring lecture was delivered.

Results and Discussion

The group of students who received the message before the lesson were more motivated and showed higher levels of engagement during the lesson. This impact increased as the lesson progressed, with a 25% difference in motivation by the end of the class. After the lesson, the group of students who received the message reported more interest in the subject and rated that the subject was "more important" than the group of students who didn't receive the message before the lesson. In addition, the group of students who received the message showed an 11% higher level of factual and conceptual knowledge of the lecture topic.

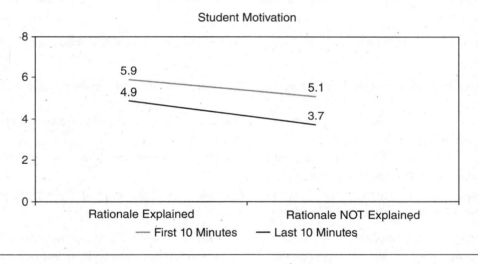

Adapted from Jang, H. (2008). Supporting students' motivation, engagement, and learning during an uninteresting activity. *Journal of Educational Psychology,* 100(4), 798–811. https://doi.org/10.1037/a0012841

Source B

Introduction

Researchers from the University of Iowa and University of Oklahoma sought to answer the research question: How do teachers' choices about instruction during class impact student motivation? Researchers partnered with teachers, providing them with training on autonomy-supporting teaching techniques. The study then investigated whether student motivation was impacted when teachers used these autonomy-supporting teaching techniques.

Participants

20 high school teachers were recruited for the study from two school districts. The participants taught math, economics, English, and science classes. 9 female and 11 male teachers participated in the study. The teachers had an average of 14.8 years professional teaching experience and their average class size was 24 students. The two districts participating in the study were similar in class offerings, graduation rates, standardized test scores, and socioeconomic status.

Method

The research took place over a 10-week period. Participating teachers were first taught the autonomy-supporting teaching techniques. Researchers assessed whether all teachers were skilled in the techniques at the end of the training.

Researchers then worked with the teachers to designate specific lessons and classes. These classes were divided into 4 groups:

1. Classes not given any rationale about why they should try hard (Not an autonomy-supporting teaching technique)
2. Classes that included information that there would be a major test over the lecture topic (Not an autonomy-supporting teaching technique)
3. Classes in which teachers told students they were expected to try hard during the lecture (Not an autonomy-supporting teaching technique)
4. Classes given a message that what they would learn was a new skill that will help them grow in the future. (An autonomy-supporting teaching technique)

Teachers taught the designated classes using each of the 4 techniques. Researchers gathered information from students after the lesson about how important they thought the lesson was, their levels of intrinsic and extrinsic motivation before and after the lesson, and how much effort they put in during the class.

Results and Discussion

Data from all 4 groups indicated that group 4, the group that received the autonomy-supporting message about the value of the information from the lecture, learned more. (These students outperformed the other groups on tests over the material.)

In addition, students in the group 4 classes:

- Rated the lesson as more important (up to 25% more important than the indications given by students in other groups)
- Reported higher levels of intrinsic motivation rather than extrinsic motivation
- Were far more likely to put forth more effort during the lesson.

Adapted from Reeve, J., Jang, H., Carrell, D., Jeon, S., & Barch, J. (2004). Enhancing students' engagement by increasing teachers' autonomy support. *Motivation and Emotion,* 28(2), 147–169. 10.1023/B:MOEM.0000032312.95499.6f

Source C

Introduction
Can teachers be trained to create more effective learning environments? That's the question researchers from four universities in the United States and Canada decided to try to investigate in this large study of high school classrooms in Virginia. Specifically, the researchers focused on a specific teacher-training technique, noted how that training impacted interactions between students and teachers, and then measured the impact these interactions had on student achievement.
Participants
This study involved training teachers in a specific professional learning program: the My Teaching Partner–Secondary program (MTP-S). This program is designed to help teachers create more high-quality and impactful teacher-student interactions. The research included 78 teachers (28 male and 50 female) in Virginia. Teachers had an average of 8.7 years of experience (SD = 8.8). Teacher race/ethnicity was as follows: 83% white, 8% African American, 6% two or more races, and 3% other. 35% of the teachers had a B.A. degree, and 65% had graduate degrees. Informed consent was gathered from all teachers, and parent consent was gathered from the families of the students in these classes.
Method
Participating teachers were divided into two groups: ■ Intervention group: received training in the MTP-S workshop ■ Control group: received regular professional development (not the MTP-S training) Teachers assigned to the intervention group received MTP-S training. This training was designed to be the same approximate length and involvement level as the regular professional development classes experienced by teachers in the control group. Researchers worked with this group of 78 teachers for 2 years in order to evaluate the impact of the MTP-S training. Data from the teachers' classrooms were collected from over 2,000 students. Data were collected on how well teachers in the intervention group implemented the MTP-S techniques and on the quality of teacher-student interactions in all classes. Students took a version of the Virginia state standards assessment at the end of each participating year. Students' previous test achievement (from the end of the prior year) was used as the pre-test score, and their score on the same exam after participating in the class as the post-test score.

Results and Discussion

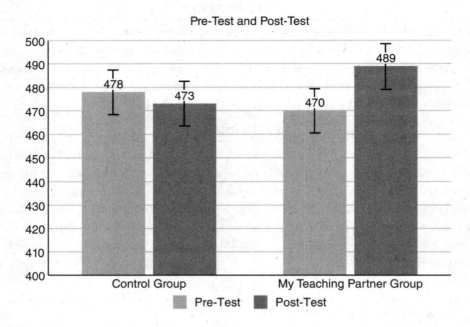

Pre-Test and Post-Test

As researchers analyzed the differences in teacher-student interactions between the control group and the intervention group, they documented five major aspects of interactions that were positively correlated with higher student test scores:

- A classroom climate that students perceived as positive (as defined by student ratings of communication and relationship with the professor).
- When students perceived the professor was responsive, flexible, and had high levels of empathy.
- Students who reported that their professor used a variety of engaging instructional techniques along with clear learning goals.
- Professors encouraged students to focus on metacognition: thinking about how problems are solved and analyzing their own thinking.

Note that these correlations were higher in smaller classrooms than in large, lecture-style classes.

Adapted from Allen, J., Hamre, B., Pianta, R. Gregory, A., Mikami, A., & Lun, J. (2013). Observations of effective teacher-student interactions in secondary school classrooms: Predicting student achievement with the classroom assessment scoring system. *School Psychology Review* 42, 76–98.

Answer Explanations

Section I: Multiple-Choice Questions

1. **(D)** Authoritarian parents tend to make harsh rules and implement them without exception. Authoritative parents are more flexible with the creation and implementation of rules; this style of parenting has also been termed democratic. Indulgent and neglectful parents typically eschew rules, the former because they want to be kind and the latter because they don't pay enough attention to their children's needs.

2. **(B)** Calinda may suffer from dissociative identity disorder, formerly known as multiple personality disorder. This disorder, while questioned by some, manifests itself in breaks in consciousness and memory as the sufferer shifts from one personality to another. Conversion disorder is a type of somatoform disorder in which someone complains of a physical problem (e.g., deafness) for which no organic cause can be found. Schizophrenia, often confused with dissociative identity disorder, does not involve multiple personalities. Rather, someone with schizophrenia suffers from profoundly disordered thought. Post-traumatic stress disorder is an anxiety disorder that typically plagues people who have experienced tragic events like wars and natural disasters.

3. **(C)** Since Curie, Madison, and Gandhi are all thought of as intelligent, an intelligence test on which they scored poorly would be criticized as lacking validity. A test that lacks validity does not test what it is supposed to test. Projective tests are typically used by psychodynamic psychologists to measure personality. It is possible for a test to be standardized, normed, and reliable but not valid.

4. **(A)** Saluja is probably in the identity versus role confusion stage during which adolescents try on a variety of roles in an effort to define themselves. The other choices are all stages that Erikson proposed occur at other times during one's life.

5. **(D)** Daniel is learning conservation of number, a skill that Piaget believed children learn in the concrete operational stage (ages 8–12).

6. **(D)** Procedural knowledge, your knowledge of how to perform skills such as tying your shoes, is thought to be stored in the cerebellum.

7. **(A)** It is easier for people and animals to learn new things when they are reinforced continuously. If something is reinforced every time, it is easier to form a link between the action and its consequences. Partial reinforcement schedules, however, are more resistant to extinction.

8. **(C)** Difference threshold, or just-noticeable difference, is the amount a stimulus needs to be changed in order for a person to detect a difference. Absolute threshold is the smallest amount of a stimulus necessary for one to detect its presence. If you were to add salt to a plain glass of water until someone could first taste it, you would be testing absolute threshold. Since the soup already has some salt in it, this question is about difference threshold.

9. **(D)** We know that when objects get closer to us they do not grow larger because, through experience, we have learned size constancy. Damage to the fovea would impair vision, and an inability to use binocular cues would limit depth perception.

10. **(C)** Negative reinforcement is when a behavior (e.g., picking up a baby) is strengthened because it results in the removal of an aversive stimulus (e.g., crying). Insight learning, in this case, would involve parents suddenly realizing that holding their babies is a good thing. Positive reinforcement is when a behavior is strengthened by the addition of a pleasant stimulus; if babies applauded their parents when picked up, the babies would be positively reinforcing them. Latent learning is learning that occurs in the absence of reinforcement.

11. **(C)** According to Noam Chomsky, children's innate language acquisition device enables them to decode grammatical rules amazingly quickly. Sometimes, in the process, they apply the rules when it is incorrect to do so; that is, they overgeneralize. A child who understands the idea that the past tense in English is often denoted by the addition of -ed therefore might add -ed to irregular verbs like go.

12. **(A)** Whorf's linguistic relativity hypothesis holds that language influences (or, in its initial pronouncement, determines) thought. Therefore, referring to women as "girls" could affect the way people think about women. Bandura's social learning theory explains how people learn by modeling the behavior of others. The nativist theory of language refers to Chomsky's school of belief that human beings are wired in such a way that we learn language quickly and easily. Signal detection is a perceptual theory.

13. **(C)** An approach-avoidance conflict is when one is attracted to and repelled by different features of the same thing. In this case, Mari is attracted to the idea of seeing Ben Folds but repelled by spending the evening with Jenna. In an approach-approach conflict, one must choose between two attractive alternatives. In an avoidance-avoidance conflict, one must choose between two unattractive alternatives. In a multiple approach-avoidance conflict, one must choose between several options, each of which has an attractive and an unattractive feature.

14. **(D)** A test that measures potential is an aptitude test. A power test is comprised of items in increasing level of difficulty and is intended to ascertain the highest level at which one can perform, whereas a speed test contains many easy items and is meant to discern how fast one can solve the problems. Achievement tests measure what someone has learned.

15. **(A)** Door-in-the-face is a compliance technique in which one begins with a request that is likely to be perceived as too large and follows up with a smaller request that will surely be seen as more reasonable. Lowballing is when unattractive features of a decision are hidden until after someone agrees. Norms of reciprocity is the idea that people feel obliged to treat others as those others have treated them. Self-fulfilling prophecy is when one person's expectations of someone else elicit behavioral confirmation in the second person.

16. **(D)** Cognitive dissonance theory posits that it is stressful to hold a thought (e.g., I hate my boss) that contradicts one's actions (e.g., I am really nice to my boss). The stress motivates people to reduce the dissonance by bringing their beliefs into line with their actions. Therefore, since Elsa cannot change her behavior, she is likely to change her beliefs about her boss.

17. **(D)** Bystander intervention studies have shown that the fewer people around, the more likely it is that someone will help another person in need. One reason posited for this phenomenon is diffusion of responsibility, the idea that when others are present, any single person experiences a decreased feeling of responsibility to help. Interestingly, religious beliefs have not been found to predict helping behavior.

18. **(C)** Achievement motivation is typically defined as a person's drive to be successful in work or school. Achievement motivation is more closely linked to how good a job one seeks to do than to the type of job (e.g., doctor) that one has. People with high achievement seek to do their best, not merely to make money or gain other extrinsic rewards but because they want to challenge themselves.

19. **(D)** Our tendency to approach problems in ways that have been successful for us in the past is known as mental set. Proactive interference is when something we learned first interferes with our ability to remember something we learned later. Functional fixedness is the tendency to overlook novel uses for items we are accustomed to using in a particular way. Belief bias is when people's preexisting beliefs interfere with their logical reasoning.

20. **(B)** Motion parallax is a depth cue. Nearby objects appear to move faster as we pass them than do objects that are far away. Texture gradient is also a depth cue; we can see more texture in objects that are close by than in those that are far away. Stroboscopic motion is what movies use to create the appearance of motion. The phi phenomenon explains why we perceive the light in a movie marquee or traffic sign as moving.

21. **(D)** A correlation shows a relationship but not necessarily a cause-and-effect relationship. Therefore, choice (C) is incorrect. A negative correlation is when the presence of one variable (e.g., hours spent meditating) predicts the absence of a second variable (e.g., stress); therefore, choice (D) is correct, and choice (B) is incorrect. Finally, choice (A) is wrong for several reasons, including that it does not suggest an inverse relationship between the variables and that when research is done on a group of people, one cannot infer anything about particular individuals.

22. **(C)** Standard deviation is measure of variability. The greater the standard deviation, the more varied or diverse the group. We would expect a lot of variability in the IQ scores of students in a large public school system. Conversely, we would expect all the other groups to have less variability as they are narrower groups who are unlikely to differ from one another as much in terms of IQ.

23. **(B)** Raising your hand to answer a question is a voluntary motor movement controlled by the somatic nervous system. The parasympathetic and sympathetic systems are the two parts of the autonomic nervous system; they control involuntary functions such as heart rate and digestion. Although they would have played a role in telling Gonzo to raise his hand, taking that action was ultimately enabled by the motor neurons in his somatic system.

24. **(C)** Bottom-up processing is when an object is perceived only by examining the object itself. Signal detection theory and perceptual set are theories about how one's expectations and past experiences can impact perception. Since Olivia's experience is limited to the concrete jungle of New York City where cows are unusual and she saw the cow in a place one would not have expected to see a cow, her perception of the cow would have relied on bottom-up processing. Difference threshold is the amount a stimulus needs to change in order for someone to perceive that it has changed.

25. **(C)** The opponent-process theory of color vision explains that some of the cells that help us to see color are organized in opponent pairs: red and green, blue and yellow, black and white. If we fatigue one-half of the pair and then look at a white surface that reflects all wavelengths of light, we will see an image in the opponent colors (a negative color afterimage). Hence, the red of the original parrot is seen as green and the yellow appears blue.

26. **(B)** Reaction formation is a defense mechanism in which one expresses the opposite of what one feels; Roscoe feels hate but professes love. Displacement is when one takes out one's feelings on a less threatening target than the cause. Projection is when one attributes one's own undesirable traits to others. Sublimation is when one channels one's sexual energy into more acceptable pursuits.

27. **(D)** Bipolar disorder has been linked to an excess of acetylcholine receptors. The manic phase responds well to lithium, and the depressed phase responds well to antidepressant medications. In addition, much research suggests that bipolar disorder runs in families. Though we may be predisposed to develop certain phobias more easily than others, phobias are well explained by and treated from other perspectives, particularly the behaviorist perspective. The existence of dissociative identity disorder is hotly debated; those who believe in its existence generally posit a traumatic event in childhood as a cause.

28. **(D)** The false consensus effect is the tendency of people to overestimate the number of people who share their views. Deindividuation is a loss of self-restraint under conditions of anonymity and arousal. The just-world bias is people's belief that good things happen to good people and that bad things happen to bad people. Norms of reciprocity is the idea that we feel obligated to treat others as they have treated us.

29. **(B)** Dr. Lupin's approach is a cognitive behavioral one; she challenges her clients' beliefs (cognitive) and gives them homework assignments to practice new behaviors (behavioral). Rational emotive behavior therapy (REBT), developed by Albert Ellis, does just that. Existential and Gestalt therapies are humanistic approaches. Psychoanalysis involves probing patients' unconscious in order to discover the repressed roots of their complaints.

30. **(D)** If Artie acts competitively in situations where others do not (low consensus), people are likely to attribute his behavior to something in himself (a person attribution) rather than something in the situation. If Artie always acts this way (high consistency), people are likely to make a stable (as opposed to unstable) attribution.

31. **(A)** Behaviorist therapies tend to be relatively brief and focus on replacing behaviors that make clients unhappy with ones that will make them happier. Psychodynamic therapies tend to be long, in part, because they involve a search for the underlying cause of a patient's issues, a search that often involves a discussion of someone's entire life. Since people from the sociocultural perspective see society as the cause of mental illness, short-term therapy that focuses on the individual is difficult. Humanistic therapies tend not to be as focused as behaviorist ones; they may focus on more abstract issues, such as how to find meaning in one's life, rather than on how to alter a particular behavior.

32. **(A)** Isabella's memory of the first time she went skydiving is a declarative or explicit memory because it is a conscious memory she can actively recall. It is also an example of an episodic memory, but that term is not a choice. Semantic memory is our memory for facts. Implicit memory, as opposed to explicit memory, contains memories we don't even realize we have. Eidetic memory is another name for photographic memory.

33. **(D)** Observational learning is when one member of a species observes a behavior in another member of that species and then copies it. The same species aspect of the definition means that a girl howling like a wolf and a parrot imitating its owner saying "mama" are not examples of observational learning. The other choice involves no observation or imitation.

34. **(B)** Discrimination in operant conditioning is learning that a behavior will result in reinforcement only under certain conditions. Since earthworms are easier to find after it rains, Melissa has learned to discriminate between the good and bad times to dig for earthworms.

35. **(D)** Experimenter bias refers to the idea that researchers' beliefs in their own hypotheses may inadvertently cause them to influence the results of the research so as to confirm those hypotheses. Confirmation bias refers to a similar tendency in all people to pay more attention to information that supports their preexisting beliefs than to information that refutes them. The availability heuristic is the tendency to draw conclusions about the frequency of something based on how easily it can be recalled to memory. Functional fixedness is the tendency not to recognize that a familiar object can be used in a novel way. The representative heuristic is the tendency to reason by similarity and, in the process, to underweight base rate probability. For instance, people might believe that a tall, very thin, attractive woman would be more likely to be a supermodel than a librarian.

36. **(D)** Scores on the WISC are normally distributed. The WISC has a mean of 100 and a standard deviation of 15. Banu, therefore, scored 2 standard deviations above the mean: $(130 - 100)/15 = 2$. Remember that z-scores are a measure of the distance from the mean in units of standard deviation. So Banu has a z-score of $+2$, making possible answers (C) and (D). Percentile is a measure of the percent of test takers who scored at or below a particular score. We know that 50 percent of the test takers scored at or below the mean. We know that an additional 34 percent of scores fall between the mean and 1 standard deviation above the mean, and we know that another 13.5 percent of scores fall between 1 and 2 standard deviations above the mean. Adding these numbers together tells us that Banu scored at the 97.5th percentile, making the correct answer (D).

37. **(D)** Positive symptoms of schizophrenia are ones that are related to excesses rather than deficits. Having hallucinations, which is perceiving sensory stimulation when none exists, is a positive symptom. Flat affect and catatonia are negative symptoms since they are deficits in emotion and movement, respectively. Greater sensitivity is a positive thing, but it is not symptoms of schizophrenia.

38. **(D)** Group polarization is the phenomenon that, given time together to discuss something, groups of like-minded individuals will often come to hold more extreme ideas than those with which they entered the group. One possible reason for this phenomenon is that in the group, the responsibility for the extreme decision seems to be divided among the group's members. Out-group bias is the prejudice people feel against members of other groups. Self-fulfilling prophecy is the idea that one person's expectations about another person can influence the second person's behavior. Self-serving bias is the tendency to take greater responsibility for successful outcomes than unsuccessful ones.

39. **(D)** Myelin is a fatty tissue that surrounds the axons of some neurons and helps speed the movement of the action potential (essentially an electric charge) down the neuron. Neurotransmitters are chemicals that are stored in the terminal buttons and ultimately released into the synapse. Hormones are part of the endocrine system and are not involved in neural transmission.

40. **(A)** The learning process described would best be labeled classical conditioning because Marva's children have come to associate the sound of a car door slamming and their mother's screaming. Instrumental learning and operant conditioning are similar in that they involve learning to pair a consequence with a behavior. Observational learning, or modeling, is learning via observation and imitation.

41. **(B)** The fact that the children now cringe when they hear any car door slam is an example of generalization since the children have generalized their response (CR) to the sound of their mother's car door slamming to the sound of all car doors slamming. Acquisition in this example is when the children began to cringe to the sound of their mother's slamming car door. Spontaneous recovery would be if, after extinguishing the cringe response, the children at a later date cringed again upon hearing a slamming car door. Discrimination would be the opposite phenomenon—if the children learned to cringe

only to the sound of their mother's car door and not other car doors.

42. **(C)** A low level of glucose in Sam's bloodstream is most likely to make him want to eat a meal. Low blood sugar levels are an important cue that one is hungry. None of the other choices are tied directly to blood sugar levels.

43. **(B)** The siblings have different circadian rhythms. These approximately 24-hour cycles in biological and behavioral processes, including those that regulate alertness, body temperature, and heart rate. Sleep cycles are an example of an ultradian rhythm, a cycle that happens multiple times a day. The sleep cycle is approximately 90 minutes long, and we cycle through it several times over the course of a night's sleep. Even though the siblings may differ in terms of their daily activities and personalities, these are unlikely to account for their consistent differences in peak alertness time.

44. **(D)** The feeding tubes represent a somatic treatment, the discussion of how her beliefs are irrational involves a cognitive approach, and the belief that her early family relationships are important belies a psychoanalytic bent. The combination of these three different perspectives signals that an eclectic approach is being used.

45. **(B)** Psychodynamic theorists would say that Max is sublimating. Sublimation is a Freudian defense mechanism that involves taking inappropriate emotions (for example, fury) or desires and redirecting them toward more socially acceptable behaviors (for example, artwork). The other choices are all other defense mechanisms. If Max used displacement, he would take his anger out on a less threatening target than Dylan. If Max used rationalization, he might think to himself that he can get a better prom date. If Max repressed his fury, he would basically forget about the event by pushing the memories into his unconscious.

46. **(D)** Daniel is most likely to be diagnosed with autistic spectrum disorder, an impairment of social development. Common symptoms include delayed speech, avoiding eye contact, and a preference for routine. A description of Down syndrome, or trisomy 21, is likely to mention an extra chromosome on the 21st pair and a degree of intellectual impairment. A description of fetal alcohol syndrome would probably include mention of a mother who drank while pregnant and would likely also mention intellectual impairment. The hallmark of intellectual disability is intellectual functioning that is significantly below average.

47. **(C)** The fact that people's ears are located on opposite sides of their heads is most adaptive because it helps us identify the origin of a sound. We locate sound by comparing the time it takes a sound wave to reach each ear and the intensity of the sound wave when it hits each ear. Sounds that come from our right reach our right ear more quickly and with greater intensity than sounds that come from the left and vice versa. The location of our ears does not increase the range of frequencies we can hear, help us gauge sound intensity, or respond to noises behind us.

48. **(A)** Selye's general adaptation syndrome explains how the body deals with stressors. It has three stages: alarm, resistance, and exhaustion. After working so hard to deal with the stress of finals, Conrad reached what Selye termed exhaustion and succumbed to illness. The Yerkes-Dodson law explains the relationship between arousal and performance. Thorndike's law of effect explains the relationship between the consequences of an action and repetition of that action. Festinger's cognitive dissonance theory proposes that we are motivated to maintain consistent attitudes.

49. **(C)** The right hemisphere controls the left side of the body and is important in recognizing faces, doing spatial tasks, and all sorts of creative pursuits. The left hemisphere plays a larger role in speech and language, logical problems, and controlling the right side of the body. Plasticity is the brain's ability to change as the result of experience, and one way it is illustrated is when the functions of a damaged part of a brain are taken over by another part of the brain. Since most of Genna's right hemisphere was damaged and removed, plasticity is shown by her ability to perform functions associated with that hemisphere after the surgery. The only listed behavior associated with the right hemisphere is moving her left hand.

50. **(B)** About an hour into one's first sleep cycle, people are typically in stage 3 or 4. In these stages, people experience deep, slow-wave sleep, which is marked by the presence of delta waves. Alpha waves indicate drowsiness, and both sleep spindles and K complex waves occur mostly in stage 2.

51. **(A)** The photo seen—either with or without facial hair—is the independent variable, because it's what the researchers manipulate.

52. **(D)** The term validity refers to how accurate something is; if the dependent variable of interest is trustworthiness, it's important that the way that variable is measured reflects trustworthiness. None of the other choices reflect an issue with validity.

53. **(C)** To find the median, you should reorder the numbers so that they go in either ascending or descending order and then identify the one in the middle. Given that this distribution has an even number of numbers, you have to average the middle two, which are the 5th and 6th values; fortunately for you, those values are both 5.

54. **(A)** The distribution is negatively skewed because all the ratings fall between 4 and 6 except for one outlier, which is 1. This low score will pull the mean down, thus skewing the distribution in a negative direction.

55. **(C)** The table shows that 70% of the team members indicate that their team was simply better. Although this may be true, it also is likely to reflect the self-serving bias—the tendency to take credit for positive outcomes and distance oneself from taking responsibility for negative outcomes.

56. **(D)** The amygdala, which is part of the limbic system, plays an important role in emotion.

57. **(C)** PET scans measure the metabolism of glucose. Warm, bright colors like red and orange indicate high activity, while cooler colors like blue and green indicate lower levels of activity. The results of PET scans are not typically portrayed as waves.

58. **(B)** The most common effects of cannabis include feelings of relaxation and, in the case of marijuana, mild hallucinations. Feelings generally become less intense, so an intense feeling of joy would be surprising.

59. **(C)** Because Sylvia will be gathering qualitative data from interviews, she will not be able to compute numerical statistics like mean, median, and *p*-value. She will, however, be able to report the mode, which is the most common effect or effects.

60. **(D)** Although cannabis products are legal in the state where Sylvia goes to school, her participants still might be concerned about their use being known by their professors and future employers; therefore, it is important that Sylvia protects their privacy by keeping the data confidential. In an interview, consent and deception are less likely to be big issues, and long-lasting harm is unlikely to occur due to one's participation in an interview.

61. **(D)** A *z*-score is a measure of how far the score lies from the mean in units of standard deviation. The WISC is normed to have a mean of 100 and a standard deviation of 15. Therefore, a score of 115 is 1 standard deviation above the mean $(115 - 100)/15$.

62. **(D)** A standardized test like the WISC yields a normal distribution of scores. In a normal distribution, 68% of scores fall within 1 standard deviation of the mean: 34% above the mean and 34% below the mean. A score right at the mean is at the 50% percentile. Seeing that Cal has scored 1 standard deviation above the mean, his score is at the 84th (50 + 34) percentile.

63. **(A)** IQ tests are intended to show aptitude, which is ability or potential, as opposed to achievement, which is what one has learned. The WISC is not a projective test—typically used by psychodynamic psychologists to probe the unconscious—nor is it a speed test in that it does not ask many easy items in a limited amount of time to see how fast one can work.

64. **(C)** The modal response is the most common one; given that 9 out of 10 infants do not cross the bridge, not crossing is the modal response. This kind of behavior does not have a numeric mean, and no independent variable is mentioned. The dependent or measured variable is whether or not the infants cross, not specifically that they do not cross.

65. **(A)** The research described closely resembles the work done with the visual cliff to see when humans and other animals developed depth perception.

66. **(C)** This graph is a scatterplot; it plots the relationship between two numerical variables, one on each axis. A histogram is a type of bar chart, and this graph clearly does not include any bars; likewise, it is not a pie chart.

67. **(D)** Given that a straight line drawn through the points with the goal of minimizing their collective distance from the line would slope upward to the right, the variables appear to have a positive or direct relationship to one another. A negative relationship would slope downward from the left. A curvilinear relationship would not be linear. For instance, the points might trend upward for part of the graph and then begin to trend downward. The term skew is not typically used to describe scatterplots.

68. **(B)** The range is the greatest value minus the smallest value. By looking at the graph, we can see that the anxiety scores range from 1 to 8 and the attention scores range from 4 to 9. Since 7 (8 − 1) is greater than 5 (9 − 4), the anxiety scores have a greater range.

69. **(A)** The technique described is based on using counterconditioning, a behavioral technique.

70. **(D)** The therapy described is essentially systematic desensitization in which the patient is taught how to relax and is helped to create an anxiety hierarchy. The goal is to replace the feelings of anxiety with ones of relaxation via repeated pairings. Although also a behavioral technique, flooding involves trying to extinguish a feared object or situation by experiencing it at a high level without negative effects until the fear ceases. Mindfulness, choice (C), is a more general technique that involves becoming more aware of our awareness in the present moment. Systematic desensitization is a more gradual approach.

71. **(C)** Experimenter bias is when the researcher unintentionally influences or creates an environment that increases the likelihood that their hypothesis will be supported. By recording and using the same set of instructions for all participants, Adrian will limit the potential that what she says to the different groups or how she says it will influence their subsequent responses. Choice (A) will prevent participant bias but not experiment bias. Having a control group won't get rid of experimenter bias, and greeting each participant could make the problem worse.

72. **(C)** Random assignment helps control for confounding variables. Confounding variables are any differences between groups other than the independent variable. By dividing people into groups randomly, Adrian can decrease the likelihood that such differences will exist. Choice (A) is a specific confounding variable that could exist between the groups. Confounding variables are introduced in the assignment process, not the sampling process, and they do not have anything to do with how easy or difficult a variable is to measure.

73. **(B)** A p-value provides the probability that a result occurred by chance. A p-value of 0.05 or less is the commonly accepted threshold for statistical significance, which allows the researcher to conclude that the finding was probably not due to chance but, rather, likely reflects a true difference between groups. The r-value is the correlation coefficient. Group medians and means are used by various statistical tests in order to compute p-values.

74. **(A)** Minimal risk is the level of risk that is typically encountered in one's daily life. For college track team members, running is a common activity and therefore presents no more risk than that which they usually face. Although injuries can occur, choice (C), injuries can also occur to people simply crossing a street or even getting out of bed. Choice (B) would make the risk greater as one ethical obligation researchers have to participants is to make participation voluntary. Although experiments can involve more than minimal risk, they do not automatically increase risk, making choice (D) incorrect.

75. **(B)** The bar graph shows that both groups of runners improved but the praised ones improved more. Criticism didn't lead to as much of an improvement as praise, but it didn't hurt the runners' performance. Although the praised runners improved more, we don't know anything about how fast each group was at the outset, so we don't know which group ran faster. It is possible that a combination of praise and criticism would lead to even more improvement, but it is also possible that the combination does not work well; the study described does not provide us with the data we would need to answer that question.

Section II: Free Response

Question 1: Article Analysis Question (AAQ)—Sample Student Response

Part (A)

Identify the research method used in the study.

> This study used the correlational research method. I know it was a correlation because the researchers measured at least 2 things about each participant, like neuroticism level and heart rate.

Scoring Guide

To get a point for (A), students need to correctly identify the research method used in the study.

> This response earns 1 point because the student correctly identified the method used in the study as correlation.

Part (B)

State the operational definition of personality in this research study.

Sample Student Answer

> In this study, the researchers measured personality by the Big Five personality test. The scores on the Big Five Inventory were the operational definition of personality.

Scoring Guide

To get a point for (B), students need to explain the measurable definition of the variable identified in this study. In this case, that variable is personality.

> This response would score 1 point because the student correctly identifies that personality in this study is measured by the Big Five personality inventory

Part (C)

Describe the meaning of the r-values found between the variables described in the graphs.

Sample Student Answer

> The r-value between neuroticism and cortisol levels was -0.5 and between neuroticism and heart rate was -0.38. That means that there is a negative correlation between neuroticism and both these variables. Participants with higher neuroticism scores had lower cortisol levels and lower heart rates, indicating less physiological reaction to stress. This relationship is seen in the scatterplots: higher neuroticism means lower cortisol levels and lower heart rates.

Scoring Guide

To get a point for (C), students need to accurately explain the relevant statistic within the context of the study.

> This response would score 1 point because the student accurately explained the meaning of the statistic—the *r*-scores that showed negative correlations.

Part (D)

Identify at least one ethical guideline applied by the researchers.

Sample Student Answer

> In this study, one of the potential ethical problems might be whether the participants in the Dutch Famine Birth Cohort knew what was going to happen with the data they provided. However, the researchers got signed informed consent from the participants at every stage of the study, so it's OK.

Scoring Guide

To get a point for (D), students need to identify at least one relevant ethical consideration about the study.

> This response would score 1 point because the student actually identified one ethical element of the study: the student mentioned informed consent and how informed consent was treated in this study.

Part (E)

Explain the extent to which the research findings may or may not be generalizable using specific and relevant evidence from the study.

Sample Student Answer

> This study is probably generalizable because the researchers used a large sample size: 352 people from the Dutch Famine Birth Cohort. There isn't much detail about who the participants were. With this large a sample size from this important data set, though, the relationships they found between personality types and reactions to stress can probably be generalized to the larger population.

Scoring Guide

To get a point for (E), students need to explain why they think the results of the study are or are not generalizable using relevant evidence from the research summary.

> This response would score 1 point because the student used relevant evidence—the large sample size—and how the relationship between the variables they found in the sample from the study are probably also true of the larger population.

Part (F)

Explain how at least one of the research findings supports or refutes the researchers' hypothesis that there is a relationship between personality and physiological reaction to stress.

Sample Student Answer

> These findings support the researchers' hypothesis about personality and physiological reaction to stress. The negative correlation they found between neuroticism and cortisol levels alone provides evidence for their hypothesis. The participants who scored high on the neuroticism part of the Big Five test had lower cortisol levels and that relationship was consistent. This negative correlation is evidence that the researchers' hypothesis was supported: there is a relationship between personality and physiological reaction to stress.

Scoring Guide

In (F), students can get 1 point for using appropriate evidence but not having a complete explanation. Students can get 2 points for using appropriate evidence AND including a complete argument/explanation for how that evidence shows that the hypothesis is or is not supported.

> This response would score 2 points because the student used both relevant evidence— the negative correlation found between neuroticism and cortisol levels—and includes an argument about why that result shows that the hypothesis is supported.

Question 2: Evidence-Based Question (EBQ)—Sample Student Response

Part A

Using the sources provided, develop and justify an argument about how teachers can help students be more motivated and engaged.

> Propose a specific and defensible claim based in psychological science that responds to the question.

Sample Student Answer

> Teachers should make sure students know the point of what they are learning and how to think about the value of the lesson.

Scoring Guide

To earn the point for Part A, students just need to propose a claim that is relevant to the question.

> This sample response would score 1 point because it is a claim relevant to the question.

Part B (i)

Provide one piece of evidence from one of the sources.

> Support your claim using at least one piece of specific and relevant evidence from one of the sources.

Sample Student Answer

> In Source A, students in the group where the teachers explained the rationale or reason behind the lesson and why it would help them in the future were more motivated both at the beginning and at the end of the class.

Scoring Guide

To earn the point for Part B (i), students need to describe one relevant piece of evidence and cite the source.

> This sample response would score 1 point because the evidence is correctly cited and it is relevant to the claim about student motivation

Part B (ii)

Explain how the evidence supports your claim using a psychological concept.

> Explain how the evidence from Part B (i) supports your claim using a psychological perspective, theory, concept, or research finding learned in AP Psychology.

Sample Student Answer

> The finding about rationale and motivation in Source A makes sense because of self-determination theory. We are generally more motivated by things that help us feel more in control of our lives and our future. Knowing how a skill can help us, like the students in the group did when the teachers explained the reason behind the lesson, might make us as students feel more motivated because it increases our sense of being in control of our future.

Scoring Guide

To earn the 2 points for Part B (ii), students need to explain how the piece of evidence they chose supports their claim, using at least one relevant psychological concept in the explanation.

> This sample response would score 2 points because it is a correct interpretation of the evidence from Source A and because the student uses a psychological concept (scheme theory) correctly to explain the evidence and its relationship to the claim.

Part C (i)

Provide another piece of evidence from another one of the sources.

> Support your claim using an additional piece of specific and relevant evidence from a different source than the one that was used in Part B (i).

Sample Student Answer

> In Source B, the results showed that providing students information about what they will learn and how the new skill will help them grow in the future helped that group of students learn more from that lesson.

Scoring Guide

To earn the point for Part C (i), students need to describe one relevant piece of evidence and cite the source.

> This sample response would score 1 point because the evidence is correctly cited and is relevant to the claim about retrieval practice.

Part C (ii)

Explain how the evidence supports your claim using a psychological concept.

> Explain how the evidence from Part C (i) supports your claim using a different psychological perspective, theory, concept, or research finding learned in AP Psychology than the one that was used in Part B (ii).

Sample Student Answer

> The study showed that giving students information about what they would learn helped that group of students learn more from that lesson. This makes sense because of semantic encoding. Semantic encoding is more effective than other kinds of encoding (like acoustic or visual) because we are actually thinking about the meaning of something and that helps encode it in long-term memory. The students who knew more about what they were going to learn and why it was important had more of a chance to think about what the ideas in the lesson meant to them (semantic encoding).

Scoring Guide

To earn the 2 points for Part C (ii), students need to explain how the piece of evidence they chose supports their claim, using at least one relevant psychological concept in the explanation.

> This sample response would score 2 points because it is a correct interpretation of the evidence from Source B and because the student uses a psychological concept (self-determination theory) correctly to explain the evidence and its relationship to the claim.

ANSWER SHEET
Practice Test 2

1. Ⓐ Ⓑ Ⓒ Ⓓ   20. Ⓐ Ⓑ Ⓒ Ⓓ   39. Ⓐ Ⓑ Ⓒ Ⓓ   58. Ⓐ Ⓑ Ⓒ Ⓓ
2. Ⓐ Ⓑ Ⓒ Ⓓ   21. Ⓐ Ⓑ Ⓒ Ⓓ   40. Ⓐ Ⓑ Ⓒ Ⓓ   59. Ⓐ Ⓑ Ⓒ Ⓓ
3. Ⓐ Ⓑ Ⓒ Ⓓ   22. Ⓐ Ⓑ Ⓒ Ⓓ   41. Ⓐ Ⓑ Ⓒ Ⓓ   60. Ⓐ Ⓑ Ⓒ Ⓓ
4. Ⓐ Ⓑ Ⓒ Ⓓ   23. Ⓐ Ⓑ Ⓒ Ⓓ   42. Ⓐ Ⓑ Ⓒ Ⓓ   61. Ⓐ Ⓑ Ⓒ Ⓓ
5. Ⓐ Ⓑ Ⓒ Ⓓ   24. Ⓐ Ⓑ Ⓒ Ⓓ   43. Ⓐ Ⓑ Ⓒ Ⓓ   62. Ⓐ Ⓑ Ⓒ Ⓓ
6. Ⓐ Ⓑ Ⓒ Ⓓ   25. Ⓐ Ⓑ Ⓒ Ⓓ   44. Ⓐ Ⓑ Ⓒ Ⓓ   63. Ⓐ Ⓑ Ⓒ Ⓓ
7. Ⓐ Ⓑ Ⓒ Ⓓ   26. Ⓐ Ⓑ Ⓒ Ⓓ   45. Ⓐ Ⓑ Ⓒ Ⓓ   64. Ⓐ Ⓑ Ⓒ Ⓓ
8. Ⓐ Ⓑ Ⓒ Ⓓ   27. Ⓐ Ⓑ Ⓒ Ⓓ   46. Ⓐ Ⓑ Ⓒ Ⓓ   65. Ⓐ Ⓑ Ⓒ Ⓓ
9. Ⓐ Ⓑ Ⓒ Ⓓ   28. Ⓐ Ⓑ Ⓒ Ⓓ   47. Ⓐ Ⓑ Ⓒ Ⓓ   66. Ⓐ Ⓑ Ⓒ Ⓓ
10. Ⓐ Ⓑ Ⓒ Ⓓ   29. Ⓐ Ⓑ Ⓒ Ⓓ   48. Ⓐ Ⓑ Ⓒ Ⓓ   67. Ⓐ Ⓑ Ⓒ Ⓓ
11. Ⓐ Ⓑ Ⓒ Ⓓ   30. Ⓐ Ⓑ Ⓒ Ⓓ   49. Ⓐ Ⓑ Ⓒ Ⓓ   68. Ⓐ Ⓑ Ⓒ Ⓓ
12. Ⓐ Ⓑ Ⓒ Ⓓ   31. Ⓐ Ⓑ Ⓒ Ⓓ   50. Ⓐ Ⓑ Ⓒ Ⓓ   69. Ⓐ Ⓑ Ⓒ Ⓓ
13. Ⓐ Ⓑ Ⓒ Ⓓ   32. Ⓐ Ⓑ Ⓒ Ⓓ   51. Ⓐ Ⓑ Ⓒ Ⓓ   70. Ⓐ Ⓑ Ⓒ Ⓓ
14. Ⓐ Ⓑ Ⓒ Ⓓ   33. Ⓐ Ⓑ Ⓒ Ⓓ   52. Ⓐ Ⓑ Ⓒ Ⓓ   71. Ⓐ Ⓑ Ⓒ Ⓓ
15. Ⓐ Ⓑ Ⓒ Ⓓ   34. Ⓐ Ⓑ Ⓒ Ⓓ   53. Ⓐ Ⓑ Ⓒ Ⓓ   72. Ⓐ Ⓑ Ⓒ Ⓓ
16. Ⓐ Ⓑ Ⓒ Ⓓ   35. Ⓐ Ⓑ Ⓒ Ⓓ   54. Ⓐ Ⓑ Ⓒ Ⓓ   73. Ⓐ Ⓑ Ⓒ Ⓓ
17. Ⓐ Ⓑ Ⓒ Ⓓ   36. Ⓐ Ⓑ Ⓒ Ⓓ   55. Ⓐ Ⓑ Ⓒ Ⓓ   74. Ⓐ Ⓑ Ⓒ Ⓓ
18. Ⓐ Ⓑ Ⓒ Ⓓ   37. Ⓐ Ⓑ Ⓒ Ⓓ   56. Ⓐ Ⓑ Ⓒ Ⓓ   75. Ⓐ Ⓑ Ⓒ Ⓓ
19. Ⓐ Ⓑ Ⓒ Ⓓ   38. Ⓐ Ⓑ Ⓒ Ⓓ   57. Ⓐ Ⓑ Ⓒ Ⓓ

Practice Test 2

Section I: Multiple-Choice Questions

90 MINUTES

DIRECTIONS: Each of the questions or incomplete statements below is followed by four suggested answers or completions. Select the one that is best in each case.

1. Cyan has come up with a test to identify people with the potential to be great civil rights lawyers. Such a test would be classified as a(n)

    (A) speed test.
    (B) achievement test.
    (C) EQ test.
    (D) aptitude test.

2. Approximately what percent of the population scores between 70 and 130 on the WISC?

    (A) 34
    (B) 50
    (C) 68
    (D) 84

3. Young Tina had never seen the space shuttle until her parents pointed out a picture of it ready to launch. When she next saw a picture of it flying, she had difficulty recognizing it.

    Which concept best explains this problem?

    (A) Autokinetic effect
    (B) Dishabituation
    (C) Summation
    (D) Shape constancy

4. Alyssa presents one group of shoppers with an advertisement for milk that is 99 percent fat free and another group of shoppers with an advertisement for milk that is 1 percent fat. What is Alyssa most likely testing?

    (A) Representativeness heuristic
    (B) Confirmation bias
    (C) Schema
    (D) Framing

5. Jupiter pilots his newly created perfectionism scale on a high school psychology class. He returns one month later to administer the same test to the same students, and then he correlates the two sets of results. What is Jupiter probably doing?

    (A) Checking for outliers
    (B) Standardizing the test
    (C) Looking to see if the mean level of perfectionism has changed
    (D) Measuring the test's reliability

6. If the College Board neglected to put any questions that had to do with neuroscience on the AP Psychology exam one year, the test would lack

    (A) construct validity.
    (B) predictive validity.
    (C) concurrent validity.
    (D) content validity.

7. An American teenager's prototype of a chair is most likely to include

   (A) a desk and/or table.
   (B) four legs and a seat.
   (C) a feeling of anxiety associated with school.
   (D) an armchair, a chairlift, and a wheelchair.

8. In studying for the AP Psychology exam, good advice would be to

   (A) store as much as possible in your short-term memory.
   (B) read this book over and over as many times as you can.
   (C) rely heavily on the serial position effect.
   (D) study from multiple sources.

9. Of the following, most children will develop which skill first?

   (A) Write with a pencil
   (B) Cut with a knife
   (C) Say a sentence
   (D) Clap their hands

10. Antonia has a cat. The first time Antonia sees a rabbit, she calls it a cat. Her mistake is due to the process of

   (A) discrimination.
   (B) generalization.
   (C) accommodation.
   (D) assimilation.

11. Four-year-old Kate positions herself squarely in front of all the other kids to watch a magician. Piaget would attribute this to Kate's

   (A) egocentrism.
   (B) lack of object permanence.
   (C) inability to conserve.
   (D) animism.

Questions 12 and 13 refer to the following.

The school librarian wants to encourage children to read over the summer. Therefore, she sets up a system where students get a prize for every five books they read over the summer.

12. The librarian is using

   (A) continuous reinforcement.
   (B) a fixed-ratio schedule.
   (C) a variable-ratio schedule.
   (D) a fixed-interval schedule.

13. The librarian is pleased to find that students report reading more books over the summer than ever before. However, the number of books borrowed from the library decreases in the fall. Psychologists would likely explain these findings with

   (A) the overjustification effect.
   (B) social learning theory.
   (C) the Premack principle.
   (D) the law of effect.

14. Coach Perry is training Lana to be the kindergarten soccer team's goalie. Coach Perry starts by rolling the ball to Lana slowly so she can stop it; he gradually begins to roll the ball faster and to different parts of the goal, all while praising her successful attempts. The technique Coach Perry is using is called

   (A) the law of effect.
   (B) the partial reinforcement effect.
   (C) shaping.
   (D) second-order conditioning.

15. Which of the following is the strongest piece of evidence for the idea that animals are capable of developing and using a sophisticated language?

   (A) The discovery of physical structures in animal brains are analogous to the language acquisition device in humans.
   (B) Primates quickly learn words that result in food rewards.
   (C) Systems of communication have been documented in species from honeybees to dolphins.
   (D) Apes have been able to use the words they know to express novel concepts.

16. Research has shown that people who read a job description written only with male pronouns (e.g., he, his) are more likely to think of an employee as male than people who read a description that uses gender-neutral language (e.g., he or she). This finding is most closely linked to

(A) the linguistic relativity hypothesis.
(B) gender schema theory.
(C) the social role hypothesis.
(D) modeling.

17. Which of the following graphs best represents the relationship between arousal and performance?

(A)
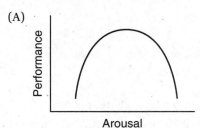

(B)
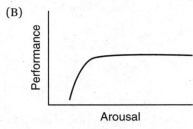

(C)
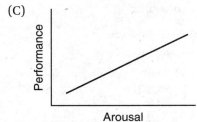

(D)
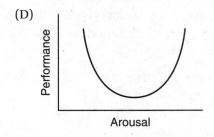

18. Faye believes that victims of natural disasters are foolish because they should have developed better advance detection and warning systems. Faye is manifesting the

(A) false consensus effect.
(B) self-fulfilling prophecy effect.
(C) self-serving bias.
(D) just-world bias.

19. Ani believes that her attitudes and behavior play a central role in what happens to her. Such a belief is likely to be associated with

(A) a strong superego.
(B) low self-esteem.
(C) low self-efficacy.
(D) an internal locus of control.

20. Sal meets Petunia for the first time. She is outgoing and funny. He walks away with the opinion that Petunia is a fun person, whereas in actuality Petunia is temporarily gleeful because she just won the lottery. Sal's opinion that Petunia is funny is best explained by

(A) the mere-exposure effect.
(B) self-serving bias.
(C) equipotentiality.
(D) the fundamental attribution error.

21. As part of her campaign for school president, Edy personally gives out cookies that say "Vote for Edy" on them. Which of the following is one reason that this approach might improve Edy's chances in the election?

(A) Foot-in-the-door
(B) Mere-exposure effect
(C) Central route of persuasion
(D) Pluralistic ignorance

22. After taking AP Psychology and doing well in the class and on the exam, Donald goes to college. If Donald is interested in psychology and has high achievement motivation, as a first-year student, he is most likely to

(A) take an introductory psychology class in which he knows that he will excel.
(B) enroll in an upper-level graduate seminar in which he will be exposed to a lot of new information but is likely to struggle to pass.
(C) avoid psychology classes since he has already mastered the material.
(D) sign up for an upper-level undergraduate course in which he will have to work hard to succeed and will learn new things.

23. Runners in a park were found to pick up their pace when another runner came into view; this finding illustrates the phenomenon of

(A) social facilitation.
(B) conformity.
(C) deindividuation.
(D) norms.

24. Vance's therapist believes Vance is psychotic. From which of the following medications would he most likely believe Vance would benefit?

(A) L-Dopa
(B) Neuroleptics
(C) Benzodiazepines
(D) SSRIs

25. Odette is nearing her 70th birthday. Over the last year, she has suffered a loss of appetite and began to experience difficulty sleeping. She has lost interest in her favorite pastimes: gardening and bridge. Odette is most likely to be diagnosed as having

(A) Alzheimer's disease.
(B) seasonal affective disorder.
(C) insomnia and bulimia.
(D) major depressive disorder.

26. A doctor examining a car crash victim in order to determine whether the crash caused structural damage to the brain would use what kind of brain scan?

(A) MRI
(B) PET
(C) EEG
(D) fMRI

27. Children who suffer brain damage may be able to regain their physical and mental abilities more quickly than older patients with brain damage due to which of the following properties of the brain?

(A) Contralateral control
(B) Klinefelter's syndrome
(C) Effective psychological environment
(D) Brain plasticity

28. Which of the following kinds of brain scans would be most useful in disproving the statement "Most people only use 10 percent of their brains"?

(A) CAT
(B) MRI
(C) EEG
(D) PET

29. Turning up the volume on a music player changes which aspect of sound?

(A) Amplitude of the wave
(B) Frequency of the wave
(C) Pitch of the tone
(D) Transduction of the tone

30. A research study establishes that most people can taste 1 gram of salt in 1 quart of water. Which of the following concepts is most closely related to the goal of this study?

(A) Difference threshold
(B) Absolute threshold
(C) Taste constancy
(D) Sensory adaptation

31. A musician's ability to make a distinction between two very similar pitches depends on which of the following concepts?

   (A) Absolute threshold
   (B) Signal detection theory
   (C) Bottom-up processing
   (D) Difference threshold

32. Adrian dreams she has discovered a new restaurant in the city with really good salads. Her analyst suggests that the dream reflects Adrian's discontent with her current life situation and her desire for change. The analyst's interpretation best exemplifies a

   (A) cognitive perspective.
   (B) psychoanalytic perspective.
   (C) sociocultural perspective.
   (D) behaviorist perspective.

33. Someone with brain damage who has difficulty making the muscle movements needed to produce accurate speech might have damage to which area of the brain?

   (A) Wernicke's area
   (B) Hippocampus
   (C) Broca's area
   (D) Amygdala

34. A researcher tests the problem-solving skills of twenty 10-year-old, twenty 20-year-old, and twenty 30-year-old participants for a study on age and problem solving. What research method is this researcher using?

   (A) Longitudinal
   (B) Stage
   (C) Developmental
   (D) Cross-sectional

35. Knowledge of different categories of trees and where they grow best is an example of what kind of long-term memory?

   (A) Episodic memory
   (B) Semantic memory
   (C) Procedural memory
   (D) Eidetic memory

36. Which of the following is an example of an implicit memory?

   (A) Describing the taste of the cake at your last birthday party
   (B) Remembering how to tie a tie
   (C) Recalling the name of your junior high school shop teacher
   (D) Recognizing a celebrity

37. Which classical conditioning term best describes the following scenario? Later in his classical conditioning experiments, Ivan Pavlov's dogs began to salivate whenever they heard any sound similar to a bell, such as a doorbell or someone accidentally clinking a water glass.

   (A) Discrimination
   (B) Spontaneous recovery
   (C) Trace conditioning
   (D) Generalization

38. What is the major difference between classical and operant conditioning?

   (A) Operant conditioning was established well before classical conditioning.
   (B) Classical conditioning involves pairing stimuli, and operant conditioning involves pairing a response with a stimulus.
   (C) Operant conditioning is used to train organisms to perform specific acts, and classical conditioning is used to get organisms to stop performing specific acts.
   (D) Classical conditioning is more difficult to use but more effective than operant conditioning.

39. A nonprofit environmental group includes a free gift of address labels in a letter asking for contributions. Which social psychological principle is the nonprofit group trying to use to increase contributions?

   (A) Self-fulfilling prophecy
   (B) Stable attribution
   (C) Compliance strategy
   (D) Fundamental attribution error

40. A math teacher refuses to look at the grades her students received in the past in math classes. The teacher is worried that looking at their past grades might influence the ways she reacts to her students. What effect is the teacher trying to avoid?

    (A) Cognitive dissonance
    (B) Self-fulfilling prophecy
    (C) Fundamental attribution error
    (D) False-consensus effects

41. Which social psychological principle best explains prejudice?

    (A) Individualism
    (B) Collectivism
    (C) Self-serving bias
    (D) In-group bias

42. Someone who fails an important exam and reacts by spending more time studying in the library and less time socializing probably has which kind of locus of control?

    (A) Internal
    (B) External
    (C) Subconscious
    (D) Unconscious

43. Which of the following techniques would be most helpful in avoiding the problems associated with groupthink?

    (A) Responding to deindividuation among group members
    (B) Encouraging contrary opinions within the group
    (C) Increasing group polarization within different groups
    (D) Identifying approach-avoidance conflicts

44. What would a psychometrician conclude about a personality test that tells a person she is an extreme extrovert the first time she takes the test and an extreme introvert the next time she takes it?

    (A) This personality test has low reliability but high validity.
    (B) The test is probably high in construct validity but isn't very predictive.
    (C) These test norms and standardization probably need improvement.
    (D) The results indicate that the test has low test-retest reliability.

45. A person who experiences flashbacks and nightmares after being involved in a serious car accident is likely to be diagnosed with which psychological disorder?

    (A) Dissociative identity disorder
    (B) Bipolar disorder
    (C) Schizophrenia
    (D) Post-traumatic stress disorder

46. In what way would a person diagnosed with schizophrenia most likely differ from a person diagnosed with a dissociative disorder?

    (A) A person with schizophrenia is likely to have more than one personality.
    (B) A person diagnosed with a dissociative disorder is likely to have delusions.
    (C) A person diagnosed with schizophrenia is likely to experience hallucinations.
    (D) A person diagnosed with a dissociative disorder may have difficulty keeping a job.

47. A psychologist who advises a patient to write about his depressed thoughts and prescribes an antidepressant medication is using a combination of which of the following perspectives?

    (A) Therapeutic and psychoanalytic
    (B) Behavioral and social-cultural
    (C) Humanist and evolutionary
    (D) Cognitive and biopsychology

48. Which psychological perspective would be most likely to attribute the greater rate of ADHD diagnoses in boys to the way schools are structured?

    (A) Biological
    (B) Cognitive
    (C) Humanistic
    (D) Sociocultural

49. Juana has been feeling down for nearly a year. Although she is still able to go about her daily activities, she does not experience the same level of pleasure from them as she used to. Juana would be most likely to be diagnosed with

    (A) Persistent depressive disorder
    (B) Bipolar disorder I
    (C) Major depressive disorder
    (D) Seasonal affective disorder

50. Dr. Akbar often asks her patients about their memories of childhood and dreams. What type of therapist is Dr. Akbar most likely to be?

    (A) Humanistic
    (B) Psychodynamic
    (C) Behaviorist
    (D) Somatic

Questions 51 through 55 refer to the following.

One of your high school classmates, Paula, is researching the effect of keeping a daily gratitude journal on happiness. She first gets a baseline measure of happiness using a standard 10-point scale and then asks all the students to keep a daily gratitude journal during the first 5 minutes of English class each day during the month of March. Paula then has the students complete the same measure of happiness again. The data she collected are shown below, including the difference between posttest and baseline scores.

	Baseline Happiness Score	Posttest Happiness Score	Posttest–Baseline Difference
Zebron	5.2	5.5	0.3
Yolanda	6.2	6.6	0.4
Xavier	4.9	6.1	1.2
Walt	8.2	8.3	0.1
Velma	1.7	9.2	7.5
Ursula	3.4	3.7	0.3
Tomeo	4.8	4.7	−0.1
Sandy	6.6	6.8	0.2
Rachel	7.5	7.6	0.1
Quincy	5.9	6.2	0.3

51. Whose baseline score could be considered an outlier?

    (A) Zebron's
    (B) Xavier's
    (C) Velma's
    (D) Tomeo's

52. What is the mode of the change in happiness scores?

    (A) 7.6
    (B) 1.3
    (C) 0.3
    (D) 0.1

53. Which measure of central tendency would be most useful in describing this distribution?

    (A) Mean
    (B) Median
    (C) Range
    (D) Mode

54. Given her design, what confounding variable does Paula need to be most concerned about?

    (A) When she collected the data
    (B) Where she collected the data
    (C) Who she chose to be in the study
    (D) Why she chose to run the study

55. Which *p*-value would indicate that Paula found a significant effect for journaling?

    (A) 1.0
    (B) 0.5
    (C) 0.1
    (D) 0.05

Questions 56 through 58 refer to the following.

Juniper is interested in the relationship between vision and hearing. She finds 12 volunteers to come into her university lab to determine the faintest sounds they can hear (in decibels) and the smallest letters they can see (in centimeters)—both from 5 meters away. A graph of the data appears below.

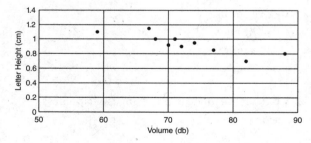

56. Based on the graph, what type of relationship appears to exist between the two variables?

    (A) Positive
    (B) Negative
    (C) Symmetrical
    (D) Curvilinear

57. What value would be most useful in interpreting the graph?

    (A) Mean
    (B) Standard deviation
    (C) Correlation coefficient
    (D) Percentile

58. Juniper's research is most closely related to the concept of

    (A) absolute threshold.
    (B) top-down processing.
    (C) signal detection theory.
    (D) just-noticeable difference.

Questions 59 and 60 refer to the following.

Dr. Patel, a neurologist, is researching the effect of a new drug on brain plasticity in older adults. He recruits 50 volunteers from his patients who are over 60 and have recently sought help for cognitive decline. Half the participants are given the new drug, while the other half are given a placebo. All come back for evaluation at 1 month, 3 months, and 6 months.

59. Dr. Patel's assistant, Jorge, thinks that Dr. Patel's control group should not take anything. What do you think?

    (A) Jorge is correct. The control group should not receive anything and will need to come in for all the evaluation sessions.
    (B) Jorge is correct. In addition, the control group will not need to come in for any of the evaluations.
    (C) Jorge is incorrect. The placebo ensures differences between groups are not due to the belief that patients are taking medication.
    (D) Jorge is incorrect. It is unethical not to give everyone some form of "treatment" even if it does not really work.

60. How should Dr. Patel decide which patients get the new drug and which get the placebo?

  (A) He should ask them which they prefer.
  (B) He should assign the patients with the most severe symptoms to get the drug.
  (C) He should assign the patients with the least severe symptoms to get the drug.
  (D) He should use random assignment to divide the patients into groups.

Questions 61 through 63 refer to the following.

After a few disappointing scores on his Introduction to Psychology exams, Andre goes to see his teaching assistant (TA), Jenny. Jenny asks how Andre usually studies for the exams, and Andre tells her that he devotes the entire night before the exam to studying for at least 3 hours. Jenny explains that she has been testing two different study strategies with her students. One strategy is massed practice where she helps students identify what to study and for how long the day before the test. The other strategy is distributed practice where she also helps identify what to study and for how long but then helps them divide that material into chunks to study on each of the 4 days preceding the test. Jenny then shares some informal data she has been keeping since she began working as a TA; the table below presents that data.

Student Number	Assigned Study Pattern	Improvement (in points)
1	Massed	5
2	Massed	2
3	Massed	11
4	Distributed	12
5	Distributed	8
6	Distributed	18
7	Distributed	6

61. What is the difference between the means of the two groups?

  (A) 3
  (B) 5
  (C) 6
  (D) 7

62. Which statement best describes how conclusive Jenny's findings are?

  (A) They are not very conclusive because the sample is too small.
  (B) They are not very conclusive because more people used the distributed method.
  (C) They are very conclusive because the difference between the two groups is more than 0.05.
  (D) They are very conclusive because one group scored about twice as much as the other.

63. Andre wants to know whether Jenny's students are improving relative to their classmates. Which statistic would be most helpful to him to understand this?

  (A) The modes on all the tests
  (B) The standard deviation on all the tests
  (C) How far the students are from the median on each of the tests
  (D) The students' percentile scores on each of the tests

Questions 64 and 65 refer to the following.

To prepare his students for the AP Psychology test, Mr. Rosales conducts review sessions and gives practice tests in the room where the test will be given. On the practice tests, he carefully examines both the mean class performance and the standard deviation.

64. Mr. Rosales is trying to take advantage of

  (A) depth of processing.
  (B) mood congruence.
  (C) the serial position effect.
  (D) context-dependent memory.

65. What information can the standard deviation give Mr. Rosales?

  (A) Whether his practice test is reliable
  (B) Whether his practice test is valid
  (C) How varied his students' scores are
  (D) Students' average performance

Questions 66 and 67 refer to the following.

Ms. Rashid has 6 children: Aaron, Aubrey, Audrey, Annie, Alfred, and Alexa. When they turn 5, she teaches them how to make their beds. For the first 3, she checked their rooms every day to see if their beds were made and gave them $1 if they were, but for the last 3 children she only checked every Saturday. The table below shows how many times each child needed to be given a dollar and therefore how much they earned before they learned to make their bed consistently.

Child	Checking Schedule	Number of Dollars Paid to Each Child
Aaron	Daily	8
Aubrey	Daily	6
Audrey	Daily	11
Annie	Weekly	7
Alfred	Weekly	16
Alexa	Weekly	12

66. What is the median number of dollars it took Ms. Rashid's children to learn to make their beds?

    (A) 9
    (B) 9.5
    (C) 10
    (D) 10.5

67. What might explain why the children checked daily learned faster than the children checked weekly?

    (A) Continuous reinforcement typically results in faster learning than intermittent reinforcement.
    (B) The older children probably helped teach the younger ones to make their beds.
    (C) Variable schedules are more resistant to extinction.
    (D) Ms. Rashid probably became used to a more authoritarian parenting style as she got older.

Questions 68 through 71 refer to the following.

Andrea has been trying to train her dog, Trigger, to bring in the morning paper. She started by giving him a treat for going near the paper, then for touching the paper with his mouth, and then for carrying it in the direction of the house. Once Trigger started bringing in the paper, Andrea started to time how long it took him. That data appear below.

Day Number	Seconds to Return with Paper
1	42
2	35
3	20
4	18
5	19
6	20

68. Based only on this data, how many days did it take Trigger to learn to bring in the paper?

    (A) 1
    (B) 2
    (C) 3
    (D) 4

69. What is the range of the times shown in the table?

    (A) 26
    (B) 24
    (C) 22
    (D) 20

70. What technique did Andrea use to teach Trigger to get the paper?

    (A) Classical conditioning
    (B) Shaping
    (C) Chaining
    (D) Spontaneous recovery

71. What type of reinforcer did Andrea use with Trigger?

    (A) Generalized
    (B) Secondary
    (C) Positive
    (D) Negative

Questions 72 through 75 refer to the following.

Recently, Evergreen School District decided to merge its two high schools: Evergreen North and Evergreen South. For years, the two have been rivals, which has helped breed negative stereotypes in both directions. Over the course of the first year, the staff at the new campus, Evergreen Central, implemented a series of activities meant to unify the student body. The staff surveyed a random sample of students about their attitudes toward their new classmates on the first day of school using a standard scale from 1 to 7, where 1 indicated the most negative attitudes and 7 indicated the most positive attitudes. The staff then administered the same survey during the last week of school. Below are the means (M) and standard deviations (SD) separated by grade. Although the grades scores differed, each grade's scores were normally distributed.

Grade	Pretest Attitudes		Posttest Attitudes	
	M	SD	M	SD
9	3.3	1.2	6.7	0.9
10	3.1	0.5	5.9	1.0
11	2.4	0.5	4.1	0.9
12	2.3	0.2	2.9	0.6

72. Which grade's attitudes improved the most?

(A) 9
(B) 10
(C) 11
(D) 12

73. Which grade started the school year with the most diverse views about their classmates?

(A) 9
(B) 10
(C) 11
(D) 12

74. About 95% of which grade's students ended the year with attitudes that fall between 2.3 and 5.9 on the 7-point scale?

(A) 9
(B) 10
(C) 11
(D) 12

75. If the Evergreen administration had consulted you in planning their activities, which of the following would you have recommended they try?

(A) Friendly competitions between North and South students
(B) Jigsaw classroom activities to mix students from the two schools
(C) Separate student lounges for North and South students to provide safe spaces
(D) A schoolwide Battle of the Bands

STOP If there is still time remaining, you may review your answers.

Section II: Free-Response Questions

70 MINUTES

> **DIRECTIONS:** You have 70 minutes to answer the TWO questions that follow. Your answer should present an argument rather than a list of facts. Make sure to incorporate psychological terminology into your answers whenever possible.

Question 1: Article Analysis Question (AAQ)

Note that the text of the question below is adapted from the *AP Psychology Course and Exam Description*.

Your response to the question should be provided in six parts: A, B, C, D, E, and F. Write the response to each part of the question in complete sentences. Use appropriate psychological terminology in your response.

Using the source provided, respond to all parts of the question.

(A) Identify the research method used in the study.

(B) State the operational definition in this study of "belief in a conspiracy theory."

(C) Describe the meaning of the differences in percentages between the treatment group and the control group.

(D) Identify at least one ethical guideline applied by the researchers.

(E) Explain the extent to which the research findings may or may not be generalizable using specific and relevant evidence from the study.

(F) Explain how at least one of the research findings supports or refutes the researchers' hypothesis that a discussion between a person and a large language model can reduce belief in a conspiracy theory.

Source

Introduction

Many people are concerned about the number of people who believe in conspiracy theories and how difficult it can be to convince people to think critically about the evidence for and against conspiracy theories people encounter on social media sites. Researchers investigated past research about what techniques help encourage people to rethink their beliefs in potentially harmful conspiracy theories. They found that most research findings indicate that it is very difficult to get people to evaluate their beliefs and change their minds. Most interventions used in past research studies resulted in very few people changing their minds (and sometimes caused a strengthening of the belief in the conspiracy theories).

The researchers noticed that one of the only moderately effective techniques is one-on-one conversations with experts. Research indicates that when an expert is able to take time to converse with individuals who believe in a conspiracy theory and patiently walks them through evidence about the conspiracy theory in a nonconfrontational way, that conversation can result in a reduction in conspiracy theory belief.

This finding caused the psychological researchers to wonder whether an artificial intelligence "bot" could replace the expert in these kinds of conversations. If conversations with online large language models (like ChatGPT) have the same impact on reducing belief in conspiracy theories, it might be a powerful technique in the overall effort to reduce belief in potentially dangerous conspiracy theories. These researchers wondered: can a large language model talk someone out of believing in a conspiracy theory?

Participants

The researchers recruited 1,055 volunteer participants (all from the United States) to take their initial survey. These participants were selected in order to be a representative sample: the proportions of participants matched the percentages of the U.S. population for age, gender, and race/ethnicity demographic groups.

The survey began with a consent statement letting possible participants know that if they take the survey, their results might be used to invite them to participate in the next phase of the study. The survey included questions designed to measure belief in common conspiracy theories. Researchers used results from the survey to identify a subset of participants to participate in the next phase of the study.

Responses from 75.2% of the participants in the initial study indicated that they had substantial belief in one or more common conspiracy theories measured by the survey.

This group moved on to the next phase of the study.

Researchers randomly divided these participants into two groups:

- Treatment group: These participants experienced a 3-round conversation with the large language model about their favored conspiracy belief (as indicated by the initial survey).
- Control group: These participants experienced a similar conversation about a neutral topic with the large language model.

Method

The research with the treatment group involved several specific phases:

1. Researchers examined survey responses from participants in the treatment group to identify the specific conspiracy theories these participants believed in.
2. They then developed prompts based on these conspiracy theories for the artificial intelligence large language model (GPT-4 Turbo). The prompts uploaded to the large language model included both the specific conspiracy theory indicated by the participant and evidence supporting the theory mentioned by the participant.
3. Participants then engaged in a back and forth "conversation" with the large language model. The large language model used knowledge it gleaned from elsewhere on the web to try to reduce the participant's belief in the targeted conspiracy theory.
4. After the conversation with the large language model, treatment group participants took a version of the initial survey again, answering questions about their current level of belief in the targeted conspiracy theory.

The control group experienced a similar conversation:

1. Researchers developed prompts about a neutral topic, unrelated to conspiracy theories identified in the initial survey.
2. These prompts were provided to the artificial intelligence large language model (GPT-4 Turbo).
3. Participants then engaged in a back and forth "conversation" with the large language model about this neutral topic. The large language model used knowledge it gleaned from elsewhere on the web to continue the conversation and respond to control group participant questions.
4. After the conversation with the large language model, control group participants took a version of the initial survey again, answering questions about their current level of belief in conspiracy theories.

At the end of the research study, participants in both groups were debriefed about all the details of the research, including the purpose, hypothesis, processes used with the treatment and control groups, and findings of the study.

Results and Discussion

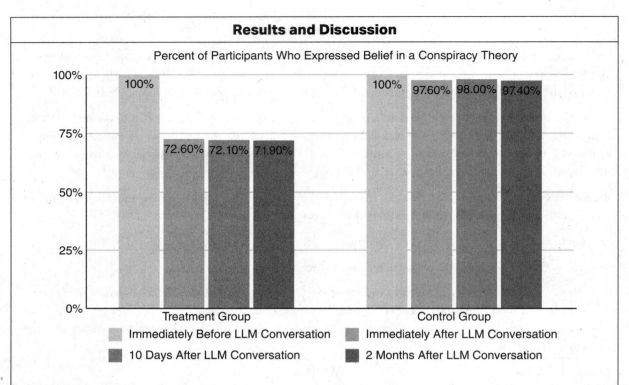

Percent of Participants Who Expressed Belief in a Conspiracy Theory

Here are the overall findings from the study:

- The impact of the conversation with the large language model (LLM) was consistent across all types and examples of conspiracy theories.
- The impact of the LLM on conspiracy belief in the treatment group was statistically significant ($p < 0.001$).
- The treatment effect was similar for deeply held beliefs in conspiracy theories (as indicated by extremely high scores on the initial survey) and less intense or less certain beliefs in conspiracy theories (as indicated by moderate to low scores on the initial survey).
- The follow-up survey after the LLM conversation also asked participants questions designed to measure beliefs in conspiracy theories other than the targeted conspiracy theories. After the LLM conversation, there was a 3.05-point decrease in generic conspiracy belief in the treatment group, compared to a 1.64-point increase in the control group.
- A post-hoc analysis of the LLM's conversations with the participants in the treatment group indicates that an evidence-based strategy was the most frequently used strategy chosen by the LLM. Transcripts of the conversations indicate that the LLM used evidence-based argumentation extensively in a majority of conversations (83%). The transcripts reveal that LLMs encouraged participants to use critical-thinking skills in approximately half the conversations (47%).
- Overall, analysis of the conversations reveal that the LLM was mostly persuasive due to actual use of evidence and arguments to change people's minds.

Adapted from Costello, T. H., Pennycook, G., & Rand, D. G. (2024, April 3). Durably reducing conspiracy beliefs through dialogues with AI. https://doi.org/10.31234/osf.io/xcwdn

Question 2: Evidence-Based Question (EBQ)

Note that the text of the question below is adapted from the *AP Psychology Course and Exam Description.*

This question has three parts: Part A, Part B, and Part C. Use the three sources provided to answer all parts of the question.

For Part B and Part C, you must cite the source that you used to answer the question. You can do this in two different ways:

- Parenthetical Citation: For example: " … (Source A)"
- Embedded Citation: For example: "According to Source A, … "

Write the response to each part of the question in complete sentences. Use appropriate psychological terminology.

Using the sources provided, develop and justify an argument about how attention and distraction influence how much students learn during class.

(A) Propose a specific and defensible claim based in psychological science that responds to the question.

(B) (i) Support your claim using at least one piece of specific and relevant evidence from one of the sources.

(ii) Explain how the evidence from Part B (i) supports your claim using a psychological perspective, theory, concept, or research finding learned in AP Psychology.

(C) (i) Support your claim using an additional piece of specific and relevant evidence from a different source than the one that was used in Part B (i).

(ii) Explain how the evidence from Part C (i) supports your claim using a different psychological perspective, theory, concept, or research finding learned in AP Psychology than the one that was used in Part B (ii).

Source A

Introduction
Teachers often feel that they are teaching an engaging, valuable lesson but that their students don't pay enough attention to learn what they need to learn during a class. What causes students to pay attention or not pay attention during a lesson? Specifically, how often does daydreaming impact students' learning?
Participants
Researchers at the University of Waterloo asked all the students enrolled in a physiological psychology course whether they would agree to participate in this study. Students knew that participation would count for partial course credit.
154 students from the course agreed to participate. These students ranged from age 16 to age 38 and had between 12 and 20 years of education. 97 of the participants identified as female, and 57 identified as male.
After completing informed consent documents, participants were informed of the rest of the data collection procedures and that they could stop participating at any time without penalty to their course grade or their relationship with the instructor or anyone else at the university.

Method
Researchers designed "mind-wandering" questions that were asked at planned moments during course lectures. These thought probes were placed at various points during lectures in order to try to catch examples of students daydreaming at those moments. Participating students attended the lectures and lessons as usual. At predesignated times during the lessons, the 154 participating students answered a short series of questions about what they were thinking about at that moment. Students used a clicker system to answer the mind-wandering questions, and data were collected in real time during the lecture. Overall, over 5,000 questions were answered by participating students over the course of the semester.

Results and Discussion
Data from the mind-wandering questions indicated that most students were able to maintain attention and focus during lectures, but the researchers found significant evidence of mind wandering or daydreaming: - 20% of the responses to the mind-wandering questions indicated that the students were intentionally focusing on something other than the class at that moment in time (intentional mind wandering). - 14% of the responses indicated that students happened to be daydreaming at that moment without intending to (unintentional mind wandering). In additional to these overall data, researchers analyzed the patterns of the mind-wandering events during the classes in order to identify common patterns: - Attention levels do not generally start high at the beginning of a class and then decrease. Rather, they may increase and decrease for each student in less predictable ways during a typical class period. Overall, students had the most incidents of mind wandering during the third 15 minutes of a 60-minute lecture. - Students were slightly more likely to experience mind wandering on Mondays and Fridays and were the least likely to experience daydreaming on Wednesdays. - Students experienced more daydreaming at the end of the term (just before finals) rather than at the beginning or middle of the semester. - Students who reported more episodes of daydreaming performed worse on class tests than students who reported little or no mind wandering.

Adapted from Wammes, J., et al. (2016). Mind wandering during lectures I: Changes in rates across an entire semester. *Scholarship of Teaching and Learning in Psychology.* 2(10),), 13–32. https://doi.org/10.1037/stl0000053

Source B

Introduction
Many teachers (especially teachers of younger students) spend a considerable amount of time planning the visual appearance and environment of their classrooms. Bulletin boards, wall posters, and other visual decorations are often carefully planned in an attempt to help remind students of important rules and reminders about learning goals in the classroom. How much do students learn from these classroom decorations? Are some kinds of visual reminders more effective than others? Do the bulletin boards and posters help students learn? Or are they sometimes distracting and lessen student attention? Researchers wanted to answer these questions in order to provide advice to teachers about how (and whether) to add visual reminders to their classrooms.

Participants
Researchers chose one kindergarten classroom with 12 girls and 12 boys for the study. They worked with school officials to obtain informed consent from the parents of the elementary students in these classrooms. These students all knew each other because they were part of the same kindergarten class at a local elementary school. Participating students were predominantly white (74% white, 26% students of color) and predominantly from families of high socioeconomic status.

Method
Then researchers used a laboratory at the university to set up their kindergarten classroom. The 24 students were brought to the laboratory classroom several times during the year to experience lessons. During some of the lessons, the classroom walls were relatively free of visual material like posters or bulletin boards. During other lessons, many posters and other educational materials were hung on the walls. The kindergarten teacher taught six science lessons in the laboratory classroom. The kindergarten teacher was not informed of the goal of the study and did not know that the research focused on the impact of the wall decorations. Researchers used observational methods to assess how often students in each of the classrooms were paying attention to teacher instructions versus behaviors that might indicate distraction. Students participated in pretests and posttests designed to measure how much science content they learned during the lesson.

Results and Discussion

When students experienced the science lessons in the highly decorated classroom, they were far more likely to engage in distracted behaviors (e.g., looking away from the teacher and at the walls, asking questions about something on the wall that didn't relate to the topic of the lesson, etc.):

- Across the lessons in the highly decorated classroom, students engaged in distracted behaviors 20% of the time.
- During lessons in the nondecorated classroom, researchers observed these same distracted behaviors only 3% of the time.

Researchers also recorded how long students were able to maintain on-task behaviors during the lesson (participating in discussions and following other lesson directions):

- In the highly decorated classroom, students were off task 38.5% of the time.
- In the nondecorated classroom, students were off task 28.4% of the time.

Students in the nondecorated classroom seemed to gain more skills and knowledge from the science lessons:

- In the highly decorated classroom, students' pretest scores on average were 20% correct, and this increased to 40% correct on the posttest.
- In the nondecorated classroom, students' pretest scores on average were 20% correct, and this increased to 85% correct on the posttest.

These findings indicate that wall decorations may affect students' attention and that posters and bulletin boards may have unintended, negative consequences for learning in kindergarten classrooms.

Adapted from Fisher, A., & Godwin, K., & Seltman, H. (2014). Visual Environment, Attention allocation, and learning in young children: When too much of a good thing may be bad. *Psychological Science.* 25(7).

Source C

Introduction

Cognitive psychologists are always interested in how people interpret and process different kinds of information. Some researchers investigate a phenomenon called the split-attention effect: this occurs when people have to interpret two or more different sources of information at the same time as they are trying to learn new knowledge or skills. For example, a teacher shares a poorly designed diagram with students with the written labels included but it's not clear what parts of the diagram each of the labels refer to. If students constantly have to mentally switch from reading the labels to trying to interpret the rest of the components of the diagram and figure out what the labels refer to, the split-attention effect might lessen students' abilities to learn from that diagram. The split-attention effect might interfere with the amount or speed of learning that can occur because students have to spend mental effort (cognitive load) to integrate the different parts of the diagram.

These researchers decided to investigate the impact of the split-attention effect on learning in the context of reading and interpreting research reports in an introductory psychology course.

Participants

20 students from the University of South Wales volunteered to participate in the study. All of these students were enrolled in an introductory educational psychology course.

Method

After an informed consent process was completed, the student participants were randomly assigned to two groups:

- Conventional group: This group of students read a research summary about a study that involved participants studying computer programming content. In this research summary, information about the study was separated into the conventional areas journal articles are usually organized into, using typical headings (literature review, participants, methods, results, and discussion).
- Integrated group: This group of students read a summary of the same research study as the conventional group, but all the information about the study was integrated into one overall narrative instead of being separated into different sections by headings.

Both research summaries were of similar length and used similarly difficult vocabulary.

Both groups were asked to study their research summary at their own pace. They were told that after the reading period, they would be asked to take a quiz about the content of the research summaries. Students were asked to tell the researchers when they were done studying the research summaries, and the time elapsed was noted for each participant.

After the reading phase, the test phase began. Students answered 34 questions about the content of the research summaries they studied. Students were allowed as much time as they needed to complete the 34 questions.

Results and Discussion

Overall, the students who were assigned to read the integrated research summaries seemed to comprehend the material more quickly and learn more than the students who read the conventionally presented research summary.

The following describes the specific findings:

- Students in the conventional summary group took on average 216 seconds to read their summaries. Students in the integrated summary group took an average of 190 seconds. This difference in reading time required was statistically significant ($p < 0.05$).
- Students in the conventional summary group answered an average of 17.5 of the 34 items correctly on the comprehension quiz. In contrast, students in the integrated summary group answered 21.4 of the items correctly on the comprehension quiz. This difference in correct answers was statistically significant ($p < 0.05$).

Since the students in the integrated research summary group took less time to read through the material but answered more items correctly on the comprehension quiz, researchers concluded that the students who had read the conventional research summary were likely hampered by the split-attention effect: students had to mentally switch between the different sections of the conventional research summary in order to integrate all the information from the research summary and conclude about what the study might indicate as well as evaluate limitations of the study. In contrast, the integrated research summary was designed to help readers integrate information about the study in a logically arranged narrative, reducing the split-attention effect, and increasing learning.

Adapted from Chandler, P. And Sweller, J. (1992), The split-attention effect as a factor in the design of instruction. *British Journal of Educational Psychology*, 62(2): 233–246. https://doi.org/10.1111/j.2044-8279.1992.tb01017.x

Answer Explanations

Section I: Multiple-Choice Questions

1. **(D)** Cyan's test would be classified as an aptitude test because it is intended to show a person's potential to be a great civil rights attorney. A speed test is comprised of many items and is meant to demonstrate how quickly a person can answer questions. An achievement test measures people's knowledge of a given area. An EQ test would measure emotional intelligence.

2. **(D)** Approximately 95 percent of the population scores between 70 and 130 on the WISC. The WISC has a mean of 100 and a standard deviation of 15, which means that the scores between 70 and 130 represent all the scores within 2 standard deviations of the mean.

3. **(D)** Young Tina had never seen the space shuttle until her parents pointed out a picture of it ready to launch. When she next saw a picture of it flying, she had difficulty recognizing it. Tina's problem can best be explained by shape constancy. Shape constancy is a perceptual constancy that we learn from experience. An unfamiliar object looks different from different angles, and we have to learn that it is the same object. Until we do, we make errors like Tina's. The autokinetic effect is when a spot of light in a dark room appears to move on its own. Dishabituation refers to an increase in response that occurs to a novel stimulus. Summation refers to the way the layers of the retina are set up: multiple rods and cones synapse with one bipolar cell. and multiple bipolar cells synapse with a single ganglion cell.

4. **(D)** Alyssa is testing the impact of framing. Milk that is 1 percent fat is the same as milk that is 99 percent fat free; the only difference is how the milk is framed. Representativeness heuristic is when people judge the likelihood of an event by comparing it to something they believe to be similar and assuming the probabilities of the events will be the same. Confirmation bias is the tendency to pay more attention to information that supports our preexisting beliefs than information that contradicts it. Schema are cognitive structures that influence how we process information.

5. **(D)** In correlating the two sets of results, Jupiter is measuring the test's reliability. This type of reliability is known as test-retest reliability. Since perfectionism should not change over the course of the month, a low correlation would indicate that the test was not reliable. Outliers are extreme scores, and Jupiter does not appear to be looking for them. To standardize the test, Jupiter would have to give it to a standardization sample and then look to assemble a group of questions that yielded a normal distribution of scores. Nothing in the question suggests Jupiter believes the mean level of perfectionism should have changed, and the correlation will not necessarily show whether it has.

6. **(D)** If the College Board neglected to put any questions that had to do with neuroscience on the AP Psychology exam one year, the test would lack content validity. A valid test measures what it is supposed to measure. A test with high content validity covers all the areas it is supposed to in the appropriate level of depth. Predictive and concurrent validity are two types of criterion validity. A test with predictive validity provides a measure of how someone will perform on a task in the future, whereas concurrent validity provides a measure of how someone will perform at the present time. Construct validity, choice (A), is a term that applies to tests that attempt to measure one overall idea or construct, not a test like the AP Psychology exam that measures many different areas of knowledge.

7. **(B)** An American teenager's prototype of a chair is most likely to include four legs and a seat. A prototype is the most typical example of category. Although there are many types of chairs such as the armchair, chairlift, and wheelchair listed in choice (D), most chairs we encounter have the features described in choice (B). Through classical conditioning, someone may have come to associate certain types of chairs with anxiety.

8. **(D)** In studying for the AP Psychology exam, good advice would be to study from multiple sources. Studying from your class notes, homework, old

tests, and review book involves a fairly deep level of processing and will result in more elaborative encoding. Short-term memory lasts only about 20–30 seconds, so it's not a place to store information you're going to need hours later. Even though we hope you find our book helpful, reading any one source over and over again is a relatively shallow form of processing, and you would do better to study from multiple sources. Since what you need to know for the exam is not a long list of items, the serial position effect would not be particularly helpful.

9. **(D)** Most children will develop the ability to clap their hands before any of the other skills listed. Typically, infants learn to clap hands in the second half of their first year. In general, gross motor skills (e.g., clapping) tend to develop before fine motor skills (e.g., writing or cutting with a knife). Most children do not speak in anything resembling full sentences until they are well over 2 years old.

10. **(D)** Antonia has a cat. The first time she sees a rabbit, she calls it a cat. Her error results from the process of assimilation. Assimilation, as defined by Piaget, is the ability to take in new information using one's existing schemata. Antonia had a schema for a cat and used it to make sense of a new animal, a rabbit. Accommodation will occur if Antonia is corrected and told that this new animal with longer ears and a shorter tail is a rabbit and she then creates a new schema for rabbits. Discrimination and generalization are terms used together in discussing learning. Discrimination is when one can tell the difference between a stimulus and similar stimuli, and generalization is when one responds the same way to similar stimuli as one did to the stimulus with which one was originally trained.

11. **(A)** Four-year-old Kate positions herself squarely in front of all the other kids to watch a magician. Piaget would attribute this to Kate's egocentrism. Piaget would say that Kate does not have the cognitive capacity to realize that she is blocking others' view; she is only capable of seeing things from her own perspective. Piaget believed infants develop object permanence, the understanding that an object still exists even when no longer in view, toward the end of the first year. According to Piaget, children learn to conserve around age 7, when they enter concrete operations. Conservation is the knowledge that a change in the form of matter does not change the amount of matter that exists. Animism is a limitation in the thought of the preoperational child. It is when one attributes life or consciousness to inanimate objects.

12. **(B)** The school librarian's system of giving students a prize for every five books they read uses a fixed-ratio reinforcement schedule. The schedule is fixed (as opposed to variable) because students are rewarded for every five books they read—a fixed or constant number. The schedule is a ratio (as opposed to an interval) schedule because what controls the reinforcement is the number of responses the person makes and not the passage of time.

13. **(A)** The fact that students read more books in the summer but fewer books in the fall is probably due to the overjustification effect, the finding that extrinsic rewards can undermine intrinsic motivation. Students who previously read because they liked to read may have come to think they read for the prizes and not because they liked reading. As a result, when the prizes were withdrawn, they no longer had a reason to read and therefore may have read less.

14. **(C)** The technique Coach Perry is using is called shaping. Shaping is defined as rewarding successive approximations of a desired behavior. Coach Perry would love 5-year-old Lana to be able to stop his hardest kick, but he knows that in order to reach that goal he must begin by letting her stop slow-moving balls. The law of effect is Thorndike's pronouncement that pleasant consequences will increase the likelihood of a behavior and unpleasant consequences will decrease the likelihood of a behavior. The partial reinforcement effect is the finding that partial reinforcement schedules are more resistant to extinction than continuous reinforcement. Second-order conditioning is when, in classical conditioning, you use something that was initially a CS as a US to condition a new CS.

15. **(D)** One of the more impressive feats cited by those who believe that animals are capable of true language is that some apes have been able to use words they were taught to express novel concepts. For instance, Washoe, who didn't know the word for refrigerator, was able to describe it as a "cold box." Chomsky speaks of a language acquisition device, but the term does not refer to a physical structure in the brain. Even though primates are able to learn words that result in food rewards, critics of the idea animals have language say these words are merely the result of operant conditioning and do not evidence true language. There is no doubt that animals including honeybees and dolphins can communicate with one another and with people to some extent; however, there is much debate over what should be considered "language."

16. **(A)** The finding that people who read a job description written only with male pronouns (e.g., he, his) are more likely to think of an employee as male than people who read a description that uses gender-neutral language (e.g., he or she) is most closely linked to the linguistic relativity hypothesis. The linguistic relativity or Sapir-Whorf hypothesis holds that language influences thought. Therefore, people who read a job description written using only male pronouns are influenced to think of the person who holds the job in a particular way. Gender schema theory holds that children learn about the gender roles of their culture and that the expectations they develop then guide their behavior. The social role hypothesis theorizes that society's expected roles can influence people to act in various ways. Modeling, or observational learning, is Bandura's theory that people learn by watching and imitating others.

17. **(A)** The relationship between arousal and performance is known as the Yerkes-Dodson law and is expressed by a graph that looks like an inverted "U." As arousal increases, so does performance—up to a point. When arousal becomes too high, performance suffers.

18. **(D)** Faye believes that victims of natural disasters are foolish because they didn't develop better advance detection and warning systems. Faye is manifesting the just-world bias, which is the belief that because the world is a fair place, good things happen to good people and bad things happen to bad people. The false consensus effect is our tendency to overestimate the number of people whose views are similar to our own. The self-fulfilling prophecy effect is the ability of one person's expectations to elicit behavioral confirmation in another. Self-serving bias is the tendency to take more credit for good outcomes and less credit for bad outcomes than one deserves.

19. **(D)** Ani's belief that her attitudes and behavior play a central role in what happens to her is associated with an internal locus of control. Although people with an external locus of control feel that fate and luck play a large role in their lives, people with an internal locus of control believe that they control their destinies. A strong superego is associated with being concerned with morals and ethics. People with low self-esteem have negative thoughts about themselves. People with low self-efficacy doubt their ability to get things done.

20. **(D)** Sal's conclusion that Petunia is a funny person after their brief meeting is best explained by the fundamental attribution error, the tendency for people to underestimate the role of the situation in explaining the behavior of others. The mere-exposure effect would hold that the more time Sal spent with Petunia, the more he would like her; it says that exposure to a person or thing increases liking. Self-serving bias is the tendency to take more credit for positive outcomes than negative ones. Equipotentiality is a learning principle, the belief that we have an equal opportunity to teach all organisms all things.

21. **(B)** Since Edy is giving out the cookies herself and they have her name on them, the act of distributing will increase the student body's familiarity with her. According to the mere-exposure effect, increased exposure increases liking. Foot-in-the-door is a compliance technique that involves getting someone to agree to a small request in order to increase the likelihood they will agree to a larger, subsequent request. Edy's technique utilizes the peripheral route more than the central route; the central route to persuasion would involve Edy explaining why she is the best candidate. Pluralistic ignorance is one explanation for the bystander effect.

22. **(D)** After taking AP Psychology and doing well in the class and exam, Donald goes to college. If Donald is interested in psychology and has high achievement motivation, as a first-year student, he is most likely to sign up for an upper-level undergraduate course in which he will have to work hard to succeed and will learn new things. His interest in psychology will lead Donald to want to take more psychology classes and learn new things, while his high achievement motivation will lead him to select a class that will be challenging but not overly difficult.

23. **(A)** Runners in a park were found to pick up their pace when another runner came into view; this finding illustrates the phenomenon of social facilitation since it shows that the presence of others improved performance. Conformity involves a change in attitude or behavior to fit in with a group; if a runner ran faster to keep up with her soccer teammates, conformity could be at work. Deindividuation is a loss of self-restraint under conditions of high arousal and anonymity. Norms are standards of expected behavior.

24. **(B)** Neuroleptics are commonly prescribed to treat schizophrenia, the most common psychotic disorder. L-Dopa is used to treat Parkinson's disease and would likely have an adverse effect on Vance since it would lead to an increase in dopamine and an excess of dopamine is a hypothesized cause of schizophrenia. Benzodiazepines are commonly used to treat anxiety. SSRIs (serotonin selective reuptake inhibitors) are used to treat major depressive disorder.

25. **(D)** Odette has several classic symptoms of major depressive disorder—loss of appetite, disrupted sleep, and a loss of interest in her usual activities. Although Odette is at an age when many people sadly begin to suffer from Alzheimer's, she is not experiencing the rapid degeneration in memory and cognitive function associated with that disease. Since her problems began about a year ago, they do not seem to be associated with winter. So she is unlikely to be diagnosed with seasonal affective disorder. There is no indication that she is engaging in the binge-purge cycle associated with bulimia.

26. **(A)** MRI and CAT scans provide detailed information about the structure of the brain (and other body parts). These scans would reveal any structural brain damage caused by the car crash. The PET, EEG, and fMRI scans are primarily used to detect brain function, not structure (although the fMRI would also provide structural details).

27. **(D)** Dendrites grow more quickly in children, so brains of younger people are more "plastic," or changeable. A young person who suffers brain damage is more able to make new connections in nondamaged parts of the brain and regain lost functions. The other brain-related concepts listed are not related to brain plasticity.

28. **(D)** PET scans provide information about which parts of the brain are most active, which would reveal that all parts of the brain are used (although different areas of the cerebral cortex are more active than others on different tasks). CAT and MRI scans only provide information on the structure of the brain, not brain activity. An EEG scan does provide information about brain wave activity but does not tie this activity to specific areas of the brain.

29. **(A)** Volume is determined by the amplitude (height) of the sound wave. Wave frequency determines the pitch of the sound. Transduction is the process where signals, such as sounds, are changed into neural impulses.

30. **(B)** The absolute threshold represents the minimum amount of stimulus we can usually detect, such as the minimum amount of salt we can taste in water.

31. **(D)** Detecting the difference between two very similar pitches depends on the difference threshold, which is the minimum difference between two stimuli that we can perceive.

32. **(B)** Psychoanalysts would view the salad restaurant as the manifest content of the dreaming masking the more important latent content. Clinicians from other perspectives tend not to analyze dreams.

33. **(C)** Broca's area of the brain (located in the left frontal lobe in most people) helps control the muscles in the jaw, throat, and tongue needed to produce speech. Wernicke's area is also involved in spoken language but primarily with meaning and interpretation of language. The hippocampus and amygdala areas of the brain are not involved in spoken language.

34. **(D)** Cross-sectional studies use groups of subjects of different ages in order to infer the impact of age on a variable. Longitudinal studies follow one group of people over a long period of time in order to infer the impact of age on a variable.

35. **(B)** Semantic memories are general knowledge about the world. Episodic memories are memories of specific events, and procedural memories are memories of skills and how to perform them. Eidetic memory is not a specific kind of long-term memory.

36. **(B)** Explicit memories are memories of facts and events. Implicit memories (or nondeclarative memories) are memories of procedures or skills that we may not even realize we have, such as the skill of tying a tie.

37. **(D)** Generalization occurs in classical conditioning when an organism responds to any stimuli similar to the conditioned stimuli, such as salivating to any sound similar to a bell.

38. **(B)** Classical conditioning involves pairing conditioned stimuli with unconditioned stimuli, producing a conditioned response. Operant conditioning involves providing a stimulus (a reinforcer or a punishment) after a specific response is performed. The other possible answers provided about classical and operant conditioning are not accurate.

39. **(C)** Including the free address labels is an example of norm of reciprocity, one of the compliance strategies. People are more likely to help if they feel someone has done them a favor, such as including a gift in a letter asking for contributions.

40. **(B)** Self-fulfilling prophecies occur when our preconceived ideas about someone influence the ways we act toward them, which may increase the likelihood that our preconceived ideas about the person may seem to be confirmed.

41. **(D)** We tend to see members of our own group (the in-group) as more diverse and more favorable than people outside our group (the out-group). This bias could contribute to discrimination and prejudice.

42. **(A)** A person who buckles down and studies more after failing an exam must believe that her studying will benefit her and that she will do better on the next exam because of her efforts. This is the definition of an internal locus of control: the belief that our actions have impact and that we are in control of what happens to us.

43. **(B)** Groupthink occurs when a group makes a bad decision because members of the group did not want to contradict each other (often due to mutual admiration of group members). Any techniques used to encourage contrary opinions within the group will work against this groupthink tendency.

44. **(D)** Test-retest reliability is a measure of a test's ability to deliver similar results each time it is administered to the same person.

45. **(D)** The symptoms described best match PTSD, post-traumatic stress disorder.

46. **(C)** Schizophrenia is associated with hallucinations and delusions. Both schizophrenia and dissociative disorders involve splits from reality, and both disorders are very disruptive and may interfere with careers and jobs.

47. **(D)** This psychologist is advising the patient to examine her or his own thinking (cognitive perspective) and prescribing a psychoactive medication (biopsychology perspective).

48. **(D)** The structure of schools is a social construction. Even for young children, American schools typically involve long periods of sitting still, which may be more difficult for boys than girls for a combination of reasons. People who believe the structure of schooling plays a role in the rate of diagnoses are giving a sociocultural explanation rather than a biological, cognitive or humanistic one.

49. **(A)** The persistence and relative mildness of Juana's symptoms are their defining features—hence she would most likely be diagnosed with persistent depressive disorder. A diagnosis of major depressive disorder would be more severe, seasonal affective disorder would be linked to the lack of sun in winter, and bipolar disorder I would require at least one episode of mania.

50. **(B)** Psychodynamic therapists are most interested in their patients' early lives because they believe these early years play a major role in shaping people's lives. Their interest in dreams emanates from the belief in the importance of the unconscious.

51. **(C)** Velma's baseline score is way below everyone else's and therefore can be considered an outlier or extreme score.

52. **(C)** The mode is the most frequently occurring value, and 0.3 appears three times in the column representing change in happiness.

53. **(B)** Because of Velma's low score, the distribution is negatively skewed. In skewed distributions, the median is a better measure of central tendency than the mean because the median is affected less by the extreme score. The median is always the middle score when the scores are ordered in either ascending or descending order, while the mean is the arithmetic average of all the numbers.

54. **(A)** A confounding variable in this type of design is always time. Since scores from two different times are being compared, it's possible that the happiness level changed because of the passage of time rather than the journaling.

55. **(D)** A *p*-value of 0.05 or less is the commonly accepted threshold for statistical significance.

56. **(B)** The pattern in the scatterplot suggests a negative or inverse relationship because the dots seem to cluster in the upper left and slope downward to the lower right. Such a pattern indicates that a high score on one variable correlates with a low score on the other.

57. **(C)** The correlation coefficient would quantify the relationship between the variables. The further away the value is from 0 and the closer it is to 1 or -1, the stronger the relationship is. The sign of the correlation coefficient shows whether the relationship between variables is positive (direct) or negative (inverse). None of the other values are particularly useful in interpreting the relationship between two values in a correlation.

58. **(A)** Absolute threshold is one's ability to detect a stimulus 50% of a time. Juniper is interested in the relationship between absolute thresholds in different sensory modalities.

59. **(C)** A placebo is typically used as a control in drug studies to isolate the actual pharmacological effect of the drug from any improvement that might result just from thinking one is taking medication.

60. **(D)** It is essential that Dr. Patel randomly assign patients to conditions so that the two groups are equivalent at the start. If he does not, Dr. Patel will not be able to tell whether improvements are due to the new drug or something about the patients who chose it (A), regression to the mean in patients that have been struggling a lot lately (B), or a tendency for cognitive decline to get worse (C).

61. **(B)** The mean of the massed group is $(5 + 2 + 11) = 18/3 = 6$. The mean of the distributed group is $(12 + 8 + 18 + 6) = 44/4 = 11$. $11 - 6$ is 5.

62. **(A)** Jenny's onto something here, but 7 people is not enough from which to draw a conclusion. Although it is ideal to keep the groups the same size, a difference of a few people does not pose a problem. There is no set number that indicates how far the means of two groups need to differ for the difference to be statistically significant. This is because the size of this difference is only one of several factors that affect statistical significance; sample size is another very important factor.

63. **(D)** Percentiles tell you how many people score at the same level or below you. So, if Andre learns that Jenny's students' percentile scores increased, he would be able to see they were improving relative to their peers.

64. **(D)** Memory has been found to be context dependent, which means that the context (or place) in which information is learned can later provide retrieval cues.

65. **(C)** Standard deviation is a measure of variability. The higher the standard deviation, the more varied Mr. Rosales' students' scores are.

66. **(B)** The median is the middle number when values are ordered by size. When listed this way, the data set looks like 6, 7, 8, 11, 12, 16. Because there are an even number of values, there is no one middle number. So we need to average the middle two numbers, which are 8 and 11. The median is $8 + 11 = 19/2 = 9.5$.

67. **(A)** Continuous reinforcement is most effective in teaching new skills. If a child receives a dollar every time they make their bed, they quickly learn that association. If they have to wait a week for the reward, it will take longer for them to link the action and result.

68. **(C)** By day 3, Trigger is consistently bringing in the paper in around 20 seconds. Although it may take a second or two longer on some days, acquisition has occurred by day 3.

69. **(B)** The range is the highest value minus the lowest value, which in this case is $42 - 18 = 24$.

70. **(B)** Shaping is the reinforcement of successive approximations of a behavior. Because it was unlikely that Trigger was going to wake up one morning and trot out to get the paper, Andrea reinforced steps toward that end goal—going toward the paper, touching the paper with his mouth, and so on.

71. **(C)** The positive in positive reinforcer refers to the fact that something pleasant is added when a behavior is performed. Treats are positive, and Trigger gets a treat when he gets the paper. A negative reinforcer, on the other hand, is when behavior is reinforced by removing something unpleasant—like that pesky collar Trigger wears. Treats are also primary reinforcers—which means they are naturally reinforcing—no one has to learn to value food. Secondary reinforcers have to be learned. Generalized reinforcers, like money, are things that have broad value because they can be traded for a variety of other valued objects.

72. **(A)** To answer the question, you need to subtract the pretest means from the posttest means. Grade 9's changed the most—by 3.4 points.

73. **(A)** To see how the attitudes within a grade differed, you need to look at the standard deviation, a measure of variability equal to the average distance of all the numbers in a distribution from the mean. Grade 9 has the greatest standard deviation in attitudes at the pretest.

74. **(C)** To answer this question, you need to know that 95% of scores in a normal distribution fall within 2 standard deviations of the mean. Therefore, all you need to do is find which grade had a posttest mean that was 2 standard deviations away from both 2.3 and 5.9. The 11th grade had a mean score of 4.1 with a standard deviation of 0.9 because $2.3 + 1.8 = 4.1$ and $5.9 - 1.8 = 4.1$. The easiest way to find the answer is simply to average 2.3 and 5.9, which also gives you 4.1.

75. **(B)** The jigsaw classroom is a technique to get students to work together on a superordinate goal. Each student participates in a group where they are the only one who knows some of the material; hence, everyone's information is needed to complete the "puzzle." Superordinate goals have been shown to be effective in breaking down prejudices. Competitions and separation, on the other hand, tend to reinforce negative feelings.

Section II: Free Response

Question 1: Article Analysis Question (AAQ)—Sample Student Response

Part (A)

Identify the research method used in the study.

Sample Student Answer

> This study is definitely an experiment.

Scoring Guide

In order to get a point for (A), students need to correctly identify the research method used in the study.

> This response earns 1 point because the student correctly identified the method used in the study as an experiment.

Part (B)

State the operational definition of "belief in a conspiracy theory."

Sample Student Answer

> The way the researchers measured belief in conspiracy theory in this study was by using scores on the initial survey that were designed to measure belief in conspiracy theories. The scores on this survey measured how much people believed in some conspiracy theories.

Scoring Guide

In order to get a point for (B), students need to explain the measurable definition of the variable identified in this study. In this case, that variable is belief in conspiracy theories.

> This response would score 1 point because the student correctly identifies that belief in conspiracy theories in this study is measured using the initial survey participants took. Researchers used the scores from that survey to measure whether people believed in conspiracy theories.

Part (C)

Describe the meaning of the differences in percentages between the treatment group and the control group.

Sample Student Answer

> The people in the treatment group had their belief drop after the artificial intelligence (AI) conversation, and the people in the control group didn't have that same change happen. Before the AI conversation, 100% of the treatment group and the control group believed in the conspiracy theories. After the AI conversation, that dropped to 72.6% in the treatment group and barely dropped in the control group (to 97.6%). That difference between the groups indicates that the AI conversation had an impact on lessening belief in conspiracy theories.

Scoring Guide

In order to get a point for (C), students need to accurately explain the relevant statistic within the context of the study.

> This response would score 1 point because the student accurately explained the meaning of the differences in percentages between the treatment and control groups. The student accurately explained the meaning of the drop in percentage of people who believed in conspiracy theories after the conversation with the large language model.

Part (D)

Identify at least one ethical guideline applied by the researchers.

Sample Student Answer

> In this study, the researchers included the important ethical requirement of debriefing at the end of the study. It's important to tell participants what really happened during a study, especially when some participants didn't experience part of the study that might be beneficial to them (like the AI conversation that the treatment group got and the control group didn't).

Scoring Guide

In order to get a point for (D), students need to identify at least one relevant ethical consideration about the study.

> This response would score 1 point because the student actually identified one ethical element of the study: the student mentioned debriefing and how debriefing was used in this study.

Part (E)

Explain the extent to which the research findings may or may not be generalizable using specific and relevant evidence from the study.

Sample Student Answer

> The findings of this study are probably generalizable because the researchers were careful when they recruited the 1,055 volunteers to take the survey. They made sure that this group was proportionally the same as the proportions in the general population. Since it was a representative group, that helps the results be more generalizable to the population.

Scoring Guide

In order to get a point for (E), students need to explain why they think the results of the study are or are not generalizable using relevant evidence from the research summary.

> This response would score 1 point because the student used relevant evidence—the fact that the sample was representative of the overall population—and how this representativeness increases the chances that the results generalize to the population.

Part (F)

Explain how at least one of the research findings supports or refutes the researchers' hypothesis that a discussion between a person and a large language model can reduce belief in a conspiracy theory.

Sample Student Answer

> The findings in this study totally support this hypothesis. The fact that about 30% of the people in the treatment group stopped believing so much in the conspiracy theory after the conversation with the AI bot (and that the same didn't happen in the control group) is good evidence for the hypothesis that a conversation with an AI "expert" might reduce belief in a conspiracy theory.

Scoring Guide

In (F), students can get 1 point for using appropriate evidence but not having a complete explanation. Students can get 2 points for using appropriate evidence AND including a complete argument/explanation for how that evidence shows that the hypothesis is or is not supported.

> This response would score 2 points because the student used relevant evidence, which is the drop in the percentage of treatment group participants who believed in a conspiracy theory after the AI conversation, and specifically describes why that result shows that the hypothesis is supported, which is the impact of the conversation in the treatment group as compared to the control group.

Question 2: Evidence-Based Question (EBQ)—Sample Student Response

Part A

Using the sources provided, develop and justify an argument about how attention and distraction influence how much students learn during class.

> Propose a specific and defensible claim based in psychological science that responds to the question.

Sample Student Answer

> Students need to be paying attention to the meaning of what they are trying to learn instead of being distracted by irrelevant information in order to learn effectively.

Scoring Guide

In order to earn the point for Part A, students just need to propose a claim that is relevant to the question.

> This sample response would score 1 point because it is a claim relevant to the question.

Part B (i)

Provide one piece of evidence from one of the sources.

> Support your claim using at least one piece of specific and relevant evidence from one of the sources.

Sample Student Answer

> In Source A, students who experienced more mind-wandering or daydreaming episodes didn't learn as much as other students (who scored worse on the tests than students who didn't daydream much).

Scoring Guide

In order to earn the point for Part B (i), students need to describe one relevant piece of evidence and cite the source.

> This sample response would score 1 point because the evidence is correctly cited and it is relevant to the claim about attention, distraction, and learning.

Part B (ii)

Explain how the evidence supports your claim using a psychological concept.

> Explain how the evidence from Part B (i) supports your claim using a psychological perspective, theory, concept, or research finding learned in AP Psychology.

Sample Student Answer

> According to the multistore model of memory, information must pass through the sensory memory and working memory stages in order to stand a chance at getting encoded into long-term memory and being "learned." If a student is daydreaming a lot, they aren't paying attention (or selectively attending) to the information in the class. This reduces the chance that the information goes from sensory memory into working memory and then into long-term memory, which could hurt their learning and their test scores.

Scoring Guide

In order to earn the 2 points for Part B (ii), students need to explain how the piece of evidence they chose supports their claim, using at least one relevant psychological concept in the explanation.

> This sample response would score 2 points because it is a correct interpretation of the evidence from Source A and the student uses a psychological concept (multistore model of memory) correctly to explain the evidence and its relationship to the claim.

Part C (i)

Provide another piece of evidence from another one of the sources.

> Support your claim using an additional piece of specific and relevant evidence from a different source than the one that was used in Part B (i).

Sample Student Answer

> In Source C, the students who read the integrated summary of the research study were able to read it more quickly and learn more from that summary (as measured by the quiz).

Scoring Guide

In order to earn the point for Part C (i), students need to describe one relevant piece of evidence and cite the source.

> This sample response would score 1 point because the evidence is correctly cited and it is relevant to the claim about attention and learning.

Part C (ii)

Explain how the evidence supports your claim using a psychological concept.

> Explain how the evidence from Part C (i) supports your claim using a different psychological perspective, theory, concept, or research finding learned in AP Psychology than the one that was used in Part B (ii).

Sample Student Answer

> This finding from Source C makes sense because of the concept of chunking. Chunking occurs when we can group information together into meaningful units. When we can chunk lots of information into a meaningful group, it's easier for us to encode it into long-term memory and remember it later. In the Source C study about the split-attention effect, the students who read the integrated research summary read faster and learned more than the students who read the conventional research summary. I think chunking can help explain the split-attention effect. In the integrated research summary, the information was organized in a logical narrative. So students could chunk it into meaningful units more easily and avoid the split-attention effect. In the conventional group, those students had to jump around between the conventional section headings. This made chunking more difficult and split their attention. So chunking can help explain why students in the integrated research summary group read faster and learned more.

Scoring Guide

In order to earn the 2 points for Part C (ii), students need to explain how the piece of evidence they chose supports their claim, using at least one relevant psychological concept in the explanation.

> This sample response would score 2 points because it is a correct interpretation of the evidence from Source C and because the student uses a psychological concept (chunking) correctly to explain the evidence and its relationship to the claim.

Index